THE ULTIMATE COMPANION TO

MEAT

ON THE FARM ~ AT THE BUTCHER ~ IN THE KITCHEN

THE ULTIMATE COMPANION TO

MEAT

ON THE FARM ~ AT THE BUTCHER ~ IN THE KITCHEN

ANTHONY PUHARICH
LIBBY TRAVERS

FOREWORD BY ANTHONY BOURDAIN

THE COUNTRYMAN PRESS
A division of W. W. Norton & Company
Independent Publishers Since 1923

CONTENTS

For my father, Victor Puharich: my role model, my business partner, my best friend. – **AP**

FOREWORD

My dear friend Anthony Bourdain penned this generous foreword for the book just weeks before he passed away. I will miss you, Tony. – **AP**

It is the single most beautiful butcher shop I've ever seen—though 'butcher shop', while descriptive of a place where a fine and noble and quite ancient profession is practised, does not seem adequate to describe Victor Churchill. A temple of meat. A dream. A gift.

Everything is perfect. Beyond perfect. It is perhaps the most famous and certainly the most envied shop of its kind in the world. White-coated butchers break down primal cuts in a refrigerated glass cutting room. Old-school charcuterie of many wonderful kinds beckons like jewels from a display case. Another case contains fat slabs of rib eyes and sirloins and boutique cuts of boutique breeds of pampered animals. Chickens turn slowly on a magnificently restored rotisserie, filling the room with a smell that both comforts and compels.

Anthony Puharich created this wonderland around the bones of the already pretty damn cool Churchill's, the oldest continuously operating butcher shop in Australia. It was an act of love, an homage to his father, a hard-working meat cutter and butcher who emigrated to Sydney and built a thriving business. What Anthony did was create the perfect space to cut meat. A fantasy of a butcher shop: theatre, retail shop, eatery and school.

Anthony has applied that same thinking, methodology and attention to detail to this lavish book. *The Ultimate Companion to Meat* is the perfect place to learn how to understand meat and what to do with it to maximum strategic and emotional effect. Anthony knows meat in ways that even I will never know. His deep history and experience with sourcing, ageing, handling, cutting and preparing animal protein is unparalleled. His extraordinary good taste and culinary instincts are obvious from the number of internationally famous chefs you often find huddled in the shop's back room, greedily devouring the results.

You hold the right book in your hands. Learning from it will be delicious.

Anthony Bourdain

PREFACE

Following in the footsteps of his six siblings before him, my father Victor Puharich came to Australia from Croatia in search of opportunity. Each child in his family had been sent for a three-year stint, most of them finding work in the mines of Western Australia, after which they returned to their homeland to carry on the butchery trade. Unlike his siblings, however, Dad continued on to Sydney where he found love with my mother, Stephanie, a job in a butchery and a home. He stayed.

I was also told to break with tradition. My parents wanted their children to seek a 'better life'. Butchery was labour intensive: it meant early starts and cold conditions, and it did not mean good money. They wanted their children to get an education.

I was the first person in both my father's and mother's families to graduate from university. Mum wept with pride the first day I put on a suit and left for a job in merchant banking. It was civil, decent, clean work and yet, nine months into the role, I realised something wasn't right.

Despite the vastly different working hours of a butcher and banker, we always ate dinner together as a family. One night over dinner I mustered the courage to tell my parents that I wanted to be a butcher and work with Dad. It took me three months to convince my mum and dad to mortgage the house and my dad to leave the job he had worked at for 30 years and open a butchery with his son.

In February 1996, we opened Vic's Premium Quality Meat, a traditional retail butchery in Sydney's Oxford Street. Our philosophy was simple: to pay respect to an animal by using every part of it. We were looking to re-create what our forefathers had done in Croatia, bringing in whole animals and butchering them on site: it was to be a place where offal was celebrated and the whole animal was consumed. Working side by side with my father was just what I had dreamt of, yet the business wasn't succeeding: within six months we had burned through our capital. There were not enough families, not enough people cooking at home. We needed a community, but we hadn't found it in Sydney.

Full of desperation, I set off in search of our community and started knocking on restaurant doors. It worked! The chefs understood and appreciated the dedication to the craft, the quality of our produce, the offal. Our community expanded to include farmers and producers too, as Dad and I sought out Australia's best. We became wholesalers of Australia's best meat to many of Australia's best restaurants. Vic's Meat quickly grew into one of the most revered meat companies in Australia.

In 2009, Churchill's Butchery—the oldest continuously run butchery in Australia—was put up for sale. I saw this as an opportunity to open a neighbourhood butchery, something that had eluded us in the early years. When we reopened it as Victor Churchill, we returned the butchery to the community. Our business set the bar for butcheries around the world, putting meat on a pedestal as never before.

I'm incredibly proud of my dad and of the business we have built together. Now we're also working with my sister, Anita: the family business has become a reality. We have had the pleasure of working with many other great families over the decades, from chefs to producers and, perhaps most importantly, our many excellent employees.

When I met Libby in 2005, she was running the Produce Awards for *Vogue Entertaining + Travel*, finding and celebrating producers all over the country. She worked with us at Vic's Meat for a number of years, putting the work of our butchers into words and sharing these stories with our customers and chefs. Over the past decade we have had many (strong-minded!) conversations about the industry.

Libby and I hope that, by writing this book, we can bring your family into our community as well.

Anthony

INTRODUCTION

It wouldn't be an exaggeration to suggest that culture was created over a steak.

When early humans first wrangled fire it brought them warmth and light, while their hunting skills brought meat in quantity; however, it was only when the two came together that they created the defining moment for humans. Cooked meat reduced the time our bodies required for digestion. Our brains had space to develop, time to think. We created conviviality, we created culture and we also created a damn fine meal.

Hunting was the first of the natural contracts between animal and man: you ate what you could catch and kill. Things changed around 10,000 years ago when agriculture started to take shape. Ruminants (sheep, goats and cows) could feed on the stubble of wheat crops, while omnivores (pigs and chickens) could feed on the scraps of the household. As they ate, their fertiliser gave back to the soil, their foraging snouts and hoofs helped to plough and turn the soil, their grazing helped to tame the weeds.

The growth of towns and cities meant these personal connections to the land and the animals diminished. The butcher became the link between farmer and cook. Early archaeological evidence for a butchery dates back to Persia 8500 years ago. In Roman times, they had distinct words for the *boarii* (butchers), the *suarii* (pork butchers) and the *pecuarii* (poultry and game butchers).

As tactics and tools evolved, we began to make decisions about what we were comfortable eating. These questions are interesting and enormous: why chickens, ducks and geese, but not swans, peacocks and swallows? Furthermore, we started to celebrate certain qualities in the animals we chose to farm and consume, highlighting strengths by selective breeding, feeding and farming.

Butchery also evolved. As agriculture became more centralised, so too did the trade. Abattoirs were logical and well organised: did you know that Henry Ford learnt the ways of the industrial production line from butchery?

As the trade spread from the old world to the new, generations of migrant families brought with them the traditions of both farming and butchering from their own countries. The Puharich family, with five generations of butchers from Croatia, have such a heritage.

Sadly, this relationship between farmer, butcher and cook is fracturing. Agriculture is concentrated in the hands of fewer and fewer, with large feedlots and industrialised systems raising animals *en masse*: the animals' proximity means food is trucked in, activity is minimal and, often, antibiotics are employed to keep the animals healthy.

The local butchery is disappearing into the vast cavern of the supermarket, meaning that the closest many get to a conversation about meat is reading the label on the plastic wrapping. This is not just a shame for your kitchen, but a shame for your health—eating good food is the best pre-emptive medicine—and for the environment.

The recipes chosen for this book have been developed by Emma Knowles from classic dishes to celebrate the whole animal, in portion sizes that allow you to purchase better-quality meat. We've taken culinary cues from all over the globe: new versions of recipes from many cultures that have become generational favourites for a reason, as well as a handful of absolute classics, from well-known chefs and cooks, that we've reproduced with permission. This is not restaurant cooking, but family cooking, gathered from all corners of the world.

Among the many choices we make every day, the decision as to what we put on our plates—and into our bellies—has to be one of the most important. And yet, with three meals a day, it can also be the one that feels the most tedious.

This book is designed to help.

SOME THOUGHTS ABOUT MEAT

What was originally a luxury for few is now an expectation for many; yet the population is growing, cities are growing, the middle class is growing. All that growth is putting incredible pressure on farms and the way agriculture sustains us. This book will walk you through the world of meat: from the eyes of the farmer, the butcher and the cook, to help you with the questions you might want to ask yourself before you buy your meat. Thoughtful consumption requires one key ingredient: knowledge.

We have split the chapters into the three key components of an animal's life; the three choices you should be aware of: their breed, their feed and their life and death. In the butchery sections, we explain the key techniques you can use to get the most from your meat, while each cut is described and attributed its own recipe.

BREED

Many scientists believe that we are staring down the barrel of the world's sixth mass extinction. This phenomenon is not just limited to obscure species of tree frogs, but extends to breeds of cattle, chickens and sheep: animals that were regularly served at our parents' and grandparents' tables. The statistics are scary; it is estimated that we are losing almost one breed per month, with one in five species of farm animal in danger of extinction.

In part, this comes down to the industrial nature of much farming: there are only 14 species that provide 90 per cent of the meat we eat! As the breed pool dwindles, so, too, do the small farms, the abattoirs and the infrastructure that supported those businesses. The community suffers too, and we are at risk of losing the traditional ways of working with these breeds and eating them, the old lessons from generations gone by.

Once we lose these breeds, they are gone forever. Supporting barnyard diversity generally comes down to one, perhaps surprising, solution: to save them, we must eat them.

FEED

It was Jean Anthelme Brillat-Savarin, the famous eighteenth-century gastronome, who suggested that we are what we eat. From that idea, it is not a great stretch to suggest that we are also what we eat eats.

As it is with humans, animals with a balanced, nutritious diet are healthier. Nutrients from the soil enter the grass and in turn the animal (which we then eat). Consequently, meat from grass-fed animals is higher in omega–3s and –6s—the 'good' fats—than that of their grain-fed cousins. On the other hand, grain and corn-fed animals offer tenderness that is harder to produce consistently in the wild. Between the grass and the grain there are a number of wild and supplemented feeds, solutions to different terroirs, that have their own delicious impact on the flavour of meat.

What the animal has eaten changes the texture, taste and health benefits of the meat you eat. You are careful about what you eat, so why not extend those thoughts to what you eat eats.

ON THE FARM

The final decision when choosing the meat you put on your table is how you want the animal to have lived (and died). This is largely an ethical question, and thus it comes down to the individual. Do you think animals should live their lives in the outdoors, and what value do you put on that?

The dream solution, a polyculture, with agricultural systems that return to the symbiotic peace and harmony of yesteryear, may not be realistic with our growing global population, but nor is turning to vegetable monocultures and feeding the world a vegan diet. It's all about balance.

Unfortunately, the science on this point is complicated. It is, for example, possible to conclude that industrial farms have a smaller carbon footprint. By centralising the industry, inputs can be brought in once, animals can be moved once, slaughter and processing can also be simplified. There are advantages.

There are also problems. Concentrating animals in one place means concentrating refuse and a whole lot of it. Run-off from feedlots and industrialised farming can wreak untold damage on the local waterways and the greater environment. Antibiotics are often increased to cope with the stress on the animals. In fact, approximately half the antibiotics produced in the USA are fed to animals, not humans, with the situation exaggerated in developing countries such as India and China. We don't deliberately take unnecessary antibiotics, so we should not inadvertently take them either.

There are flavour ramifications, too: free-range animals build up muscle that intensively reared animals do not. These muscles result in more flavour. Unstressed animals will also deliver better-quality meat. This is, perhaps, Mother Nature taking care of these creatures; stressed animals release hormones that change the taste, shelf-life and colour of the meat. Stress is obvious to the buyer and is carefully guarded against by good farmers. This is an important point: farmers don't want to damage their animals. In fact, it is in their interests to protect their assets and to bring them to market in the best shape, if only to make the best profit.

Farmers are not the demons here: it is the market. It's supply and demand. It's the cost the market will bear. Essentially, it is you. Make these choices wisely and the world will be a better place.

THREE GUIDING PRINCIPLES

1. EAT BETTER QUALITY MEAT, BUT EAT LESS OF IT.

Make the choices that matter to you about the animal's breed, feed, life and death, and spend the money to support that choice. March with your wallet. While you are being selective, you can choose to spend a little more, but eat less: perhaps an unusual suggestion from the butcher, but an important one. There is no reason to eat meat with every meal nor to have servings of 250 g (9 oz) per person. The majority of recipes in this book are aimed towards 150 g (5½ oz) per person. Our serving suggestions have been included to balance out each dish with this in mind.

2. EAT THE WHOLE ANIMAL.

We made a conscious decision to avoid 'primary' and 'secondary' cuts when describing the cuts we work with. All cuts were not created equal, but in the hands of a good cook, all cuts can create greatness! However, here, we're not just talking about unloved cuts and offal, we are also talking about using the trimmings from your meat to render fat for your dish; using the bones to make a quick stock; freezing leftovers for later meals. The average household throws away one-third of the groceries they buy. Be aware of this and only buy what you need, when you need it.

3. EAT MORE WILD ANIMALS.

One way we can reduce the burden on industrial agriculture is by eating outside the system. Animals that are endemic to a region tend to have a lighter footprint on the land. When well managed, their numbers will be protected and their lives will be good ones. This is eating in the circle of life. A nice way to eat.

CHAPTER ONE

BIRDS

**CHICKEN ~ DUCK ~ TURKEY ~ GOOSE
SQUAB ~ QUAIL ~ GAME BIRDS**

BIRDS

BEYOND THE FLESH: EGGS, FEATHERS (BEDDING & CUSHIONS), QUILLS, EMU OIL & LEATHER, BONES (STOCK & SOUP)

PRIZED CUTS

TO ROAST *Whole chicken or duck*

TO GRILL *Skin-on supreme (breast fillet with wing attached), butterflied squab, poussin*

TO BRAISE *Bone-in thighs*

TO POACH *Turkey breast*

SELECT & STORE

Where possible choose a free-range bird that has not been frozen. Poultry generally has a very short shelf-life and should be consumed within a few days of purchase. Store in the coolest part of the fridge, preferably at the lowest point. Ensure the bird is set on a plate to catch any juices that could contaminate or drip on other food in your fridge. Always defrost poultry in the refrigerator.

COMPLEMENTS TO THE CHICKEN

EVERYTHING! BUT ESPECIALLY GARLIC, BACON, OLIVES, MUSHROOMS, BUTTER, TARRAGON, CREAM, ONION, LEMON, CHILLI, THYME, PAPRIKA, CUMIN, SAFFRON, SESAME, SOY SAUCE, WINE, CHORIZO, PROSCIUTTO, MAYONNAISE, AÏOLI, LEMON, RICE.

COMPLEMENTS TO THE DUCK & GOOSE

ORANGE, ALL PEPPERS, GARLIC, PEAS AND BEANS, CHERRIES, TURNIPS, CIDER, FIGS, JUNIPER, PORT, PLUMS, CHINESE FIVE SPICE, SOY SAUCE, CHILLI, GINGER, ASIAN GREENS.

COMPLEMENTS TO GAME BIRDS (PHEASANT, PARTRIDGE, QUAIL)

FRUIT, BERRIES, MUSHROOMS, WALNUTS, HAZELNUTS, RED WINE, PORT, SHERRY (DARK FLESH AND DARK WINE ARE PARTICULAR FRIENDS), APPLE, PEAR, QUINCE, CREAM, ONION, PUFF PASTRY, ROOT VEGETABLES.

BIRD FAMILY

TURKEY   **CHICKEN** *AND* **POUSSIN**   **DUCK**   **SQUAB**   **QUAIL**

LEARN MORE ABOUT THE DIFFERENT CUTS AND HOW TO USE THEM ON PAGES 55–63.

CHICKEN LABELS

Corn fed
distinctive for their yellow skin.

Chemical free
processed without chemicals, namely chlorine.

Free range
provided with access to the outdoors at a set ratio, depending on local regulations.

Organic
All organic birds must also be free range. Their diet must be free of antibiotics and vitamin or mineral supplements. These birds are generally slaughtered older (65–80 days rather than 35–55 days).

SKIN OFF VS SKIN ON

Chicken is one of the few animals that is sold at the butchery with the skin still intact. This is a win for flavour hunters, but not for the big supermarkets and processors, as the skin shows the first signs of ageing. This is why much chicken is sold skinless.

—ALL ABOUT—
COOKING
BUY THE WHOLE BIRD

There is a very simple economic argument for buying one, whole, beautifully raised bird and using it all in the kitchen: it is significantly cheaper. Taking apart a chicken is a very simple process, a skill that will stand you in great stead when it comes to both cooking and carving (see page 480). There is also a culinary argument: all the pairs will be the same size, all the skin (where much of the flavour resides) is still attached and the carcass—the chicken bones—in all its flavourful glory remains at the end to be boiled down for your next soup or stock.

BROWN MEAT VS WHITE MEAT

It is the white meat—the breasts—that are often favoured at the family table. This is a terrible shame, as much of the flavour resides in the darker flesh of the bird. As with all animals, it is these darker cuts (the thighs, wings and drumsticks) that do most of the work in the field. With the greatest work-out comes the greatest flavour.

DARK MEAT

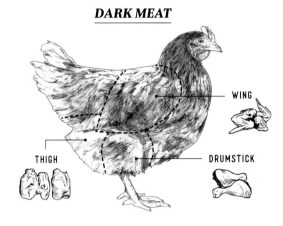

THIGH · WING · DRUMSTICK

⊢ LEFTOVERS ⊢

Stock, stock and stock: learn how to quickly turn your leftover carcass (even after a roast) into a speedy stock for the basis of your next soup, risotto or stew (see page 460). Soup will also be a great home for any leftover roasted chicken meat. One bird, two stones.

BUTCHER'S TREATS

THE CHICKEN OYSTER (OR, AS THE FRENCH CALL IT, *LE SOT L'Y LAISSE*, TRANSLATING AS 'THE IDIOT LEAVES IT BEHIND')

THE PARSON'S NOSE

LIVER AND HEART

THE SKIN

RENDERED DUCK AND CHICKEN FAT

TIP: *Rest your roasted chicken breast-side down so that all the juices flow back into the breast.*

HISTORY

The world has turned to a comforting chicken soup to nurture the body and soul for centuries, if not millennia. One of the great natural medicines, this broth has been used as a treatment for both the common cold and the winter blues.

Chicken bones, with or without a little flesh still clinging to them, simmered for a number of hours, give up a delicious golden elixir with an intrinsic comfort, the warmth of a great hug in big arms.

The Jewish philosopher and physician Maimonides prescribed chicken soup for respiratory problems as far back as the twelfth century and, to this day, there is nothing quite so efficient at countering colds as 'Jewish penicillin': a chicken broth bolstered with matzo balls bound with *schmaltz* (rendered chicken fat).

In Greece, they boost the restorative properties of their chicken soup, *avgolemono*, with lemon and egg white; while in Columbia, it's *ajiaco*, thickened with corn and potato; the Vietnamese have their *pho gà*, embellished with fresh herbs, ginger and lime.

In China, they serve chicken soup during the traditional period of self-imposed 'internment' following childbirth (indeed, they also use whole chickens, some women eating up to one entire chicken each day during this period); there is a similar period of care for new mums in some parts of Africa, where it is the native guinea fowl that is slowly braised in a little liquid.

King Henry IV of France, in the sixteenth century, was such an admirer of the humble chicken and its soup, that he proclaimed his desire that every home in his kingdom should have the means to regularly enjoy *poule au pot*, the traditional French version.

How terrible to think how we, in return, treat the chicken. The majority of chickens live in large barns with little room to move; scant, if any, access to natural lighting; and no access to the outside world. Their breeding pool has been narrowed to the tipping point and they are designed to put on bulk at a rate their legs can barely sustain; these are Frankensteinian animals that hardly resemble their barnyard ancestors of only a few decades ago. Furthermore, their existence has been reduced to as few as 28 days of hard and fast labour: eat, grow, die. Those few weeks are less than half the time it took their forebears to mature. It is hard to imagine how an animal so maltreated can offer care and sustenance to us.

Of course, these systems have meant that, at least financially, Henry IV's ideal is now a possibility. In Australia, for example, we eat 10 times more chicken than we did 60 years ago. Taking into account that the overall consumption of meat has changed very little in this period—remaining at around 110 kg (240 lb) of protein per person per annum—this is an incredible shift. For those with tight budgets and big families to feed this, of course, can be viewed as a positive.

But what if King Henry was wrong? What if chicken should be a special occasion treat? Or, at the very least, respected in totality: each chicken valued and utilised for every part the bird offers up? One beautiful bird, bought in its entirety—if you're lucky, with the neck and feet still attached and, as in France, sold with the liver and heart, not just a cook's treat but proof of the freshness of the bird—can feed a couple or a small family a number of times over. The breasts can be removed and diced for quick cooking in a stir-fry or flattened for schnitzels; the thighs, wings and legs make for fantastic slow cooking in tagines, curries and stews; while the bones will always offer up that precious restorative elixir, stock: use it as a soup on its own or as the base of your next risotto, polenta or gravy.

What value should we place on one purchase that can achieve all of that?

Chickens, *in fact all poultry, are omnivores, eating vegetable matter along with insects, lizards, grass and grains. See pages 42–43 for more on feed.*

BREED

The vast majority of the chicken we eat comes from only two breeds: Ross (from Scotland) and Cobb (from North America). In our quest to streamline production of this bird, with high productivity and fast growth rates at the forefront, the ubiquitous chicken we now eat comes from the tiniest genetic pool. It was not always this way.

It is believed that chickens, descendants of the megapode, a jungle bird of Malaysia, were first domesticated in the Indus Valley more than 4000 years ago, before making their way to Europe. The reason behind their arrival in Europe was not food, but rather entertainment (if we can call cockfighting 'entertainment').

→ Cockfighting was a popular blood sport. Terminology such as the word 'cockpit' remains as testament to this.

Chickens quickly found favour beyond the arena, on the sacrificial table and dining table. All manner of birds, including peacocks, swans and flamingos (in fact, pretty much all except the turkey, with its roots in the Americas), were served at Roman feasts. To keep their supply up the Romans used hot vapour to incubate chickens.

It is the Egyptians, however, who are credited with creating the first incubators by storing eggs in very gentle ovens fuelled by manure and straw. The Chinese also used an oven of sorts for their prized ducks, supplementing man-made heat with the natural warmth produced by older eggs to heat the younger ones.

Poultry breeding really hit its straps at the turn of last century. There is a thriving industry producing beautiful backyard chickens with plumage ranging from browns through spots to white, deep red cockscombs to puffs of white feathers on their heads that would rival a racegoer's fascinator. But it's not all about the feathers.

For the nonmigratory chicken, the predominant story of breeding is one of consumer preference and greed: white feathers are prized more highly than dark, white breast meat finds favour over darker thighs, resulting in busty birds barely able to hold their own weight on their less-appreciated legs. (Don't be fooled by the simplicity of the breast, so much more flavour resides in the thighs and wings!) Breeding programs have focussed on meat production (egg-laying chickens are drawn from another genetic pool entirely: see page 48), and have edged out many of the natural traits of these jungle birds.

The implications of narrowing the chicken's genetic pool were driven home in Hugh Fearnley-Whittingstall's excellent documentary *Hugh's Chicken Run*.

Cockscomb
The cockscomb is the fleshy growth on top of the chicken's head. It is generally larger on a male. See page 54 for more information.

Fearnley-Whittingstall wanted to understand the differences between organic, free-range chickens and intensively reared battery chickens. In order to compare the two methods of farming, Fearnley-Whittingstall set up two sheds side by side: one free range, one intensive. The farming methods were different, but intriguingly so too were the breeds of bird: it seems the intensively reared birds have had the curiosity, the adventure—indeed, their very nature—bred out of them.

American farmer, author and advocate for holistic farming Joel Salatin confronted these issues when he chose the birds to use in his circular polyfarm system; a symbiotic system designed to thrive on the different stomachs that pass over his land. Salatin steered away from commercial breeds to find birds that still had the brains to run from predators and the brawn to effectively forage in the fields.

Intelligence, ingenuity and intrigue are important for more than survival; birds that only stay beside the feed bin will not only miss the opportunity to put on muscle mass, they will also miss out on the varied diet available in the field. These are two crucial elements in the development of a flavourful bird. Chicken is an incredible vehicle for flavour, but it should also have excellent flavour of its own.

There are some commercial exceptions to this rule. The *poulet de Bresse*, considered by many connoisseurs to be the best tasting chicken in the world, is bred from a highly protected genetic pool in the region of Bresse, France. Their production method is also carefully controlled, if a little controversial, and they are sold with tags on their black feet to confirm the breed and farm of origin. Juicy and rich in flavour, they deserve the extra attention; however, with the Bresse genetics so fiercely guarded and the stranglehold of the intensively raised breeds Ross and Cobb so tight, it is hard work to break free from these genetic shackles.

In Australia, poultry-breeder and farmer Michael Sommerlad joined a dozen different Australian heritage breeds to create a bird that is strengthened by this genetic variety. A motley crew, full of varieties your great-grandmother would have recognised, these birds are up to four months old when they are processed and can grow to 5 kg (11 lb 4 oz), compared to industrially reared chickens processed at around one month and 1.6 kg (3 lb 8 oz). The conformation of these birds is incredible: strong thighs, dark meat and rich flavour, this animal has lived a good life in an environment where they belong. All the Sommerlad birds retain the characteristics that allowed them to live in the jungles and are raised accordingly.

Tracing the origin of other breeds of fowl we enjoy at the table is more complicated for a very simple reason: they fly. (In fact, the chicken and the guinea fowl—from the African bush—are the only nonmigratory birds that we consume regularly.)

Traditionally, eating migratory birds was more closely connected with the seasons and solar calendar than their terroir. As they left northern European homes in autumn to fly to the tropics, opportunists below would take advantage of the moveable feast above. This remains the case with many game birds in the UK and Europe: they aren't suited to captivity and remain a score for opportunists to this day.

→ Hugh's Chicken Run *aired on the UK's Channel 4, as part of their Food Fight series. It is an excellent documentary and one of the few that actually allow the viewer to see the reality behind industrial chicken farming.*

→ *Joel Salatin's farming methods were brought to international attention by Michael Pollan, in his excellent book* The Omnivore's Dilemma: A Natural History of Four Meals *(Penguin, 2007). Pollan also coined the phrase: 'you are what what you eat eats'.*

Ortolan

→ *Hunting and eating this little wild bird is illegal in the European Union, but the legendary manner of its preparation and eating is a story for the ages: kept in a darkened cage to simulate night (its feeding time), it is fattened, then roasted and eaten whole with one's head under a napkin, supposedly so as to hide one's gluttony from God.*

Their breeds are as diverse as their homes: with fewer industrial constraints they have bred and interbred to suit their environment and, perhaps consequently, they all offer incredible treats at the table. The variety of game birds found in Europe—the bécasse (snipe), pheasant and partridge—herald the arrival of autumn. They are something to make the passing of summer a little easier to bear.

DUCKS AND GEESE

And then, of course, there is the duck, a wonder all of its own: whether roasted whole, lacquered and served golden and crisp at Chinese feasts; adding its rich flavour to South-East Asian curries; or confit in its own fat to preserve the duck.

The duck fat is a culinary marvel that is also used to make deliciously crisp potatoes in southwestern France. There is a lot to love about the logical evolution of French cookery, the way different regions have been moulded over the centuries by their own terroir, seasons and produce. In some regions the correlation is obvious. The glittering olive trees that thrive along the Mediterranean coast provide the oil that is intrinsic to the cooking of the south, while the lush green pastures of the north nurture a dairy industry and consequently a diet rich in butter and cream. In the west, and particularly the southwest of France, it is duck and goose fat that adds a unique flavour to the cuisine.

It was the migratory path of wild geese and ducks that inspired this reliance on duck and goose fat. While most of the birds are now farmed, traditionally the turning of the autumn leaves was accompanied by the arrival of these birds, heading south to avoid the harsh winters and frozen lakes of their northern breeding grounds. They arrived fat from months of preparatory gorging, a feast designed to sustain them on journeys that can be as long as three to four thousand kilometres. Some birds can put on up to 50 per cent of their weight (in fat) in just a couple of weeks before they fly!

Dishes rich in the fat that is carefully rendered from these birds are found all over the region, from the cassoulet to *confit de canard* (duck slowly cooked in its own fat, so it can be stored in the cooled fat for months).

The rich fattiness of duck, coupled with the slight sweetness in the flesh is a delicacy adored the world over. With this extra richness, duck can be more forgiving to cook, but there is a greater disparity between the time required to cook the breast and the legs. Thus, there is a lot to be said for removing the legs and getting them started first, before adding the rest of the carcass.

Pound for pound, ducks provide less meat than chickens: they have a heavier carcass, thicker skin and often a lot of fat. This fat can (and should) be put to use in your kitchen and this is another bird we strongly recommend you buy in its entirety and joint at home.

Ducklings, *originally migratory, are now often bred for meat on farms. Read more about life on the farm on pages 48–49.*

HERITAGE BREED MAP: BIRDS

EUROPE

Aylesbury duck

Named for a small town in the UK, this is a great meat duck: it is slightly leaner than the Pekin of North America, but has delicious sweet fat.

Pigeon

Squab is the culinary term for a pigeon, but more specifically refers to a pigeon that has not actually flown yet.

Quail

The quail is usually solitary. They are migratory and can fly, but some species walk in a small flock for protection.

Rouen duck

The drake (male) is light grey with a green neck, the female is light brown. A heavy breed and good layers.

Bécasse (snipe)

Cooked and consumed in their entirety: stomach, brains and all.

Poulet de Bresse

Bresse chickens spend four months in the field before being fed for the final two weeks on a diet of skim milk, oats and maize.

Partridge

Partridges are medium-sized nonmigratory game birds, with wide distribution throughout Europe.

Grouse

The flesh is dark and gamey. Be careful not to overcook them, as they can become bitter and iron-y.

Goose

A trophy bird for the Christmas table, the goose has a similar flavour profile to the duck, but is larger of form.

EURASIA AND NORTH AFRICA

Mallard ducks

The wild mallard has been eaten since Neolithic time. It has a delicious flavour and is easy to prepare, not necessarily requiring hanging.

AFRICA

Guinea fowl (bim)

A nonmigratory bird, descended from birds of the African savannahs. Smaller than chicken with slight bones and amber flesh, it has a slightly gamey taste.

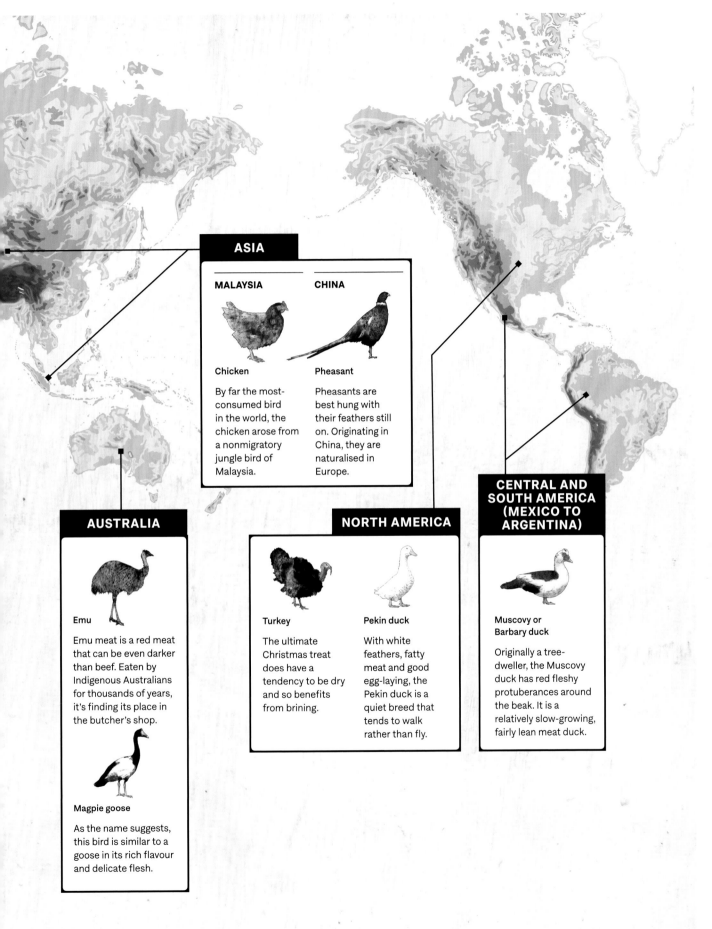

ASIA

MALAYSIA

Chicken

By far the most-consumed bird in the world, the chicken arose from a nonmigratory jungle bird of Malaysia.

CHINA

Pheasant

Pheasants are best hung with their feathers still on. Originating in China, they are naturalised in Europe.

AUSTRALIA

Emu

Emu meat is a red meat that can be even darker than beef. Eaten by Indigenous Australians for thousands of years, it's finding its place in the butcher's shop.

Magpie goose

As the name suggests, this bird is similar to a goose in its rich flavour and delicate flesh.

NORTH AMERICA

Turkey

The ultimate Christmas treat does have a tendency to be dry and so benefits from brining.

Pekin duck

With white feathers, fatty meat and good egg-laying, the Pekin duck is a quiet breed that tends to walk rather than fly.

CENTRAL AND SOUTH AMERICA (MEXICO TO ARGENTINA)

Muscovy or Barbary duck

Originally a tree-dweller, the Muscovy duck has red fleshy protuberances around the beak. It is a relatively slow-growing, fairly lean meat duck.

FEED

Chickens, along with the occasional pig, traditionally played the role of composters and waste consumers in the farmyard. The implicit contract between farmer and bird was one of much mutual respect.

On the farm, chickens have tacitly bartered their eggs in return for kitchen scraps (thus also minimising the farmer's waste) and a safe place to scavenge for worms and bugs. When their laying days were up, the chickens' lives—perhaps less romantically—would end in the pot.

Chickens—in fact, almost all poultry—are omnivores, eating vegetable matter along with insects, lizards, grass and grains. It is in their natural habitat that they perform best, with the four Gs to keep them happy: grains, greens, grubs and grits (including small stones, sand and often crushed oyster shells for calcium, that aid digestion; a component of the diet that is particularly important for turkeys). It's a good life for those that can get it.

For most chickens, these days are long gone and instead the standard broiler, or meat chicken, is fed a prepared high-protein crumble from start to finish. In Australia, this is largely composed of grains, while in America the chickens are predominantly corn-fed: just as with their cattle, this largely comes down to corn being such a cheap commodity. The corn lends a yellow tone to the skin, a sweeter flavour and fattier flesh, which adds a juiciness to the meat.

From birth to around four days before processing, that feed will often be medicated: they may receive antibiotics, although it is a myth that hormones are used to promote growth in chickens in most Western countries. The antibiotics are a precaution used particularly for barn-raised chickens; with up to 40,000 birds in a shed a single bug will spread like wildfire. Recent scientific evidence has suggested this also aids weight gain, but at what cost to us, the consumers? This is a question that is yet to be definitively answered.

There are alternatives to this kind of production, but sadly not much that still incorporates the varied diet of yesteryear; even organic chickens are fed a prepared mix, albeit one made with organic grains or corn.

The solution, if you want to find a truly flavourful bird, is to find a producer you trust, or a butcher who has done that work for you. Keep in mind that even if the predominant feed is a crumble, the free-ranging and organic birds benefit from time outside not just for the access to grubs and grass, but for the exercise to build muscle mass: just as it is with all animals, this work-out helps the muscles to develop flavour.

FOIE GRAS

Foie gras—literally translating to 'fat liver'—is perhaps the most controversial of the duck and goose products. Of course, we eat duck and chicken liver in pâtés and parfaits regularly; however, foie gras are livers that have been purposely fattened to the point of atrophy. These livers, often served as whole lobes, are celebrated for their rich, buttery yet delicate flavour and considered a culinary delicacy across France and throughout the world. However, it is the process of *gavage*—a system whereby the birds are force-fed corn, much of it poured down their throat through a funnel—that has polarised diners for decades, with some countries even banning the practice.

For an alternative, seek out the foie gras produced by Eduardo Sousa and Diego Labourdette in Extremadura, Spain. The region was traditionally a resting place for geese en route to the tropics during their migration. Sousa's grandfather noticed the birds would often stay on, enjoying the habitat; however, their natural instinct to gorge in the autumn remained. Working with the natural life cycle of these geese, the birds are left to wander the 500 hectare (1235 acre) property, feasting on acorns (the region is perhaps most famous for its acorn-fed black pigs: see page 210) and grasses. Their foie gras has won awards around the world, even in the French motherland. It's worth seeking out!

Chickens

ON THE FARM

Chickens and many of the other birds we eat are gregarious animals, foraging, roosting and travelling—often on the wing—in small or vast flocks to search far and wide for their sustenance. Sadly, intensive farming has taken the concept of flocking to extremes.

The life of a chicken has long been connected to that of the deities. The weathervane found its place on the rooftops of churches as the image of St Peter (who was said to have betrayed Jesus three times before the cock crowed). In India, the cock is associated with the sun, while the Greeks consecrated the cock to both the lunar and solar deities. There are similar tales of divinity seen from Africa to Mexico, Vietnam to China. In some Muslim cultures, they say if the cock crows outside the regular morning hours it is an angel passing by.

Sadly, the twentieth century saw many changes for the chicken and the rooster. The romantic sound of the crowing of the rooster to start the day is becoming a rarity. So, too, are the dual-purpose birds, providing both eggs and meat, their multiple talents exchanged for a life in pursuit of one part of the equation or the other. We now have two specific breeding pools: one for the egg producers, one for the meat.

In most cases, the farmyard has been replaced with massive air-conditioned barns. Egg-laying hens are packed in cages or barns and forced to live out their producing days pumping out all the eggs they can; the female chicks are bred to become layers, while the male chicks are discarded soon after hatching to avoid wasted feed. Artificial lights are controlled to provide extra hours of 'daylight', consequently avoiding the inconvenient traditional lull in winter months. Some breeds of chicken can now lay up to 300 eggs per annum. For all intents and purposes the egg-laying chicken has become an industrialised machine.

Meat chickens (known as broilers in the USA) are spared this fruitless quest for egg accumulation; however, their lives are no better. They are not subjected to cages, but only a small percentage of them have access to the outdoors or any sunlight. They too live a life with a controlled temperature—the birds too feeble to handle fluctuations—and artificial lights are used to maximise time at the feed bin. Regulations set for the number of dark hours in the shed vary from country to country, but can be as low as three or four hours per day. While it has now been

How did le coq become the emblem of France?

→ *For the fighting? For its sexual prowess, perhaps its pride? The truth, a little less excitingly, lies in the origin of the breed's scientific name,* Gallus gallus. *The Latin word for rooster,* gallus, *is similar to the word* Galli, *meaning the people of Gaul (the French).*

discovered that the dark hours help the birds to regenerate their melatonin stores and thus aid immune function and disease resistance, that is no match for the desire to encourage weight gain.

The much-maligned battery farm is not new; in fact, it dates back to Roman times, when chickens were traditionally fattened from the new moon to the last quarter. Pigeons were also battery farmed, with their legs first broken to prevent flight and the consequent change in texture and flavour. Geese have been force-fed since the times of the Ancient Greeks. This style of farming does not offer much in the form of dietary variety or activity for the bird, and thus neither does it for those who consume them.

It is important to note that these production techniques, refined breeds and high-protein feeds do mean that the intensive chicken meat and egg industry can produce more with less: less space, less water, less energy. It is no life for the chicken, but it does feed many people with less outputs, on paper. With world production sitting at around 60 billion birds per year, the cumulative effect of these small gains can be massive. It's a numbers game and the figures and arguments can be viewed to present a strong case for either side. Many of the decisions for your kitchen will be based on your own gut feeling. Do you want chickens that have fed from the earth, that have acquired muscle and thus flavour from time outside? Does happiness come into the equation? These are personal questions, ones that only you can answer.

There are some great free-range and organic producers—from chicken producers to duck and quail—working to provide an alternative for those who seek it. Beyond access to the outdoors—providing a lifestyle that allows them to build muscle and bone at a rate that is in keeping with the nutrients around them—some of these producers are also restoring the breeding stock of the birds of yesteryear (see page 36). These production methods also have many shades of grey: commercial free range may have different stocking density to a local family farm.

There has also been significant growth in the numbers of people raising their own backyard chickens. Chickens (and in fact many of the birds we eat) are gregarious animals; social creatures who like to live in a flock. If keeping your own chickens, be warned that this social system is delicate—those at the top of the pecking order will have first dibs on the feed and the best roosting spot—and losing one of these birds will require some adjustment for the flock. Conversely, bringing other birds into the mix can cause friction: the term 'hen-pecked' is literal when used in the chicken yard. It's not nice.

→ *In spite of their apparent ease in big cities, pigeons are considered the most difficult bird to raise in numbers for their meat.*

There remain many breeds of bird that are not domesticated, but hunted with much delight when the season allows: pheasants, grouse, partridges and jungle fowl are thought to have been hunted since the Stone Age. And then there are pigeons, now bred in captivity (a squab is actually a pigeon that has never flown), that have been hunted from woods to town squares (in particular times of need) across the globe.

Chickens

While chickens can be commercially processed from around 28 days old, some farmers are turning to heritage breeds that take longer to reach maturity.

AGE AT SLAUGHTER

Capon or cockerel? The stage of development of the chicken dictates the name it is sold under.

Poussin – baby chicken 450–500 g (1 lb–1 lb 2 oz) weight. In Australia this is often mistakenly called a spatchcock, which is a butchery method, not a bird.

Chicken or broiler – young birds, generally processed at six to eight weeks (but can be as fast as 28 days and as long as five months; they technically can be called chickens up to a year old). Commercially reared birds can be male or female and there is very little difference in their flavour at this young age.

Cockerels – males less than one year, praised for their flavour. (A *coquelet* is a young cockerel.)

Pullets – females less than one year. A fattened pullet is smaller than a cockerel at 2 kg (4 lb 8 oz). Also the name used for small eggs laid before the chicken has reached maturity.

Capon – castrated young male (often castrated chemically). A capon will grow much bigger than a cockerel or a pullet, between 3 and 3.5 kg (6 lb 12 oz and 7 lb 14 oz). Many believe the capon has a better flavour than a hen.

Hens – females, one year or older.

Boiler – old laying hen, great for stocks. A laying hen usually ends her career in a pot, thus fulfilling the wish of King Henry IV (see page 30). Not to be mistaken for a broiler, which is a young bird for grilling.

Roosters – male, one year or older, a fully grown cock can grow to 5 kg (11 lb 4 oz) at 18 months. Not suitable for roasting but better jointed and cooked. Cocks' kidneys and cockscombs are considered a delicacy in some parts of the world.

→ *The capon is credited to the Romans. To preserve grain rations it was forbidden to eat fattened hens, so they castrated cockerels and fattened them instead. The serendipity of the discovery led to a much bigger bird and much more flavour.*

DUCKS

Most ducks are processed at less than eight weeks, when their pin-feathers become too hard to remove.

Duckling – generally less than three or four weeks of age, they officially turn into ducks when they are fully in feather.

Duck (hen) – more prized than the drake, the female duck is softer in both texture and flavour.

Drake – a male duck, which can be quite lean and muscly with a tighter texture and more robust flavour than the female.

Average processing age of other birds

→ **Turkey** *12–14 weeks*
→ **Quail** *5–6 weeks*
→ **Squab** *4 weeks*
→ **Goose** *16–20 weeks*

EGGS

Eggs are a nourishing and perfectly balanced food, providing all the amino acids essential to human nutrition. Harold McGee, in his book *On Food and Cooking: The Science and Lore of the Kitchen*, points out that eggs, along with 'their botanical counterparts the seeds, and milk, are among the most nutritious foods on earth, and for much the same reason. Unlike meats or vegetables, they are all designed to be foods, to support chick embryo, seedling, and calf until these organisms are able to exploit other sources of nourishment.' (Scribner, 1984.)

The true beauty of the egg lies in its ability to be transformed into many different dishes. Eggs are used to bind ingredients together, such as hamburger patties and meatballs. Gently beaten, they make an excellent glaze for a pie. Yolks are used to thicken sauces and soups and to emulsify mayonnaise, aïoli and hollandaise sauce. Beaten egg whites are used to make light meringues and crisp batters.

→ *If you want to really understand the wonder of the egg pick up Harold McGee's brilliant book,* On Food and Cooking, *and read through the process of an egg being developed inside the chicken: it is absolutely fascinating. In fact, this is the absolute go-to for all food-based science questions. A fundamental book for your cookery collection.*

The cheapest and most versatile of all ingredients you can conquer, eggs are nutritious: it only takes one to provide all those amino acids! Eggs are cheap: even the most prized egg comes in at a tiny cost per gram. Eggs are versatile: the flavour of an egg can be complemented by many different flavours.

The key to a good egg dish is undeniably in the quality of the egg. Fresh eggs, produced by hens that are able to run around and eat a good diet, are a world apart from the cage-laid egg sitting on a supermarket shelf that you may be familiar with.

Try to buy eggs that have been refrigerated, as this has a big impact on their freshness. Eggs will deteriorate more in one day at room temperature than one week in the fridge. Eggs should be stored unwashed (washing strips the already porous shell, exposing the egg to odours in the fridge) with the pointed end down, in the least cold part of the fridge.

Cooking with eggs

→ *Older eggs are great used in a meringue as the eggs will form peaks more easily. If you are using fresh eggs, add a generous pinch of salt.*

→ *Bring eggs to room temperature if combining with other ingredients. This is particularly important when the eggs need to emulsify with those ingredients as in mayonnaise or meringues.*

Look for eggs that have at least a month left on their use-by date. It takes 21 days for an egg to hatch and not much more for a fresh egg to deteriorate (about one month). The air bubble, intended to provide oxygen to the chicken, grows as the egg gets older.

To test the freshness of an egg, plunge it into 160 g (5¾ oz/½ cup) of salt dissolved in 1 litre (35 fl oz/4 cups) of water: an egg up to three days old will instantly fall to the bottom (small air bubble); at three to six days old it will float halfway up; if it is bad it will float horizontally on top of the water. Another test for freshness is to crack the egg onto a plate (you can do this if you are ready to use it immediately). If the yolk sits up tall amid the white and the egg white sits up off the plate (as opposed to running all over the plate like water) then the egg is fresh.

Storing eggs with truffles allows the beautiful truffle flavour to permeate the porous shells and makes delicious scrambled eggs. Seek organic or biodynamic eggs, as these classifications must all be truly free range.

AT THE BUTCHER

Look to other cultures that always use the whole bird with bones and all: the stews, curries and tagines from all corners of the globe, with bones for flavour and different cuts for contrast.

Of the chicken we eat, how much of it is bought as a whole bird? The answer is very little. It's a terrible shame that so many people buy their chicken in individual pieces, especially when there are so many creative things to do with the whole bird. Buying a whole bird is economical: it can offer multiple meals, and it also means you have a number of pairs, meaning you can work with equal cooking time for the wings, breasts, drumsticks and thighs. In many European countries, chickens are sold with head and feet on, and giblets inside, to prove their freshness.

THE CARCASS

Chicken **breasts** are generally sold with skin off because the skin shows the age first. They are excellent cooked skin-side down on the barbecue, where the skin will render and become crisp, while also preventing the breast from drying out.

Chicken **thighs** have a beautiful deep flavour and don't dry out as easily as the breast. The **drumstick** also carries this deeper flavour and has the advantage of a built-in handle. The drumstick with the thigh still attached is known as a **Maryland** or leg quarter.

Chicken **wings** are a crowd pleaser, when marinated and slowly roasted until unctuous and sticky. **Wing tips**, **necks**, **feet** and the **carcass** are great for stock: freeze these and wait until you have enough to make a rich brown chicken stock.

In the Piedmont region of northern Italy, **cockscomb** is a vital ingredient in a stew known as *finanziera*, a dish that also uses the rooster's **wattles** (the flaps under the beak) and **testicles**. Cockscombs are used in conjunction with chicken livers and eggs in a sauce served with tagliatelle known as *cimabella con cibreo*. They have an excellent gelatinous texture. The chicken **liver**, best known in pâté and parfait, may be quickly pan-fried and served on some bread as the ultimate cook's treat. The **heart** is also delicious when grilled and served blushing pink in the middle. It's a favourite in yakitori restaurants.

→ *The best way to ascertain the freshness of your poultry is to look at the processing date. Ideally you want to be eating chicken within two to three days of processing.*

CHICKEN CUTS

*Buy a beautifully raised whole chicken and celebrate
the sum of its parts.*

For more about chicken cuts, see pages 58–60.

DUCK CUTS

Many people just buy duck breasts, leaving behind the carcass (an excellent addition to your next poultry stock), the unctuous thighs and, of course, the fat.

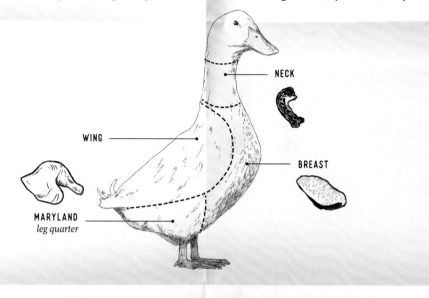

TURKEY CUTS

On the American Thanksgiving table, it is the native turkey that is at the centre of the feast. This large endemic bird is thought to have saved the Pilgrims.

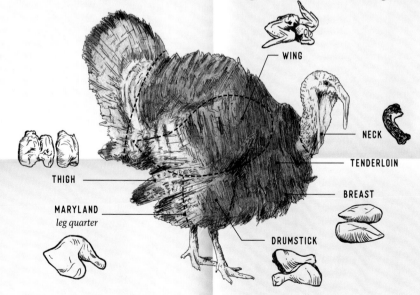

SQUAB CUTS

Gamier than chicken, squab is particularly delicious roasted.
The bird is best butterflied before a quick grilling.

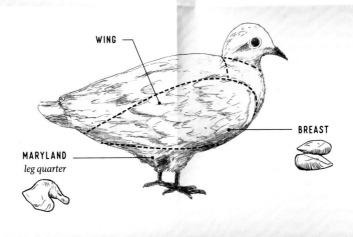

QUAIL CUTS

Due to their size, quails are best allotted one per person, either roasted whole,
tea-smoked or butterflied and grilled on the barbecue.

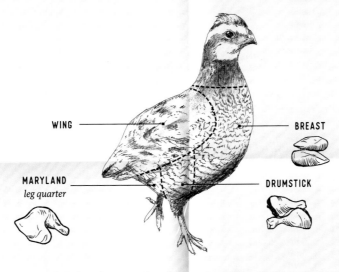

For more about bird cuts, see pages 61–63.

CHICKEN CUTS

WHOLE CHICKEN

The comfort of a whole roast chicken is undeniable: it's a classic family dinner, an awesome contrast of crisp skin and soft flesh. However, a whole chicken should also be seen as the sum of its parts; especially when there are so many creative things you can do if you buy the whole bird. Beyond the standard chicken stock or broth, the whole chicken holds precious treats including the parson's nose and two little nuggets underneath the chicken known as the oysters. While its clean flavour makes it the most popular of animals, it also presents a canvas for the creative cook.

→ Buy a whole chicken, joint it at home and use carcass and wings for stock.

→ Ask your butcher to butterfly your chicken for the barbecue; alternatively, see page 484 to learn how to do it yourself.

→ Carve a cooked chicken as you would joint a raw one: separate wings, thighs and drumsticks; take the breasts off whole, then slice horizontally.

CUT WEIGHT: 1.6–1.8 KG (3 LB 8 OZ–4 LB)
BEST COOKED: ROASTED
OPTIMAL FINISH: COOKED THROUGH
RECIPES: PAGES 70–77

BREAST

The breast is perhaps the most popular part of the chicken. It's an amazing carrier of flavour, but doesn't really have a lot of flavour on its own. Unlike any other meat, it has an incredible purity to it; however, the breast does need attention so it does not overcook and become dry. A breast with all or part of the wing attached makes for a nice presentation and is called a supreme or airline breast.

Two breasts together on the bone, known as a crown or buffet, make a great roast for two or three. Chicken breasts are lean and great for pan-frying, poaching, grilling and smoking.

→ Try to buy chicken breast with the skin on for extra flavour and protection when cooking (they are often sold with the skin removed because the skin shows age first).

CUT WEIGHT: 220–280 G (7¾–10 OZ)
BEST COOKED: POACHED
OPTIMAL FINISH: COOKED THROUGH
RECIPES: PAGES 80–87

WINGS

Every child's favourite, a chicken wing slow-roasted and sticky is a finger food like no other. They are also inexpensive, rich and fatty and are a great flavour burst. Chefs will caramelise chicken wings with onions, cover with water and simmer to make a rich brown chicken stock that is great for risotto or soup and can be a good alternative to veal stock.

This is the perfect piece of chicken to marinate, with a world of flavours at your fingertips.

→ The wing comprises three parts: the wing tip, the drumette and the mid-wing.

→ If you are making a brown chicken stock (see page 460), cut the wings into three parts to maximise the surface area for browning.

CUT WEIGHT: 80–90 G (2¾–3¼ OZ)
BEST COOKED: SLOWLY ROASTED
OPTIMAL FINISH: UNCTUOUS AND STICKY
RECIPES: PAGES 92–93 AND 460

MARYLAND

LEG QUARTER

The Maryland is the whole leg, including both the bone-in thigh and the drumstick attached. Both these cuts work well with slow, gentle cooking and the bone adds excellent flavour to your braise or casserole. The Maryland can also be boned and stuffed, creating a delicious package full of the best flavour of the bird.

→ Sometimes the Maryland will be sold with the spine still attached, but you can ask your butcher to remove this.

→ Found where the thigh attaches to the spine is the ultimate cook's treat: two small oyster-shaped nuggets of flesh that can be slipped from their sockets on each side of the spine. They are super-tender and incredibly tasty: somewhere between the brown and white meat of the chicken.

CUT WEIGHT: 250–300 G (9–10½ OZ)
BEST COOKED: BRAISED
OPTIMAL FINISH: COOKED THROUGH
RECIPES: PAGES 88–91

THIGH

This is a flavour-packed, juicy and tender cut of chicken. The chicken thigh is a great option for dinner for one. The thigh will have more flavour and darker meat than the breast and will enjoy a little slower cooking time. It is great for braises or stews as it will remain juicy. The thigh fillet can come with the drumstick attached, which is called a chicken Maryland (leg quarter). This cut is perhaps the most forgiving and certainly has the most flavour.

→ Try to get your thighs with the skin on for added flavour.

→ Bone-in thighs also offer an extra boost of flavour.

CUT WEIGHT: ABOUT 120 G (4¼ OZ)
BEST COOKED: BRAISED
OPTIMAL FINISH: TENDER
RECIPE: PAGES 78–79

DRUMSTICKS

Chicken drumsticks have made themselves known to the world deep-fried and served in a bucket. By playing with different marinades, you can do great things with drumsticks at home.

Their natural shape makes them a great option for the kids and the flavour of this cut makes it an easy one to dress up. For a bigger meal, you can serve them attached to the thigh, when they are known as a Maryland or leg quarter.

→ If marinating drumsticks, carefully score the skin, to help the marinade penetrate better.

→ Soaking drumsticks in buttermilk overnight, before crumbing and frying, will help the complex muscles break down and become more tender.

CUT WEIGHT: 100 G (3½ OZ)
BEST COOKED: DEEP–FRIED
RECIPE: PAGES 92–93

Please note that all weights are approximate, as animals will differ based on their age, breed and feed.
For more information on cooking styles, roasting times, etcetera, see pages 448–455.

BONES, NECK, FEET

Chicken and duck bones, including (or, perhaps more correctly, particularly with) the necks and feet, are most excellent for making stocks. Whether it's a raw carcass or the picked carcass after your roast dinner, this simple frame is full of minerals and has a lot to offer. Good butchers will happily sell you carcasses to add to your stock. Necks and feet may need to be ordered in, but are worth the effort: the necks are rich in collagen, while the feet are all tendons, bone and cartilage, providing nourishment as well as a gel-like texture to your stock.

→ Broth is technically made with the meat still clinging to the bones, while stock is made with just the bones.
→ Chicken necks are multifaceted, meaning there's more surface area exposed to the hot water, making for a more flavourful stock or broth.
→ Necks, like wings, can be roasted before they are used for a chicken stock, lending a deep, rich flavour.
→ Duck necks are particularly prized and, in the hands of a skilled chef or butcher, can be turned into the most amazing duck neck sausages.

GIBLETS

Gizzards: The gizzard is a muscle that forms part of the digestive tract in a bird: it's used to grind food with previously swallowed stones and grit, an evolutionary tool to make up for the lack of teeth. Duck, chicken and turkey gizzards can all be found at a good butcher. As hardworking muscles they require long, slow cooking, but reward with a rich, dark chicken meat flavour. They are an excellent source of iron.

Hearts: Chicken and duck hearts are delicious grilled and served medium-rare. To prepare, remove the outer membrane, trim the ventricles and pick out any blood clots. Duck hearts have a little more sweetness, while chicken hearts can have a slight bitterness.

Liver: Predominantly used in pâtés and parfaits (see page 97) for their creamy texture, chicken and duck livers can be quickly sautéed and served on toast, or paired with an acidic sauce in a salad. Wash in cold water and remove any sinews. Livers are fragile and can turn to mush if handled heavily. They will deteriorate and oxidise quickly, so be sure to use within two days. Avoid any with green tinges (or cut them out) as they can be bitter.

RECIPES: PAGES 94–97

DUCK CUTS

WHOLE DUCK

A whole duck offers so many treats to the thoughtful cook. Of course, you can cook it whole, taking care to protect the breasts as they will cook faster than the rest. Alternatively, joint the duck and cook the legs and breasts separately. The breasts can be removed for fast cooking, served medium-rare, with crisp skin. The legs can be reserved for slow cooking or confit. The fat reserves can be rendered down for cooking your roast potatoes. Finally, the carcass and wing tips can be reserved in the freezer until you are ready to make your next stock: they will add a deep, umami flavour.

→ Wild duck benefits from being hung (aged) to allow the meat to become more tender (see dry-ageing on page 456).
→ Leave duck on a plate on a tea towel (dish towel) to help the skin to dry out, for excellent crisp skin.
→ To learn how to render your own duck fat, see page 468.

CUT WEIGHT: 1.8–2.5 KG (4 LB–5 LB 8 OZ)
OPTIMAL FINISH: COOKED THROUGH
RECIPES: PAGES 98–103

BREAST

Duck, a waterfowl, has a layer of subcutaneous fat between the skin and the breast which needs to be rendered carefully before cooking the rest of the breast, also known as *magret de canard*. Score the skin (as you would pork crackling) and place the breast skin-side down in a cold pan, allowing the temperature of the fat to come up with the heat (for more details, see page 69). While duck breasts are an excellent, easy cut to buy, they can be as expensive as buying the whole duck, but without the bonus of the fat to render, the legs to cook and the carcass for a rich stock.

→ We recommend scoring the skin on your duck breast before pan-frying to help it render better. See page 468 for the best way to render duck fat.

CUT WEIGHT: 230–250 G (8¼–9 OZ)
BEST COOKED: MEDIUM-RARE
OPTIMAL FINISH: 55°C (130°F)
RECIPE: PAGES 104–105

MARYLAND
(LEG QUARTER)

The Maryland, with the thigh and leg joined, is a cut with a lot of flavour. Richer and deeper in flavour than the breast, duck Maryland likes long and slow cooking or confit, as in the recipe on page 106. Traditionally, the French would then store the confit Marylands for the winter months under its protective layer of fat.

CUT WEIGHT: 250–280 G (9–10 OZ)
OPTIMAL FINISH: COOKED THROUGH
RECIPES: PAGES 106–109

Please note that all weights are approximate, as animals will differ based on their age, breed and feed. The internal temperatures given are the rested temperatures. For more information on cooking styles, roasting times, etcetera, see pages 448–455.

OTHER BIRDS

QUAIL

TURKEY

TURKEY BREAST

So often seen as a fiddly and specialty bird that you might order at a restaurant, quail is a fantastic bird to try cooking at home. A true treat for those who like to nibble the meat from around the bone, quail is an excellent entrée into the game-bird world. With delicate flesh and a slightly more gamey flavour than chicken, quails are excellent roasted whole or butterflied and cooked on the barbecue. As most quails we eat are now farmed, they tend to be more juicy; however, they do still require careful attention in the kitchen so as not to overcook them. Traditional quails are the perfect size for one as a starter or two for a main; however, there are now jumbo quails available that will work as one quail per person for a main course.

CUT WEIGHT: 150–200 G (5½–7 OZ):
    JUMBO QUAIL 200–230 G (7–8¼ OZ)
BEST COOKED: BUTTERFLIED AND
    PAN–FRIED OR BARBECUED
OPTIMAL FINISH: COOKED THROUGH:
    BREASTS MEDIUM–RARE
RECIPE: PAGES 110–111

Native to North America, turkey is much admired in the USA for the deep flavour compared to chicken. Obviously, being significantly larger than a chicken, care needs to be taken in the kitchen to ensure it doesn't dry out when cooking. It is for this reason that many people will brine their turkey, adding extra moisture before starting the cooking process. The turkey's conformation is much the same as the chicken and, while the size will change the approach slightly, each cut will generally have the same attributes.

→ For more information on brining a turkey, see page 470.

CUT WEIGHT: 4–10 KG (9–22 LB)
BEST COOKED: BRINED THEN ROASTED
OPTIMAL FINISH: COOKED THROUGH
RECIPE: PAGES 113–115

The size of the turkey breast is both its greatest attribute and its biggest complication; a great cut to feed the family, it can be hard to cook in its entirety as it does tend to dry out. Lean and virtually fat free, turkey is great cut into strips to keep it moist for fast cooking.

→ Turkey breast could also be used to great effect in many of our chicken recipes.

CUT WEIGHT: 1.5–2 KG (3 LB 5 OZ–
    4 LB 8 OZ)
BEST COOKED: POACHED
RECIPE: PAGES 116–117

GOOSE

SQUAB

Perhaps the most festive of the bird family, the goose is an excellent special occasion dish. A waterfowl like the duck, geese also have a layer of fat between the skin and flesh to keep them warm in the water. This is particularly delicious, but does need to be rendered carefully to cook it out.

Rich in flavour, a goose will hold up against other deep flavours and fruits to balance it. Goose fat can be rendered down and is excellent for roasting potatoes or frying croutons, while the liver is also highly prized.

→ An intriguing mix of deep-flavoured meat and fat, the goose is one of the richest animals on the plate.

CUT WEIGHT: 3 KG (6 LB 12 OZ)
BEST COOKED: ROASTED
OPTIMAL FINISH: COOKED THROUGH
RECIPE: PAGES 120–121

Squab, the culinary term for pigeon, refers to a pigeon that has not yet flown. While the squab we eat has dark flesh and a gamey flavour, it is now most often farmed. It benefits from fast cooking and being served just cooked to medium rare. Rest this bird well after cooking.

Domestic pigeons do not have the same colour and flavour as wild pigeons (including those that were poached in town squares during the food shortages of World War II). A wild pigeon will be deep in colour and have a rich, gamey flavour.

→ The breasts and legs cook at different rates, which is why you will often see the legs confit (see page 468) and the breasts grilled.

CUT WEIGHT: 500 G (1 LB 2 OZ)
BEST COOKED: ROASTED OR PAN-FRIED
OPTIMAL FINISH: RARE TO MEDIUM–RARE
RECIPE: PAGES 118–119

Please note that all weights are approximate, as animals will differ based on their age, breed and feed. For more information on cooking styles, roasting times, etcetera, see pages 448–455.

IN THE KITCHEN

When people think of poultry, they tend to think of chicken: we eat a lot of chicken. It is the dish we are most likely to order when we are out to dinner and it's a fabulously easy meal to prepare at home.

Around the world chicken consumption continues to grow, perhaps due to the size of the bird, its cost or its versatility. It was only recently that chicken knocked beef from the number two spot on the list of most consumed meat, and now it is on the tail of number one: the pig. Understandably so, as the roast chicken is a perfect family meal: popped into the oven, surrounded by roast potatoes, it's the ultimate comfort food.

SELECT AND STORE

Generally, chickens will be sold according to their weight: a 1.6 kg (3 lb 8 oz) bird is about perfect for a family of four. Look for a bird that has been raised outdoors, and is labelled free-range or preferably organic.

A whole, raw chicken should be cooked within three to four days of processing. (Ask your butcher when the chicken was processed. Packaged chicken will have the date on the label.) Portioned fresh chicken and livers should be eaten within two days. Always store chicken in the fridge, below vegetables to avoid spillage and contamination, and be conscious of use-by dates (ask your butcher when you purchase the birds).

FREEZING CHICKEN

If freezing chicken for a couple of weeks, it is fine to freeze the chicken in its original packaging. If you are freezing for longer, remove the packaging and wrap it in plastic or foil then in a plastic bag with as much air removed as possible, as it is the air that causes 'freezer burn', an ugly discolouration that occurs when frozen meat is exposed to air in the freezer.

Thaw frozen chicken in the fridge, on a plate, and make sure it's completely thawed before cooking.

→ *Time left exposed in the dry air of the fridge will make for better skin on the roast.*

SKIN OFF VS SKIN ON

Unfortunately the skin will show its age before the meat of the chicken and it also can house bacteria, which is the reason much of the chicken you will see is sold with the skin removed. Just like crackling on a pig, the chicken skin has incredible flavour and can provide brilliant textural contrast. There are a number of ways you can get the most out of this treat—the Maillard reaction (see page 472) applies here—and don't forget the importance of rendering the fat. If roasting a chicken or duck, store the whole bird uncovered in the fridge overnight before you cook it: this will help dry out the skin, ensuring it cooks to crisp and golden.

DARK MEAT VS WHITE MEAT

There is much debate around every family table as to who gets which cut from the chicken roast. Unfairly, many have had an aversion to the browner meat of the thighs and drumsticks. This is a shame, as so much flavour resides in these cuts. The misconception may come from an issue with the idea this is blood (haemoglobin) … it is not. Rather, this is the oxygen-storing myoglobin, used by the body in muscles that do a lot of work in the field and thus require more oxygen.

KITCHEN HYGIENE

Working with poultry in the kitchen requires careful attention. Raw poultry juices can contain contaminants such as salmonella or *E. coli* if not carefully cooked, and these can be transferred if the raw chicken or its juices come into contact with any products that are not going in the pot. The skin also carries bacteria and therefore needs to be treated with great care.

When chopping raw poultry you must be particularly conscious of cross-contamination. Always wash the board (some have a specific board in the kitchen just for chicken) and knife straight after they have come in contact with raw poultry. Always wash your hands with warm soapy water too. Nothing else should touch raw chicken or anything that has been in contact with raw chicken.

Rinsing your poultry is now considered a thing of the past: rather than cleaning, it is thought to spread germs with splashes of water around your kitchen. Don't do it. Instead, pat the chicken with paper towel and discard the towel afterwards.

COOKING CHICKEN

Chicken needs to be cooked through for safety: it should not be served raw. To check when a chicken is cooked, insert a skewer or knife into the thickest part of the thigh and ensure the juices run clear. If you have a temperature probe, it should reach 75°C (165°F) at the thickest part of the thigh.

RESTING CHICKEN

Chicken should be given time to rest after cooking, as should all meat. When resting a whole roast chicken, turn it breast-side down, allowing the juices to flow back through the breast, keeping it moist.

DUCK

A whole duck will naturally give up a lot of fat when roasting, but there are two jewels of fat found just inside the cavity that you can remove before cooking and render separately (see page 468). You can also save any of the fat that is left in the bottom of your roasting tin and, once strained, this can be stored in a jar in your fridge to become friends with your next batch of roast potatoes.

COOKING DUCK BREAST

Duck breast presents a quandary, with excellent fat that needs time to become crisp, and delicate flesh that will quickly turn tough, bitter and unpalatable if overcooked: duck breast is generally best served medium-rare.

As you would for pork crackling, you can carefully score the skin of the duck breast, creating more surface area to crisp up. Rub the skin with salt and perhaps some crushed juniper berries or peppercorns. Aim to do this at least half an hour before you start to cook; this will allow the duck to come to room temperature and help the skin to dry out a little.

Place the breast skin-side down in a cold frying pan over medium heat and allow the pan to heat. The fat will begin to render, helping to fry the skin. Once the skin is crisp, transfer the breast to a moderate oven and cook gently to your liking. Reserve the fat from the pan. Be sure to rest, skin-side up, for at least five minutes before carving.

Butchery techniques

→ **Brining** *see page 470*
→ **Stock** *see page 460*
→ **Confit** *see page 468*
→ **Rendering** chicken and duck fat *see page 468*

GAME BIRDS

Due to their more active lifestyle and thus leaner flesh, game birds are often hung (or dry-aged) in the butchery to help them become more tender. This can be done with or without the feathers.

Game birds will often have a defined season, based on local regulations; however, a number of types of game bird are now farmed with varying levels of access to the outdoors. These farmed birds will be milder in flavour and more tender.

SERVES 4–6

ROAST CHICKEN

Prep time *10 minutes*
Cook *1 hour (plus resting)*

Simon Hopkinson's delightful book, Roast Chicken and Other Stories, *is a treasure trove of words, ideas and recipes for all of his favourite ingredients. His roast chicken is simple, classic and truly delicious.*

1. Preheat the oven to 230°C (450°F). Smear the butter with your hands all over the bird. Put the chicken in a roasting tin that will accommodate it with room to spare. Season liberally with salt and pepper and squeeze over the juice of the lemon. Put the herbs and garlic inside the cavity, together with the squeezed out lemon halves—this will add a fragrant lemony flavour to the finished dish.

2. Roast the chicken in the oven for 10–15 minutes. Baste, then turn the oven temperature down to 190°C (375°F) and roast for a further 30–45 minutes with further occasional basting. The bird should be golden brown all over with a crisp skin and have buttery, lemony juices of a nut-brown colour in the bottom of the tin.

3. Turn off the oven, leaving the door ajar, and leave the chicken to rest for at least 15 minutes before carving. This enables the flesh to relax gently, retaining the juices in the meat and ensuring easy, trouble-free carving and a moist bird.

4. Carve the bird to suit yourself; I like to do it in the roasting tin. I see no point in making a gravy in that old-fashioned English way with the roasting fat, flour and vegetable cooking water. With this roasting method, what you end up with in the tin is an amalgamation of butter, lemon juice and chicken juices. That's all. It is a perfect homogenisation of fats and liquids. All it needs is a light whisk or a stir, and you have the most wonderful 'gravy' imaginable. If you wish to add flavour, you can scoop the garlic and herbs out of the chicken cavity, stir them into the gravy and heat through; strain before serving.

INGREDIENTS

7 tablespoons (110 g) good butter, at room
  temperature
1.8 kg (4 lb) free-range chicken
Salt and pepper
1 lemon
Several sprigs of thyme or tarragon,
  or a mixture of the two
1 garlic clove, crushed

NOTES

→ *Another idea, popular with the Italians, is sometimes known as 'wet-roasting'. Pour some white wine or a little chicken stock, or both, or even just water around the bottom of the tin at the beginning of cooking. This will produce more of a sauce and can be enriched further to produce altogether different results. For example, you can add chopped tomatoes, diced bacon, cream, endless different herbs, mushrooms, spring vegetables, spices— particularly saffron and ginger—or anything else that you fancy.*

→ *From* Roast Chicken and Other Stories, *by Simon Hopkinson with Lindsey Bareham (Hyperion Books, 1994).*

Cut Whole chicken
See page 58

COQ AU VIN

Prep time *35 minutes*
Cook *4½ hours (plus overnight marinating)*

1. Combine the chicken, wine, onion, carrot, celery, half the thyme and 1 bay leaf, cover and leave overnight in the refrigerator. Drain, reserving the marinade, and pat dry with paper towel.

2. To make the brown chicken stock, preheat the oven to 200°C (400°F). Remove the fat and skin from the carcass after jointing the chicken. Place the carcass and chicken wings in a roasting pan and roast for 30–40 minutes until browned.

3. Meanwhile, combine the vegetables for the stock in a separate roasting pan and roast, stirring occasionally, for 20–25 minutes until browned. Transfer the chicken carcass and roasted vegetables to a large saucepan, add the remaining ingredients and cover generously with cold water. Bring to the boil, reduce the heat to medium and simmer, skimming scum from surface for 1–2 hours until well flavoured. Strain, discarding solids, and refrigerate the stock until required.

4. To prepare the coq au vin, fry the lardons in a large enamelled cast-iron casserole over medium–high heat for 3–4 minutes to render the fat, then transfer the lardons to a plate.

5. Pour off the rendered fat and reserve it for browning the chicken, leaving about 2 tablespoons in the casserole. Add the mushrooms and fry over high heat for 8–10 minutes until golden brown. Add to the lardons.

6. Add the baby onions to the casserole and fry for 3–4 minutes to brown lightly. Add to the lardon mixture.

7. Put a little of the reserved fat in the casserole if necessary. Add the jointed chicken in batches and fry for 6–8 minutes, turning occasionally, to brown well all over.

8. Pour the brandy into the casserole, bring to the boil and light it with a long match (this is optional). When the flames die down, add the reserved marinade, the lardon mixture, 375 ml (13 fl oz/1½ cups) of the brown chicken stock, the garlic, vinegar and remaining thyme and bay leaf. Season with salt and pepper.

9. Bring to the boil, reduce heat to low, cover and simmer for 15–20 minutes until cooked through. The chicken breast pieces will cook more quickly than the legs, so check at 15 minutes and remove as they are ready.

10. Transfer the chicken and vegetables to a plate and cover with foil. Strain the sauce, return to a clean casserole and boil for 25–30 minutes until reduced to 500 ml (17 fl oz/2 cups).

11. Whisk in the butter mixture and simmer for 2–3 minutes to emulsify and thicken the sauce. Season and return the chicken and vegetables to the casserole, spooning the sauce over.

INGREDIENTS

1 chicken, about 1.6 kg (3 lb 8 oz), jointed into 8 pieces, carcass and wings reserved
1 bottle (750 ml) full-bodied red wine
1 small brown onion, coarsely chopped
1 small carrot, coarsely chopped
1 celery stalk, coarsely chopped
6 thyme sprigs
2 fresh bay leaves
100 g (3½ oz) bacon lardons
200 g (7 oz) mixed mushrooms, such as button and Swiss brown, smaller ones left whole, larger ones halved
12 baby onions, trimmed, larger ones halved
125 ml (4 fl oz/½ cup) brandy or Cognac
1 garlic bulb, halved
1 tablespoon red wine vinegar, or to taste
1 tablespoon butter, at room temperature, mixed with 1 tablespoon plain (all-purpose) flour

Brown chicken stock
Carcass and wings (reserved from chicken)
1 brown onion, coarsely chopped
1 carrot, coarsely chopped
1 celery stalk, coarsely chopped
1 teaspoon black peppercorns
3 thyme sprigs
1 handful of parsley stalks
1 fresh bay leaf

SERVING SUGGESTION

mash or parsley potatoes

Cut Whole chicken
See page 58

CHICKEN AND LEEK PIE

Prep time *40 minutes*
Cook *2 hours 20 minutes (plus resting, cooling, standing)*

1. Put the chicken in a stockpot with the carrot, celery, green parts of the leek and the stalks of the herbs (reserve the leaves for the pie filling). Cover with cold water to submerge the chicken and place a plate on top. Bring to a simmer over medium–high heat and cook for 20–25 minutes. Cool the chicken in the poaching liquid for 2 hours, then remove and coarsely shred the meat (discard the sinews, skin and bones).

2. Strain the poaching liquid into a large saucepan, discarding the solids, and boil over medium–high heat for 20–25 minutes until reduced to 500 ml (17 fl oz/2 cups). Strain and set aside.

3. To make the thyme shortcrust pastry, combine the flour, butter, thyme and salt in a food processor and process until it resembles fine crumbs. Add the egg, yolk and the iced water and pulse to bring dough together; add a little extra water if necessary. Form the dough into a disc, wrap in plastic wrap and rest in the refrigerator for 1 hour. Pastry can be made up to a day ahead and refrigerated until required.

4. Fry the bacon in a large enamelled cast-iron casserole over medium–high heat for 3–4 minutes to render the fat, then use a slotted spoon to transfer the bacon to a bowl.

5. Add the butter to the casserole and cook until foaming, then add the white parts of the leek and the thyme leaves. Sauté for 5–6 minutes until tender, adding the garlic in the last minute of cooking. Stir in the flour and cook, stirring, for 1–2 minutes until it has a sandy texture. Gradually add the poaching liquid and the wine, then the crème fraiche, stirring until smooth. Season with salt and pepper. Simmer for 2–3 minutes until thickened.

6. Remove from the heat, stir in the chicken meat, bacon, tarragon leaves and lemon zest until well combined. Check the seasoning. Cool to room temperature, cover and refrigerate to chill completely. The filling can be made up to 2 days in advance.

7. Preheat the oven to 180°C (350°F). Roll out just over half the pastry on a lightly floured work surface to 3 mm (⅛ inch) thick and line a lightly buttered 25 cm (10 inch) diameter pie tin, allowing the edges to overhang. Spoon in the chicken filling and brush pastry edges with egg wash.

8. Roll out the remaining pastry to 3 mm thick, lay it over the filling and press the edges together to seal. Trim off excess pastry, cut a few vents in the pastry lid to let steam escape, brush with egg wash and bake for 1 hour to 1 hour 15 minutes until golden brown. Remove from the oven and set aside for 15 minutes before serving.

INGREDIENTS

1.8 kg (4 lb) whole chicken
1 carrot, coarsely chopped
1 celery stalk, coarsely chopped
2 leeks, white parts thinly sliced, green parts reserved to poach the chicken
8 thyme sprigs
4 tarragon sprigs
3 bacon rashers, rind removed, chopped
4 tablespoons (50 g) butter, chopped
2 garlic cloves, finely chopped
45 g (1½ oz) plain (all-purpose) flour
100 ml (3½ fl oz) dry white wine
125 g (4½ oz/½ cup) crème fraiche or sour cream
Finely grated zest of ½ lemon
1 egg yolk whisked with 1 tablespoon milk, for egg wash

Thyme shortcrust pastry
500 g (1 lb 2 oz/3⅓ cups) plain flour
½ lb (250 g) chilled butter, chopped
3 thyme sprigs, leaves picked and finely chopped
1 teaspoon sea salt
1 egg
1 egg yolk
2–3 tablespoons iced water

SERVING SUGGESTION

a crisp green salad, dressed with your favourite vinaigrette

N O T E

→ *You can use ready-made puff pastry instead of making the shortcrust pastry if you like.*

Cut Whole chicken
See page 58

HAINANESE CHICKEN

Prep time *30 minutes*
Cook *40 minutes (plus steeping)*

1. Remove excess fat surrounding the chicken cavity and set aside for the rice. Stuff the chicken cavity with the spring onion, ginger and garlic and secure the opening with a skewer.
2. Place the chicken breast-side down in a stockpot large enough to hold it quite snugly and cover with cold water. Add the Shaoxing rice wine, 55 ml (1¾ fl oz) of the soy sauce, 1 teaspoon of the sesame oil and the salt. Bring to the boil, then reduce the heat so the surface of the water is barely moving and a steady stream of bubbles breaks the surface. Cover and poach gently for 8–10 minutes, skimming off any scum. Turn off the heat, cover and leave in the pot for 40–45 minutes until the chicken is cooked through.
3. Transfer the chicken to a plate. (Reserve the poaching liquid for the chicken rice and keep warm.) Combine the remaining soy sauce and remaining sesame oil in a small bowl. Rub the mixture all over the chicken and set aside.
4. To make the chicken rice, heat the chicken fat with a splash of oil in a large saucepan over medium–high heat. When the chicken fat has rendered, discard the solids. Add the shallots and sauté for 4–5 minutes until fragrant and golden, adding the ginger and garlic in the final minute of cooking. Stir in the rice to coat and lightly toast, then add the chicken poaching broth, the pandan leaf, if using, and stir to combine.
5. Season with salt and pepper, bring to a simmer, reduce the heat to low, cover with a tightly fitting lid and cook for 15 minutes without uncovering, until the liquid is absorbed. Remove from the heat, leave the lid on for 5 minutes, then uncover and fluff with a fork.
6. Meanwhile, to make the chilli sauce, process the ingredients in a food processor or blender until smooth and season with salt.
7. To make spring onion sauce, heat the oil in a small saucepan over medium–high heat, add the ginger and garlic and fry for 1–2 minutes until fragrant. Add the spring onion and sesame oil, remove from the heat and season with salt and pepper.
8. To make soy dressing, stir the ingredients together in a bowl.
9. To serve, bring 2 litres (70 fl oz/8 cups) of the remaining poaching liquid back to the boil and season with salt and pepper. Cut the chicken, Chinese-style, through the bone into bite-sized pieces using a cleaver or large sharp knife and arrange on a plate. Spoon the soy dressing over and serve with chicken rice, cucumber, coriander, chilli sauce, spring onion sauce and individual bowls of the poaching liquid.

INGREDIENTS

1.8 kg (4 lb) whole chicken
4 spring onions (scallions), knotted together
5 cm (2 inch) piece of fresh ginger, bruised and thickly sliced
3 garlic cloves, crushed
2½ tablespoons Shaoxing rice wine
70 ml (2¼ fl oz) light soy sauce
2 teaspoons sesame oil
1 teaspoon sea salt
Lebanese (short) cucumber, sliced, to serve
Coriander (cilantro) sprigs, to serve

Chicken rice
50 g (1¾ oz) reserved chicken fat
Vegetable or grapeseed oil, for frying
4 golden shallots, thinly sliced
1 tablespoon finely grated fresh ginger
2 garlic cloves, finely chopped
400 g (14 oz/2 cups) jasmine rice
700 ml (24 fl oz) chicken poaching broth
1 pandan leaf, tied in a knot (optional)

Chilli sauce
70 ml (2¼ fl oz) white vinegar
4–5 long red chillies, coarsely chopped
3 garlic cloves
1 tablespoon caster (superfine) sugar
½ teaspoon salt

Spring onion sauce
2½ tablespoons vegetable oil
1 tablespoon finely chopped fresh ginger
2 garlic cloves, finely chopped
4 spring onions (scallions), thinly sliced
2 teaspoons sesame oil

Soy dressing
2½ tablespoons light soy sauce
1 teaspoon sesame oil
100 ml (3½ fl oz) reserved chicken broth

Cut Whole chicken
See page 58

GREEN CHICKEN CURRY

1. To make the curry paste, preheat the oven to 200°C (400°F). Wrap the shrimp paste in foil and roast for 5–10 minutes until fragrant. Dry-fry the peppercorns and coriander seeds in a small saucepan over medium–high heat for 30 seconds or until fragrant. Finely grind in a mortar and pestle or spice grinder and set aside.

2. Pound the chillies in a mortar and pestle with the salt to form a paste. One at a time, add galangal, lemongrass, kaffir lime leaves, kaffir lime zest, coriander roots, turmeric, shallots and garlic and pound to crush, then add the shrimp paste and pound to combine. Once all the ingredients have been added, continue pounding until you have a smooth paste. Alternatively, you can make the curry paste in a small food processor, blending all the ingredients together. You may need to add a splash of water to help form the paste.

3. Cook half of the coconut cream in a large saucepan over high heat for 8–10 minutes until the fat starts to separate from the white coconut (this is known as 'cracking').

4. Add the curry paste to the coconut cream and fry for 6–8 minutes, stirring frequently to prevent the paste scorching, until aromatic and the raw taste cooks out. Add the chicken and stir to coat. Add the remaining coconut cream, eggplant, kaffir lime leaves, chillies, fish sauce, palm sugar and 375 ml (13 fl oz/1½ cups) of water, then simmer for 15–20 minutes for the flavours to develop and until the chicken is cooked through.

5. Add the lime juice and then taste to check the seasoning: the curry should be a balance of hot, sour, salty and sweet. Add extra fish sauce, lime juice or palm sugar to balance out the flavours.

6. Green curry will keep, refrigerated, for up to 3 days and is even better a day after making it.

INGREDIENTS

6 chicken thighs, bone in, skin on, about
   180 g (6¼ oz) each
600 ml (21 fl oz) tinned coconut cream
300 g (10½ oz) Thai eggplants, such as apple
   or pea, larger ones halved
6 kaffir lime (makrut) leaves, crushed
6 long red chillies, halved lengthways
80 ml (2½ fl oz/⅓ cup) fish sauce
1½ tablespoons finely grated palm sugar
Juice of 1 lime, or to taste

Green curry paste
1½ teaspoons shrimp paste
1½ teaspoons white peppercorns
½ teaspoon coriander seeds
10–12 Thai green chillies
1½ teaspoons sea salt
30 g (1 oz) galangal, finely chopped
4 lemongrass stems, white part only, finely
   chopped
4 kaffir lime (makrut) leaves, finely chopped
1½ teaspoons finely grated kaffir lime
   (makrut) zest (optional)
9 coriander (cilantro) roots with a little of the
   stem attached, soaked in water to remove
   grit, then drained and finely chopped
2½ teaspoons finely chopped fresh turmeric
   or ground turmeric
6 red Asian shallots or golden shallots,
   coarsely chopped
12 garlic cloves, coarsely chopped

SERVING
SUGGESTION

steamed jasmine rice,
coriander (cilantro) leaves,
Thai basil leaves and lime wedges

***Cut** Chicken thigh*
See page 59

CHICKEN KIEV

Prep time *40 minutes (plus chilling)*
Cook *25 minutes*

1. To make the herb and garlic butter, beat the ingredients together in a small bowl to combine and season with salt and pepper.

2. To prepare the chicken, make an incision along one side of each breast, creating a deep pocket. Spoon a quarter of the butter mixture into each pocket, pushing to the back of the pocket. Brush edges of the pocket with a little of the egg, dust with a little flour and press together to seal. Refrigerate until butter is firm (1 hour).

3. Put the seasoned flour, remaining egg and the breadcrumbs in separate bowls. Dip each piece of chicken in flour, then egg, shaking off excess. Dip into the breadcrumbs, pressing so the breadcrumbs stick to the chicken, coating it completely. Dip once again into the egg and breadcrumbs to double coat. Lay the crumbed pieces on a tray and refrigerate for 30 minutes to set the coating.

4. Preheat the oven to 180°C (350°F). Heat 3 cm (1¼ inches) of the vegetable oil in a large, deep frying pan over medium–high heat to 160°C (315°F), or until a cube of bread dropped into the oil browns in 30 seconds. Shallow-fry the chicken pieces in two batches, turning occasionally for 5–6 minutes until golden brown (be careful, the hot oil will spit). Transfer to a wire rack on a baking tray and bake for 10–12 minutes until cooked through. Set aside to rest for 5 minutes before serving.

INGREDIENTS

4 skinless chicken breasts with wings attached
Plain (all-purpose) flour, seasoned with salt and pepper, for dusting
4 eggs, lightly whisked
240 g (8¾ oz/4 cups) panko (Japanese) breadcrumbs
Vegetable oil, for shallow-frying

Herb and garlic butter
12 tablespoons (150 g) butter, at room temperature
2 garlic cloves, finely chopped
⅓ cup finely chopped mixed herbs, such as flat-leaf (Italian) parsley, tarragon and chives
Finely grated zest of 1 lemon

SERVING SUGGESTION

mashed potato, steamed peas and extra chopped chives

NOTE

→ *Panko breadcrumbs create a very crisp and crunchy coating, but if you prefer, you could use fresh breadcrumbs.*

Cut Chicken breast
See page 58

CHICKEN SCHNITZEL SANDWICHES

Prep time *20 minutes (plus chilling)*
Cook *15 minutes*

1. Halve each chicken breast horizontally to create two flat pieces, then flatten with a meat mallet to an even 4 mm (⅛ inch) thickness.

2. Put the seasoned flour and whisked eggs in separate bowls. Combine the breadcrumbs, parmesan, thyme and lemon zest in a separate bowl and season with salt and pepper. Dip each piece of chicken in the flour, then the egg, shaking off excess. Dip into the breadcrumb mixture, pressing the breadcrumbs onto the chicken, coating it completely. Lay the coated pieces in a single layer on a tray and refrigerate for 30 minutes to set the coating.

3. Heat 2 cm (¾ inch) of olive oil in a large frying pan over medium heat, add the chicken in batches and shallow-fry, turning occasionally, for 5–6 minutes until golden brown and cooked through. Drain on paper towel.

4. To serve, spread bread rolls with a little mayonnaise or aïoli. Top with schnitzel, season with salt and pepper, squeeze a little lemon juice over, then add lettuce and pickles. Sandwich and serve with lemon wedges.

INGREDIENTS

2 skinless chicken breast fillets

Plain (all-purpose) flour, seasoned with salt and pepper, for dusting

3 eggs, lightly whisked

185 g (6½ oz) day-old coarse white breadcrumbs

35 g (1¼ oz/⅓ cup) finely grated parmesan cheese

1½ tablespoons finely chopped thyme

Finely grated zest of 1 lemon, plus the lemon cut into wedges to serve

Olive oil, for shallow-frying

White or sourdough rolls, buttered if desired

Mayonnaise or aïoli, to serve

Shredded baby cos (romaine) lettuce and sliced cucumber pickles, to serve

NOTE

→ *If you prefer a crunchier schnitzel, use panko or dried breadcrumbs, or for a different flavour, try using rye breadcrumbs.*

Cut Chicken breast
See page 58

SERVES 4

BANG BANG CHICKEN

1. Put the chicken in a saucepan with enough cold water to cover, bring to the boil then remove from heat and set aside to steep for 20–25 minutes until cooked through. Transfer to a plate and set aside to cool, reserving the poaching liquid.
2. Meanwhile, to make the sesame sauce, dry-fry the sichuan peppercorns in a small saucepan over medium–high heat, stirring occasionally, for 30 seconds or until toasted and fragrant. Cool slightly, transfer to a mortar and use the pestle to grind to a powder, then pound in the ginger and garlic to form a paste.
3. Whisk the sichuan pepper mixture with the remaining sauce ingredients in a bowl and set aside. Thin with a little of the poaching liquid to make a drizzling consistency (the remaining poaching liquid can be used as a light chicken stock in other recipes).
4. Shred the chicken into small pieces and combine in a bowl with the sesame sauce to taste. Toss to combine and serve topped with the spring onion, cucumber and sesame seeds.

INGREDIENTS

2 skinless, boneless chicken breast fillets, about 600 g (1 lb 5 oz) total weight
5 spring onions (scallions), thinly sliced diagonally
1 Lebanese (short) cucumber, cut into matchsticks
Roasted sesame seeds (black or white)

Sesame sauce
2 teaspoons sichuan peppercorns (see note)
2 teaspoons finely grated fresh ginger
1 garlic clove, coarsely chopped
80 g (2¾ oz) sesame paste or tahini
2½ tablespoons light soy sauce
2½ tablespoons Chinese black vinegar (see note) or rice vinegar
1 tablespoon sesame oil
1 teaspoon roasted chilli oil, or to taste

SERVING SUGGESTION

rice noodles

NOTES

→ *Sichuan peppercorns are dried seed pods from a species of prickly ash and have a distinctive mouth-numbing effect. They are available from Asian grocers and spice specialists.*

→ *Chinese black vinegar is a dark vinegar made from glutinous rice and has a deep smoky flavour. Chinkiang vinegar is widely considered to be the best. It's available from some supermarkets and Asian grocers, or you can substitute regular rice vinegar.*

Cut Chicken breast
See page 58

DAVID THOMPSON

Thai Food

SERVES 4 AS A STARTER

SPICY MINCED CHICKEN SALAD
~ LARP GAI ~

Prep time *20 minutes*
Cook *10 minutes*

If you enjoy cooking Thai food then you simply must have this book on your shelf. David Thompson is indisputably an excellent chef, but he is also an excellent thinker and a methodical writer.

1. Mince the chicken with salt and garlic, if using. If using offal, wash in salted and acidulated water to clean and remove any coarseness, then finely slice.

2. Heat stock and season with salt and sugar. Add mince and offal, if using, and simmer, stirring often until just cooked (about 3–4 minutes); do not overcook or the meat will toughen.

3. Season with lime juice, chilli powder and fish sauce.

4. Mix in shallots and herbs.

5. Check the seasoning—the salad should taste hot, sour and salty—and adjust accordingly.

6. Sprinkle with roasted rice.

INGREDIENTS

150 g (5½ oz) skinless chicken breast
or thigh fillets
50–100 g (3–3½ oz) chicken offal, such
as liver, heart and giblets, optional
Pinch of salt
1 small garlic clove, finely chopped (optional)
3 tablespoons chicken stock
Extra pinch of salt
Pinch of white sugar
3 tablespoons lime juice
Large pinch of roasted chilli powder
1 tablespoon fish sauce
3 red Asian shallots, sliced
1 handful of mixed mint and coriander leaves
1 tablespoon shredded pak chi farang
(long-leaf coriander)
1 tablespoon ground roasted rice

Eat with rice and raw vegetables such as cabbage, snake beans and cucumber. Top with fried egg and a squeeze of lime juice.

SERVING
SUGGESTION

NOTES

→ *Originally from the north-east, this style of larp is now popular throughout Thailand.*

→ *From* Thai Food, *by David Thompson (Pavilion Books, 2002).*

Cut Chicken breast
See page 58

JERK CHICKEN

Prep time *40 minutes (plus overnight marinating)*
Cook *55 minutes (plus resting)*

1. To make the jerk marinade, blitz all of the ingredients in a food processor to combine.

2. Divide the Marylands through the joint and put the chicken pieces in a large bowl, add the jerk marinade and the bay leaves. Mix well to coat thoroughly, cover and refrigerate to marinate overnight, for up to 36 hours.

3. Meanwhile, set up a kettle barbecue for indirect grilling, pushing the coals to one side and set an oiled rack into the barbecue, at least 30 cm (12 inches) away from the coals. Cover barbecue with a lid for 10–15 minutes to heat and for smoke to appear. Alternatively, heat one side of a gas barbecue to medium–high.

4. Remove the chicken from the marinade and lay pieces skin-side up on the rack away from the heat source. Cover with the barbecue lid and cook for 30 minutes.

5. Uncover and, if using a coal barbecue, top up the coals if necessary. Turn the chicken, cover and cook for 15–25 minutes until evenly browned and cooked through: the chicken thigh pieces will cook more quickly than the legs. To check whether it is cooked, insert the tip of a knife into the thickest part of each chicken piece. If juices run clear, not pink, the chicken is cooked. Alternatively, an instant-read thermometer inserted should read 71°C (160°F). Transfer to a tray, cover loosely with foil and set aside to rest for 15 minutes.

6. Meanwhile, to make the rice and beans, pan-fry the bacon in a large enamelled cast-iron casserole over medium–high heat for 3–4 minutes to render the fat. Add a splash of oil if necessary, stir in the rice for 1–2 minutes to toast and coat in fat. Add the spring onion, garlic, thyme and allspice, stir until fragrant. Add the coconut milk and water, season with salt and pepper and bring to the boil. Reduce the heat to low, cover with a lid and cook without uncovering for 12 minutes or until the liquid is absorbed. Remove from the heat, set aside for 5 minutes. Drain and rinse the beans, then stir them into the rice mixture and check the seasoning.

7. To make the pineapple relish, combine all of the ingredients in a bowl and season with salt and pepper.

8. Serve the jerk chicken with the rice and beans, pineapple relish and halved limes to squeeze over, if desired.

INGREDIENTS

6 chicken Marylands (leg quarters)
10 fresh bay leaves

Jerk marinade
80 ml (2½ fl oz/⅓ cup) vegetable oil
80 ml (2½ fl oz/⅓ cup) soy sauce
40 g (1½ oz) fresh ginger, coarsely chopped
8 garlic cloves
6 spring onions (scallions), coarsely chopped
5 Scotch bonnet chillies, coarsely chopped
Finely grated zest and juice of 3 limes
12 thyme sprigs, leaves picked
2 tablespoons soft brown sugar
2 tablespoons golden rum
1 tablespoon ground allspice
1 tablespoon malt vinegar
2 teaspoons sea salt
1 teaspoon freshly grated nutmeg

Rice and beans
3 bacon rashers, rind removed, chopped
300 g (10½ oz/1½ cups) long-grain rice
3 spring onions (scallions), thinly sliced
2 garlic cloves, crushed
2 thyme sprigs
1 pinch of ground allspice
400 ml (14 fl oz) tinned coconut milk
250 ml (9 fl oz/1 cup) hot water
400 g (14 oz) tin kidney beans

Pineapple relish
½ pineapple, chopped
Juice of 1 lime
1 tablespoon soft brown sugar, or to taste
1 golden shallot, finely chopped
1 handful of coriander (cilantro), chopped

***Cut** Chicken Maryland*
See page 59

CHICKEN BALLOTINE
~ WITH SAUTÉED MUSHROOMS ~

Prep time *45 minutes*
Cook *40 minutes (plus resting)*

1. To make the pork and sage stuffing, heat a splash of oil in a saucepan over medium–high heat, add the shallot and garlic and sauté for 4–5 minutes until tender and translucent. Transfer to a bowl to cool completely. Add the remaining ingredients to the bowl, season generously with salt and pepper and mix well to combine.

2. To bone the chicken Maryland, follow the instructions on page 483.

3. Open out the boned thigh on your chopping board, skin-side down. Cover with a piece of plastic wrap and pound with a meat mallet to an even thickness. Spoon about 2 tablespoons of stuffing into each thigh, then fold the meat and skin around the stuffing, pulling it tightly. Wrap each leg in pancetta slices, overlapping to enclose completely.

4. Preheat the oven to 180°C (350°F). Heat a splash of oil in a large frying pan over medium–high heat. Add the chicken ballotines and pan-fry, turning occasionally, for 4–5 minutes until browned all over. Transfer to a baking tray and roast for 15–20 minutes until cooked through. Transfer the chicken to a plate, cover loosely with foil and set aside to rest for 10 minutes.

5. Meanwhile, to make the sautéed mushrooms, slice larger mushrooms and leave smaller mushrooms whole. Heat the butter and olive oil in a large frying pan over medium heat until foaming. Add the shallots, season with salt and pepper and sauté for 4–5 minutes until tender and translucent, adding the garlic in the last minute of cooking. Remove from the pan, increase heat to high, add mushrooms and sauté for 6–8 minutes until browned and tender. Return shallot mixture to pan, add the lemon zest and juice and the parsley. Season with salt and pepper.

6. Return the pan you used to brown the chicken to medium–high heat. Pour the wine into the pan and scrape the base of the pan to remove all the lovely caramelised bits. Boil for 2–3 minutes to reduce by half. Add the butter a piece at a time, swirling to combine, and season with salt and pepper.

7. Serve ballotine with sautéed mushrooms and pan sauce.

INGREDIENTS

4 chicken Marylands (leg quarters)
16 thin slices flat pancetta or prosciutto
Olive oil, for pan-frying
300 ml (10½ fl oz) dry white wine
2 tablespoons (30 g) butter, chopped

Pork and sage stuffing
Olive oil, for sautéing
1 golden shallot, finely diced
1 garlic clove, finely chopped
200 g (7 oz) minced (ground) pork shoulder
1 tablespoon finely chopped sage
1 tablespoon finely chopped flat-leaf
  (Italian) parsley

Sautéed mushrooms
400 g (14 oz) mixed mushrooms, such as
  pine, Swiss brown and field mushrooms
4 tablespoons (60 g) butter, chopped
2 tablespoons olive oil
2 golden shallots, thinly sliced
2 garlic cloves, thinly sliced
Finely grated zest and juice of ½ lemon,
  or to taste
1 handful of coarsely chopped flat-leaf
  (Italian) parsley

NOTE

→ *Dried mushrooms add rich flavour and texture to the sautéed mushrooms. Soak 10 g (¼ oz) of dried mushrooms in water for 20 minutes. Strain through a fine sieve (add the liquid to the pan gravy). Rinse the mushrooms to remove any grit. Add with the fresh mushrooms.*

Cut Chicken Maryland
See page 59

BUTTERMILK FRIED CHICKEN

Prep time *30 minutes (plus overnight marinating)*
Cook *50 minutes (plus chilling)*

1. Combine the buttermilk, hot sauce, mustard powder and salt in a bowl. Add the chicken pieces and mix well until coated, cover and refrigerate overnight.

2. Combine the flour, onion powder, garlic powder, paprika, cayenne and thyme leaves in a bowl, season generously with salt and pepper and mix well. Drain the chicken pieces from the buttermilk and dredge heavily in the flour mixture. Shake off excess and lay on a wire rack, making sure the chicken is in a single layer. Refrigerate for 30 minutes to help the coating set.

3. Preheat 3 cm (1¼ inches) of oil or lard in a deep saucepan to 170°C (325°F) or until a cube of bread dropped into the oil turns golden brown in 20 seconds. Shallow-fry the chicken in batches, turning occasionally for 15–25 minutes until golden brown and cooked through. The chicken breast pieces will cook more quickly than the legs, so if using jointed chicken, check at 15 minutes and remove when they are ready. To check for doneness, insert a meat thermometer into the thickest part of each piece: it should read 71°C (162°F). Drain on paper towel and serve with extra hot sauce.

INGREDIENTS

1.8 kg (4 lb) chicken, jointed into 8 pieces or 12 chicken drumsticks

600 ml (21 fl oz) buttermilk

2½ tablespoons hot sauce of your choice, such as Cholula or Tabasco, plus extra to serve

1 teaspoon mustard powder

1 tablespoon sea salt

300 g (10½ oz/2 cups) plain (all-purpose) flour

2 teaspoons onion powder

1 teaspoon garlic powder

1 teaspoon sweet paprika

½ teaspoon ground cayenne

2 thyme sprigs, leaves picked

Vegetable oil or lard, for shallow-frying

NOTE

→ *Try drizzling the fried chicken with honey: warm some honey in a saucepan, add a good pinch of chilli flakes and drizzle it over the hot chicken.*

Cut Jointed chicken or drumsticks
See pages 58–59

SERVES 4

YAKITORI

Prep time *45 minutes*
Cook *25 minutes*

1. Soak 20 bamboo skewers in cold water for 20 minutes to prevent burning.

2. Meanwhile, to make the tare sauce, stir all of the ingredients together in a small saucepan to combine. Bring to the boil, then reduce the heat and simmer for 6–8 minutes until sauce thickens to a glaze consistency. Strain and set aside.

3. To prepare the chicken skin, scrape most of the fat from the inside of the skin, cut into 2.5 cm (1 inch) strips and thread onto four skewers.

4. To prepare the chicken hearts, rinse under cold running water and peel off the skin. Trim off any veins or sinew, cut in half lengthways, then thread onto four skewers.

5. To prepare the livers, separate the livers into lobes. Trim off sinew and any blood vessels. Cut crossways into bite-sized pieces and thread onto four skewers.

6. Thread spring onion pieces onto four skewers and mushroom halves onto another four skewers and drizzle with a little oil.

7. Heat coals to white hot in a hibachi, konro or kettle barbecue or preheat a gas barbecue or chargrill plate to medium–high heat. Grill the mushroom and spring onion skewers, turning occasionally, for 2–3 minutes until golden brown. Brush with tare sauce after the first minute of cooking to glaze. Season with salt and pepper to taste.

8. Grill hearts and livers, turning occasionally for 2–2½ minutes until almost cooked through, brush with tare sauce and grill for 10 seconds. Remove from the heat and season with sansho pepper to serve.

9. Grill the chicken skin, turning occasionally, for 3–4 minutes until crisp and golden brown. Season to taste.

10. Serve yakitori as it's ready from the grill.

INGREDIENTS

150 g (5½ oz) chicken skin, preferably from the neck
6 chicken hearts
4 chicken livers
8 spring onions (scallions), trimmed and cut into 3 cm (1¼ inch) batons
12 large shiitake mushrooms, halved and stems trimmed
Vegetable oil or grapeseed oil, for drizzling
Sansho pepper, to serve (see note)

Tare sauce
125 ml (4 fl oz/½ cup) light soy sauce
60 ml (2 fl oz/¼ cup) sake
2½ tablespoons mirin
3 spring onions (scallions), coarsely chopped
10 g (¼ oz) fresh ginger, coarsely chopped

NOTE

→ *Sansho pepper comes from the Japanese species of prickly ash and has a citrus-like flavour with sichuan pepper bite. It's available from specialist Japanese grocery shops and specialist spice shops, but if it's unavailable, you can leave it out.*

Cut Chicken skin and giblets
See page 60

LIVER PARFAIT

1. Separate the livers into lobes and trim, removing any blood vessels and sinew.

2. Melt 2 tablespoons (20 g) of the butter in a large frying pan over medium–high heat until foaming. Add the shallots to the pan and sauté for 3–4 minutes until tender and translucent, adding the garlic in the final minute of cooking, then transfer to a food processor or blender.

3. Wipe out the pan and add another 2 tablespoons (20 g) of the butter. When the butter foams, add the livers and sear, turning once, for 2–3 minutes until browned (be careful, as the livers will spit and pop a little). Make sure you don't overcook the livers at this stage; you want them to still be a little pink in the centre. Transfer to the food processor with the shallot mixture.

4. Pour in the Port to deglaze the pan, bring to the boil and scrape any of the delicious browned bits from the base of the pan. Cook for 1–2 minutes to reduce by half. Add to the liver mixture in the food processor with the thyme and allspice and cool slightly.

5. Add the vinegar and remaining butter to the food processor, season and process until very smooth. Add the cream, process to combine, then pass through a sieve. Transfer to ramekins and refrigerate for 2 hours until set and chilled.

INGREDIENTS

350 g (12 oz) chicken livers or duck livers
11 tablespoons (150 g) butter, chopped
2 golden shallots, thinly sliced
1 garlic clove, finely chopped
70 ml (2¼ fl oz) Port or tawny
2 thyme sprigs, leaves picked
1 pinch of ground allspice
1 teaspoon red wine vinegar
100 ml (3½ fl oz) pouring (pure) cream

*sourdough crostini, cornichons
and bitter salad leaves (such
as endive or radicchio)*

SERVING
SUGGESTION

NOTE

→ *If you're not using the parfait straight away, cover the surface with a thin layer of clarified butter. Cook 9 tablespoons (120 g) of chilled diced butter over low heat until the fat and milk solids separate. Strain off the clear yellow butter (discarding the milky white solids) and pour it over the surface of the parfait to form a thin layer (which helps prevent oxidation). Refrigerate for 2 hours until set. The parfait will keep refrigerated for up to 2 weeks, but once the butter seal is broken, eat it within a day or two.*

Cut Chicken livers
See page 60

DUCK À L'ORANGE

1. Heat the excess duck skin and fat in a large heavy-based saucepan over medium heat and cook to render the fat. Discard the solids, then add the wings, carcass, onion, carrot, celery and garlic and cook, stirring occasionally, for 6–8 minutes to brown.

2. Pour off excess fat (reserve for the pilaf), add the thyme, bay leaf and 2 litres (70 fl oz/8 cups) of cold water and bring to the boil. Skim off any scum, reduce the heat to medium and simmer for 1 hour. Strain, discarding solids; measure out 750 ml (26 fl oz/3 cups) for the sauce and use the remainder for the pilaf.

3. To make the wild rice pilaf, heat a little of the rendered duck fat in a large saucepan over medium–high heat. Add the shallot, season and sauté for 4–5 minutes until tender and translucent, adding the garlic in the final minute of cooking. Stir in the rice.

4. Measure the remaining stock and top up with hot water to make 1.5 litres (52 fl oz/6 cups). Pour into the pan with the rice, stir and season. Reduce heat to low, cover and cook for 45–50 minutes, until rice is tender and liquid is absorbed. Set aside with the lid on for 15 minutes. Season with salt and pepper and stir in the parsley. Cover and set aside.

5. Meanwhile, make the orange sauce. Scatter sugar in the base of a saucepan and cook over medium–high heat for 2–3 minutes, swirling occasionally, until it turns to caramel. Add the reserved stock, orange juice, Grand Marnier, thyme and spices (be careful, hot caramel will spit) and stir to combine. Simmer for 30–35 minutes until reduced and thickened, then discard the thyme. Meanwhile, put the orange zest in a small saucepan with cold water to cover, bring to the boil and drain. Add the zest, the orange slices and the vinegar to the sauce and season with salt and pepper. Remove from the heat and set aside.

6. Prick the duck skin all over with a skewer and season with salt and pepper. Place duck pieces skin-side down in a large non-stick frying pan over medium heat and cook for 20–25 minutes, until the skin is a deep golden brown. Spoon off any fat.

7. Turn the duck over and cook for 1–2 minutes until the breasts are medium-rare; a thermometer should read 53°C (127°F) and the duck will continue to cook as it rests. Transfer the breasts to a baking tray and cover with foil to rest while the legs finish cooking. Continue to cook the legs for 10–15 minutes until cooked through; a thermometer should read 70°C (160°F) and juices should run when the meat is pierced with a skewer.

8. Bring the sauce back to the boil. Arrange the duck pieces on a platter, spoon the orange sauce over and serve with the pilaf.

INGREDIENTS

1 duck, about 2 kg (4 lb 8 oz), jointed into
    4 pieces; carcass, wings, excess skin and
    fat reserved
2 onions, coarsely chopped
2 carrots, coarsely chopped
1 celery stalk, coarsely chopped
1 garlic bulb, halved
5 thyme sprigs
1 fresh bay leaf

Wild rice pilaf
2 golden shallots, thinly sliced
1 garlic clove, finely chopped
255 g (9 oz/1⅓ cups) wild rice
1 handful of coarsely chopped flat-leaf
    (Italian) parsley

Orange sauce
55 g (2 oz/¼ cup) caster (superfine) sugar
Juice of 3 oranges, zest of 1 orange, plus
    1 extra orange, peeled and sliced
2½ tablespoons Grand Marnier
4 thyme sprigs
4 whole cloves
2 cinnamon sticks
1 tablespoon sherry vinegar

*braised witlof or a bitter leaf salad,
such as frisée (curly endive), shredded
witlof (chicory) or torn radicchio*

SERVING
SUGGESTION

NOTE

→ *If blood oranges are in season, use half blood
oranges and half regular oranges for the sauce.*

Cut Whole duck
See page 61

CHERRY ROAST DUCK

Prep time *20 minutes*
Cook *1 hour 10 minutes (plus resting)*

1. Preheat the oven to 220°C (425°F). Remove and reserve three strips of peel from the orange using a peeler; juice half of the orange and reserve; chop the remaining half of the orange for stuffing the duck.

2. Remove excess fat from around the duck cavity (reserve for rendering). Pat the duck dry inside and out with paper towel. Season generously inside and out with salt and pepper and stuff the cavity with the chopped orange, the garlic and half the thyme.

3. Prick the skin of the duck breast all over with a skewer (this helps to render the fat from the duck, but make sure you don't pierce the flesh). Set aside at room temperature for 30 minutes.

4. Lay the duck breast-side up on a wire rack set over a roasting tin and roast for 20–30 minutes until the skin is starting to brown. Pour off any fat that pools in the tin (strain and reserve for another use). Reduce the oven temperature to 180°C (350°F).

5. Carefully remove the rack with the duck and set aside. Put the cherries, wine, shallots, reserved orange zest and juice, bay leaf and remaining thyme into the roasting tin, season with salt and pepper and stir to combine.

6. Replace the wire rack with the duck over the roasting tin and roast for 30–35 minutes until the duck is just cooked: a thermometer inserted into the thigh should read 70°C (160°F) and the juices should run clear. Remove the duck, cover loosely with foil and set aside to rest for 15–20 minutes.

7. Add the vinegar to the cherry mixture and season with salt and pepper to taste. Serve the duck with the cherry sauce.

INGREDIENTS

1 whole duck, about 2 kg (4 lb 8 oz)
1 orange
½ garlic bulb, cloves separated
10 thyme sprigs
350 g (12 oz) cherries, pitted (see note)
185 ml (6 fl oz/¾ cup) full-bodied red wine
2 golden shallots, thinly sliced
1 fresh bay leaf
1 teaspoon sherry vinegar

a radicchio salad dressed with a sherry vinaigrette, to cut through the richness, and duck fat–roasted potatoes

SERVING SUGGESTION

NOTES

→ *If cherries are out of season, use frozen cherries instead.*

→ *Excess fat removed from the cavity can be rendered and reserved for another use.*

→ *Use the duck fat poured from the roasting tin to roast potatoes to serve alongside the duck.*

→ *If you prefer your duck breasts medium-rare, remove them from the duck before cooking. Score the skin and lay them in a cold frying pan, skin-side down, and cook for 6–7 minutes over medium–high heat until the skin is crisp and the fat renders. Turn and sear the other side. Put the breasts in the oven with the rest of the duck for the last 5 minutes of cooking.*

Cut Whole duck
See page 61

LACQUERED DUCK

Prep time *45 minutes*
Cook *1 hour 10 minutes (plus 24–36 hours drying, resting)*

---

1. Working from the base of the breasts and using your fingers, carefully separate the duck skin from the flesh, ensuring you don't tear the skin. Once you can no longer reach with your fingers, use the handle of a wooden spoon to work between the skin and the flesh. Work around to separate the skin where the thigh meets the body. This ensures delicious crisp skin.

2. Bring a large saucepan of water to the boil. Lay the duck breast-side up on a wire rack in the kitchen sink. Pour the boiling water over, making sure it gets inside the cavity and all over the duck. Alternatively, if you have a large enough saucepan, you can dunk the duck into the boiling water instead. When cool enough to handle, pat thoroughly dry inside and out with paper towel.

3. Combine the maltose and soy sauce in a small saucepan over low heat and stir until smooth and combined. Place the duck breast-side up on a wire rack in a roasting tin and rub it all over with maltose mixture, massaging well into the skin.

4. To make the five-spice salt, combine the ingredients in a bowl. Rub some of the five-spice salt inside the duck cavity. Refrigerate the duck, uncovered, for 24–36 hours to dry the skin. The skin will be dry to touch and look like leather.

5. Preheat the oven to 240°C (475°F). Roast the duck for 20–30 minutes until starting to brown, then reduce the heat to 180°C (350°F). Roast for 30–35 minutes until glossy and lacquered and the duck is just cooked: a thermometer inserted into the thigh should read 70°C (160°F) and the juices should run clear. Set aside to rest for 10 minutes, then carve.

6. Serve lacquered duck with warmed mandarin pancakes, hoisin sauce, spring onion, cucumber and remaining five-spice salt.

INGREDIENTS

1 whole duck, about 2 kg (4 lb 8 oz)
90 g (3¼ oz/¼ cup) maltose or honey (see note)
1 tablespoon dark soy sauce
Mandarin pancakes, warmed, to serve (see note)
Hoisin sauce, to serve
Spring onions (scallions), cut into strips, to serve
Lebanese (short) cucumber, cut into batons, to serve

Five-spice salt
1 tablespoon sea salt
2 teaspoons Chinese five-spice

NOTES

→ *Maltose and mandarin pancakes are available from Asian grocers. Honey is a good substitute for maltose, but it will make the dish slightly sweeter.*

→ *Leftover lacquered duck is excellent added to fried rice.*

Cut *Whole duck*
See page 61

DUCK SAN CHOY BAU

Prep time *15 minutes*
Cook *10 minutes*

1. Finely chop the duck breasts with a very sharp knife and put them in a bowl with the pork, mixing well with your hands to combine.

2. Heat a splash of peanut oil in a wok over high heat, add the ginger and garlic and stir-fry for 30 seconds or until fragrant. Add the sausage, water chestnuts and shiitake mushrooms and stir-fry for 2–3 minutes until browned.

3. Add the duck mixture and stir-fry for 5–6 minutes until browned and the moisture has evaporated, breaking up any clumps with a wooden spoon.

4. Pour in the Shaoxing rice wine and boil, stirring for 30 seconds to deglaze the wok. Reduce the heat to medium, add the soy sauce, oyster sauce, sesame oil and sugar and toss to combine.

5. Spoon the duck mixture into the lettuce cups, top with the cucumber, carrot and spring onion and serve.

INGREDIENTS

3 duck breasts (about 200 g/7 oz), skin removed (see note)
200 g (7 oz) minced (ground) pork shoulder
Peanut oil, for frying
1 tablespoon julienned fresh ginger
3 garlic cloves, finely chopped
1 lap cheong sausage, thinly sliced (see note)
50 g (1¾ oz/ ⅓ cup) tinned water chestnuts, diced (see note)
100 g (3½ oz) shiitake mushrooms, stalks trimmed, thickly sliced
100 ml (3½ fl oz) Shaoxing rice wine
2½ tablespoons light soy sauce
2 tablespoons oyster sauce
2 teaspoons sesame oil
1 teaspoon caster (superfine) sugar
12 iceberg lettuce cups
1 Lebanese (short) cucumber, cut into julienne strips
1 small carrot, cut into julienne strips
Thinly sliced spring onions (scallions), to serve

NOTES

→ *Lap cheong sausage is a Chinese dried pork sausage with a distinctive red colour. Lap cheong sausage and tinned water chestnuts are available from Chinese food shops.*

→ *The duck skin can be rendered and reserved for other cooking, such as duck fat–roasted vegetables. It also makes excellent crackling: cut into thin strips and cook in a large non-stick frying pan over medium heat for 6–8 minutes until crisp and golden.*

Cut Duck breast
See page 61

SERVES 8
DUCK CONFIT

Prep time *20 minutes*
(plus overnight curing)
Cook *2 hours*

INGREDIENTS

8 duck Marylands (leg quarters)
100 g (3½ oz) sea salt
5 thyme sprigs, leaves picked
1 rosemary stalk, leaves picked
3 garlic cloves, crushed
2 golden shallots, coarsely chopped
1 pinch of finely grated nutmeg
1.5 kg (3 lb 5 oz) tinned duck or goose fat
   (see note)

1. Pulse the salt, thyme, rosemary, garlic, shallot and nutmeg in a food processor to combine. Lay the duck pieces in a single layer in a ceramic baking dish, and rub the salt mixture well all over the duck. Scatter any remaining salt mixture over the top, cover with plastic wrap and refrigerate to cure for 12 hours.

2. Preheat the oven to 100°C (200°F). Brush excess salt mixture from the duck, pat dry with paper towel and lay in a single layer in a deep roasting tin.

3. Melt the duck fat in a saucepan over low heat, then pour it over the duck Marylands to completely cover. Bake for 1½– 2 hours until very tender and the meat is just beginning to fall from the bone.

4. Scatter a little salt in the base of a ceramic baking dish. Remove the duck from the fat and lay it in a single layer in the baking dish. Strain the duck fat over the top, ensuring the duck is completely submerged. Cover and refrigerate for up to 3 months.

5. To use the duck confit, warm the baking dish gently until the fat softens enough to remove the pieces you need, then crisp them in a heavy-based frying pan over high heat until golden and warmed through. Serve with duck fat–fried potatoes or braised cabbage or, for a lighter take, shred the meat and toss through a salad of bitter leaves and sliced pear, dressed with a mustard-spiked vinaigrette.

N O T E S

→ *Duck fat is available in tins or jars from selected delicatessens, or you can accumulate it over time by rendering it down from whole birds. To render fat yourself, heat pieces of duck fat in a saucepan with 2–3 tablespoons of water until the fat melts and becomes clear. Strain and refrigerate in sterile containers.*

→ *The duck fat can be strained and refrigerated almost indefinitely, to be re-used for confit or other cooking.*

→ *To make duck rillettes, shred the duck meat from the bone and combine in a bowl with a splash of brandy, a pinch of quatre épices or ground cloves and season with freshly ground black pepper. Spoon into a ramekin, packing to remove air pockets, smooth the top and pour over enough duck fat to cover and form a thin layer. Refrigerate until the fat is solid, for up to 2 weeks. Serve with toasted baguette and cornichons.*

***Cut** Duck Maryland*
See page 61

DUCK CASSOULET

Prep time *1 hour*
Cook *4 hours (plus overnight soaking)*

1. To make the pork stock, combine the pork skin, onion, carrot, garlic and bouquet garni in a large saucepan with 4 litres (140 fl oz/16 cups) of cold water, season with salt and pepper and bring to the boil. Reduce the heat to medium, cover and simmer for 1 hour to develop the flavours. Strain the stock, discarding the solids. You'll need 3 litres (105 fl oz/12 cups), so top up with water if necessary.

2. Meanwhile, combine the soaked beans with enough cold water to cover generously in a wide, large enamelled cast-iron casserole. Bring to the boil, cook for 5 minutes, drain the beans and return them to a clean casserole.

3. Add the pork stock to the casserole with the beans, bring to the boil, then reduce the heat to low and simmer for 1–1¼ hours until the beans are just tender. Strain the beans, reserving the stock separately. Season the beans with salt and pepper to taste.

4. Heat the duck fat in a clean casserole over medium–high heat, add the duck Marylands skin-side down and pan-fry for 3–4 minutes to brown well, then transfer to a plate. When cool enough to handle, divide the Marylands through the joint.

5. Add the sausages and pancetta to the casserole. Pan-fry, turning occasionally, for 4–5 minutes to brown well, then transfer to a plate. When cool enough to handle, cut the sausages into thirds and pancetta into rough 2.5 cm (1 inch) chunks. Pour off the fat from the casserole (reserve it for another use), leaving 1 tablespoon in the casserole.

6. Put the onion and garlic in the casserole, season with salt and pepper and sauté for 4–5 minutes until tender and translucent. Add the beans, stir to combine and season again.

7. Preheat the oven to 150°C (300°F). Tuck the duck, sausages and pancetta into the bean mixture, making sure they are partially covered. Scatter with the bay leaves and thyme, pour in the reserved pork stock to just cover the beans and add any resting juices from the meats. Bake for 1–1½ hours until golden and beans are very tender, topping up with extra pork stock if necessary. Remove from the oven and set aside for 15 minutes.

8. Meanwhile, to make the garlic crumbs, stir the breadcrumbs, duck fat and thyme in a bowl to combine, season with salt and pepper and spread on a baking tray lined with baking paper. Bake, stirring occasionally, for 12–15 minutes until crisp and golden brown. Stir in the garlic and parsley, then drain on paper towel and set aside.

9. Serve the cassoulet scattered with the garlic crumbs.

INGREDIENTS

3 confit duck Marylands (leg quarters), plus
2 tablespoons duck fat (see page 106)
400 g (14 oz) dried cannellini beans, soaked
in cold water overnight, drained
2 thick pork sausages, such as Toulouse,
pricked all over using a small knife
or skewer
150 g (5½ oz) flat pancetta
1 brown onion, finely diced
4 garlic cloves, finely chopped
2 fresh bay leaves
3 thyme sprigs

Pork stock
300 g (10½ oz) pork skin, cut into 5 cm
(2 inch) pieces
4 brown onions, coarsely chopped
3 carrots, coarsely chopped
1 garlic bulb, halved
Bouquet garni, made with 5 thyme sprigs,
4 parsley stalks, 2 small celery stalks and
2 fresh bay leaves, tied together with
kitchen string

Garlic crumbs
80 g (2¾ oz) coarse sourdough breadcrumbs
2½ tablespoons melted duck fat or olive oil
1 thyme sprig, leaves picked
1 garlic clove, finely chopped
1 handful of coarsely chopped flat-leaf
(Italian) parsley

SERVING SUGGESTION

a crisp bitter-leaf salad, dressed with a tangy vinaigrette, to cut through the richness

Cut Duck Maryland
See page 61

TEA-SMOKED QUAIL

Prep time *20 minutes*
Cook *15 minutes (plus standing)*

1. Combine the rice, brown sugar and tea in a large wok lined with a double layer of foil. Heat over high heat. Place the quail on a rack in the wok, cover tightly with foil (don't let the foil touch the quail) and smoke for 5 minutes, then turn off the heat. Stand for 5 minutes before uncovering.

2. Meanwhile, to make the salad, blanch the beans in a saucepan of boiling salted water for 1–2 minutes until tender and bright green. Drain, refresh under cold running water and transfer to a bowl. Add the frisée, sliced mandarin, shallots and parsley.

3. Whisk the olive oil, sherry vinegar, mandarin juice and mustard in a separate bowl to combine and season with salt and pepper. Drizzle over the salad and toss lightly.

4. Heat the vegetable oil in a large frying pan over medium–high heat, add the quail in batches and pan-fry, skin-side down, for 1–2 minutes until browned. Cut each quail in half and arrange on serving plates or a platter. Scatter the salad over and serve drizzled with any remaining dressing.

INGREDIENTS

6 butterflied quail, about 100 g (3½ oz) each
150 g (5½ oz/¾ cup) jasmine rice
60 g (2¼ oz) soft brown sugar
1 tablespoon tea leaves, such as jasmine
  or oolong
Vegetable oil, for pan-frying

Mandarin and witlof salad
100 g (3½ oz) green beans, trimmed and
  sliced lengthways
1 large handful of frisée (curly endive) leaves
2 mandarins (clementines), peeled and
  sliced into rounds, plus juice of 1 extra
1 golden shallot, thinly sliced
1 large handful of flat-leaf (Italian) parsley
  leaves
60 ml (2 fl oz/¼ cup) extra virgin olive oil
1 tablespoon sherry vinegar
1 teaspoon dijon mustard

Cut Whole quail
See page 62

*Brined roast turkey
(see pages 114–115).*

BRINED ROAST TURKEY

Prep time *30 minutes (plus overnight brining, drying)*
Cook *3½–4 hours (plus resting)*

1. To make the brine, put all of the ingredients with 4 litres (140 fl oz/16 cups) of water in a large stockpot, bring to the boil, then simmer for 10 minutes over medium heat. Remove from the heat, add another 4 litres of water, then strain (discarding the solids) and set aside to cool completely.

2. Pour the brine into a container large enough to hold the whole turkey. Submerge the turkey in the brine and use a heavy plate to weigh it down. Cover and refrigerate for 24 hours (see note). Five hours before cooking, drain the turkey, discarding the brine, and pat dry inside and out with paper towels.

3. Preheat the oven to 220°C (425°F). Season the turkey generously with salt and pepper, inside and out. Loosely fill the body cavity and neck cavity with stuffing (any remaining stuffing can be cooked separately in a buttered baking dish). Secure the cavity with a skewer and tuck the wings underneath the body.

4. Weigh the stuffed turkey to calculate the cooking time, allowing 20 minutes per 500 g (1 lb 2 oz).

5. Spread the onion slices in a large roasting tin to form a trivet and place the stuffed turkey, breast-side up, on top. Drizzle generously with olive oil and rub well into the skin. Season with salt and pepper.

6. Roast for 20 minutes, then reduce the oven temperature to 180°C (350°F) and roast, basting every 30–40 minutes with the pan juices, until golden brown, referring to your calculated cooking time. If the turkey browns too quickly, cover with a piece of buttered foil. To check whether it is cooked, a thermometer inserted into the thickest part of the thigh should read 71°C (160°F).

7. Transfer the turkey to a platter, cover loosely with foil and rest for at least 1 hour.

8. Tip any excess fat from the roasting tin. Heat the tin over medium–high heat, pour in the wine and verjuice and scrape the base of the pan to remove all the lovely caramelised bits. Reduce by half, add the stock and boil for 10–15 minutes to reduce to a rich-flavoured sauce. Season with salt and pepper.

9. Serve the turkey and sauce with your favourite trimmings.

INGREDIENTS

1 whole turkey, about 5.5–6 kg (12–14 lb)
1 quantity of stuffing (see recipes at right)
2 brown onions, thickly sliced
Olive oil, for drizzling
½ bottle (375 ml) dry white wine
100 ml (3½ fl oz) verjuice
500 ml (17 fl oz/2 cups) chicken or turkey stock (see note)

Brine
500 g (1 lb 2 oz/2 cups) fine salt
220 g (7¾ oz/1 cup) white sugar
2 tablespoons peppercorns
10 sprigs each thyme and sage
2 fresh bay leaves

NOTES

→ For extra-crisp skin, brine the turkey a couple of days in advance, drain and pat dry with paper towel. Refrigerate uncovered for up to 2 days for the skin to dry out.

→ If the turkey comes with giblets, remove them before brining and use them in your gravy.

→ Remove the neck and use it to make a simple stock for the base of your gravy.

→ Resting the turkey after cooking is important: it's the perfect time to roast your vegetables. At least 1 hour resting is recommended, but you can rest the turkey for up to 2 hours.

→ Leftover roast turkey is great tossed through a salad of boiled potatoes, bitter leaves, walnuts and peaches, dressed with a vinaigrette.

SOUR CHERRY, PISTACHIO AND ORANGE STUFFING

Heat a splash of olive oil in a saucepan over medium–high heat, add 1 chopped brown onion and 3 finely chopped garlic cloves and sauté until tender and translucent (4–5 minutes). Transfer to a bowl to cool, add 200 g (7 oz) of fresh sourdough breadcrumbs, ½ cup of coarsely chopped flat-leaf (Italian) parsley, 60 g (2¼ oz) of dried sour cherries or dried cranberries, 50 g (1¾ oz) of coarsely chopped pistachios, 2 tablespoons of finely grated orange zest and 2 lightly whisked eggs. Season with sea salt and freshly ground black pepper and mix to combine.

RYE, BACON AND SAGE STUFFING

Heat a saucepan over medium–high heat, add 4 chopped bacon rashers and fry for 2–3 minutes to render the fat. Add a splash of olive oil to the pan if necessary, then add 1 diced brown onion and 3 finely chopped garlic cloves. Sauté for 4–5 minutes until tender and translucent. Transfer to a bowl to cool, then add 200 g (7 oz) of fresh rye breadcrumbs, 1 small handful of coarsely chopped sage, 50 g (1¾ oz) of coarsely chopped hazelnuts, 2 tablespoons of finely grated lemon zest and 2 lightly whisked eggs. Season with salt and pepper and mix to combine.

WILD RICE, SAUSAGE AND APPLE STUFFING

Cook 200 g (7 oz) of wild rice in a saucepan of boiling water until tender (40–45 minutes), then drain and set aside to cool completely. Heat a splash of olive oil in a saucepan over medium–high heat. Squeeze the meat from the skins of 500 g (1 lb 2 oz) of pork and fennel sausages into the pan. Fry for 6–8 minutes to brown well, breaking up the pieces with a wooden spoon. Add 1 chopped brown onion, 1 coarsely chopped granny smith apple and 3 finely chopped garlic cloves and sauté for 4–5 minutes until tender and translucent. Transfer to a bowl to cool, then add the wild rice, 1 cup of coarsely chopped flat-leaf (Italian) parsley and 2 tablespoons of chopped sage, season with salt and pepper and mix to combine.

Cut Whole turkey
See page 62

TURKEY MOLE

Prep time *1 hour (plus soaking)*
Cook *3½ hours (plus resting)*

1. Dry-fry the chillies in a large enamelled cast-iron casserole over medium–high heat for 20–30 seconds. Transfer to a large heatproof bowl. Pour boiling water over the chillies to cover and set aside for 20 minutes to soften. Drain, reserving the water, and transfer to a blender. Add 250 ml (9 fl oz/1 cup) of chicken stock and 200 ml (7 fl oz) of the reserved soaking water and blend to a smooth purée. Strain and discard the solids.

2. Dry-fry the pepitas in the casserole for 1–2 minutes. Add the reserved chilli seeds and cook, stirring, for 2–3 minutes until toasted, adding the aniseed and dried herbs in the last minute of cooking. Cool, then use a spice grinder or mortar and pestle to grind to a fine powder. Transfer to a large bowl.

3. Heat the peanut oil in the casserole over medium–high heat, add the almonds and fry, stirring, for 3–4 minutes until browned, adding tortilla strips in the final 2 minutes of cooking. Use a slotted spoon to transfer them to the spice mixture.

4. Add a splash of extra oil if necessary, then add the onion and garlic to the casserole and sauté for 8–10 minutes. Add the tomatillo and tomato and sauté for a further 8–10 minutes until beginning to soften. Add to the spice and tortilla mixture.

5. In a blender, process the spice and tortilla mixture, with the raisins and another 500 ml (17 fl oz/2 cups) of the stock to a fine purée: you may need to do this in batches. Pass through a fine sieve (discarding the solids) and season with salt and pepper.

6. If necessary, add a splash of extra oil to the casserole and heat over medium–high heat. Season the turkey with salt and pepper and lay it skin-side down in the dish. Pan-fry, turning once, for 10–15 minutes until golden brown. Transfer to a plate.

7. Put the chilli purée into the same casserole and cook, stirring occasionally, for 10–15 minutes until reduced and thick. Add the spice purée and the remaining stock, reduce the heat to low and simmer, stirring occasionally, for 20–25 minutes to develop the flavours. Stir in the chocolate, add the cinnamon and bay leaf and season with salt and pepper. Half-cover with a lid and simmer, stirring occasionally, for 25–30 minutes until rich. Season to taste, adding sugar if you like.

8. Preheat the oven to 160° (320°F). Put the turkey in the sauce, spooning a little over the top of the meat. Cover with a lid and bake, turning occasionally, for 45 minutes to 1 hour until cooked through: a thermometer inserted into the thickest part of the breast should read 68°C (154°F). Set aside to rest for 20 minutes.

9. To serve, slice the turkey and spoon the sauce over.

INGREDIENTS

1 turkey breast, skin on (about 2 kg/4 lb 8 oz)
75 g (2¾ oz) dried poblano chillies (about 6), stems removed, deseeded, 1 tablespoon seeds reserved
40 g (1½ oz) dried guajillo chillies (about 6), stems removed, deseeded, seeds reserved
50 g (1¾ oz) dried pasilla chillies (about 4), stems removed, deseeded
Boiling water, to soak
1.75 litres (61 fl oz/7 cups) chicken stock, turkey stock or water
40 g (1½ oz/¼ cup) pepitas (pumpkin seeds)
1 teaspoon aniseed
1 teaspoon dried thyme
½ teaspoon dried oregano
80 ml (2½ fl oz/⅓ cup) peanut oil
160 g (5¾ oz/1 cup) almonds
2 corn tortillas, torn into strips
1 large brown onion, chopped
6 garlic cloves, crushed
2 large tomatillos, chopped
1 large ripe tomato, chopped
65 g (2¼ oz/⅓ cup) raisins, soaked in warm water for 20 minutes, drained
100 g (3½ oz) Mexican chocolate, finely chopped
2 cinnamon sticks
1 fresh bay leaf
60 g (2¼ oz) caster (superfine) sugar (optional)

SERVING SUGGESTION

coriander (cilantro) sprigs, warm tortillas, extra toasted pepitas

Cut Turkey breast
See page 62

BUTTERFLIED SQUAB

Prep time *5 minutes*
Cook *15 minutes*

1. Take the butterflied squab out of the fridge 20 minutes before cooking to bring them to room temperature. Season with salt and freshly ground black pepper.

2. Put a splash of olive oil in a heavy-based frying pan over high heat. When the oil is slightly smoking, put the squab skin-side down and sear for 5–7 minutes until crisp and light brown.

3. Add the butter, garlic and thyme. Turn the squab and spoon the pan juices over for 1 minute. Transfer the squab to a plate lined with paper towel to rest.

4. Deglaze the frying pan with the sherry, light it with a long-handled match to burn off the alcohol for 1 minute (be careful of the flame). Add the stock and reduce until the mixture coats the back of a spoon. Season with salt, pepper and fresh lemon juice. Serve the squab with the gravy drizzled over.

INGREDIENTS

2 x 500 g (1 lb 2 oz) squab, butterflied
2 tablespoons olive oil
1 tablespoon butter
2 garlic cloves, unpeeled and crushed
2 thyme sprigs
2½ tablespoons dry sherry
1 tablespoon game stock or chicken stock
Lemon juice

SERVING SUGGESTION

fluffy mashed potatoes, French beans and pickled cherries

NOTES

→ *To learn how to butterfly a bird, see page 484.*

→ *Squab is best served rare to medium-rare, with an internal temperature of 50–53°C (120–127°F) before resting. If you would like the thighs and wings cooked a little further, joint the squab and cook them in the pan for a little longer, while the breast rests.*

Cut Whole squab
See page 63

ROAST GOOSE
~ WITH CIDER GRAVY ~

Prep time *40 minutes (plus standing, resting)*
Cook *2 hours 40 minutes*

INGREDIENTS

1 whole goose, about 5 kg (11 lb 4 oz)
4 brown onions, coarsely chopped
12 sage sprigs
12 thyme sprigs
3 rosemary sprigs
3 fresh bay leaves
Oil, for drizzling
350 ml (12 fl oz) dry apple cider

Goose stock
Goose wings, reserved
2 brown onions, coarsely chopped
1 carrot, coarsely chopped
12 sage sprigs
12 thyme sprigs

SERVING SUGGESTION

potatoes, shallots and pink lady apples, roasted in goose fat

1. To prepare the goose, remove any fat from the opening of the cavity. Remove the first and second joints of the wings and set aside for the stock.

2. Prick the skin of the breasts and legs all over with a skewer, or lightly score the skin with a sharp knife to form a crosshatch pattern, being careful not to pierce the flesh: this helps the fat below the skin to render during roasting.

3. Place the goose on a wire rack in a flameproof roasting tin, season the cavity with salt and pepper and stuff with the onion and herbs. Loosely tie the legs together with kitchen string, drizzle with a little oil, rubbing it in well, and season with salt and pepper. Set aside at room temperature for 30 minutes.

4. Preheat the oven to 220°C (425°F). Roast the goose for 20 minutes until golden brown, then reduce the oven temperature to 180°C (350°F). Ladle out excess fat from the pan from time to time (or use a turkey baster). Roast for a further 1 hour 40 minutes to 2 hours until well browned, with an internal temperature of 71°C (162°F). Cover with foil if it is browning too quickly.

5. Meanwhile, to make the stock for the gravy, heat a little of the fat reserved from the pan in a saucepan over medium–high heat, add the reserved wings and fry for 4–5 minutes until browned. Add the vegetables and fry, stirring occasionally, for 8–10 minutes until caramelised. Pour off excess fat, add the herbs and 1.5 litres (52 fl oz/6 cups) of water, bring to the boil, then reduce the heat to medium. Simmer for 1–1½ hours until well flavoured, skimming off any scum that forms on the surface. Strain (discarding the solids) and set aside. Skim off the fat that rises to the surface as it cools.

6. When the goose is cooked, transfer to a platter or board, cover loosely with foil and set aside to rest for 30 minutes.

7. Tip excess fat from the pan and heat the pan on the stovetop over medium–high heat. Pour in the cider, scraping the base of the pan to remove all the lovely caramelised bits. Cook for 4–5 minutes until reduced by half, add 500 ml (17 fl oz/2 cups) of the stock and boil for 10–15 minutes to reduce to a rich-flavoured sauce. Season with salt and pepper to taste.

8. To carve the goose, cut off the legs and cut each one in half through the joint. Carve the breasts off the bird, then slice thinly. Serve with cider gravy and your choice of trimmings.

NOTES

→ *Fat removed from the cavity can be rendered for roasting or frying. Melt very slowly in a saucepan over low heat and strain. The fat from the roasting tin can also be strained and reserved. Refrigerate for up to 6 months. Use in the same way as you would duck fat.*

→ *Leftover goose can be kept refrigerated for up to 3 days, or frozen for up to 3 months. Leftover breast meat is excellent cold in sandwiches (don't reheat it, or it will be very dry), while leg meat can be gently reheated in leftover gravy.*

Cut *Whole goose*
See page 63

CHAPTER TWO

SHEEP

LAMB ~ MUTTON ~ GOAT

SHEEP

LAMB, MUTTON, LANOLIN, WOOL, MILK & CHEESE, PARCHMENT, TALLOW, COLD CREAM, GLUE, KNUCKLEBONES

PRIZED CUTS

TO ROAST *Cap-on lamb rack*

TO GRILL *Lamb loin chops, tail on*

TO BRAISE *Neck*

PRIZED OFFAL *Kidneys, brains, liver (lamb's fry) and sweetbreads*

COMPLEMENTS TO THE LAMB

ROSEMARY	ONION	OUZO
MINT	YOGHURT	SUMAC
THYME	LEMON	CORIANDER SEEDS
ANCHOVIES	ALMONDS	CHAMOMILE
OLIVES	APRICOTS	OREGANO
POTATOES	POMEGRANATE	RAISINS
GARLIC	CUMIN	TOMATO
EGGPLANT	CINNAMON	BEANS

LAMB LEFTOVERS Shepherd's pie is a recipe designed for leftovers: use remaining meat picked from a leg or shoulder roast. Lamb fritters, made with leftover meat, mash, herbs and an egg to bind, are excellent fried in a hot pan. Lamb fat is not friends with the fridge and will become hard and unpalatable, so remove any fat from lamb that you plan to use in a salad or a sandwich. Chutney is a cold lamb sandwich's best friend.

SIMPLE CUTS VS COMPLEX CUTS

When deciding the best way to cook lamb, it's best to think about how this animal works in the field to determine the best use for each cut: there's a lot of activity up the front of the lamb, with strong shoulders and neck muscles that do a lot of the work, but these cuts make up for their muscle with collagen and sinews that melt with slow cooking.

Simple cuts, requiring minimal intervention:
RIBS · LOIN · LEG

Complex cuts, requiring longer cooking time:
NECK · SHOULDER · BREAST · SHANK

COMPLEX CUTS

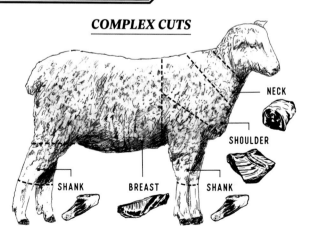

NECK

SHOULDER

SHANK · BREAST · SHANK

LEARN MORE ABOUT THE DIFFERENT CUTS OF SHEEP AND HOW TO USE THEM ON PAGES 148–154.

SELECT & STORE

Sheep are good at living on meagre pastures and rocky areas, so the lamb you find at the butcher's is most likely free ranging and grass fed. Look for lamb that is pink in colour with clean white fat. Lamb will have a beautiful fresh smell. Buy cuts such as the rack and rump with the fat cap still on, to keep your roast juicy. Consider buying cutlets and rack unfrenched, with the delicious meat still on the bones. Lamb roasts and chops can be stored, wrapped in butchers' paper, in the fridge for two to three days.

BUTCHER'S TREATS

CAP-ON LAMB RACK AND RUMP

LAMB BELLY AND RIBLETS

NECK

—ALL ABOUT—
AGE

LAMB: less than 12 months of age, no permanent incisors (teeth). It will be mild on flavour and tender.

HOGGET: sheep of either sex, generally one year old with no more than two permanent incisors. A hogget will have a deeper flavour than lamb, but this can be a mere matter of days or a month's difference.

MUTTON: a female or castrated male (wether) with more than two permanent incisors (around two years old). Mutton has a much deeper sheep flavour than lamb. It can be tough and is great stewed with spices to balance the intensity, or citrus or yoghurt to cut the richness.

SHOULDER vs LEG

THIS IS THE QUESTION OF THE ULTIMATE LAMB ROAST. TRADITIONALLY THE LEG HELD SWAY. BUT NOW IT'S THE SHOULDER—WITH ITS EXTRA CONNECTIVE TISSUE, SINEW AND FLAVOUR— JOSTLING FOR A SPOT AS FAMILY FAVOURITE.

FRENCHED RACK OF LAMB

The bones of a rack of lamb can be 'frenched', meaning they have been tidied up by scraping away the meat that clings to them. It's great for presentation, but if you want to pick them up and gnaw on the bone you may want to leave all that flavour attached. Cut between the bones of the rack for little lamb cutlets, perfect for simple grilling or crumbing.

⊣ CAP ON/CAP OFF ⊢

Due to its size, there are a number of cuts on a lamb that we get to appreciate in conjunction with the cap of fat that sits above them. This is a treat for the cook as the fat will protect the cut as it roasts and will baste the meat, keeping it moist. A lamb rack with the cap on, or a lamb rump with the cap on, are two delicious cuts that can be purchased with this advantage.

TIP: *The goat is anatomically similar to the lamb, so many of the slow-cooking recipes for lamb work beautifully with goat too.*

HISTORY

The histories of many nations have been woven in wool: sheep, with their ability to adapt to different climates and food sources, accompanied (and, indeed, financed) explorers and settlers as they conquered lush mountain pastures and arid plains.

In Australia, children played knucklebones in the schoolyard, candles were fashioned from tallow, to tell a story was to spin a yarn and lanolin was a cure-all. In the kitchen, the lamb roast became a cultural staple between the wars (although, it was more often mutton—meat procured from sheep that had served their purpose providing wool first—that the family sat down to). Iconic paintings such as Tom Roberts' *The Golden Fleece* eternalised this image and took it to the world, cementing Australia's reputation as the country that 'rode on the sheep's back'.

However, Australia is not the only country that has profited from sheep. Since the Middle Ages, trading fine wool has been an incredibly lucrative business and consequently the genetics of flocks were fiercely guarded by monarchies. Money made from these flocks sent ships to conquer the world.

The best example of this is the merino, the great fine-wool breed of Spain. While it is revered for its fleece, the merino has a lot going for it beyond its cloak; it thrives in semi-arid climates and is well suited to nomadic farming. The Spanish monopoly on the fine-wool market helped fund exploration around the globe. Wool was such a treasure that up until the eighteenth century the export of merinos was a crime punishable by death, as Spain rightly realised that the value was ensured by the protection of the genetic stock.

Tracing the sheep's path from Central Asia to Europe and later the New World, we can also track a path of some of the best culinary solutions for this animal. In Central Asian cuisines it is mutton, not lamb, that sits at the centre of the table. It will most often be made into curries and other one-pot dishes that use slow cooking to break down the older, tougher meat: dishes such as lamb biryani and rogan josh. In these countries, it is not unusual to see the word mutton used interchangeably between sheep and goat.

Lamb and mutton have long been the favoured meats of the Middle East, marrying beautifully with their rich spices and fireside cooking: think of lamb kofta and

→ *In England, 'owling'—the smuggling of sheep or wool out of the country—was also forbidden. In the House of Lords the speaker still sits on a wool bale, or more recently a cushion stuffed with wool, known as the woolsack. (In 1938, it was discovered this cushion was actually stuffed with horse hair. It has since been restuffed with a mixture of wool from all over the Commonwealth, in a sign of unity.)*

shish kebabs, or, coupled with cracked wheat such as burghul (bulgur) and other grains and nuts to make kibbeh and kibbeh nayeh, a raw meat dish spiced up with lemon juice and chilli.

As sheep made their way across the seas of the Mediterranean, the taste of young lamb made itself known and loved. Yoghurt, lemon, garlic, herbs and spices cut through the fatty meat and rich flavour, helping lamb find a place at the summer table. Both sheep and goats thrived on the rocky shores of the sea and the animals found an easy home in salty pastures that, in essence, seasoned the lambs from the inside out.

Sheep also found a place in the highlands of Europe. Their wool provided ample coverage for the animals in the cold winters and the warm fibre was also a boon for the humans of these cold lands. When flavoured by the rich herbaceous grasses of the highlands, the sheep's milk is also highly sought after, making some of the world's most renowned cheeses, including the French Roquefort and the Basque Ossau-Iraty. This industry subsequently brings another treat to the table—young milk-fed lamb—a by-product of the sheep dairy.

In Australia, sheep have found their place across all pastures, from the arid and semi-arid inland tracts to the lush pastures on the coast. In a country where most of the meat that is eaten comes from animals that are introduced, it is astonishing to see how well adapted sheep are to the climate. They cope with the weather and love the rocky land that most other animals can't endure, as do goats. In fact, it is the lack of local appetite for the latter, coupled with their natural affinity to the land, that is one of the reasons Australia is one of the world's biggest exporters of goat. Perhaps it should be considered as a local option.

➡ *For more on the story of sheep in Australia, read C.E.W. Bean's book,* On the Wool Track, *first published by John Lane Company, New York, in 1910.*

The story of sheep in Australia is not simply one of glory. The old soils have laboured under the sheep's hoofs. As historian C.E.W. Bean stated, the 'delicate country responds like a piano to whatever touches it'. Times of drought, coupled with the hard-compacted earth caused untold damage to the land (aided by the rabbits, which in times of need ate the grasses to the roots while digging burrows under the earth, exacerbating the damage to an already fragile system). Careful soil and mob management can now help to temper this.

Sheep remain beholden to the humans who tend them—due to their small stature there are many predators and thus very few examples of wild sheep in the world—but they remain largely outdoors, free-ranging on grass pastures. In fact, their adaptability allows them some of the most beautiful grazing lands on the planet.

Sheep

As the idiom suggests, sheep like to follow each other. For more on life in the flock, see pages 142–143.

BREED

Historically, sheep have been domesticated as much for a source of clothing as for meat and milk, and humans have looked to sheep for more than 10,000 years to clothe and nourish.

In Neolithic days we see the first evidence of herding and domestication of both sheep and goats; their manageable size, herding mentality and placid nature all played a role in endearing sheep to early farmers and herdsmen. The relationship between man and sheep has become symbiotic and, in fact, sheep now largely rely on humans for their existence. Consequently, there are very few examples of wild sheep and certainly not in the numbers we still find horses, pigs, goats and dogs; there are a couple of exceptions, limited to islands such as Corsica and Sardinia where natural predators can be kept at a minimum.

As we have sought to breed sheep with a view to having the very best wool or the very best meat, we have somewhat lost the multitalented sheep in the process. With distinct breeds, we use one for wool, discarding or exporting the mutton at the end; likewise with the meat from milk-producing sheep; while our taste for lamb, cooked pink, means that the sheep bred for their meat are processed at under a year, before they cut their first teeth.

The history of genetics and breeds is interesting, with the breeding programs of sheep—particularly the work of eighteenth century agriculturist Robert Bakewell—thought to have paved the way for Darwin's theories of selective breeding or artificial selection, theories that later led to his ideas and works on natural selection. Bakewell was one of the first to illustrate that from one family of sheep you can breed out specific traits while exaggerating others by careful selection.

Today, sheep are bred for three distinct purposes—wool, meat or milk—rather than remaining the all-rounders they once were. For example, it is believed that the mutton flavour is more pronounced in fine-wool breeds, while the milk breeds put all their energy into producing significant quantities of milk.

Generally, unless a sheep is being raised for the purebred market or registered breeding, they will be a first-cross or second-cross animal (where two breeds are

→ *The majority of lamb production today is conducted using crossbreeds and composites (selecting traits from different breeds). Farmers select certain maternal traits in their breeding stock, crossing them each season with rams chosen for growth rates and meat production.*

→ A first cross, where one purebred is crossed with another, is the same as an F1 in cattle (see page 284); a second cross, when a crossbred animal is paired with a purebred, is known as an F2.

brought together, or 'crossed' over each other). By crossing one breed over another the farmer can achieve hybrid vigour or heterosis: a crossbreed that will show superior qualities to both parents. There are now considered to be more than a thousand sheep breeds across the world.

When selecting breeds for meat, the farmer is looking for two key attributes: growth rate and good carcass size. They will also consider birthing rates, as a ewe that can produce two lambs each year will, of course, provide double the profits. Lamb breeds are significantly affected by the amount of fat and the way in which the fat is deposited on the carcass, whether it is intramuscular, intermuscular or internal.

Lambs produced for meat are known as prime lambs and may come from a combination of breeds: dorper, Suffolk, merino, border Leicester and a number of other key breeds (see the heritage breed map, page 136). Given these variations and possibilities, work is still being done to enhance breeds for the current market. And yet it is interesting to note that sheep appear to be behind the eight ball when it comes to celebrating breeds on menus. In Australia, this has recently led to the Australian White, a breed that is being described as the Wagyu of the sheep world.

Goat breeds, on the other hand, were originally chosen for their wool—the cashmere and Angora—while the Boer goat is predominantly a meat breed. With the goat we note another interesting phenomenon: despite the most careful breeding, animals have an uncanny ability to return to their original form. A great example of this is the rangeland goat in Australia. Feral goats have been found in Australia in quite large numbers since the 1900s, having been abandoned in unprofitable times or escaped from flocks. They have reverted to a species that is almost unrecognisable compared to the tame breeds they sprouted from, whether out of a need to adapt or an adverse reaction to a forced breeding regime. Perhaps it is time for a celebration of the different breeds and their attributes on the table.

Goats *range further than sheep: their mountain-climbing abilities allow them to access hills and scrub that other animals cannot reach.*

HERITAGE BREED MAP: SHEEP & GOATS

BRITAIN

BRITAIN

English Leicester

A large-framed animal, with good-quality long wool.

Border Leicester

Also large framed, they make good mothers, due to their protective instincts and milk production.

Wiltshire

Predominantly a meat breed, it is unusual for its ability to moult its short wool and hair in spring.

Dorset (Wales horned x Spanish merino)

The dorset and poll dorset (US) are dedicated meat breeds with a fast growth rate and high carcass yield.

Cheviot

Originating in Scotland (and named for the region), this is a small meat breed with a well-muscled carcass.

Southdown

Now also in the USA, the original breed from Sussex is shorter but with a larger frame than their US cousins. Renowned for their high fertility.

Ryeland

Considered to be a descendant of the merino, docile with high fertility and good wool production. Great for smallholdings.

Suffolk (Norfolk cross Southdown)

A large sheep with rapid growth; good maternal instincts. Their genetics are used in many composite breeds.

MIDDLE EAST

TURKEY

Angora goat

Produce mohair, a soft and silky fibre used for fabric and knitting yarn.

EUROPE

NETHERLANDS (& GERMANY)

Texel

Lean but heavily muscled, with a reputation for ideal muscle-to-bone ratio and less carcass fat than other breeds.

Blue texel

Unique colouration of the fleece. Considered to have better birthing rates than the texel.

East Friesian

Excellent quality and prolific milk production.

SPAIN

Merino

Thrive in semi-arid conditions, good herders, excellent fine wool with crimp.

FRANCE

Lacaune

Produces flavourful milk; this is the breed used to make Roquefort cheese.

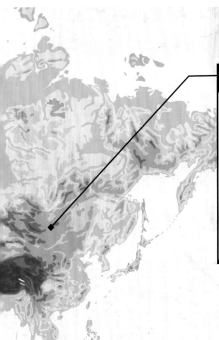

ASIA

MONGOLIA

Cashmere goat

Produce luxurious fibres.

AFRICA

SOUTH AFRICA

Van Rooy

Wool variety for shearing, meat-producing; well suited to arid environments. This is one of dozens of fat-tailed breeds farmed in Africa and the Middle East.

Dorper (from Dorset horn and blackhead Persian)

Fast-growing, meat-producing, typically early maturing with a small carcass that butchers love.

Boer goat

Renowned for delicious meat, easy to manage; the name comes from the Afrikaans word meaning farmer.

AUSTRALIA

Australian white (cross)

Good body weight and muscle conformation with intramuscular fat, well suited to Australian conditions.

Australian rangeland goat

Well adapted to the environment, but with mixed eating quality.

NEW ZEALAND

Coopworth (cross border Leicester and romney, another British breed)

This dual-purpose sheep has good fertility and growth rates. Excellent meat production has taken it around the world.

FEED

Perhaps due to the way sheep can be crossbred quickly to exhibit certain characteristics, sheep find a home in many different landscapes, albeit with the implicit protection of humans (or beautiful maremma sheepdogs).

Sheep have earned a loving place in the heart of many farmers due to the ease with which they will graze on meagre pastures and thrive in marginal, rocky areas. Romantically, the flowers and herbs of beautiful hilly pastures can easily be traded for sea succulents on windswept salty plains. The adaptability of sheep has given them the most picturesque of homes and the most diverse of diets.

Imagine life, for example, on Pag, a small Croatian island in the Adriatic Sea, where sheep roamed wild across traditionally unowned lands for centuries. The island is nestled close to the mainland, under a large mountain range, the Velebit. The *bora* wind travels down this mountain range, gathering strength, and rushes over the island, depositing salt crystals across the island's vegetation, which is predominantly an indigenous sage plant. It is on these salty herbs that the sheep fed, in essence flavouring the meat from within.

The story of Pag sheep is also unique due to the lack of predators, meaning the sheep could roam free around the island. The free-roaming sheep were identifiable to their owners by cuts made in their ears, similar to the tradition of slashing shapes into bread in France or Morocco, where the scalpel cuts distinguished loaves in the communal bread oven.

The benefits of salty pastures are also seen in the French *agneau de pré-salé* (literally meaning 'presalted lamb') that graze on the salty shores of Brittany and Normandy. The sea succulents and grasses grow wild in these areas and so the grazing is generally completely natural: no fertilisers, no sprays.

In England, this is known as salt-marsh lamb, where sheep graze coastal estuaries for their salt-tolerant grasses and herbs—samphire, sorrel, *Spartina* (sparta) grass and sea lavender—plants that are washed by the daily tides. In Australia it is the rugged saltbush, a plant suitably adapted to the arid land in the centre of the country, that provides both moisture and salty sustenance.

Most lamb, however, is still traditionally grass fed. Lamb, particularly grass-fed lamb, is a great source of omega-3s. In fact, in countries with limited access to the ocean, lamb can form the key source of this essential fatty acid. Furthermore, up to 40 per cent of the fat in grass-fed lamb comes from oleic acid (the same fat for which olive oil is praised). Long considered an integral part of Mediterranean cuisine, these oils play a role in the lauded diet of these people.

Different flavours in grass-fed lamb can be affected by the seasons (and the available grasses) and it is believed that lamb fed on aromatic herbs will develop some of the taste of the aromatics in the meat. There are some studies that also suggest different breeds will feed on different pastures. For example, merinos are more selective in the field, seeking out the soft grasses, while dorpers are nonselective and are thus less likely to go in search of greener pastures.

Increasingly lamb may now be ration or lot fed, in a similar manner to cows: they start their life on a pasture and will be moved to outdoor pens to be 'finished' on a diet of grains and hay. The grains are often cracked and steamed to enlarge the surface area, making them easier to digest. Silage is also a regular feature of a supplementary diet: the grains are covered and allowed to begin to ferment, making digestion easier.

Goats range even further than sheep, with their mountain-climbing abilities allowing them to access hills and scrub that other animals cannot. These varying pastures and grasses contribute to their intense, earthy flavour.

Goats are browsers, rather than grazers like cattle and sheep. While they eat a wide variety, they can also be picky; for example, they are used to browse between the tea plantations in China, as they will avoid the bitter tea leaves in favour of weeds.

Due to their free-ranging ways and curious nature, there will often be seasonal variation in the flavour of goat meat.

Most lamb in Australia *is free ranging and grass fed. Improved pastures, like this one, are also common for extra sustenance.*

ON THE FARM

Sheep like to be together; as the idiom suggests, they follow each other and will generally stay in a mob. The collective nature of sheep makes them quite easy to manage; and sheep herding— tending a flock—is considered one of the earliest professions.

The traditional shepherd would take a flock into the mountains without fences, knowing that in finding one he would generally find them all. Grazing common land—often in mountainous regions where more lucrative crops could not be grown—these shepherds, with their flocks, would practise a migratory flocking system. As the seasons changed and the grasses were consumed, sheep would be moved from one fertile pasture to another, while the shepherd would protect them and ensure they were kept together.

In England, shepherds and their flocks practised a more sedentary life. 'Hefted to the land', breeds were established based on their terroir. Like homing pigeons, these animals have been known to return, over vast plains, to their hefted home. Over generations the mob's territorial instincts were honed to their own place on the hilltops where they grazed without fences, without guidance. Often flocks grazed side by side, each acutely aware of the end of their own boundaries. Beatrix Potter had one such flock and her property was sold on the provision that these sheep were left connected to their home.

→ *The book* The Shepherd's Life *by James Rebanks (Allen Lane, 2015) covers the subject of sheep herding in amazing detail and is recommended reading.*

It is an incredible example of animal terroir; in some cases even proving that animals can form natural resistance to the ticks and diseases connected to their home turf, such as Louping ill, and iron and mineral deficiencies that the land may enforce upon other introduced flocks. The system is largely reliant on the spaces around the pasture also being occupied, the other animals acting as a barrier to movement. While examples of this kind of herding are on the decline, they can still be found in northern England and Wales.

TRADITIONS

The fate of the sacrificial lamb is a story long told in religious texts, particularly in the monotheistic religions; and Abraham, Isaac, Moses and King David were all shepherds. In the Christian tradition, Christ was known as the lamb of God, sacrificed to atone for the sins of others, while the scapegoat is a concept oft-too-well understood in society. Beyond the religious, it's an interesting idea of the importance of a life and the respect of death.

Traditions, both religious and otherwise, are important components in celebratory feasts. The Easter lamb is one such tradition for many; however, it raises an interesting question of seasonality with meat. Easter in the northern hemisphere coincides with spring, and so may make sense of eating the suckling lambs, but in the southern hemisphere Easter is in autumn, of course.

Now, with the wonders of crossbreeding, we can produce sheep with two lambing periods in the year: one in spring and one in autumn, with lambs processed at six to eight months of age. The main difference with these lambs will be the grasses they are fed on. In regions with long summers, grass-fed spring lamb may work harder to find lush pastures, while those born in autumn have the benefits of winter pastures, and vice versa.

SHEEP AGE

Mutton dressed up as lamb: it's an odd concept. It's odd to strive to be something that you're not. Young people try to look older, but the older you get, the younger you hope to look. Being your age is a beautiful thing and the same rings true with animals. For example, we classify lamb as an animal that has not 'cut' its teeth, which generally happens at a year old. Once the teeth show, the animal's price will drop dramatically as its classification moves from lamb to hogget. This is a crazy tightrope we expect farmers to walk. While classifications are necessary and have a place, it is a terrible shame to see the value of a sheep drop by almost a quarter with the growth of their first teeth.

→ *Generally, the younger an animal the milder the flavour and the more tender the meat. Both the fat and the bones harden as the animal gets older. The colour of the flesh will deepen as the animal gets older: lamb will be light to dark pink; yearling mutton medium pink to light red; mutton is light to dark red.*

In England, there has been a recent campaign aimed at reinstating mutton as a quality product, with pride of place in the butcher's cabinet. Mutton will be darker, coarser and firmer, with more intensely flavoured fat.

As with veal, we find an excess of young lambs that are surplus to milk production, particularly in cheesemaking regions such as Roquefort, Sardinia and the Pyrenees. Known as suckling lambs or milk-fed lambs, these young sheep have less fibrous tissue; however, perhaps of more import is their underdeveloped rumen, meaning they have a monogastric stomach, like pigs and chickens, and are unable to process grasses yet. Essentially this means their fat composition is more similar to their mother's milk than to the fat of older sheep, thus giving a milky flavour.

As sheep age the levels of hormones and, specifically, polyunsaturated fatty acids increase, which can lead to lipid oxidisation. The resulting mutton can have 'rancid' or 'stale' flavours. This is also attributable to the fat deposits, which are influenced by diet and by the shifting chemical balance of the sheep. It is also in older animals that the difference between the sexes in terms of taste becomes more pronounced. The flavour decreases in strength from ram to ewe to wether. Lamb under a year old is not said to differ dramatically in taste due to its sex.

AGE AT SLAUGHTER

Lamb, hogget or mutton? The age of the sheep dictates the name it is sold under.

Milk-fed (suckling) – typically four to six weeks old (5.5–8 kg or approximately 12–18 lb). These lambs are often by-products of the sheep dairy and cheesemaking industry. They are delicate in flavour and texture, with a milky taste.

Spring lamb – the traditional Easter lamb, three to five months old, is a treat in the northern hemisphere, where the spring and summer pastures are lush.

Lamb – from around four months to one year old. In Australia to be classified as lamb they will have no permanent incisors, while in New Zealand the definition allows for no incisors 'in wear'.

Hogget – classified after it has its first pair of permanent teeth, between one and two years old. Can be of either sex.

Mutton – more than two years old; generally, given the hormones in a ram, it is more likely that this will be a wether (castrated male) or a ewe (female). In some countries hogget will be classified as mutton. In India and much of the Middle East the term 'mutton' is used interchangeably between sheep and goats.

GOATS

A kid goat, also known as a ***capretto*** (Italian) or ***cabrito*** (Spanish) is a goat under six months of age. It will generally weigh between six and 12 kilograms (between about 14–27 lb).

Chevon, the word used for goat meat generally, technically refers to an older goat.

→ ***Wether*** – *castrated male sheep*
→ ***Ewe*** – *female sheep*
→ ***Ram*** – *male sheep*
→ ***Buck*** – *male goat*
→ ***Doe*** – *female goat*

AT THE BUTCHER

Generally, a lamb will be divided into three parts: forequarter, loin and hindquarter. The forequarter includes the neck, shoulder and front legs. The hindquarter includes the rear legs, hip and rump. The loin includes everything in between.

THE CARCASS

The **neck** is great diced for stews or, with the bone in, the neck chops are slowly cooked to create favourites such as the Lancashire hotpot (see page 162). The **foreshank** is much smaller than the rear and so if used you may require two, instead of one, per person.

Traditionally known as the poor man's leg, the **shoulder** is a great cut when boned and rolled. Whether on or off the bone it is certainly better cooked a little slower and a little longer than the leg: the aim is medium, not medium-rare. Even better is to cook it super slowly. This is also where you will find the forequarter or best-end chops: they're great for grilling.

The **rack of lamb** may be the king of all lamb roasts. In restaurants, it is most often served with the cap off (the layer of fat that sits above the rack removed), but you can also get it with the cap still attached if you are a fat fan; the fat will baste the rack as it cooks and can be removed afterwards.

A boneless **loin** also makes a great roasting cut. For a real feast, leave the belly attached to the loin and stuff and roll it up for a delicious roast. More extravagant than this, you can leave the two loins together to make a saddle of lamb that can be roasted whole.

The **backstrap** is taken from the loin and is equivalent to the sirloin in a cow. If you are buying backstrap from your butcher, which is a great easy meal, ask your butcher to leave the fat cap on, which will baste this cut as it cooks, protecting it and giving you a beautifully moist little roast. Alongside the backstrap is a tiny **tenderloin**. If these two cuts are cut vertically you have lamb **loin chops**, a lamb T-bone ... a family favourite.

The **breast** or **belly** of lamb is akin to a pork belly; it has a lot of fat, which may scare some, but can also create amazing dishes. The real advantage of this cut is that it remains inexpensive compared to the rest of the lamb. This cut is often used for doner in Greece and Turkey, but is rather unfortunately referred to as mutton flaps in the UK: try Elizabeth David's Sainte Ménéhould recipe (see page 174). Lamb spare ribs are also an excellent treat and worth seeking out.

The **leg** can be prepared bone-in or boneless. It can be divided into two smaller roasts or butterflied for barbecuing. When you buy the whole leg, the shank is traditionally left on, folded over for ease; it's a cook's treat or remove it and pop it in the freezer for your next braise. The shank can also be fabulous on its own slowly cooked, bringing out the gelatinous properties of this cut. The **rump**, or chump, can be sold attached to the leg, but detached makes a lovely neat little roast for one or two. This is also where we get chump chops.

At the rear, the **shank** bones are bigger and thus the meat more generous. With rear shanks you can easily count on one per person.

GOAT

While goat may be a little harder to procure, and you may need to order ahead, it is worth seeking out. Try to find a goat that has been bred for its meat; wool- or milk-producing breeds will generally be skinnier and tougher and will require long and slow cooking to help break down the complex cuts.

The conformation of the goat is very similar to a lamb and most of the same cuts can be found; however, you will generally want to treat the meat more like mutton. That is, much gentle, long cooking with vibrant flavours to balance the rich taste.

LAMB CUTS

A young lamb will offer plenty of simple grilling cuts. There are also many excellent offal treats within.

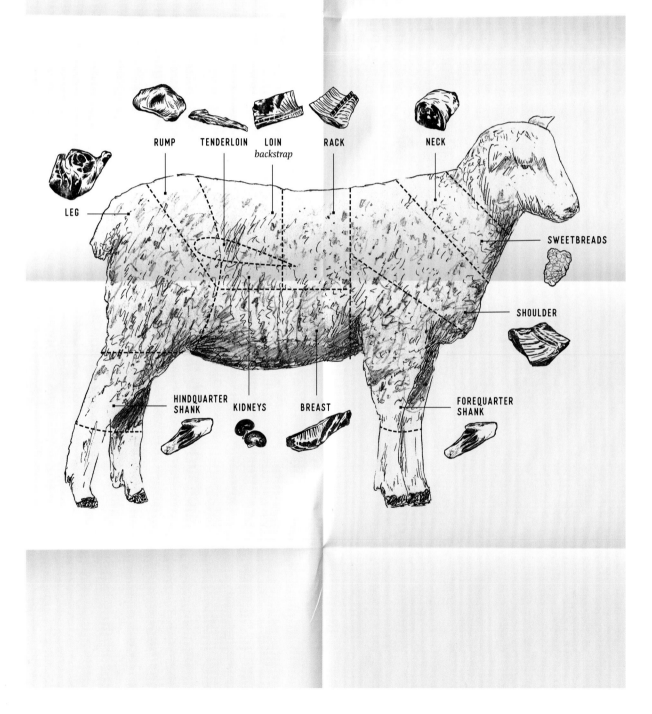

RUMP

TENDERLOIN

LOIN
backstrap

RACK

NECK

LEG

SWEETBREADS

SHOULDER

HINDQUARTER SHANK

KIDNEYS

BREAST

FOREQUARTER SHANK

GOAT CUTS

While goat cuts are very similar to lamb, the meat should generally be treated more like mutton in the kitchen.

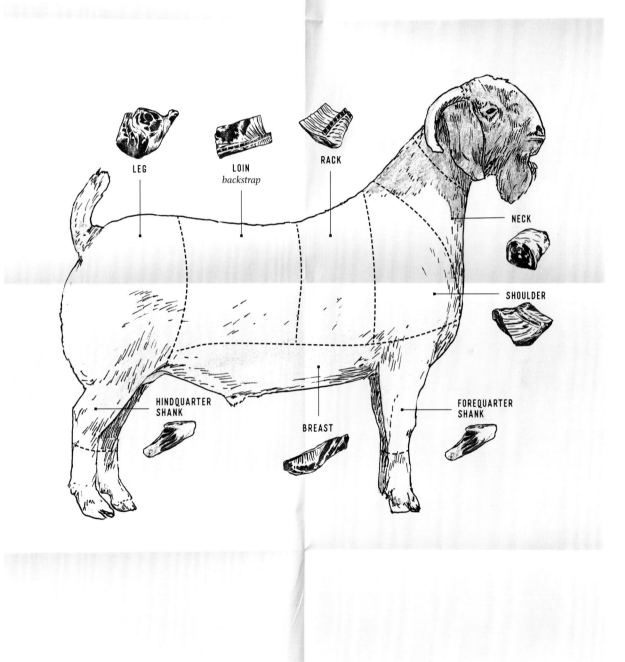

LEG

LOIN
backstrap

RACK

NECK

SHOULDER

HINDQUARTER
SHANK

BREAST

FOREQUARTER
SHANK

For more about lamb and goat cuts, see pages 150–157.

LAMB CUTS

NECK

SCRAG-END, NECK FILLET, BEST-END, NECK CHOPS

In the field, the lamb neck gets a good work-out bobbing for grass, so it is rich in collagen and sinews that melt and become gelatinous and tender with slow cooking. This cut is favoured by butchers and cooks alike for the bone-in neck chops. When you remove the bones you end up with a perfect cut for stewing, braising and curries. With the bone still in, neck chops can be slowly cooked for a Lancashire hotpot or Irish stew.

→ Ask your butcher to bone, trim and cube the neck fillet for you for a delicious stew or curry. Allow 150 g (5½ oz) per person.
→ Neck meat, when combined with the meat from the foreshank, makes a great burger.
→ Ask for scrag-end (closer to the head) for stews and super-slow cooking and best-end (the top of the rack) for neck chops.

CUT WEIGHT: 600 G (1 LB 5 OZ) TO 1.5 KG (3 LB 5 OZ)
BEST COOKED: BRAISED
OPTIMAL FINISH: SOFT AND TENDER
RECIPES: PAGES 162–165

SHOULDER

Recently this cut has taken over the leg as the go-to cut for a great family roast. The shoulder's combination of fat, collagen and meat reward with a richly flavoured, tender roast. The shoulder consists of a group of muscles reaching down from the neck, including the blade and sometimes chuck. These moderately working muscles appreciate slower cooking. It is great slowly roasted on the bone, or try it boned, stuffed and rolled. Either way it's better cooked a little slower and longer than the leg.

→ For an easy-carve option ask your butcher to bone and roll the shoulder for you. The fat will baste the lamb from the inside, creating a beautiful tender roast.
→ The lamb shoulder can be treated in much the same way as the leg. It likes the temperature a little lower and takes a little longer but rewards with more flavour.

CUT WEIGHT: BONELESS 1.5–2 KG (3 LB 5 OZ–4 LB 8 OZ); BONE-IN 2–2.9 KG (4 LB 8 OZ–6 LB 8 OZ)
BEST COOKED: ROASTED (SLOWLY)
OPTIMAL FINISH: MEDIUM, 60°C (140°F)
RECIPES: PAGES 166–169

RACK

CROWN ROAST, CUTLETS

The most expensive cut of lamb, the rack is beautiful roasted whole and even better divided into cutlets and grilled on the barbecue. The rib cage technically includes all 13 ribs running from the neck to the loin, but it is the nine ribs closest to the loin that are known as the 'best-end' or 'top-end' rack. Riding on the back of the lamb, the muscle is thicker and more tender (because it does less work). The rack responds well to quick cooking and is lovely served medium-rare. Allow three to four ribs per person. Cutlets can be quickly grilled over coals or sautéed in butter in a frying pan after being dipped in flour, egg and breadcrumbs (two cutlets per person should suffice).

→ The cap is a layer of fat and meat that protects and bastes the lamb as it cooks. If you have left the cap on, start in a cold tray, placing it fat-side down and letting it slowly heat up. This helps the fat to render evenly.

CUT WEIGHT: 500–800 G (1 LB 2 OZ– 1 LB 12 OZ)
BEST COOKED: ROASTED
OPTIMAL FINISH: MEDIUM-RARE TO MEDIUM, 55–60°C (130–140°F)
RECIPES: PAGES 170–173

LOIN
SADDLE, BACKSTRAP, SHORT LOIN, NOISETTE, LOIN CHOPS

Cooking a lamb loin requires some skill because it is so lean; it can easily end up dry and tough. The loin begins where the rack ends and continues to the rump. It can be sold boneless as lamb backstrap, essentially the sirloin of the lamb. For a great roasting cut, ask for a short saddle of lamb: a whole loin (both sides), boned, with the belly wrapped around it. With some of the belly attached, the loin can be cut vertically and sold as loin chops.

→ Have your butcher bone the loin, leaving the belly attached, and then stuff, roll and tie. Keep the belly on the outside so the loin won't dry out.
→ The combination of the eye of loin and the belly fat keeps the loin moist.
→ Lamb noisettes are made by boning and trimming the loin, then rolling, tying and slicing into medallions.

CUT WEIGHT: 800 G–1.5 KG (1 LB 12 OZ–3 LB 5 OZ)
BEST COOKED: ROASTED
OPTIMAL FINISH: MEDIUM, 60°C (140°F)
RECIPES: PAGES 176–179

TENDERLOIN
PENCIL FILLET

Petite, tender and juicy, the tenderloin is a beautiful cut to quickly grill and throw into salads, or, like the backstrap, it's great quickly pan-fried. It sits beneath the backstrap and does very little work in the paddock. It forms the central part of the lamb loin chop. As the name suggests, this cut offers serious tenderness, so it can be expensive due to this. Be sure to cook it quickly and serve it medium-rare.

CUT WEIGHT: 100–150 G (3½–5½ OZ)
BEST COOKED: BARBECUED
OPTIMAL FINISH: MEDIUM–RARE, 55°C (130°F)
RECIPE: PAGES 180–181

RUMP
CHUMP, CHUMP CHOPS

A perfectly sized mini-roast, this is an awesome cut. From the top of the hind leg, it is known as the chump (when the bone is left in) and rump when boneless. The rump cap is a particular treat, akin to a tortoise's shell; it provides the perfect little protective layer of fat to help lock in the juices while roasting. It's juicy, tender and jam-packed with flavour. This is a versatile muscle, meaning both slow roasting or quick grilling are suitable. This is also where we get chump chops.

→ Buy lamb rump with the cap on, which will help baste the lamb as it cooks. You can always remove the fat after it is cooked (at least that way it will have done its work).
→ A well-trimmed rump will be square in shape. A small rump is a lovely neat roast dinner for one or two people.

CUT WEIGHT: RUMP 250–350 G (9–12 OZ); CHUMP 400 G (14 OZ)
BEST COOKED: ROASTED
OPTIMAL FINISH: MEDIUM, 60°C (140°F)
RECIPE: PAGES 182–183

Please note that all weights are approximate, as animals will differ based on their age, breed and feed. The internal temperatures given are the rested temperatures. For more information on cooking styles, roasting times, etcetera, see pages 448–455.

LEG

The traditional Sunday roast, this economically priced cut is steeped in tradition. A lamb leg consists of four muscles: rump, topside, silverside and knuckle. It's most often enjoyed as a roast, cooked on the bone (for maximum flavour) or boneless and butterflied (for maximum convenience). Roast it fast and serve it pink, or roast it slow and serve it falling off the bone. It's no surprise this cut is so fondly thought of, it somehow miraculously feeds everyone and is the ultimate crowd-pleaser.

→ The shank is traditionally left on the leg roast, folded over, as the cook's treat. If you prefer, remove the shank and freeze it. A few of these will make a feast down the track.

→ The leg can be divided into two smaller roasts: the lamb rump and then all that is left behind (the topside, knuckle and silverside). This will leave you with a centre bone to roast, or boneless for the barbecue.

CUT WEIGHT: BONE IN 3 KG (6 LB 12 OZ); BONELESS 2 KG (4 LB 8 OZ)
BEST COOKED: ROASTED
OPTIMAL FINISH: MEDIUM 60°C (140°F)
RECIPES: PAGES 184–187

BREAST
BELLY, RIBLETS

Until recently when anybody thought about belly meat, it was all about pork; however, the same attributes can be found in lamb belly at a significantly cheaper price. The breast or belly does have a lot of fat, but it can create amazing dishes. Minced lamb breast can be added to lean lamb mince (ground lamb) for succulent meatballs or kofta or the breast can be very slowly braised and then recooked (roasted or fried) for a powerfully flavoured dinner. In Norway, they salt and dry the belly ribs in spring to be reconstituted and slowly cooked for their traditional Christmas meal.

The breast of lamb consists of the belly and riblets (the front of the rib cage as it extends down from the rack). These can be treated as US-style pork ribs and roasted until sticky and delicious.

→ Treat the lamb belly as you would pork: braise, press, portion then fry to create a crisp exterior.

CUT WEIGHT 1.5 KG (3 LB 5 OZ)
BEST COOKED: BRAISED
OPTIMAL FINISH: SOFT AND TENDER
RECIPE: PAGES 174–175

SHANK

The expression 'falling off the bone' is never so perfectly applied as when it is used with this cut. This succulent, sweet piece of meat responds incredibly well to long, slow cooking, bringing out the gelatinous properties. Slow cooking of this meat will be rewarded with flavour and a wonderful sticky texture; cooking on the bone also means that lamb shanks will be packed full of flavour.

The forequarter shank is smaller and, although not as sought after as the hindquarter shank, it is a terrific cut to braise. One hindquarter shank will feed one person, whereas you will need two forequarter shanks. The shank can be frenched, cutting through the connective tendon, allowing the meat to slip down the bone and reveal a neat white section of bone. This is predominantly done for cosmetic reasons and is not critical for successfully cooking the shank.

→ Ask your butcher to cut the shanks crossways to make lamb osso buco.

CUT WEIGHT: 250–350 G (9–12 OZ)
BEST COOKED: BRAISED
OPTIMAL FINISH: FALLING OFF THE BONE
RECIPE: PAGES 188–189

KIDNEYS

Perhaps even more than other offal, lamb kidneys need to be spanking fresh. As they age they take on a tainted, bitter flavour. You may get them still in their 'suet jacket'—the layer of fat that encases them—you will need to remove this and then peel away their outer membrane. Once they are cut in half you may want to also snip out the white, gristly core. To soften the gamey flavour, you can soak them in milk for half an hour before cooking. Juicy and flavoursome, they are traditionally served lightly dusted in flour for extra crunch and devilled. Fergus Henderson suggests they are the perfect breakfast on your birthday with a glass of black velvet.

CUT WEIGHT: 60 G (2¼ OZ)
BEST COOKED: FRIED
OPTIMAL FINISH: BLUSHING PINK INSIDE
RECIPE: PAGES 190–191

BRAINS

Creamy but firm, with a texture akin to tofu, lambs' brains have an almost sweet flavour. They degrade quickly, so eat them as soon as you buy them. Trim away excess fat nodules, blood clots and sinews and peel off the outer membrane. Soak in iced water for 1–2 hours to remove blood. Gently poach them to ensure they are cooked through, then allow to cool before shallow-frying to a crisp, golden exterior (they are also excellent crumbed) and serve with brown butter and capers.

CUT WEIGHT: 80 G (2¾ OZ)
BEST COOKED: FRIED
OPTIMAL FINISH: COOKED THROUGH

SWEETBREADS

A marshmallowy essence of lamb, the term sweetbreads is the culinary name for the glands of the thymus (neck glands) and the pancreas (heart or belly glands). The neck glands are more cylindrical in shape, while the heart glands are vaguely spherical. Cooked to crisp on the outside, while remaining juicy and succulent on the inside, this delicacy is relatively easy to prepare: remove the membrane, blanch and then fry in oil, butter or lard. As they are soft, they benefit from a crisp exterior and a contrast in flavour, a piquancy: they're delicious served with balsamic vinegar or a squeeze of fresh lemon.

CUT WEIGHT: 30–40 G (1–1½ OZ)
BEST COOKED: FRIED
OPTIMAL FINISH: COOKED THROUGH

Please note that all weights are approximate, as animals will differ based on their age, breed and feed. The internal temperatures given are the rested temperatures. For more information on cooking styles, roasting times, etcetera, see pages 448–455.

LIVER

Often referred to as lamb's fry, lamb's liver is firm and sweet with an iron flavour, a flavour that develops as it cooks. Best served quickly fried with a crisp exterior, with its jelly-like flesh still pink inside. You can soak the liver in milk before cooking, covering it liberally with spices such as pepper or paprika. Livers are exceptionally high in nutrients and can be used to boost the flavour and benefits of a lamb stew or casserole. The onion is the liver's best friend, with bacon a close second, and a spike of vinegar is also welcome at the party.

CUT WEIGHT: 600 G (1 LB 5 OZ)
BEST COOKED: FRIED
OPTIMAL FINISH: BLUSHING PINK INSIDE

GOAT

GOAT

All of the sheep cuts mentioned on the previous pages can be found on the goat carcass; however, some of these will be significantly more slight, which will impact your cooking (see page 159 for more on goat in the kitchen).

As the goat is finer of features and harder of living, you will want to consider slower cooking for even the simple cuts. Look out for goat shoulder for stews and curries, leg and loins for roasting, or a whole goat cooked on the spit.

CUT WEIGHT: UP TO 22 KG (49 LB 8 OZ)
BEST COOKED: BRAISED
OPTIMAL FINISH: UNCTUOUS
RECIPES: PAGES 192–195

Victor Puharich *gently works his knife around a lamb loin. See pages 488–489 to learn how to bone, roll and tie a loin .*

THE FAMILY OF LAMB CHOPS

From head to hind leg, these are the lamb chops you love to grill.

NECK CHOP

Sliced from the bone-in lamb neck, these chops are full of flavour and best suited to braising and stewing.

FOREQUARTER/SHOULDER CHOP

A shoulder chop will be comprised of the oyster blade, bolar blade plus some of the neck and loin fillet. It is sold bone-in. They are excellent in stews and slowly cooked braises due to the fat and connective tissue.

LAMB CUTLET

Cut from between the bones of a rack of lamb (essentially the rib eye of the sheep) the cutlet holds a delicious, tender nugget of meat. It is great quickly grilled, but also appreciates being crumbed, to protect the delicate meat. A frenched cutlet will have a clean bone, while unfrenched will still have the delicious intercostal meat clinging to it.

LOIN CHOP

Loin chops, the T-bone of the lamb world, include the loin and the tenderloin and are most often sold with a little bit of the lamb belly still attached and wrapped around the chop. This is unctuous and delicious and offers excellent contrast to the eye of the loin and the tenderloin, which can be quite lean.

BARNSLEY CHOP

Also known as a saddle chop or double loin chop, the Barnsley is cut from the entire short loin or saddle. These delicious double loin chops have the spine bone running through them and an excellent layer of fat running around the outside.

CHUMP CHOP

Cut from the rump of the lamb, where the top of the leg meets the loin. Like a rump steak, a chump chop can include a combination of up to three different muscles (tri-tip, rostbiff and rump cap) providing excellent contrast and flavour.

LEG CHOP

The leg chop can consist of a number of muscles: the topside, silverside, girello and knuckle. It is most often sold bone-in. This mix of muscles can work with both slow and quick cooking.

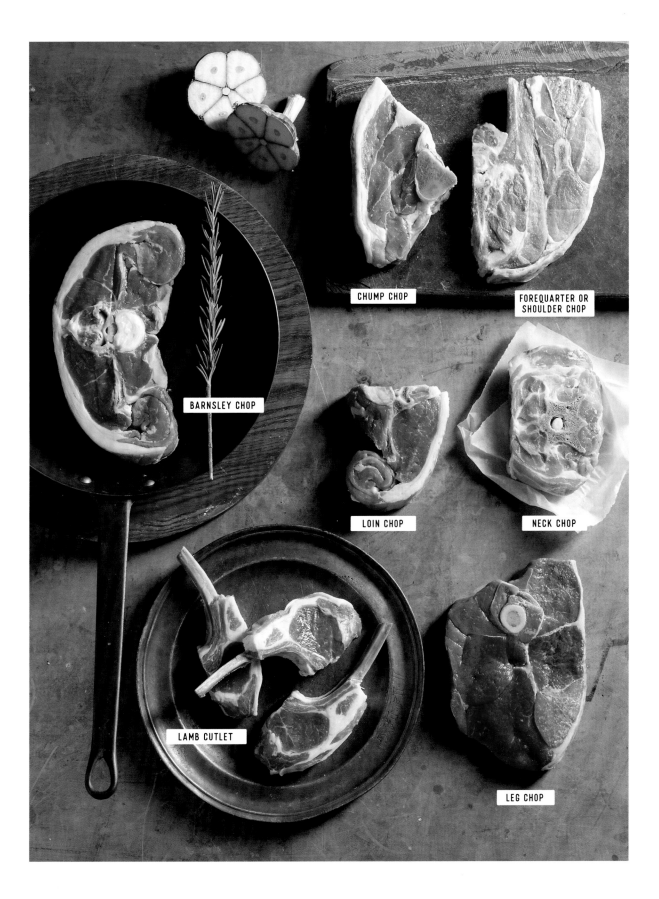

CHUMP CHOP

FOREQUARTER OR
SHOULDER CHOP

BARNSLEY CHOP

LOIN CHOP

NECK CHOP

LAMB CUTLET

LEG CHOP

IN THE KITCHEN

The relatively small size of a lamb makes it perfect for a spit and it also means these cuts are easy to butcher at home. For the aspiring chef–butcher, this is the perfect place to begin.

In Mediterranean backyards, in the streets and at markets, you will find lambs and goats gently turning over hot coals. Liberally covered in salt, from both the shaker and the sweat of the person in charge, their insides are stuffed with onions and whatever local herbs grow wild, sewn together with a couple of metal skewers or prosciutto hocks.

The spit is the ultimate sign of celebration. In the Sahara, lambs are also roasted whole, Berber style (*meshwi*), while on the plains of Argentina, they splay the animal on a cross (*asador*) and roast it over coals.

In France, there is a fabulous tradition of lamb leg *à la ficelle*: the leg is strung up in the hearth, then the string is tightly wound and allowed to spin gently first in one direction and then the other, carefully and evenly cooking the lamb with the heat from the fire. One of the joys of this method is the juices and fat falling from the lamb: be careful to catch these in a tray with a little water or stock in the bottom.

Beyond whole cuts, you can try your hand at boning out a shoulder, then roll and tie it for an easy-carve roast; or stuff a loin with the belly still attached and roll for an extravagant dinner. Alternatively, for something a little showy, ask your butcher for a baron of lamb (the saddle and the two legs together; that is, the whole back half)—Auguste Escoffier thought it 'one of the finest and best intermediate courses for a meal.' (*Ma Cuisine*, Paul Hamlyn, 1934).

SELECT AND STORE
COLOUR AND SMELL

When looking for great lamb, colour is the key. In general, the darker the colour, the older the animal. Baby lamb should be pale pink, while regular lamb is pinkish–red. In hogget and mutton the meat is darker again in colour. Lamb should have a clean fresh smell.

Butchery techniques
→ **Butterflying** a lamb leg
  see pages 486–487
→ **Rolling and tying** a lamb loin
  see pages 488–489

FAT

→ In Australia, where lamb is eaten frequently by both children and adults, recent studies have shown lamb to rank among the top omega–3 foods in the daily diet. Grass-fed lamb has been shown to average at least 25 per cent more omega–3s than conventionally fed lamb.

Generally, the lamb we purchase today is lean. Look for lamb that has beautiful white fat. The fat can be deeply flavoured, and you will want to be careful when cooking, to allow time for it to render. That said, fat is crucial to helping this lean meat baste as it cooks; it provides key omega-3s, particularly for regions away from the sea, where it can be the main source of these essential fats. Note, these higher levels are increased in grass-fed lamb.

Lamb tallow is another name for lamb fat. Just like lard, you can use the tallow to lubricate the pan and fry your onions, garlic—and indeed, lamb—in this rendered fat to add flavour, richness and 'good' fats.

Do note that lamb fat can be very strong in both smell and flavour. It is not enjoyable when cold and so remove it from any salad or cold leftovers.

STORING LAMB

Minced (ground) lamb and small lamb cuts should be wrapped in butchers' paper and refrigerated for up to three days or tightly wrapped and frozen for up to three months. Larger roasts may be refrigerated for up to five days before using or frozen for up to six months.

LAMB OFFAL

Perhaps also due to its size and manageability, a lot of the offal from the lamb is eaten. Lamb's brains, kidneys, sweetbreads and liver are all traditionally consumed and in many places considered delicacies. Lamb's offal can, however, have a deep flavour; thus it's often a balance between the smaller, more manageable size and the true offal flavour.

GOAT

Anatomically the goat is very similar to the sheep, so many of the cuts mentioned for sheep can be purchased; however, the cuts need to be treated quite differently in the kitchen. Goat is generally lean, with little external fat, and will toughen up with quick cooking, this is largely due to the way the goat puts on fat: they tend to accumulate it in the body cavity, rather than within the muscle. The cuts will also be smaller, with a higher ratio of bone to meat.

Farmed goat meat, or breeds that are raised specifically for meat (such as the Boer) will offer more flexibility in the kitchen. The age will also help with the tenderness. A capretto or kid goat is fantastic cooked whole on a spit. In many countries it is more highly prized than lamb.

Spit roasting
The size of lamb and goat carcasses make them perfect for the spit. Season well and baste with herbs and olive oil.

LANCASHIRE HOTPOT

Prep time *20 minutes*
Cook *6½ hours*

1. To make the lamb stock, preheat the oven to 220°C (425°F). Spread the lamb bones in a roasting tin and roast, turning occasionally, for 30–40 minutes until well browned. Meanwhile, spread the onion and carrot in a separate roasting tin and roast, turning occasionally, for 30–40 minutes until browned.

2. Combine the lamb bones, roasted vegetables, garlic and herbs in a large saucepan, cover with cold water by about 5 cm (2 inches). Bring to the boil, skim off any scum from the surface and simmer for 2–3 hours until well flavoured. Strain (discarding the solids) and refrigerate until required. Remove any fat from the surface before using.

3. To make the hotpot, preheat the oven to 170°C (325°F). Heat a splash of olive oil in a large enamelled cast-iron casserole over medium–high heat. Dust the lamb chops with seasoned flour, then add them to the casserole in batches, turning occasionally, for 4–5 minutes to brown well all over: the deeper the browning, the better the flavour of the finished dish, so take your time to do this well. Transfer to a plate.

4. Add the onion and garlic to the casserole and fry, stirring occasionally, for 8–10 minutes, until beginning to brown. Stir in any excess seasoned flour left over from dusting the lamb, cooking the flour until lightly golden, then gradually add the stock and Worcestershire sauce and stir to combine.

5. Return the lamb to the casserole, add the bay leaves and two-thirds of the thyme, season with salt and pepper and bring to a simmer.

6. Remove from the heat and layer the potatoes on top, seasoning with salt and pepper and scattering with the remaining thyme as you go. Brush with the melted butter, cover and bake for 1 hour 45 minutes, then uncover and bake for 20–30 minutes until the potatoes are golden brown and lamb is tender. Set aside to rest for 15 minutes.

INGREDIENTS

1 kg (2 lb 4 oz) best-end lamb neck chops
Olive oil, for cooking
2½ tablespoons plain (all-purpose) flour, seasoned with salt and pepper, for dusting
2 brown onions, thinly sliced
1 garlic clove, finely chopped
500 ml (17 fl oz/2 cups) lamb stock (see below) or chicken stock
1 tablespoon Worcestershire sauce
2 fresh bay leaves
3 thyme sprigs, leaves picked, plus extra to serve
1 kg (2 lb 4 oz) large floury potatoes, sliced into 7–8 mm (¼–⅜ inch) thick rounds
2 tablespoons (30 g) butter, melted

Lamb stock
1 kg (2 lb 4 oz) lamb bones
2 onions, coarsely chopped
2 carrots, coarsely chopped
1 garlic bulb, halved
3 thyme sprigs
1 fresh bay leaf

SERVING SUGGESTION

braised red cabbage or wilted spinach with garlic and a squeeze of lemon

Cut Lamb neck or goat neck
See page 150

LAMB SOUVLAKI
~ WITH TZATZIKI ~

Prep time *25 minutes (plus marinating, draining)*
Cook *10 minutes*

1. Combine the lamb, olive oil, onion, garlic, herbs and paprika in a bowl, season generously with freshly ground black pepper and mix well to coat the lamb thoroughly. Cover and refrigerate for at least 4 hours or overnight, to deepen the flavours.

2. To make the tzatziki, grate the cucumber, put it in a sieve with a sprinkling of salt to help draw out the liquid and set it aside for 10 minutes to drain. Squeeze out any excess liquid and put the cucumber in a bowl with all of the other ingredients, stirring to combine. Season with salt and pepper. Cover and refrigerate until required.

3. Drain the lamb from the marinade and thread it onto skewers, without packing it too closely, then season with salt.

4. Heat a barbecue or chargrill pan to high heat (a coal barbecue will give the best flavour). Grill the lamb skewers, turning occasionally, for 8–10 minutes (5–6 minutes for smaller skewers) until well browned but still a little pink in the centre. Serve with lemon wedges, tzatziki and Greek rice.

INGREDIENTS

1 kg (2 lb 4 oz) boneless lamb neck, chopped into 3 cm (1¼ inch) pieces
100 ml (3½ fl oz) extra virgin olive oil
1 red onion, coarsely chopped
3 garlic cloves, crushed
1½ teaspoons dried oregano (preferably Greek rigani)
1 teaspoon finely chopped thyme
½ teaspoon sweet smoked paprika
Lemon wedges, to serve

Tzatziki

1 Lebanese (short) cucumber, halved lengthways and seeds scooped out
375 g (13 oz) Greek-style natural yoghurt
2 tablespoons extra virgin olive oil
1 garlic clove, finely chopped
1 tablespoon red wine vinegar, or to taste

rice and chopped salad of baby cos (romaine) lettuce, Lebanese (short) cucumber, radishes, red onion, mint, dill and kalamata olives

(SERVING SUGGESTION)

NOTE

→ *If you are using bamboo skewers, soak them in water for 20 minutes to prevent them from burning during cooking.*

Cut Lamb neck
See page 150

~ SLOW-COOKED ~
LAMB SHOULDER WITH ANCHOVIES, GARLIC AND ROSEMARY

Prep time *20 minutes (plus overnight marinating)*
Cook *5½ hours (plus resting)*

INGREDIENTS

1 lamb shoulder, bone in, about 1.8 kg (4 lb)
4 garlic cloves, thinly sliced
8 anchovies, halved
2 rosemary sprigs, leaves picked
2 brown onions, thickly sliced
250 ml (9 fl oz/1 cup) dry white wine
Olive oil, for drizzling

Tomato, chickpea and farro salad
220 g (7¾ oz) farro (see note)
1 small red onion, thinly sliced
1 garlic clove, finely chopped
Finely grated zest and juice of 1 small lemon, or to taste
1 tablespoon red wine vinegar
100 ml (3½ fl oz) extra virgin olive oil
400 g (14 oz) tin chickpeas, drained and rinsed
1 teaspoon ground cumin
400 g (14 oz) mixed cherry tomatoes, halved or quartered, depending on size
1 large handful each of mint and flat-leaf (Italian) parsley

1. Make short but deep incisions at 3–4 cm (1¼–1½ inch) intervals all over the lamb. Stuff each incision with a slice of garlic, a piece of anchovy and a few rosemary leaves. Cover and refrigerate overnight for the flavours to develop: you can cook the lamb straight away, but the flavour will be deeper and richer if you have the time to let it marinate. Bring to room temperature for 1–1½ hours before cooking.

2. Preheat the oven to 150°C (300°F). Spread the onion slices in the base of a large roasting tin, add the wine and 500 ml (17 fl oz/2 cups) of water, then place the lamb on top. Drizzle with a little olive oil, season to taste, cover with a piece of baking paper then with foil and roast, basting occasionally, for 4–5 hours until fork tender.

3. Meanwhile, cook the farro for the salad in a large saucepan of boiling water for 45–50 minutes until tender, then drain and transfer to a bowl. Add the onion, garlic, lemon zest and juice, the vinegar and 80 ml (2½ fl oz/⅓ cup) of the olive oil. Season with salt and pepper and toss to combine. Set aside to cool to room temperature.

4. Increase the oven temperature to 180°C (350°F). Remove the foil and baking paper from the lamb and roast uncovered for 20–30 minutes until browned. Removed from the oven, cover loosely with foil and set aside to rest for 20 minutes.

5. Meanwhile, toss the chickpeas, cumin and the remaining oil for the salad in a small roasting tin, season with salt and pepper and roast for 15–20 minutes until golden brown, then set aside to cool slightly before adding the chickpeas to the farro mixture. Add the tomatoes and herbs, season with salt and pepper and toss to combine well.

6. Serve the lamb with the onions from the tin and any pan juices, with the tomato, chickpea and farro salad.

NOTES

→ *The same technique can be used to slow-roast a lamb leg on the bone and will result in the same melt-in-your-mouth texture.*

→ *Farro is a type of wheat grain with a nutty texture and earthy flavour. It is available from delicatessens, but if it's unavailable, you can use barley or freekeh instead.*

Cut Lamb shoulder
See page 150

LAMB KOFTA

Prep time *20 minutes*
(plus chilling, resting)
Cook *10 minutes*

1. Remove the sinew from the lamb shoulder and cut the lamb into 2 cm (¾ inch) cubes, then chop as finely as possible (or ask your butcher to coarsely mince the lamb for you). Put the lamb in a bowl with the capsicum, spices and sea salt. Mix well with clean hands, then cover and refrigerate to rest and chill thoroughly (3–4 hours).

2. Divide the lamb mixture into six equal portions, then form each portion into a ball. Wet your hands and press each ball evenly along a flat metal skewer to form a sausage along the skewer. If you are using smaller skewers, divide the mixture into 12 equal portions, then form into balls. Wet your hands and press each ball evenly along a flat metal skewer to form a sausage along the length of each skewer. Lay the skewers on a tray, cover and refrigerate to rest for 1 hour.

3. Meanwhile, to make the garlic tahini sauce, process the lemon juice and garlic in a small food processor until smooth, then strain through a fine sieve into a bowl, pressing on the solids. Whisk in the tahini and cumin (the mixture will seize and thicken, but this is OK), then thin with hot water, adding a little at a time and whisking to combine until the mixture has a drizzling consistency. Season generously with salt and pepper and set aside.

4. Preheat a gas barbecue to high heat or light a charcoal barbecue an hour before cooking and allow the coals to burn down to hot embers. Drizzle the kebabs with a little oil and barbecue, turning occasionally, for 5–6 minutes until browned, then rest on a plate for 5 minutes.

5. Serve with the garlic tahini sauce, pitta (the pitta will love a moment on the hot grill while the kebabs rest, followed by a little brush of garlic oil), parsley, onion and pickled chillies, with lemon wedges.

INGREDIENTS

900 g (2 lb) boneless lamb shoulder, fat on
1 small red capsicum (pepper), finely minced
1 tablespoon hot paprika
2 teaspoons ground cumin
2 teaspoons ground sumac
1 teaspoon sea salt
Vegetable oil, for drizzling
Pitta bread, flat-leaf (Italian) parsley, sliced red onion, pickled chillies (see note) and lemon wedges, to serve

Garlic tahini sauce
80 ml (2½ fl oz/⅓ cup) lemon juice
8 garlic cloves, unpeeled
180 g (6¼ oz/⅔ cup) tahini
½ teaspoon ground cumin
Hot water, for thinning

NOTES

→ *Pickled chillies are available from supermarkets and delicatessens.*

→ *You can make the kofta mixture a day ahead to develop the flavours even further.*

→ *You will need six 25 cm (10 inch) metal skewers or twelve 15 cm (6 inch) metal skewers.*

Cut Lamb shoulder
See page 150

ROAST LAMB RACK WITH SPRING GREENS
~ AND TARRAGON SAUCE ~

Prep time *20 minutes (plus marinating)*
Cook *35 minutes (plus resting)*

INGREDIENTS

2 lamb racks of 6 cutlets each, cap on,
about 450 g (1 lb) each
1 tablespoon olive oil, plus extra for cooking
1 teaspoon finely chopped thyme, plus extra
sprigs for roasting
1 teaspoon finely chopped rosemary,
plus extra sprigs for roasting
1 garlic clove, crushed
Finely grated zest of ½ lemon
200 ml (7 fl oz) dry white wine
200 g (7 oz/1¼ cups) peas
350 g (12 oz) asparagus, trimmed and cut
into 3–4 cm (1¼–1½ inch) lengths
200 g (7 oz) broad (fava) beans
Extra virgin olive oil and lemon juice,
for dressing

Tarragon sauce
60 ml (2 fl oz/¼ cup) milk
30 g (1 oz) day-old crustless sourdough
bread, torn
150 ml (5 fl oz) olive oil
¾ cup loosely packed tarragon leaves
½ cup loosely packed flat-leaf (Italian)
parsley
2 tablespoons lemon juice
25 ml (¾ fl oz) tarragon vinegar or white wine
vinegar
1 garlic clove, finely chopped

1. Preheat the oven to 220°C (425°F). Stir the olive oil, herbs, garlic and lemon zest in a large bowl to combine, season with salt and pepper, add the lamb and massage to coat it well. Arrange several thyme and rosemary sprigs in a roasting tin, place the lamb racks on top and set aside to marinate and come to room temperature for about 30 minutes.

2. Meanwhile, to make the tarragon sauce, combine the milk and bread in a bowl and set aside for 5 minutes until the bread softens. Squeeze out the excess milk and discard. Put the bread into a food processor or blender with the olive oil, tarragon, parsley, lemon juice, vinegar and garlic. Process until smooth and finely chopped. Season with salt and pepper.

3. Transfer the lamb to the oven and roast for 20 minutes, then reduce the oven temperature to 160°C (315°F). Add the wine to the roasting tin and roast for a further 8–10 minutes for medium-rare; internal temperature will read 52°C (125°F) on a thermometer. Cover loosely with foil and set aside to rest for 10 minutes; the meat will continue to cook as it rests and the internal temperature will reach 55°C (130°F).

4. While the lamb is resting, blanch the peas and asparagus in a saucepan of boiling salted water for 1–2 minutes until tender and bright green. Use a slotted spoon to transfer the vegetables to a bowl. Add the broad beans to the water and blanch for 1–2 minutes until bright green and just tender, then remove with a slotted spoon. Double-peel the broad beans if they're large and add to the other vegetables. Drizzle with olive oil and lemon juice, season with salt and pepper and toss to combine.

5. Serve the lamb racks and spring greens with the tarragon sauce and any resting juices from the roasting tin.

Cut Lamb rack
See page 150

CRUMBED LAMB CUTLETS
~ WITH BEETROOT RELISH ~

Prep time *25 minutes*
Cook *1 hour (plus resting)*

1. To make the beetroot relish, heat the olive oil in a large saucepan over medium–high heat, add the onion and sauté for 4–5 minutes until tender and translucent, adding the garlic in the last minute of cooking. Add the beetroot and stir occasionally for 2–3 minutes until beginning to soften, then add the remaining ingredients and 200 ml (7 fl oz) of water. Season with salt and pepper, bring to the boil, then reduce the heat to medium and simmer, stirring occasionally, for 30–35 minutes until the beetroot is tender and the liquid is completely reduced. Remove from the heat, check the seasoning and cool to room temperature. Refrigerate in an airtight container for up to 1 month.

2. Remove the lamb from the refrigerator and set aside at room temperature for 20 minutes. Put the seasoned flour and eggs in separate bowls. Combine the breadcrumbs, rosemary and lemon zest in a separate bowl and season with salt and pepper.

3. Dip each cutlet in the seasoned flour, then the egg, shaking off excess. Dip it into the breadcrumb mixture, pressing so the breadcrumbs stick to the lamb, coating completely.

4. Heat 5 mm (¼ inch) of olive oil in a large frying pan over medium heat. Add the cutlets in batches and pan-fry for 3–4 minutes on each side until golden brown. Drain on paper towel, season with salt and pepper and set aside to rest for 5 minutes. Serve hot with the beetroot relish.

INGREDIENTS

8 unfrenched lamb cutlets, about 120 g (4¼ oz) each
Plain (all-purpose) flour, seasoned with salt and pepper, for dusting
3 eggs, lightly whisked
180 g (6¼ oz/3 cups) day-old coarse white breadcrumbs
3 teaspoons finely chopped rosemary
Finely grated zest of ½ lemon
Olive oil, for shallow-frying

Beetroot relish
2 tablespoons olive oil
1 small red onion, finely chopped
1 garlic clove, finely chopped
350 g (12 oz) beetroot (beets), peeled and cut into julienne strips
220 ml (7½ fl oz) red wine vinegar
100 ml (3½ fl oz) red wine
2½ tablespoons brown sugar
1 fresh bay leaf
2 thyme sprigs

wilted beetroot leaves (see note)

SERVING SUGGESTION

N O T E

→ *If the beetroot has lovely tender leaves, they make a great accompaniment to the cutlets. Wilt in a pan with a little olive oil and garlic, season to taste and serve alongside the cutlets. Silverbeet (Swiss chard) or kale would also work well as an accompaniment.*

Cut Lamb cutlets
See page 150

SERVES 4

BREAST OF LAMB SAINTE MÉNÉHOULD

Elizabeth David's books are a constant source of delight, whether you cook her classic home-style recipes—such as this one—or just enjoy her words and evocative descriptions.

1. First you have to braise or bake the meat in the oven with sliced carrots, an onion or two, a bunch of herbs, and, if you like, a little something extra in the way of flavouring such as 55–85 g (two or three ounces) of a cheap little bit of bacon or salt pork, plus seasonings and about 475 ml (16 fl oz or a pint) of water. It takes about two and a half to three hours—depending on the quality of the meat—covered, in a slow oven.

2. Then, while the meat is still warm, you slip out the bones, leave the meat to cool, preferably with a weight on it, and then slice it into strips slightly on the bias and about 4–5 cm (one and a half to two inches) wide.

3. Next, spread each strip with a little mustard, paint it with beaten egg (one will be enough for 2½ lb of meat), then coat it with the breadcrumbs, pressing them well down into the meat and round the sides. (I always use breadcrumbs which I've made myself from a French loaf, sliced, and dried in the plate drawer underneath the oven. I know there are those who think this business of making breadcrumbs is a terrible worry, but once the bread is dried it's a matter of minutes to pound it up with a rolling pin or with a pestle—quicker than doing it in the electric blender.)

4. All this breadcrumbing finished, you can put the meat on a rack over a baking dish and leave it until you are ready to cook it. Then it goes into a moderate oven for about twenty minutes, because if you put it straight under the grill the outside gets browned before the meat itself is hot.

5. As you transfer the whole lot to the grill pour a very little melted butter over each slice, put them close to the heat, then keep a sharp look-out and turn each piece as the first signs of sizzling and scorching appear.

6. The plates and dishes should be sizzling too, and some sort of sharp, oil-based sauce—a vinaigrette, a tartare, a mustardy mayonnaise—usually goes with this kind of dish.

Prep time *25 minutes*
Cook *3½ hours*

INGREDIENTS

1.1 kg (2 lb 7 oz) lamb breast
Carrots
1–2 onions, sliced
1 handful of mixed herbs
55–85 g (2–3 oz) bacon or salt pork
Mustard
1 egg, beaten
Fresh breadcrumbs, from a French loaf
Melted butter

SERVING SUGGESTION
vinaigrette, tartare or mustardy mayonnaise

NOTE

→ *From* An Omelette and a Glass of Wine, *by Elizabeth David (Grub Street, 2009).*

Cut Lamb breast
See page 152

KIBBEH NAYEH

Prep time *20 minutes*
Cook *25 minutes (plus overnight soaking)*

1. To make the hummus, cover the chickpeas generously with cold water in a large saucepan, bring to the boil over medium-high heat and cook for 20–25 minutes until tender. Drain, reserving 300 ml (10½ fl oz) of the cooking liquid, rinse under cold running water and discard any loose skins.

2. Process the chickpeas and remaining ingredients for the hummus in a food processor until smooth, adding enough reserved cooking liquid to thin to a smooth purée. Season to taste and refrigerate until required. Hummus will keep refrigerated for up to 1 week.

3. Soak the burghul in a bowl of cold water for 4–5 minutes to soften slightly. Drain in a fine sieve, shaking well to remove all the excess moisture. Spread on a tray to dry out while you prepare the lamb.

4. Process the chopped onion, mint and a quarter of the lamb in a small food processor until finely chopped. Combine in a bowl with the remaining lamb, the burghul, allspice and chilli and season with sea salt and freshly ground black pepper. Add an ice cube or two and knead the mixture well with slightly dampened hands until the meat starts to hold together.

5. Flatten the lamb into a circular shape about 1.5 cm (⅝ inch) thick on a chilled serving plate. Scatter with the sliced onion, pomegranate seeds, if using, and extra mint leaves, drizzle with olive oil and serve with the hummus.

INGREDIENTS

500 g (1 lb 2 oz) trimmed lamb backstrap, chilled and finely minced (ground)
35 g (1¼ oz) fine burghul (bulgur)
1 onion, half finely chopped, half thinly sliced
3 mint sprigs, plus extra mint leaves, to serve
½ teaspoon ground allspice
1 pinch of ground chilli, or to taste
Sea salt and freshly ground black pepper
Pomegranate seeds (optional), to serve
Extra virgin olive oil, for drizzling

Hummus
200 g (7 oz) dried chickpeas, soaked overnight in cold water, drained
1 pinch of bicarbonate of soda (baking soda)
150 ml (5 fl oz) extra virgin olive oil
90 g (3¼ oz/⅓ cup) tahini
4 garlic cloves, finely chopped
Juice of 2 lemons, or to taste
2 teaspoons ground cumin

SERVING SUGGESTION *labneh, tabouleh and pitta bread*

NOTE

→ *As the lamb in this dish is served raw, it is imperative the lamb is minced on the day. If you have a mincer, mince the diced chilled lamb on a coarse setting and then a fine setting. Otherwise, ask your butcher to mince the lamb for you on the day you plan to serve it.*

Cut Lamb backstrap
See page 151

ROLLED LAMB LOIN
~ WITH ROAST EGGPLANT SALAD ~

Prep time *20 minutes*
Cook *1 hour 15 minutes (plus resting)*

1. Preheat the oven to 220°C (425°F). Combine the nuts, garlic, lemon zest, herbs and olive oil in a bowl and season with salt and pepper.

2. Open out the lamb on a chopping board, skin-side down, spread with the nut mixture, then roll the lamb into a cylinder and tie at 3–4 cm (1¼–1½ inch) intervals with kitchen string. Rub all over with a little more olive oil and season with salt and pepper. Set aside at room temperature for 30 minutes.

3. Meanwhile, to prepare the eggplant salad, combine the eggplant, cumin and half the olive oil in a roasting tin lined with baking paper. Bake for 15–20 minutes until tender and golden brown, then tip into a bowl.

4. Put the rolled lamb in a small roasting tin and roast for 20–30 minutes to brown. Reduce the oven temperature to 160°C (315°F) and open the door to let the heat out. Continue to roast the lamb for 20–25 minutes for medium-rare; the internal temperature should read 52°C (125°F) on a thermometer. Cover with foil and set the lamb aside to rest for 20 minutes; the meat will continue to cook while resting, reaching an internal temperature of 55°C (130°F). Discard the string.

5. Meanwhile, for the salad, whisk the vinegar, lemon juice, tahini, garlic and the remaining oil in a bowl to combine, adding a little water if necessary to thin to a drizzling consistency. Season with salt and pepper. Drizzle the tahini mixture over the roasted eggplant, toss to coat, then toss with the remaining ingredients just before serving. Serve with the sliced lamb loin and any resting juices.

INGREDIENTS

800 g (1 lb 12 oz) piece boneless lamb loin, belly on, skin on
1 small handful each of pistachio kernels and pine nuts
2 garlic cloves, finely chopped
Finely grated zest of 1 lemon
1 small handful each of coarsely chopped mint and flat-leaf (Italian) parsley
2–3 tablespoons olive oil, plus extra for cooking

Roast eggplant salad
2 eggplants (aubergines), cut into 2 cm (¾ inch) cubes
½ teaspoon ground cumin
125 ml (4 fl oz/½ cup) olive oil
2 tablespoons red wine vinegar
2 tablespoons lemon juice
2 tablespoons tahini
1 garlic clove, finely chopped
1 large handful each of torn flat-leaf (Italian) parsley, coriander (cilantro) leaves and mint leaves
Pomegranate seeds (optional)

NOTES

→ *Leftover lamb is excellent in sandwiches the following day.*

→ *For boning and rolling a lamb loin, see pages 488–489.*

Cut Lamb loin
See page 151

LAMB TENDERLOIN
~ AND ZUCCHINI SALAD ~

Prep time *15 minutes (plus marinating)*
Cook *10 minutes*

INGREDIENTS

600 g (1 lb 5 oz) lamb tenderloin
1 tablespoon finely chopped thyme
1 garlic clove, finely chopped
Finely grated zest and juice of ½ lemon
Extra virgin olive oil, for cooking
200 g (7 oz/1¼ cups) peas
1 large handful of wild rocket (arugula)
1 baby fennel bulb, thinly shaved with a
    mandolin, fronds reserved
1 small handful each of torn flat-leaf (Italian)
    parsley and mint
2 spring onions (scallions), thinly sliced
2 zucchini (courgettes), thinly sliced into
    ribbons; use a mix of yellow and green
    zucchini if available
1 tablespoon red wine vinegar

1. Combine the thyme, garlic, lemon zest and half the lemon juice in a bowl, add a splash of olive oil and the lamb, season with salt and pepper, mix well and set aside to marinate for 30 minutes.

2. Meanwhile, blanch the peas in a saucepan of boiling salted water for 1–2 minutes until bright green and tender, then drain and refresh under cold running water. Combine in a large bowl with the rocket, shaved fennel and fronds, parsley, mint and spring onion.

3. Heat a barbecue or chargrill pan to high. Toss the zucchini with a little oil and chargrill, turning occasionally, for 1–2 minutes until just tender, then set aside.

4. Drain the lamb from the marinade and chargrill, turning occasionally, for 2–3 minutes until brown all over, but still pink in the middle.

5. Rest the lamb for a minute or two, then slice thickly across the grain and add to the salad, along with the chargrilled zucchini. Add the vinegar and remaining lemon juice, drizzle generously with extra virgin olive oil, season with salt and pepper, toss to combine and serve.

NOTES

→ *Pan-frying is also a good method to cook the tenderloins: heat a splash of olive oil in a frying pan over high heat and sear well all over, then set aside to rest for a minute or two before carving.*

→ *If zucchini flowers are in season, add them to the salad. Tear the petals into pieces and thinly slice the stems into rounds.*

Cut Lamb tenderloin
See page 151

MINI LAMB ROAST
~ WITH BABY VEGETABLES ~

Prep time *20 minutes*
Cook *50 minutes (plus resting)*

1. Preheat the oven to 220°C (425°F) and bring the lamb to room temperature for 30 minutes. Put the potatoes in a saucepan and cover generously with cold salted water. Bring to the boil and cook for 8–10 minutes until just tender. Drain.

2. Combine the potatoes, carrots, radishes and pumpkin in a large roasting tin, drizzle generously with olive oil, season with salt and pepper and roast for 12–15 minutes until beginning to brown and soften.

3. Meanwhile, heat a splash of olive oil in a frying pan over medium heat. Add the lamb and fry, turning occasionally, for 5–7 minutes until well browned all over, paying particular attention to the fat on top of the rump.

4. Combine the garlic, thyme and a dash of olive oil in a bowl and season to taste. Place the lamb on top of the vegetables in the roasting tin and drizzle with the garlic mixture. Squeeze the remaining half of the lemon and add it to the tin. Roast for 20–25 minutes for medium-rare; a thermometer will read 52°C (125°F).

5. Transfer the lamb to a tray, cover loosely with foil and set aside to rest for 10–15 minutes; the meat will continue to cook while resting and will finish with an internal temperature of 55°C (130°F). Add the baby leeks to the roasting tin, drizzle with a little extra oil and roast for 5–8 minutes until the vegetables are tender.

6. To make the minty carrot-top sauce, process the carrot tops, mint, shallot, garlic, lemon zest and lemon juice in a food processor until finely chopped. Add the oil and vinegar, process until smooth and season with salt and pepper.

7. To serve, thinly slice the lamb and serve with the roasted baby vegetables and minty carrot-top sauce.

INGREDIENTS

2 lamb rump mini-roasts, cap on,
 about 450 g (1 lb) each
250 g (9 oz) kipfler potatoes, scrubbed
 and halved
2 bunches baby carrots, tops trimmed
 and reserved
1 bunch radishes, trimmed and halved
1 baby pumpkin (winter squash), cut into
 wedges
Olive oil, for drizzling
2 garlic cloves, finely chopped
2 thyme sprigs, leaves picked
4 baby leeks, trimmed, halved lengthways
 and soaked in cold water to remove grit

Minty carrot-top sauce
1 large handful of reserved carrot tops
1 large handful of mint leaves
1 golden shallot, finely chopped
1 garlic clove
Finely grated zest and juice of ½ lemon
 (reserve the other half for the roasting tin)
100 ml (3½ fl oz) extra virgin olive oil
1 teaspoon white wine vinegar

NOTE

→ *Using the fronds from the carrots is a great way to reduce food waste and makes a beautifully herbaceous sauce which goes perfectly with the lamb. If your baby carrots have been sold without the fronds, use flat-leaf (Italian) parsley instead, or double the mint.*

Cut Lamb rump
See page 151

BARBECUED BUTTERFLIED SICHUAN LAMB LEG

Prep time *30 minutes (plus marinating)*
Cook *35 minutes (plus resting)*

1. Coarsely grind the spices using a mortar and pestle and add the sea salt. Set aside half of the spice mixture.

2. Put the remaining spice mixture in a large bowl with the oil, soy sauce and vinegar and mix to combine. Add the butterflied lamb, massage well to coat thoroughly, cover and set aside to marinate and come to room temperature (alternatively you can marinate in the refrigerator overnight and bring to room temperature for 30 minutes before cooking).

3. Preheat a barbecue or large chargrill pan to medium–high. Remove the lamb from the marinade and barbecue, fat-side down, until the fat is rendered and crisp, then turning occasionally, for 20–30 minutes for medium-rare in the thickest part or until cooked to your liking; internal temperature should read 52°C (125°F) on a thermometer and the meat will continue to cook while resting. It will reach an internal temperature of 55°C (130°F). If you have a hooded barbecue, you can close the hood in between turning the lamb; the lamb will take less time to cook in this case, about 20–25 minutes. Transfer to a tray, cover loosely with foil and set aside to rest for 20 minutes.

4. While the lamb rests, drizzle the spring onions with a little oil and barbecue for 3–4 minutes until lightly charred.

5. To make the smacked cucumber, lay the cucumber on a chopping board and smack with the flat side of a cleaver or with the flat of a large knife along the length until it splits. Coarsely chop and transfer to a bowl along with the remaining ingredients and toss to combine.

6. Serve the lamb sliced with any resting juices, with the smacked cucumber, chargrilled spring onion and the reserved spice mixture to season.

INGREDIENTS

1 butterflied lamb leg, about 1.6 kg (3 lb 8 oz), fat trimmed and reserved
1 teaspoon cumin seeds
1 teaspoon fennel seeds
1 teaspoon coriander seeds
1 teaspoon sichuan peppercorns
2 teaspoons sea salt
60 ml (2 fl oz/¼ cup) vegetable oil or other neutral-flavoured oil
1 tablespoon light soy sauce
1 tablespoon Chinese black vinegar
12 spring onions (scallions), trimmed

Smacked cucumber
1 telegraph (long) cucumber, washed
2 garlic cloves, crushed
3 teaspoons Chinese black vinegar or rice vinegar
1 teaspoon sesame oil
1 pinch of caster (superfine) sugar (optional)

SERVING SUGGESTION

steamed jasmine rice

NOTES

→ *Sichuan peppercorns are dried seed pods from the prickly ash tree. They are available from Asian grocers and spice specialists.*

→ *Butterflied lamb leg is a crowd-pleaser as it has different thicknesses throughout, meaning that some parts will be more cooked than others.*

→ *See pages 486–487 to learn how to butterfly a lamb leg.*

***Cut** Lamb leg*
See page 152

SERVES 4 (WITH LEFTOVERS FOR SANDWICHES)

ROAST LAMB LEG
~ IN CHAMOMILE ~

One of the best cookbook writers of recent years, Mark Best will make you laugh, but will also help to apply logic and process to your cooking, as he does in this recipe where he has applied the simple idea that 'what grows together goes together'—and chamomile and herbs do make the very best companions.

1. Remove the lamb from the refrigerator 2 hours before preparation to allow more even cooking. Preheat the oven to 180°C (350°F).

2. Evenly score the skin of the lamb to a depth of 5 mm (¼ inch) and rub the salt all over the meat. In a food processor, blend the garlic and olive oil into a paste, then rub this all over the lamb. Sprinkle over the chamomile tea leaves.

3. Heat a heavy roasting tin in the oven until hot.

4. Put the lamb and onion in the tin and cook for 1½–2 hours (25–30 minutes per 500 g or 1 lb 2 oz), basting the meat with its fat from time to time. Cook the lamb to your preferred temperature. (I prefer medium 65–70°C (150–160°F) for the best flavour and texture.) Remove the meat from the oven to rest for 20–30 minutes prior to serving.

5. Tip off some of the fat and deglaze the tin with a splash of white wine. Reduce the wine to nothing then add a little water. Bring to the boil, scraping the tin with a wooden spoon to make a jus and pour it over the sliced lamb to serve.

6. Garnish with the fresh chamomile flowers and carve the lamb at the table.

Prep time *10 minutes*
Cook *1 hours 35 minutes (plus resting)*

INGREDIENTS

2.2 kg (5 lb) lamb leg
2 teaspoons sea salt
1 garlic bulb, cloves separated and peeled
50 ml (1¾ fl oz) olive oil
50 g (1¾ oz) best-quality chamomile tea
2 onions, roots removed, cut into quarters
Splash of white wine for deglazing
Small bunch of fresh chamomile

NOTES

→ *From* Best Kitchen Basics, *by Mark Best (Hardie Grant, 2016).*

→ *This recipe has been adjusted to use a regular lamb leg for ease of sourcing, but if you can seek out a 1.2 kg (2 lb 10 oz) suckling lamb leg (long leg, rump on) you will have particularly spectacular results. As Best points out in his book, keeping the rump on will help to hold the shape of the whole roast: it is as the French would do it.*

***Cut** Lamb leg*
See page 152

LAMB SHANK TAGINE

SERVES 4

Prep time *30 minutes (plus soaking and marinating)*
Cook *3½ hours*

1. Combine the garlic, ginger and ras el hanout in a small bowl, then rub all over the lamb shanks and season to taste. Cover and set aside at room temperature for 1 hour (alternatively, refrigerate overnight for even deeper flavour and bring to room temperature before cooking). Preheat the oven to 160°C (315°F).

2. Drain the chickpeas and bring to the boil in a saucepan of unsalted water. Cook for 30–35 minutes until almost tender, then drain.

3. Meanwhile, melt the butter in a large enamelled cast-iron casserole over medium–high heat, add the lamb shanks and sear, turning occasionally, for 4–5 minutes until browned well all over. Transfer to a plate.

4. Add the onion to the casserole and fry, stirring occasionally for 6–8 minutes until softened and starting to colour. Add the tomato and cook for a further 3–4 minutes until it is beginning to break down. Scatter the capsicum, dates and chilli over the top, add the chickpeas, lamb shanks, cinnamon sticks and saffron water, and season generously with salt and pepper.

5. Bring to the boil, then reduce the heat to very low. Make a cartouche by cutting out a round of baking paper to fit the diameter of the casserole, crumple it up, then wet it under cold running water. Lay it directly on the surface of the mixture, pressing to get rid of any air bubbles. Cover with a lid and transfer to the oven to braise for 2–2½ hours until the lamb is very tender and almost falling from the bone. Scatter with coriander sprigs and serve with lemon wedges.

INGREDIENTS

4 lamb hindquarter shanks
4 garlic cloves, finely chopped
1 tablespoon finely grated fresh ginger
1 tablespoon ras el hanout
135 g (4¾ oz/⅔ cup) dried chickpeas, soaked overnight in cold water (see note)
2 tablespoons (40 g) butter, chopped
1 large red onion, thinly sliced
4 ripe tomatoes, coarsely chopped
1 red capsicum (pepper), deseeded and thinly sliced
6 Medjool dates, pitted and halved
1 long red chilli, thinly sliced
2 cinnamon sticks
1 pinch of saffron threads soaked in 1 litre (35 fl oz/4 cups) warm water
Coriander (cilantro) sprigs and lemon wedges, to serve

SERVING SUGGESTION

steamed couscous with roasted almonds, finely chopped preserved lemon and flat-leaf (Italian) parsley

NOTES

→ *You can use tinned chickpeas in place of the dried chickpeas if you prefer. Drain a 400 g (14 oz) tin of chickpeas, rinse and add to the tagine when the lamb is cooked, simmering for a minute or two to warm through.*

→ *The flavours of this dish get even better over a couple of days: it's a great one to make in larger batches and freeze for later.*

Cut Lamb or goat shank
See page 152

FERGUS HENDERSON

Nose to Tail Eating

SERVES 2
DEVILLED KIDNEYS

Prep time *15 minutes*
Cook *15 minutes*

No meat book would be complete without reference to Fergus Henderson's Nose to Tail Eating. *If you want to learn more about the true joys of eating the whole animal, this is the book you need to buy (along with those that followed it).*

1. Nip out the white fatty gristle of the kidneys with a knife or scissors. Mix together the flour, cayenne pepper, mustard and salt and pepper in a bowl.

2. Get a frying pan very hot, throw in a knob of butter, and as this melts roll your kidneys in your spiced flour, and shake them in a sieve to remove excess.

3. Place them in the sizzling pan, cook for 2 minutes each side.

4. Add a hearty splash of Worcestershire sauce and the chicken stock, and let all the ingredients get to know each other.

5. Remove the kidneys to your two waiting bits of toast, let the sauce reduce and emulsify in the pan (do not let it disappear) and pour over the kidneys and toast.

6. Eat – Happy Birthday!

INGREDIENTS

6 lamb's kidneys, suet and membrane removed, and slit in half lengthwise, retaining the kidney shape
3 tablespoons plain (all-purpose) flour
1 teaspoon cayenne pepper
1 teaspoon dry English mustard
Sea salt and pepper
A big knob of butter
Worcestershire sauce
A healthy splash of chicken stock
2 pieces of toast (white or brown, up to you though—just an observation—white seems to sop up the juices better)

NOTES

→ *The perfect breakfast on your birthday, with a glass of Black Velvet.*

→ *From* Nose to Tail Eating, *by Fergus Henderson (Bloomsbury, 1999).*

Cut Lamb kidneys
See page 153

GOAT ADOBO

Prep time *20 minutes*
Cook *2 hours 20 minutes*

1. Put the meat in a saucepan with the ginger and enough cold water to cover completely. Bring to a simmer and cook gently for 50 minutes to 1 hour until almost tender. Remove the meat and pat dry with paper towel, reserving the poaching liquid.

2. Heat the vegetable oil in a large enamelled cast-iron casserole over medium–high heat. Season the goat generously with salt and pepper, add it to the casserole in batches and sear over medium–high heat, turning occasionally for 5–6 minutes to brown well all over. Make sure you don't overcrowd the pan, as the meat will stew rather than caramelise; the deeper the browning, the better the flavour of the finished dish, so take your time to do this well. Transfer to a plate.

3. Add the onion to the casserole and cook, stirring occasionally, for 8–10 minutes until caramelised, then stir in the garlic until fragrant. Return the meat to the casserole, add the vinegar, soy sauce, peppercorns, star anise, bay leaves and cinnamon, along with enough of the reserved poaching liquid to just cover. Bring to a simmer, reduce the heat to low, cover with a lid and simmer for 50–60 minutes until the sauce thickens and is well flavoured and the goat is tender, adding the chillies in the last 15 minutes of cooking.

4. Serve the adobo with steamed jasmine rice, scattered with fried garlic, fresh ginger and coriander sprigs.

INGREDIENTS

1 kg (2 lb 4 oz) goat shoulder, cut into 3 cm (1¼ inch) chunks
5 cm (2 inch) piece of fresh ginger, thickly sliced
Vegetable oil, for cooking
1 onion, thinly sliced
4 garlic cloves, finely chopped
110 ml (3¾ fl oz) Chinese black vinegar (see note)
80 ml (2½ fl oz/⅓ cup) soy sauce
1 teaspoon whole black peppercorns
3 whole star anise, broken into pieces
2 fresh bay leaves
2 cinnamon sticks
3 dried long red chillies
Steamed jasmine rice, to serve
Fried garlic, to serve (see note)
Fresh ginger (extra), julienned, and coriander (cilantro) sprigs, to serve

NOTES

→ *Chinese black vinegar is a dark vinegar made from glutinous rice and has a deep smoky flavour. Chinkiang vinegar is widely considered to be the best. It's available from some supermarkets and Asian grocers, but if it's unavailable, you can substitute regular rice vinegar.*

→ *Fried garlic is available from the Asian section of some supermarkets and Asian grocers, or you can fry your own.*

→ *A similar method can be used to cook lamb: diced boneless neck or shoulder work well.*

Cut Goat or lamb shoulder
See page 154

SERVES 4

ROGAN JOSH

Prep time *30 minutes (plus marinating)*
Cook *2½ hours*

1. Combine the goat, lemon juice and 80 g (2¾ oz) of the yoghurt in a bowl, mix well to combine, cover and marinate for at least 3 hours or overnight if you have time.

2. Heat the reserved fat in a large enamelled cast-iron casserole over low heat to render, adding ghee if necessary. Increase the heat to medium–high and heat until fat is almost smoking. Add the green cardamom, fennel seeds, cloves, brown cardamom (if using), dried chillies, bay leaves and cassia: be careful as the spices will pop and spit. Stir for 30–60 seconds until fragrant.

3. Add the onion to the casserole and fry, stirring frequently, for 6–8 minutes, until the onion has softened and is beginning to brown. Stir in the ginger and garlic until fragrant, then stir in the chilli powder, ground coriander, turmeric and the marinated goat mixture and stir occasionally for 8–10 minutes until the meat is well browned.

4. Stir in the remaining yoghurt and 500 ml (17 fl oz/2 cups) of water to combine, bring to a simmer, cover and reduce the heat to low. Simmer, stirring occasionally, for 1½–2 hours until the meat is very tender, topping up with extra water if necessary. Season to taste, then scatter with coriander leaves and fried garlic and serve with lime wedges.

INGREDIENTS

600 g (1 lb 5 oz) boneless goat shoulder, cut
    into 3 cm (1¼ inch) pieces, fat trimmed
    and reserved
Juice of ½ lemon
300 g (10½ oz) Greek-style yoghurt
50 g (1¾ oz) ghee or vegetable oil
1 tablespoon green cardamom pods, bruised
1½ teaspoons fennel seeds
1 teaspoon whole cloves
5 brown cardamom pods, bruised (optional)
4 small dried red chillies
2 fresh bay leaves
Two 7.5 cm (3 inch) cassia bark or cinnamon
    sticks
3 red onions, thinly sliced
1 tablespoon finely grated fresh ginger
4 garlic cloves, finely chopped
1 tablespoon chilli powder, preferably
    Kashmiri, or to taste
3 teaspoons ground coriander
1½ teaspoons ground turmeric
Coarsely chopped coriander (cilantro), fried
    garlic (see note on page 192) and lime
    wedges, to serve

*steamed basmati rice or saffron
rice and a cooling cucumber,
tomato and onion salad*

SERVING
SUGGESTION

NOTES

→ *Fresh spices and meat with a good amount of fat make for the perfect rogan josh. If you have an Indian supermarket or spice shop nearby, you'll find everything you need in one place.*

Cut Goat shoulder
See page 154

CHAPTER THREE

PIGS

PORK ~ CHARCUTERIE

PIGS

PORK, CHARCUTERIE, HAMS, PAINTBRUSHES, HAIRBRUSHES, SAUSAGES, SAUSAGE CASINGS, BACON, COLLAGEN

PRIZED CUTS

TO ROAST *Belly with crackling*

TO GRILL *Pork cutlets and neck*

TO BRAISE *Cheek*

PRIZED OFFAL *Ears and tails*

COMPLEMENTS TO THE PIG

NUTMEG	MUSTARD	PULSES
BAY	JUNIPER BERRIES	SAGE
GARLIC	MILK	ONION
APPLE	CABBAGE	CARAWAY
PEAR	FENNEL	PAPRIKA
PARSNIP	FENNEL SEEDS	PINEAPPLE
CHESTNUT	ROSEMARY	CREAM
MUSTARD FRUITS	THYME	

BELLY vs LEG

MUCH OF THE PIG IS DESTINED FOR THE CHARCUTIER. HERE IS A BRIEF GLANCE AT THE MOST POPULAR PRIMAL CUTS AND THE WAY THEY ARE USED AROUND THE WORLD.

BACON FAMILY TREE

ITALIAN PANCETTA – BELLY, SALTED AND AIR-DRIED, FLAT OR ROLLED.

BRITISH BACON – LOIN, CAP AND SOME BELLY IS KNOWN AS 'RASHERS'; BELLY ONLY IS 'STREAKY BACON'. IT IS BRINED AND OFTEN SMOKED, OR ELSE SOLD UNSMOKED AS 'GREEN BACON'.

CANADIAN/IRISH BACON – LOIN ONLY, OFTEN CUT THICKER AND CALLED 'BACK BACON'.

AMERICAN BACON – BELLY, CURED IN SALT AND SMOKED.

SPECK – AN ENGLISH WORD MEANING FAT, IN GERMANY SPECK IS BACON, IN ITALY IT IS CURED PORK.

HAM FAMILY TREE

HAM – REAR LEG, BRINED AND SMOKED.

GAMMON STEAK – RUMP, PICKLED OR CURED. MAY BE SMOKED, BUT DOES NEED TO BE COOKED BEFORE EATING.

PICNIC HAM *AKA* **BANJO HAM –** SHOULDER, BRINED AND SMOKED.

JAMON/PROSCIUTTO – REAR LEG, SALTED AND AIR-DRIED.

WET-CURED HAM – SKINNED AND CURED BY SOAKING IN BRINE. MAY BE SOLD PRECOOKED OR RAW.

BLACK FOREST HAM – BONELESS, SMOKED OVER FIR WOOD AND SAWDUST, FROM GERMANY.

LEARN MORE ABOUT THE DIFFERENT CUTS OF PIG AND HOW TO USE THEM ON PAGES 219–225.

SELECT & STORE

Look for pork from free-ranging pigs, which have spent their whole life outdoors. There are so many heritage breeds available now with good marbling and flavour, so seek these out where possible. Store pork in the fridge loosely covered in butchers' paper, not plastic wrap or it will sweat. This is the reason we store the Christmas ham in a pillowcase. If you want to encourage the best crackling, leave the pork in the fridge uncovered overnight, with the crackling exposed to the dry air of the fridge.

BUTCHER'S TREATS

EARS AND TAILS

NECK

CHEEKS

IN FACT, THE WHOLE HEAD!

–ALL ABOUT–
CHARCUTERIE

Charcuterie literally means 'cooked meat' (*chair cuite*) in Old French, but it's not about cooked meat so much as something that is not raw. Charcuterie is often not cooked at all, but cured, using, at its most basic, a combination of two ingredients: salt and air.

People have been curing meat for thousands of years. In the days before refrigeration, curing meats, especially beef and pork, guaranteed a supply of meat throughout the warmer months when spoilage was a constant danger. It was a feature of most European smallholdings, where they would kill one animal to last the household for the year. Traditionally it was done in winter (to avoid the hot weather during the initial curing) and then hung in the roofspace with a breeze created by an open window. See page 230 for more.

SIMPLE VS COMPLEX CUTS

With a delicious amount of fat to complement the collagen and sinews of the harder-working cuts, there is much to celebrate (and cook slowly and gently) in the pig.

COMPLEX CUTS

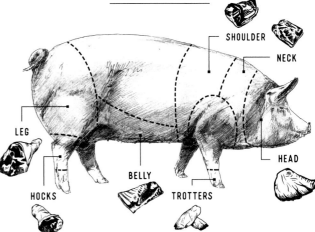

SHOULDER

NECK

LEG

HEAD

BELLY

HOCKS

TROTTERS

COOKING PORK

There has been much historical contention regarding the correct internal temperature for pork. In recent years the advice has been revised and authorities now say it is fine to cook your pork to medium, with a slight blush of pink in the middle. This is a win for our palates, because dry pork is not nice to eat! Be sure to rest your pork for at least half the time you have cooked it, as this is also fundamental for a juicy roast.

⊢ CRACKLING ⊣

Rest your pork roast crackling-side up, carve it crackling-side down. Great crackling is undoubtedly the key part of a pork roast: when it is cooked well, the family will fight for every morsel; if it's cooked poorly the disappointment is palpable. See page 227 for tips on making your crackling brilliant.

It was rumoured that New York journalist A.J. Liebling once used a piece of bacon as a bookmark.

HISTORY

Across Europe from Georgia to Spain, as the leaves begin to turn from green to shades of gold through russet, the image of the backyard pig also turns from household composter to charcuterie.

Pig day—widely practised as an annual family, or even village, highlight—is an incredible example of the way in which a whole animal can be respected, from nose to tail. While the recipes and techniques vary from region to region, it is clear that in many cultures the whole animal is put to use: some cuts may be salt-cured in their entirety, like the legs for prosciutto and the belly for pancetta, while the harder-working muscles and fat may be minced and hung in the cleaned intestines to become sausages and salamis or, with the addition of the pig's blood, *boudin noir* (black pudding) or *morcilla*; offcuts and offal are put to use to make terrines, pâtés and rillettes. It's a long day's work, but provides an incredible store cupboard of culinary treats for the year ahead.

This prewinter tradition is so engrained in Europe, the old German name for November was *Schlachtmonat*: the month of slaughter. Beyond the store-cupboard requirements, the timing is no accident: the last of the summer warmth helps to start the fermentation for the salamis, while the cooler evening temperatures are necessary to safely preserve the animal, particularly back in the days when refrigeration was scarce.

The Europeans are not alone in this: in China, the traditional pig day falls somewhere between the winter solstice and the New Year's celebrations. Pork may be cured by wind, soy, salt, smoke or a combination of the above. On the other side of the globe, in the early days of colonial America, salt pork was such a staple (one to rival bread) it became part of the everyday vernacular: salted pork, stored in barrels, led to phrases such as 'scraping the bottom of the barrel' and 'pork-barrel politics'.

In fact, as you travel the globe you will find numerous delicious solutions to the inevitable problem of curing the whole animal in different climates. Spices, leaves, salts, sugars and honey all play their role in preserving the pig, depending on the terroir.

While charcuterie itself can (and should) be considered an art form, the pig also became a tool for the arts. As all is good within the pig, there was also use for the bristles from the outside of the pig: Raphael and Michelangelo had the pig to thank for their paintbrushes, while Rapunzel also owed the pig a debt of gratitude for keeping her long hair tangle free.

The pig is also a brilliant addition to the farmyard cycle: its omnivorous appetite is well suited to deal with household waste. The animals are fed and in return they feed. Easy to raise, relatively quick to rear and helpful in the fields (pigs will turn over the earth as they scavenge), the pig traditionally presents a simple equation for a delicious symbiotic relationship.

For an animal that was so at home, well, at home, the pig has suffered in the transition to industrialised food production. The most common industrial varieties of pigs are good breeders and put on weight quickly, but as these qualities have been exaggerated, others have become weaker and their environment has thus become more controlled: they have lost access to the mud baths to help regulate their temperature; lost access to the outdoors to strengthen their immune system; relied on steel bars to protect their young rather than nests. In fact, we have treated the pig in much the same way as we have treated the chicken: that is to say we have reduced the pig to a breed of animal that can exist in a tiny space with limited access to the outdoors or to the food they would naturally enjoy and thrive on. An industrialised machine more than an animal.

The shift from prized member of the small-scale farm to the jewel in the industrialised mass-production crown, our relationship with the pig has also changed. Pig days are becoming rarities, particularly in more urbanised countries. Many of the pork products we consume now are produced with the use of boneless pork that has been shipped around the world. The industry is concentrated in the hands of a relative few and sent into the hands of the masses. Pork is now the most consumed meat in the world, and this in spite of the fact that it is not eaten by Muslims or Jews.

Pork is now cheap, but at what cost?

BREED

All modern pigs are descended from the wild boar that roamed the forests and swamps of ancient Europe and Asia around 40 million years ago. Our global appetite for pork has seen the aesthetic variety of spots, stripes and even wool—also reflected in the flavour—diminish.

At some point in the past century, the Danish succeeded in breeding two extra pairs of ribs into the pig. By crossing their local breed with the Large White, a British breed, and selectively opting for longer pigs, they evolved the Landrace pig into a bacon-making machine, with 16 or even 17 ribs as opposed to the regular 14. It changed the game.

Designed to target the bacon-loving British, while dealing with the excess whey that is a by-product of their vast dairy co-operatives, the Landrace has become one of the major genetic components of the industrial pig world. It remains the backbone (or rib-bone!) of the Danish pork industry.

Beyond the human hand, breeds of pig have naturally evolved over millennia to suit their environment and the available sources of food around them. This is particularly the case with black pigs: the Iberian pig of Spain and Portugal (also known as *pata negra* for its black hoofs), the Berkshire in England, the black Slavonian pig in Croatia (actually a cross between the *Lasasta mangulica* and Berkshire breeds). Their colouring helps them to survive in the outdoors, while in the kitchen their excellent fat content—both within the eye of the muscle (intramuscular) and their external fat—lend the meat a rich, deep flavour.

→ *In America and Australia, the wild boar is considered an invasive species. These pigs are descended from domestic species of pigs and adapted to the local environment.*

More than half the pigs in the world now live a life entirely indoors; unfortunately for the pig, they were among the first animals to be raised in an intensive farming environment. Hybrid breeds, predominantly the Large White and Landrace, have been selected for this style of farming: high-yielding, fast-growing, lean animals. Bizarrely, the industrial system also took offence to the black hairs in the pig, favouring their white cousins for the production of pork, essentially making it complicated for these industrial pigs to live in the outdoors.

The antifat mania of the second half of the 1900s, coupled with the 'other white meat' campaign, encouraged porcine breeders to turn their focus onto breeds that had little fat. Consequently we have now lost most of the succulence, and thus the flavour, in pork. It is for this reason you will find a lot of the pork in the supermarket is 'moisture enhanced', meaning it has been injected with a saline solution to try and put the tenderness back in, the tenderness that we took out through this selective breeding.

The huge demand for pork and smallgoods, coupled with the animal's relatively delicate nature (pigs cannot easily regulate their own temperature and paler pigs are prone to sunburn, among other issues, particularly if not given access to mud, their natural sunscreen), was the final nail in this industrialised coffin.

In Australia, the USA and the UK, we now rely heavily on a cross of just a few breeds. The problem is exacerbated in Australia, where stringent biosecurity laws will not allow for importation of these animals or their semen. In fact, much of the pork Australians eat is imported boneless from Canada or Denmark: up to 96 per cent of boneless smallgoods are made from imported pork.

This quest for fast growth and lean pork has had a detrimental impact on the numbers of heritage breeds such as the Berkshire, Wessex Saddleback and Hampshire. They are breeds that like to be outdoors and to live in a free-range environment; they tend to have smaller litters; and they are more expensive to grow. While difficult to find in your local supermarket, these breeds are revered for their higher fat content and their hearty flavour and texture. Of course, once they're gone, they're gone.

There is a solution: as we discussed earlier in the book, it relies on the old economic argument of supply and demand: if we want to save them, we must eat them.

HERITAGE BREED MAP: PIGS

BRITAIN

ENGLAND

Berkshire

Prized for their juiciness, tenderness and flavour. Great intramuscular marbling.

Gloucester Old Spot

Weight gain, feed efficiency, excellent foragers and grazers, high fat ratio and flavourful meat.

British large black

Superior milking and mothering abilities; excellent grazing pigs; dark colouring to withstand heat. Hardy and docile.

Small, Middle and Large White

Developed in England in the 1700s for commercial production.

Tamworth

Long snout for foraging, excellent 'plough' for clearing weeds and brambles; hardy breed; good mothering abilities; excellent bacon.

Hampshire

Lean of muscle with minimal back fat, large loin eye, good mothering ability.

Yorkshire

Good muscling with a high proportion of lean meat and low back fat.

Wessex Saddleback

Popular outdoor pig due to their ability to graze and forage; excellent milking and mothering with the ability to rear large litters.

AFRICA

Warthog

The only species of pig that has adapted to grazing savannah habitats.

EUROPE

HUNGARY

Mangulica

Great marbling, flavour and external fat. Their woolly coat helps them to survive cold winters.

CROATIA/SERBIA

Black Slavonian pig (*fajferica*)

Cross of the *Lasasta mangulica* and Berkshire. Meaty, high-fat pig.

SPAIN/PORTUGAL

Iberian pig (*el cerdo ibérico*)

Super fatty, thanks to their diet of acorns. Also known as *pata negra* for their black hoofs.

DENMARK

Landrace

Cross of native pig with Large White to meet British bacon demand; these large pigs have two extra sets of ribs.

USA

Duroc

The exact origin of the Duroc is unknown; bred for commercial production; good carcass yield, fast growth.

Razorback

Razorbacks and, indeed, wild pigs around the world, are examples of the pig's ability to return to past breed traits when their environment changes.

SOUTH-EAST ASIA

Wild boar

Considered to have originated in the islands of South-East Asia, the wild boar has spread to Eurasia, North Africa and the Greater Sunda Islands.

JAPAN

Kurobuta

The name means 'black pig': bred from Berkshires that were sent as a gift to the kingdom of Ryukyu. Soft, white and flavourful fat composition; fine, rich-textured meat.

FEED

Pigs, like chickens, are a little unusual in the farmyard world because they don't rely on pasture alone: as urban legend asserts, pigs can eat practically anything. This boon was traditionally used to help with the waste of the farmhouse, putting it to good economic use by investing the waste in the future. One man's trash is a pig's treasure.

The diet of the pig can have a wonderful impact on the flavour, and particularly the intramuscular fat, of the pork you eat. The Iberico pigs of southwestern Spain are raised on a large tract of land that runs along the border of Portugal known as the *dehesa*, a vast prairie-like grazing land that was planted with a number of varieties of oak trees, providing an abundance of acorns for the pigs' diet over a number of months (the different varieties of oak drop their acorns at different times).

Iberian pigs graze on these acorns, as well as the local grasses and herbs, during the *montanera* (acorn season). One pig can eat six to seven kilograms (13–15½ lb) of acorns each day and will put on up to 60 kg (132 lb) over the season. In order to be classified as 'pure bellota' they are required to graze on acorns for three to four months, adding an incredible nutty yet sweet flavour to this *jamón ibérico de bellota*. The fat found in the acorns is predominantly oleic acid, the same as is found in olives: leading locals to refer to these pigs as 'olives with legs'.

Of course, oak forests are not limited to Spain. In Epirus, between Albania and Greece, they have a tradition of sausage-making that makes use of the wild black pigs of the region, fattened in the oak forests of the surrounding mountains; likewise with the Rachin hams of Eastern Georgia, their pigs naturally foraging on acorns—these hams are also smoked using the oak wood, imparting a further distinct aroma and taste.

There are other ways to achieve this intramuscular marbling and flavour. In Brazil, the *nilo* pig, a breed that is considered to be the naturalised cousin of the Iberian pig, scavenges for pine seeds from araucaria trees. In Australia, there is a farm using leftover avocados from a neighbouring farm to provide a source of oleic acid. The Kelmend pig of northern Albania is fed herbs, grasses and bran—all used to give the pork better flavour—while corn is avoided. Conversely, in America the production of pigs is largely focussed in the corn belt of Iowa and their diet largely consists of corn and soy.

In Italy, the prosciutto industry in Parma was created in harmony with the production of parmesan cheese. The excess whey from the cheesemaking is fed to the pigs, creating a delicious culinary cycle. The whey lends the prosciutto an acidity and sweetness that is unique to this Italian delicacy. Excess whey is also thought to be behind the boom in pig production in Norway, where pigs outnumber humans at a rate of four to one. Pork slowly cooked in milk is one of the great culinary classics and, when you understand this connection from within as well, it makes complete sense.

Another great culinary marriage, pork and apples, has long been joined in production in England, where the Gloucester Old Spot carries the nickname 'orchard pig': they were put to use foraging for the windfall apples, while also turning up the soil in the orchard.

This kind of diet and lifestyle is rare when it comes to intensive production. In a commercial sense, pigs can still be carefully fed on the by-products of other food industries; for example, the whey from cheesemaking or spent grains from the beermaking industry. However, the pigs' feed must be carefully monitored to manage the health of the pigs; a problem that is exacerbated in large numbers. The level of biosecurity necessary for porcine production is huge and pre-emptive antibiotics are used more often than not.

THE TRUFFLE

Pigs have another uncanny ability, when it comes to seeking out food: their ability to smell the highly prized truffle. Truffles cling to the roots of the oak or hazel tree and traditionally can be sniffed out by female pigs. It turns out that the smell of the truffle is similar to the smell of the pheromones of a male pig (in a way, they are actually seeking sex); so, while perhaps the most naturally predisposed to the smell of the truffle, pigs have fallen out of favour (to be replaced by trained dogs) as their desire overwhelms them and they will, if not stopped quickly, devour the truffle in their excitement.

ON THE FARM

The life cycle of industrially reared pigs is perhaps one of the most contentious in the farmyard world. A far cry from their historical cousins, industrially reared pigs have had to contend with farrowing crates, sow stalls, tail docking and teeth removal.

From a farming perspective, pigs are a pretty brilliant proposition: four months gestation, up to 10 piglets and they can produce a couple of litters annually. Piglets grow fast and can increase their weight by five thousand per cent or more in just six months.

There is no avoiding it, the majority of pigs in the world live a pretty miserable existence. Just like chickens, they have been bred to specifications thought to appeal to the market: pale in colour, lean of muscle and fast growing for a quick financial turnaround. Although the use of gestation crates—essentially tiny prisons just large enough to house the pregnant sow—has been outlawed in the EU, some US states and Australia, farrowing crates—where the sow is housed in a crate alongside that of her young—are still used to prevent her from rolling on her piglets and squashing them (to death).

Around 1.4 billion pigs are slaughtered annually worldwide: China rears around half the world's pigs, followed by the EU and the USA. In America, the intensive pig industry is concentrated in the hands of relatively few, with 50 companies producing 70 per cent of the country's pork. Beyond the issues for the pigs, the waste and consequent pollution produced by commercial piggeries puts enormous pressure on the environment.

Australia has one of the healthiest pig herds in the world, in part due to geographical isolation and border security, and many of the porcine diseases found overseas are not present. Thus, the idea that more than half of Australian processed pork is flown in frozen, heat treated and then processed seems crazy: the local industry is known to be healthier and safer.

When searching for an alternative to this type of intensively farmed meat, the terminology is complicated. Free range can now simply mean 'meaningful access to the outdoors'. Also, be aware of the difference between 'bred free range' and free range. In many cases, breeding sows are kept in a free-range environment and give birth to their young in an outside pen; however, their progeny will be moved indoors soon (if not immediately) after weaning.

Pasture-raised has now become the standard for pigs that truly live their entire life outside. These pigs will have access to paddocks and mud wallows—used by the pigs to help them keep cool on hot days—and they will build nests before they give birth, then nurture their young in these secure homes. Access to the outdoors also provides them space to forage; to turn the land in search of food and entertainment. Pigs can be very active when it comes to working the land and, among the numerous issues facing free-range pork producers is the need for space, as you must rotate them often to allow the land time to regenerate.

Living in a natural way they get exercise that builds up muscles and produces meat with a deeper, porkier flavour. With time outdoors they also tend to develop more, and better, subcutaneous fat (under the skin) as a natural defence against the cold.

AGE AT SLAUGHTER

The Greeks had a highly defined vocabulary denoting pigs at different sizes and ages. Romans and Greeks particularly revered suckling pigs. Now, we tend to grow them so quickly that we can barely notice the difference.

The females (sows) are generally considered to have the sweetest flavour. Male pigs—boars—can develop a strong smell and flavour known as boar taint. In China, where they are particularly sensitive to this odour, the males are rarely consumed at all. It is for this reason many boars are castrated in the first week of their life; however, now they grow so quickly that many farmers don't believe it's necessary.

Suckling pigs – Two to six weeks old (at their best at three to four weeks). This is a luxury product, with the pigs generally weighing less than 20 kg (45 lb). They are normally much smaller, at somewhere between 6 and 10 kg (approximately 14 and 22 lb).

Porkers – Weighing around 50–60 kg (110–132 lb), these animals are used for fresh pork meat, generally before six months of age (most often they are processed at around 16 weeks).

Bacon – The pigs used for bacon are bigger and therefore older, weighing 70–100 kg (155–225 lb). Specific breeds are used for this purpose, particularly the Landrace with its extra ribs.

All modern pigs *are descended from the wild boar that roamed the forests and swamps of ancient Asia and Europe. For more on the brilliant variety of pig breeds, see pages 206–209.*

AT THE BUTCHER

When Homer Simpson laughed at the idea of a 'wonderful, magical animal' that could provide ham, bacon and pork chops we laughed; however, you'd be surprised if you tallied up all the ways you consume pork. The pig is a classic nose-to-tail proposition and there is not much that we won't make use of in the butchery.

THE CARCASS

The head offers delicacies including the **jowl**, **cheek** and **ears**. In its entirety it can be gently poached to make *fromage-de-tête* (headcheese) or brawn, and it is ideal for terrine. The ears are revered in many countries, with their slightly gelatinous quality and the crunch of the cartilage; they are great deep-fried. The jowl can be used to make bacon, or Italians cure it for *guanciale*. The **neck** is a butcher's favourite cut with natural marbling. It is a beautiful roast, cut into steaks, or used for curry.

The middle of the pig is easily explained by dividing it into three horizontal sections. At the top is the **back fat**, a natural protective layer for the loin. In Cortona, Italy, they cure it with rosemary and other spices and serve the *lardo* very thinly sliced on toast. The **loin** is very lean and best cooked quickly. This is where we get **pork cutlets** and **chops**. Left whole, the pork **rack** makes a great roasting cut.

The **belly** is the height of porky indulgence and conveys the true taste and flavour of pork. It is renowned for the seams of fat that run through it, making it a very forgiving cut to cook. Roasted, poached, pickled, confit, smoked or braised, the belly handles many different cooking methods and is a standout in many international cuisines. It is also where we find the pork **belly ribs**, a favourite in Chinese cooking or sweet and sticky in the US. This is where streaky bacon comes from, as well as pancetta. Full rashers of bacon contain both the eye of the loin and the belly.

At the tail end of the pig we have the **leg**, which is most commonly used to make delicious ham and prosciutto. The pork **hock** is great marinated and roasted, or smoked and used in soups (such as pea and ham). Smoked hocks star in terrines and cassoulets because they provide a complex, rich and smoky flavour. They are full of connective tissue and have superb qualities. Last, but not least, we have the **trotters** of the pig. These little gems are a great natural source of gelatine and they are also used as a key ingredient in traditional veal stocks to create body and sheen.

PIG CUTS

With much of the pig relegated to its role in charcuterie—the legs often sent to become ham and prosciutto, the belly for pancetta and bacon—we don't often see all of the cuts in the butchery.

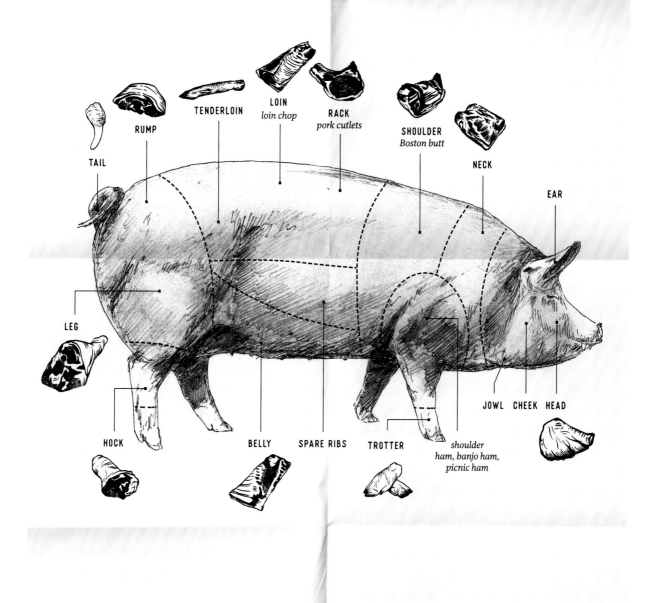

TAIL

RUMP

TENDERLOIN

LOIN
loin chop

RACK
pork cutlets

SHOULDER
Boston butt

NECK

EAR

LEG

HOCK

BELLY

SPARE RIBS

TROTTER

*shoulder
ham, banjo ham,
picnic ham*

JOWL CHEEK HEAD

For more about pig cuts, see pages 220–225.

PIG CUTS

HEAD
JOWL, CHEEK, EARS, TONGUE

The pig's head is a treasure chest of options, with delicacies including the jowl, cheek, ears and tongue. In its entirety, it can be gently poached to make *fromage-de-tête* (headcheese) or brawn, and the meat is ideal for a terrine. Among its components: the ears are prized for their gelatinous qualities and the crunch of the cartilage (braise them before frying them or crisping them in a hot pan); the cheeks have a tender, juicy, fatty flavour; the jowls are often cured and made into *guanciale;* while the tongue and even the snout can both be braised and then crisped to great effect.

CUT WEIGHT: 4–5 KG (9 LB–11 LB 4 OZ)
BEST COOKED: BRAISED
OPTIMAL FINISH: UNCTUOUS
RECIPES: SEE PAGES 238–241 AND 266–267

NECK

This cut is totally underestimated and underutilised. Revered by butchers, the neck muscle runs from the bottom of the head, through the top of the shoulder and ends at the rack (loin muscle). It is less tender than the loin, but has lots of natural marbling and, as with all working muscles, the reward is a deeper flavour. It makes a beautiful roast, is great cut into steaks, and diced it makes a great curry. The Italians use it to make their cured capocollo. When the shoulder is attached to the neck muscle it is known as the Boston butt.

→ Ask your butcher to tie some pork skin (scored at 1 cm/½ inch intervals) around the neck fillet to create beautiful crackling for your roast.
→ The neck is great sliced into 1–1.5 cm (½–⅜ inch) thick steaks and grilled on the barbecue.

CUT WEIGHT: 1.5–2 KG (3 LB 5 OZ– 4 LB 8 OZ)
BEST COOKED: ROASTED
OPTIMAL FINISH: UNCTUOUS

SHOULDER
BLADE, SHOULDER HAM, BANJO HAM, PICNIC HAM, BOSTON BUTT

Firm and hardworking, pork shoulder is deeply coloured and powerfully flavoured. A favourite among smallgoods producers due to its intense flavour, the shoulder makes wonderful sausages and salumi. A shoulder can also be made into ham and is a great, cheaper alternative to a traditional leg ham. Due to the considerable amounts of connective tissue, in the pan the shoulder responds best to longer cooking times: boneless shoulder can make a great slow roast and it's a beautiful piece of meat to mince (grind) or confit and use for pulled-pork sandwiches. With the neck muscle attached it is known as the Boston butt.

→ For an easy-carve roast ask your butcher to bone and roll the pork shoulder. A little liquid in the bottom of the pan will aid with a slow roast.

CUT WEIGHT: 3–6 KG (6 LB 12 OZ– 13 LB 8 OZ)
BEST COOKED: ROASTED
OPTIMAL FINISH: UNCTUOUS
RECIPES: SEE PAGES 242–245, 266–269 AND 390–391

RACK

PORK CUTLETS, RIB CHOPS, CARRÉ DE PORC

This cut has got it all. It's cooked on the bone, adding flavour; it's tender, coming from the middle of the animal; it has delicious crackling and a beautiful thin layer of fat that sits beneath the skin. A pork rack includes the 10 prime ribs closest to the loin, where the muscle is thicker and more tender (because it does less work). Pork racks make a terrific roast, or they can be separated into individual cutlets, which are great for pan-frying or grilling on the barbecue.

CUT WEIGHT: 10-RIB RACK 2.5 KG
(5 LB 8 OZ)
BEST COOKED: ROASTED
OPTIMAL FINISH: BLUSH OF PINK IN THE
MIDDLE, 60-65°C (140-150°F)
RECIPES: SEE PAGES 246-249 AND 270-271

LOIN

SHORT LOIN, PORK FILLET, LOIN CHOP

Sitting right next door to the rack, making it tender and tasty, this cut is great roasted whole, or cut into medallions and cooked on the barbecue. While technically the loin runs all the way down the pig's back, the pork loin roast is found between the end of the rack and the rump. The loin can be sold boneless as the backstrap or eye of loin; with the belly attached, it can be cured to make bacon. Leave the bone in and cut vertically for pork loin chops.

→ Ask your butcher to roll and tie the loin and tenderloin together with a protective layer of fat, which is scored at 1 cm (½ inch) intervals.

CUT WEIGHT: SHORT LOIN (BONELESS)
1.5-2 KG (3 LB 5 OZ-4 LB 8 OZ)
BEST COOKED: ROASTED OR PAN-FRIED
OPTIMAL FINISH: BLUSH OF PINK,
65°C (150°F)
RECIPES: SEE PAGES 250-253

TENDERLOIN

Super-tender with a mild flavour, this is a really approachable cut of meat to cook. It sits beneath the loin and does very little work in the paddock. Consequently, as the name suggests, this cut offers serious tenderness. The pork tenderloin is perfect for cutting into medallions and searing; it is also the best cut to use for pork skewers. The loin and tenderloin can be cut vertically for a porcine T-bone, which is known as pork loin chops.

→ If cooking pork tenderloin or fillet, consider stuffing it with something moist to stop it drying out, or wrap it in pancetta when cooking. While incredibly tender, it is very lean and dries out easily.
→ Buy the whole tenderloin and cut it into cubes to thread on skewers for the barbecue.
→ Ask your butcher to cut the tenderloin into large medallions for the grill.

CUT WEIGHT: 350-500 G (12 OZ-1 LB 2 OZ)
BEST COOKED: BARBECUED
OPTIMAL FINISH: BLUSH OF PINK IN THE
MIDDLE, 65°C (150°F)
RECIPE: SEE PAGES 254-255

Please note that all weights are approximate, as animals will differ based on their age, breed and feed. The internal temperatures given are the rested temperatures. For more information on cooking styles, roasting times, etcetera, see pages 448–455.

RUMP

Highly regarded for its beautiful texture and flavour, this is a great cut of meat. The square-shaped muscle that sits up on top of the leg is a relatively lean cut. Sadly, it can be quite a difficult cut to find as it is often left on the leg to round out a ham or prosciutto. When you do see it, try it roasted, or slice it to make pork steaks. It can also be found pickled as a gammon steak. This cut is great diced and threaded on skewers for the barbecue.

→ The rump is a great roast. Get your butcher to score the fat for you at 1 cm (½ inch) intervals.
→ Ask your butcher to cut the rump into cubes. Thread them onto skewers, marinate and cook on the barbecue.

CUT WEIGHT: 1.3–1.7 KG (3 LB–3 LB 12 OZ)
BEST COOKED: ROASTED
OPTIMAL FINISH: BLUSH OF PINK IN THE MIDDLE, 65°C (150°F)

LEG

The leg makes a great roast, with or without the bone, but is probably best known pickled and smoked as a delicious leg ham, or salted and hung as prosciutto or jamon. It consists of four muscles: rump, topside, silverside and knuckle, which can be separated to make smaller roasts. This cut of pork also responds well to braising. The individual muscles that make up a leg can be sliced to make a great pork schnitzel. Ask your butcher to bone and roll the leg for a great easy-to-carve roast. Allow 150–200 g (5½–7 oz) per person.

CUT WEIGHT: 7–10 KG (15 LB 12 OZ–21 LB 8 OZ)
BEST COOKED: ROASTED
OPTIMAL FINISH: COOKED THROUGH, 65°C (150°F)
RECIPE: SEE PAGES 256–259

BELLY

The Chinese refer to the pork belly as 'five-flowered meat' (*wuhuarou*) for its complex layers of fat and lean meat. The seams of fat that run through it make it a very forgiving cut to cook: roasted, poached, pickled, confit, smoked or braised, the belly handles many different cooking methods and is a standout in many international cuisines. It is where you will find the pork belly ribs and from where we make streaky bacon and pancetta. This cut conveys the true taste and flavour of pork. See page 224 for the different types of belly and rib cuts.

→ Beware of cheap bacon that has been pumped with salted liquid. If it has, it will spit ferociously in a hot pan.
→ Pancetta is pork belly that has been salted and hung (for approximately 3 months). It can be bought flat (with the fat along one side) or rolled into a log.

CUT WEIGHT: 4–6 KG (9 LB–13 LB 8 OZ)
BEST COOKED: BARBECUED
OPTIMAL FINISH: UNCTUOUS
RECIPES: SEE PAGES 260–265, 268–269 AND 278–279

Please note that all weights are approximate, as animals will differ based on their age, breed and feed. The internal temperatures given are the rested temperatures. For more information on cooking styles, roasting times, etcetera, see pages 448–455.

HOCK

Sitting just above the trotter and below the main section of the leg, the hock is great marinated and roasted, or smoked and used in soups (such as pea and ham). Smoked pork hocks star in dishes such as terrines and cassoulet, because they provide a complex, rich and smoky flavour. The hock is full of connective tissue and when treated well and given enough time it will yield all its superb qualities. There's no nationality that understands this cut better than the Germans with their traditional dish of pork knuckle and sauerkraut.

→ Rich in gelatine, smoked hocks can be added to stews to give body.
→ When buying a pork hock, be conscious of the difference between the smoked and fresh hock. The smoked hock will lend a rich (obviously smoky) flavour to your soup or stew.

CUT WEIGHT: 1 KG (2 LB 4 OZ)
BEST COOKED: SLOW ROASTED
OPTIMAL FINISH: UNCTUOUS
RECIPES: SEE PAGES 272–275

TROTTER

Where the rabbit's foot is lucky, in the culinary world it's the pig's foot that turns your sauce into liquid gold. It's a powerhouse of gelatine and provides a thickening quality to stock reductions such as jus. Chefs also use them in their veal stocks to create body and sheen. It is incredibly gelatinous and a perfect addition to boost flavour and viscosity. In the hands of a patient chef, the trotter can be made into an exceptional Italian dish known as *zampone*, where it is boned, stuffed, boiled and then slowly caramelised.

→ Rich in gelatine, the addition of a pork trotter to a pie or terrine will ensure that it sets as a jelly when cold.
→ Ask your butcher to bone the trotter, so that you can stuff and cook it.
→ The front trotters are often cut longer than the back trotters.
→ Scrub them well and then add to slow-simmering stocks or casseroles. The gelatine released by the trotter will thicken the juices.

CUT WEIGHT: 600 G (1 LB 5 OZ)
BEST COOKED: BRAISED
OPTIMAL FINISH: UNCTUOUS
RECIPE: SEE PAGES 278–279

TAIL

From nose all the way to the tail, and it would be remiss of us (and you) to ignore this particular culinary delicacy. Braise in stock until tender and so soft that you can pinch right through them. The gelatinous qualities of the pig's tail relish in the contrast of a crisp exterior: dip them in egg and then breadcrumbs before deep-frying them.

CUT WEIGHT: 150 G (5½ OZ)
BEST COOKED: BRAISED, THEN FRIED

PORK RIBS

As the name suggests, the pork ribs are all cut from the belly of the pig, where the ribs reach around under the pig: this is essentially an extension of the pork rack. Depending on where they are cut, they each offer different properties.

ST LOUIS RIBS

Taking the spare ribs as the starting point, the St Louis ribs have the sternum, cartilage and rib tips removed, but they retain a lot of the belly meat. They are considered the king among ribs, and yet you have to ruin the belly to get to them, so they are more costly to you and the butcher! There are also Kansas City ribs, which are trimmed less closely than St Louis ribs, but still have the hard bone removed.

RIB TIPS

The short, meaty sections of the spare rib, closest to the sternum. The structure is provided by the costal muscle, not the actual rib bones.

SPARE RIBS (SIDE RIBS, SPARE RIBS)

The full set of ribs, cut from the belly side of the pig's rib cage. They often contain more bone than meat, but also more fat, helping them to cook down and become tender and melting when slowly cooked. These can also be found as a half plate of ribs.

BABY BACK RIBS (BACK RIBS, LOIN RIBS, CANADIAN BACK RIBS)

Shorter than spare ribs, baby back ribs are nestled beneath the loin muscle. They will have meat between the bones and on top of the bones. They are generally more curved than spare ribs; they are lean and tender, but can also be meatier.

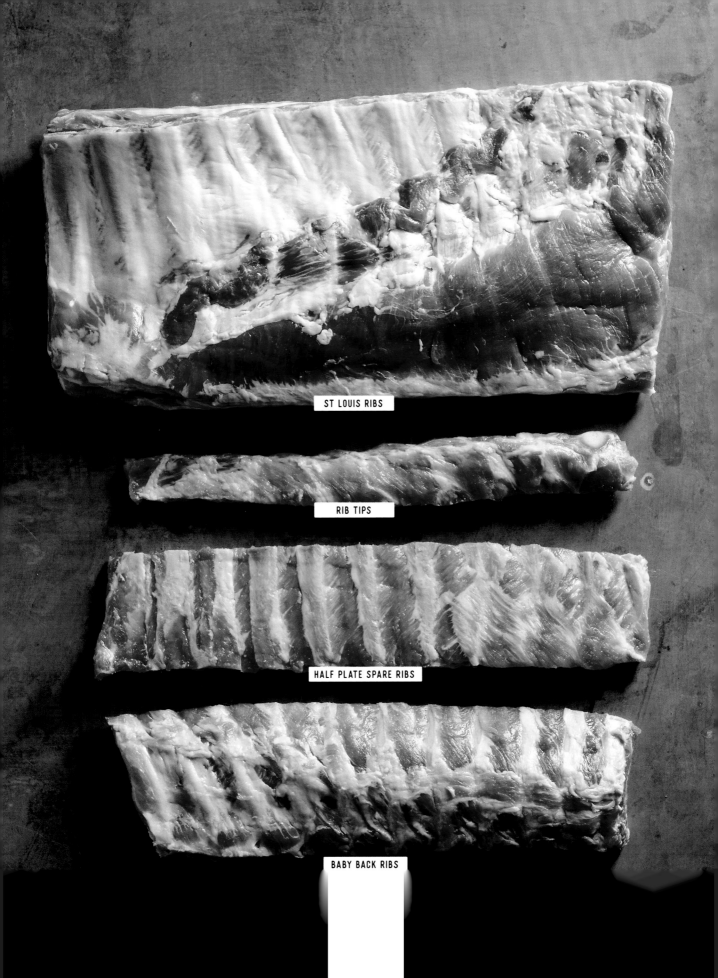

ST LOUIS RIBS

RIB TIPS

HALF PLATE SPARE RIBS

BABY BACK RIBS

IN THE KITCHEN

*Pork is consumed in so many ways: from bacon at breakfast,
a ham or salami sandwich at lunch, the little bit of pancetta in a bowl
of pasta or the skins of sausages for dinner, not to mention a pork roast
and its crowning glory, the crackling.*

SELECT AND STORE

Seek out pork that has a pink hue, white fat—potentially with a little marbling through it—and nice moist skin. Ask your butcher about sourcing heritage breeds such as Berkshire or Wessex saddlebacks, with great flavour and fat content. It should have a clean smell and not be sticky or tacky.

Many rare breeds have a higher fat content than their commercially reared cousins. Use it to your advantage. It will keep the pork moist and you can always cut it off after cooking. Don't fear the hair either. Many rare breeds have been edged out because they are not fair haired. Embrace the redheads and brunettes of the pork world: if you are anxious, you can always pluck!

STORING PORK

Be conscious of letting it breathe as much as possible, as pork tends to sweat in plastic. It is for this reason we put our Christmas hams in a pillowcase or muslin (cheesecloth). Ideally, store a pork roast in the fridge without plastic wrap for a day before you cook it. This allows the fat to dry out, resulting in brilliant crackling.

STORING HAM

To keep your ham fresh, score around the edge of the skin with a sharp knife, gently tease the skin away from the ham and remove in one whole piece. Store it with this piece of skin over the exposed ham to keep it moist in a damp ham bag or pillowcase in the coolest part of the fridge.

Soak the bag first in a solution of 1 litre (35 fl oz/4 cups) of water mixed with 2 teaspoons of white vinegar and wring it out well before using. Resoak the bag every two days and store the ham for up to a week. The pillowcase will help the ham to retain its moisture without sweating.

Butchery techniques

→ **Pork fats** *see pages 464–468*
→ **Pork stock** *see page 461*
→ **Charcuterie** *see pages 230–237*
→ **Christmas ham** *see page 485*

COOKING PORK

For decades we have been told that pork must be cooked to well done. There was good reason: a parasitic worm called trichinella had found its way into the pig population and, to kill it, the authorities had deemed high temperatures as the solution. The good news is twofold: firstly, they have discovered that a little under 60°C (140°F) is sufficient to kill the parasite; secondly, the parasite has been largely eradicated in farmed pork. Today's lean pork will taste a million times better when cooked to medium, which is not only safe, but now USDA approved (since 2011). Medium, with an internal temperature of 60–65°C (140–150°F) and a touch of pink in the middle, is what you should be aiming for.

PERFECT PORK CRACKLING

A favourite part of the pig for many, crackling is a porcine treat like no other. How do you ensure the perfect crackling? Essentially, crackling is created by melting away (or rendering) the excess moisture in the fat, leaving a bubbly, crackly, salty treat. Crackling can be made from almost any cut of the pig, as long as the fat and skin is attached. To our mind the best cut of all for crackling is the loin.

There are many methods for the best crackling, with a few certainties:

1. Score the skin at 1 cm (½ inch) intervals, making sure you cut through the skin but not the flesh). A clean craft (Stanley) knife is ideal for this. If you are unsure of yourself, ask your butcher to do this for you.
2. In many respects, the refrigerator is crackling's best friend, as the dry air encourages a crisp, bubbly crackling. Store pork uncovered in the fridge the night before you plan to cook it, or even a few hours before will help. If you don't have time to do this, make sure you have patted the pork dry, as moisture is the enemy.
3. Salt the skin liberally, massaging it into the slits. You can add fennel seeds or the like to this process for extra flavour.

And here's where it gets controversial! You could cook the crackling separately: ask your butcher to provide you with your crackling separate from the loin, in a large piece. Score and salt as above. Lay it scored-side down on a tea towel (dish towel) in the fridge overnight. It is very important that you leave it uncovered. Now it's ready to go, simply lay the crackling scored-side up on a baking tray and cook in a preheated hot oven, until crisp.

Alternatively, you can score, dry and salt the skin (still attached to the meat) and then fry it, scored-side down, in very hot oil in a pan on the stovetop. If you add pressure (pushing down on the meat, being careful of the spitting oil) you will encourage extra blistering, forcing it to pop under the pressure. Once the desired level of crackling has been achieved all over (and not a moment before) transfer the roasting joint to your preheated oven.

Finally, to carve pork, place it crackling-side down, allowing you to carve through the pork meat and then, with one swift movement, cut through the crackling.

→ *Pouring boiling water over the scored pork before chilling in the fridge overnight, or pouring hot fat over the cooked pork can also help make your crackling crisp.*

→ *If your crackling is not up to scratch, a carefully monitored blast under a hot grill will help.*

→ *Keep in mind that the crackling will firm up as it rests, so be sure to rest crackling-side up and very loosely covered. Any containment will steam the pork and ruin your hard work.*

PRESERVED MEAT

The French have always understood the virtues of the pig, and tout est
bon dans le cochon *(everything is good in the pig) has long been a catch
cry of the charcutiers. They have worked hard to make it so. The pig is
often thought to be at its best when cured: bacon, pancetta,
ham and prosciutto, salami, sausages.*

Cured meats fall into two categories: those obtained from a whole cut of meat,
such as a belly or shoulder (*prosciutto, pancetta, coppa*); and those obtained from
minced, ground or chopped meat that is stuffed into casings (salami, sausages).
There are three options for preservation: salt with herbs and spices; in a brine of
salt and sugar; or smoking. Originally intended as a way to extend the shelf-life of
pork, charcuterie products have become a delicacy in their own right.

Apart from traditional cuts (belly, neck and loin) there are the tail, ears and
intestines (used for sausage casings). Pig's liver is used for terrines and pig's trotters
are the best source of natural gelatine. Across the globe it is standard to use many
other pork innards and even the snout.

→ *The charcutiers were among the
first recognised French trade guilds.
In the fifteenth century, they were
granted the right to sell a range of
traditional cooked or salted and
dried meats, the range differing
from region to region.*

THE CARCASS

The **back legs** will commonly be salted and hung in an airy attic for between six
and 36 months: the resulting sweet, nutty ham, prosciutto or *jamon* is well worth
the wait. The **belly**, **neck** and **jowl** may be cured in salt and spices to become
pancetta, capocollo and *guanciale* respectively; while the firm white lard along the
pig's **back** will be salt cured with rosemary to become *lardo* or salted and smoked
(as in Russia and the Ukraine) to make *salo*, both served in fine slices on toast.

The **tenderloin** muscle and rack will be kept for fast cooking—the traditional family
roast—and the harder-working muscles, such as the **shoulder**, will be minced to
make sausages or salamis, stuffed into the clean intestines (these casings provide
just enough air to cure the meat without allowing bacteria to penetrate).

The **blood** will be used for *boudin noir* or black pudding, while the **liver** and other
offal may find its way into wursts, terrines and pâtés; rillettes are made from
everything that is left, the meat slowly cooked in its own fat, or confited, and then
carefully shredded and preserved under a layer of fat or the delicate spider's web
of *crépine* (caul fat) that also comes from within the pig.

Butchery techniques

→ **Pork fats** *see pages 464–468*

→ **Salt** *see pages 469–470*

→ **Smoking** *see pages 471–472*

FRENCH CHARCUTERIE

French charcutiers make the following from the pig:

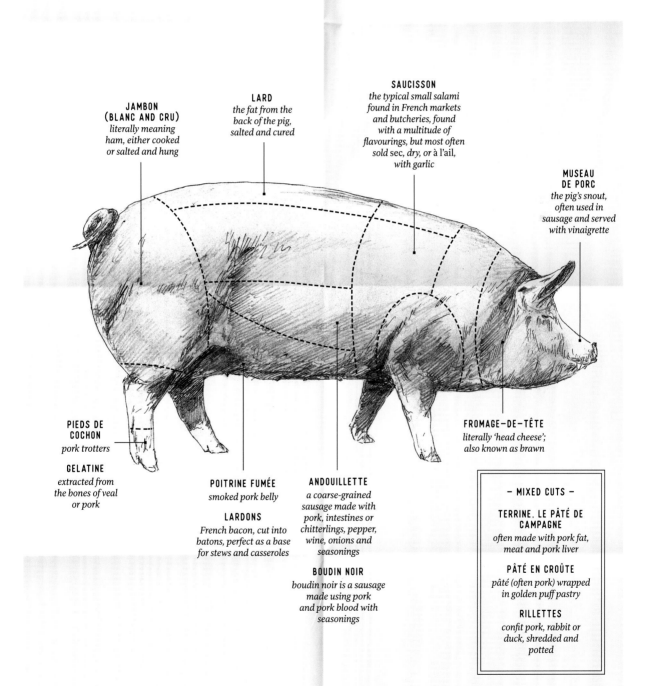

**JAMBON
(BLANC AND CRU)**
*literally meaning
ham, either cooked
or salted and hung*

LARD
*the fat from the
back of the pig,
salted and cured*

SAUCISSON
*the typical small salami
found in French markets
and butcheries, found
with a multitude of
flavourings, but most often
sold sec, dry, or à l'ail,
with garlic*

**MUSEAU
DE PORC**
*the pig's snout,
often used in
sausage and served
with vinaigrette*

**PIEDS DE
COCHON**
pork trotters

GELATINE
*extracted from
the bones of veal
or pork*

POITRINE FUMÉE
smoked pork belly

LARDONS
*French bacon, cut into
batons, perfect as a base
for stews and casseroles*

ANDOUILLETTE
*a coarse-grained
sausage made with
pork, intestines or
chitterlings, pepper,
wine, onions and
seasonings*

BOUDIN NOIR
*boudin noir is a sausage
made using pork
and pork blood with
seasonings*

FROMAGE-DE-TÊTE
*literally 'head cheese';
also known as brawn*

- MIXED CUTS -

**TERRINE, LE PÂTÉ DE
CAMPAGNE**
*often made with pork fat,
meat and pork liver*

PÂTÉ EN CROÛTE
*pâté (often pork) wrapped
in golden puff pastry*

RILLETTES
*confit pork, rabbit or
duck, shredded and
potted*

ITALIAN CHARCUTERIE

Italian salumieri preserve the parts of the pig as follows:

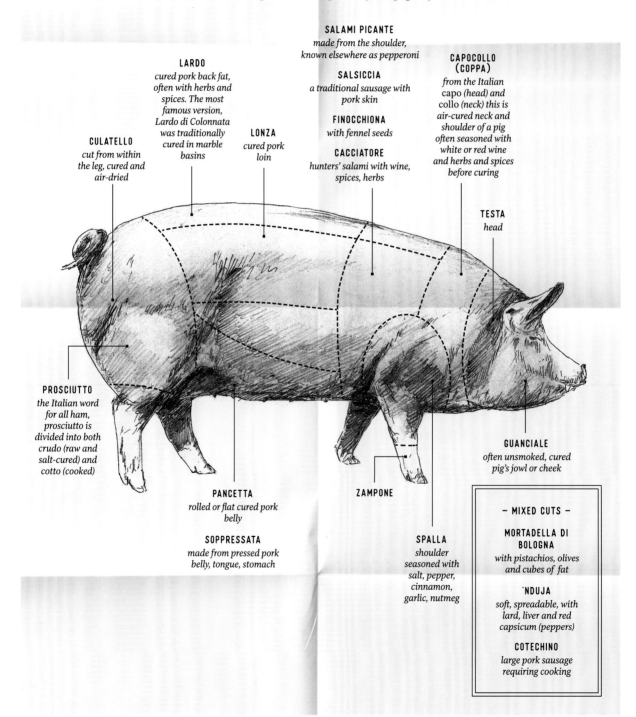

SALAMI PICANTE
made from the shoulder, known elsewhere as pepperoni

CAPOCOLLO (COPPA)
from the Italian capo (head) and collo (neck) this is air-cured neck and shoulder of a pig often seasoned with white or red wine and herbs and spices before curing

LARDO
cured pork back fat, often with herbs and spices. The most famous version, Lardo di Colonnata was traditionally cured in marble basins

SALSICCIA
a traditional sausage with pork skin

FINOCCHIONA
with fennel seeds

CACCIATORE
hunters' salami with wine, spices, herbs

CULATELLO
cut from within the leg, cured and air-dried

LONZA
cured pork loin

TESTA
head

PROSCIUTTO
the Italian word for all ham, prosciutto is divided into both crudo (raw and salt-cured) and cotto (cooked)

GUANCIALE
often unsmoked, cured pig's jowl or cheek

PANCETTA
rolled or flat cured pork belly

ZAMPONE

SOPPRESSATA
made from pressed pork belly, tongue, stomach

SPALLA
shoulder seasoned with salt, pepper, cinnamon, garlic, nutmeg

- MIXED CUTS -

MORTADELLA DI BOLOGNA
with pistachios, olives and cubes of fat

'NDUJA
soft, spreadable, with lard, liver and red capsicum (peppers)

COTECHINO
large pork sausage requiring cooking

SPANISH CHARCUTERIE

Spanish salchicheros make the following:

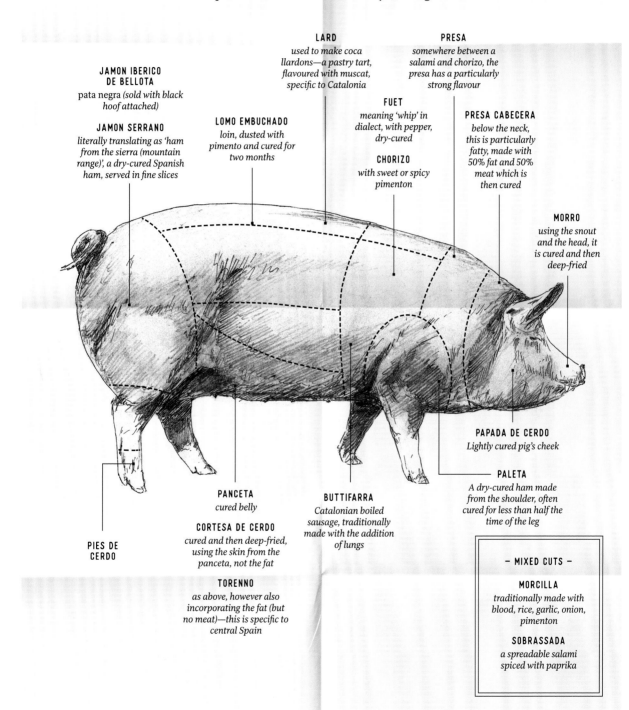

LARD
used to make coca llardons—a pastry tart, flavoured with muscat, specific to Catalonia

PRESA
somewhere between a salami and chorizo, the presa has a particularly strong flavour

JAMON IBERICO DE BELLOTA
pata negra *(sold with black hoof attached)*

JAMON SERRANO
literally translating as 'ham from the sierra (mountain range)', a dry-cured Spanish ham, served in fine slices

LOMO EMBUCHADO
loin, dusted with pimento and cured for two months

FUET
meaning 'whip' in dialect, with pepper, dry-cured

CHORIZO
with sweet or spicy pimenton

PRESA CABECERA
below the neck, this is particularly fatty, made with 50% fat and 50% meat which is then cured

MORRO
using the snout and the head, it is cured and then deep-fried

PAPADA DE CERDO
Lightly cured pig's cheek

PALETA
A dry-cured ham made from the shoulder, often cured for less than half the time of the leg

PANCETA
cured belly

CORTESA DE CERDO
cured and then deep-fried, using the skin from the panceta, not the fat

TORENNO
as above, however also incorporating the fat (but no meat)—this is specific to central Spain

BUTTIFARRA
Catalonian boiled sausage, traditionally made with the addition of lungs

PIES DE CERDO

— MIXED CUTS —

MORCILLA
traditionally made with blood, rice, garlic, onion, pimenton

SOBRASSADA
a spreadable salami spiced with paprika**

PRESERVED MEAT HERITAGE MAP

BRITAIN AND IRELAND

ENGLAND

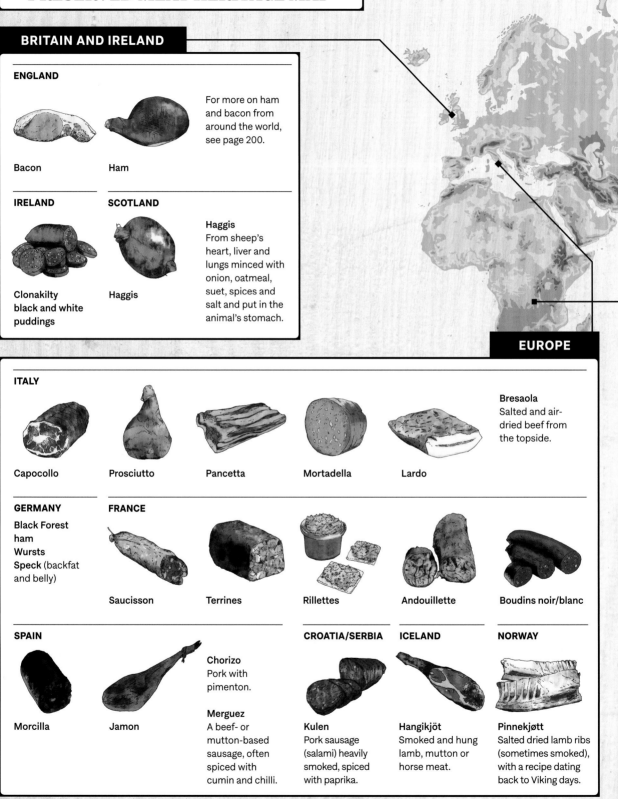

Bacon

Ham

For more on ham and bacon from around the world, see page 200.

IRELAND

Clonakilty black and white puddings

SCOTLAND

Haggis

Haggis
From sheep's heart, liver and lungs minced with onion, oatmeal, suet, spices and salt and put in the animal's stomach.

EUROPE

ITALY

Capocollo

Prosciutto

Pancetta

Mortadella

Lardo

Bresaola
Salted and air-dried beef from the topside.

GERMANY

Black Forest ham
Wursts
Speck (backfat and belly)

FRANCE

Saucisson

Terrines

Rillettes

Andouillette

Boudins noir/blanc

SPAIN

Morcilla

Jamon

Chorizo
Pork with pimenton.

Merguez
A beef- or mutton-based sausage, often spiced with cumin and chilli.

CROATIA/SERBIA

Kulen
Pork sausage (salami) heavily smoked, spiced with paprika.

ICELAND

Hangikjöt
Smoked and hung lamb, mutton or horse meat.

NORWAY

Pinnekjøtt
Salted dried lamb ribs (sometimes smoked), with a recipe dating back to Viking days.

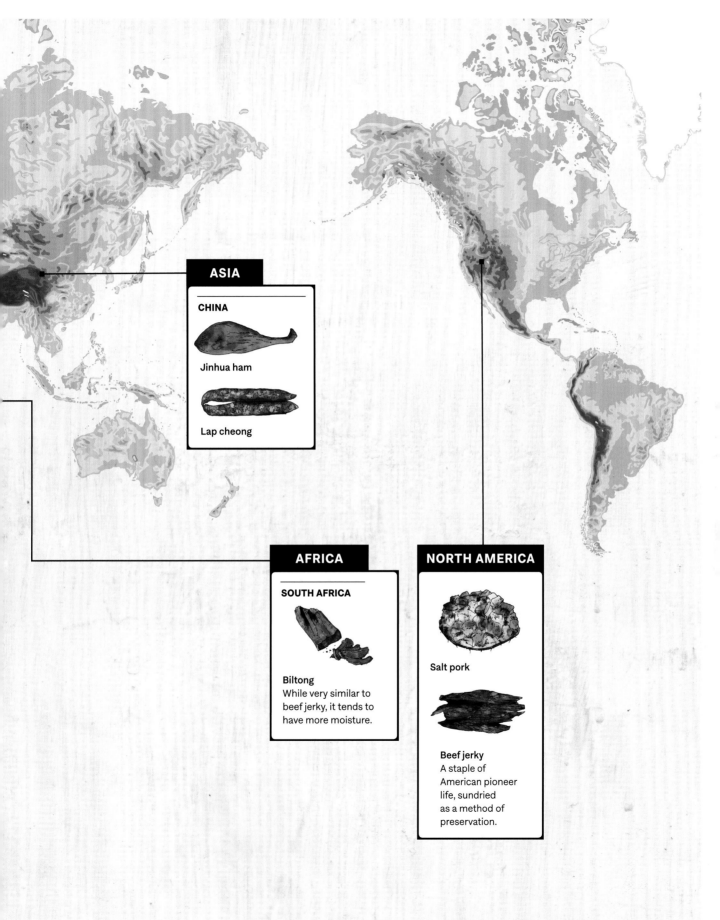

ASIA

CHINA

Jinhua ham

Lap cheong

AFRICA

SOUTH AFRICA

Biltong
While very similar to beef jerky, it tends to have more moisture.

NORTH AMERICA

Salt pork

Beef jerky
A staple of American pioneer life, sundried as a method of preservation.

Salami

Finocchiona
(Salame De Palma)

SPAGHETTI ALLA CARBONARA

Prep time *10 minutes*
Cook *10 minutes*

1. Cook the spaghetti in a large saucepan of well-salted boiling water for 8–10 minutes until al dente.

2. Meanwhile, render the fat from the guanciale in a large frying pan over medium–high heat, adding a splash of oil if necessary to the pan. Stir occasionally for 3–4 minutes until starting to crisp. Use a slotted spoon to transfer the guanciale from the pan to a plate, then remove the pan from the heat.

3. Whisk the eggs and pecorino together in a bowl and season with salt and pepper.

4. Drain the pasta, reserving 2 tablespoons of the cooking water, and put the pasta into the frying pan with the fat from the guanciale.

5. Whisk the reserved pasta water into the egg mixture, to help temper it and bring it to a similar temperature to the pasta. Add to the pasta and toss immediately for 20–30 seconds until the pasta is coated and sauce begins to thicken. Toss the guanciale through and season with plenty of freshly ground black pepper to taste. Check the seasoning (you may need to add a little extra salt, depending on the saltiness of the guanciale and pecorino). Serve immediately, scattered with extra pecorino.

INGREDIENTS

200 g (7 oz) piece of guanciale, skin removed and discarded, cut into 1 cm x 3 cm (½ inch x 1¼ inch) lardons (see note)
400 g (14 oz) dried spaghetti
Mild-flavoured extra virgin olive oil
4 eggs, lightly whisked
40 g (1½ oz) finely grated pecorino cheese, plus extra to serve
Freshly ground black pepper

NOTES

→ *Guanciale is an Italian cured pork cheek or jowl, aged for several months. It is available from specialist butchers and selected delicatessens. Alternatively, use pancetta or bacon.*

→ *For a richer sauce, add an extra egg yolk to the egg mixture.*

Cut Pig cheek
See page 220

SERVES 8

STUFFED PIGS' EARS

Prep time *45 minutes*
Cook *3 hours 10 minutes*

A beautiful, patient and nurturing man as well as an excellent chef, Janni is a true stalwart of the industry. His book, published a little while back, is definitely worth seeking out.

1. Using a pair of tongs, hold pigs' ears over an open flame to singe off any hairs. Don't leave them over the flame any longer than necessary; if the skin burns it will have an unpleasant taste. Wash thoroughly and put in a saucepan with carrots, onion, celery, garlic, bay leaves, parsley, salt, pepper, vinegar and enough water to cover. Bring to the boil, reduce heat and simmer for 2–3 hours, until a skewer goes easily through the cartilage. Leave in the cooking liquid until cool enough to handle.

2. Meanwhile, prepare stuffing by soaking the sweetbreads in plenty of salted water for 1 hour. Drain. Place sweetbreads in saucepan with chicken stock, bring to the boil, reduce heat and simmer to 10 minutes. Remove sweetbreads from stock and squeeze gently to remove excess liquid. Return stock to the saucepan and set aside. When sweetbreads are cool enough to handle, gently peel off and discard the surrounding membrane and divide into small pieces.

3. Melt butter in a large frying pan and fry onions until golden. Add mushrooms and cook for a few minutes until they are soft and most of the liquid has evaporated. Add wine to the reserved stock, bring to the boil, then simmer until reduced to a quarter of its volume—it should look like a thick sauce. Remove from heat and stir in mushroom and onion mixture, sweetbreads, ham, thyme, parsley, salt and pepper. Allow to cool.

4. Remove an ear from the cooking liquid and trim base to form a neat triangle. Using a small knife and your fingers, carefully make a pocket in the ear between the skin and one side of the cartilage. Fill the pocket with one-eighth of the stuffing. Wrap in plastic film and refrigerate cartilage-side down. Repeat with remaining ears and stuffing.

5. Preheat oven to 220°C (425°F). When ears are completely cold and set, remove from fridge. Brush both sides of ears with melted butter and cover well with breadcrumbs. Place ears on a non-stick baking tray, cartilage-side down, and bake for about 10 minutes, until golden brown.

INGREDIENTS

8 pigs' ears
2 medium carrots, roughly chopped
1 large brown onion, roughly chopped
½ stick celery, roughly chopped
6 cloves garlic, peeled
2 dried bay leaves
2 sprigs flat-leaf (Italian) parsley
125 ml (4 fl oz/½ cup) white wine vinegar
18 tablespoons (250 g) butter, melted
2 cups fresh breadcrumbs

Stuffing
500 g (1 lb 2 oz) veal sweetbreads
250 ml (9 fl oz/1 cup) chicken stock
9 tablespoons (125 g) butter
2 large brown onions, chopped
500 g (1 lb 2 oz) button mushrooms, diced
250 ml (9 fl oz/1 cup) dry white wine
250 g (9 oz) ham, diced
1 tablespoon chopped thyme leaves
½ cup chopped flat-leaf parsley leaves

SERVING SUGGESTION — *watercress salad and dijon mustard*

NOTE
→ *From* Wild Weed Pie, *by Janni Kyritsis (Penguin Books, 2006).*

Cut Pigs' ears
See page 220

~ LEXINGTON-STYLE ~
PULLED PORK

Prep time *40 minutes (plus marinating)*
Cook *7½ hours (plus resting)*

1. To make the spice rub, mix the ingredients in a bowl to combine. Rub thoroughly into the pork, massaging well into the meat. Set aside at room temperature for 1 hour.

2. To make the mop sauce, whisk the ingredients together in a bowl. Mix half of the mop sauce with the apple juice and reserve the remaining mop sauce for serving.

3. Set up a kettle barbecue for indirect grilling, with coals on one side and a foil pan filled with water on the other, and add 3–4 applewood chunks to the coals. Cover the barbecue with a lid for 10–15 minutes to heat and for the wood to smoke.

4. Place the pork on the barbecue over the foil pan. Cover and cook for 4 hours, topping up the fire with coals as necessary to maintain the temperature at 130°C (250°F). Scratch the surface of the meat to check if the spice rub has set (this is called the bark); if the bark isn't set, cook for another 30 minutes and check again.

5. Once the bark sets, continue cooking, basting with the apple juice mixture every half hour and topping up coals as necessary, for 3–3½ hours, or until very tender.

6. Wrap the pork loosely in foil and set aside to rest for 30 minutes: if there are any basting juices left, add these to the foil parcel.

7. While the pork rests, make the red cabbage slaw. Whisk the vinegar and mayonnaise in a large bowl until combined and season with salt and pepper to taste, adding a splash of the mop sauce if you like. Add the cabbage, apple and onion and toss to combine. Scatter the parsley on top.

8. Pull the pork into large pieces (discarding any fat and sinew). Transfer the pulled pork and resting juices to a bowl and run a knife once or twice through the meat to cut up any longer bits of muscle. Drizzle with the reserved mop sauce and mix well to combine. Serve with red cabbage slaw and soft rolls.

INGREDIENTS

4 kg (9 lb) bone-in skinless Boston butt (including neck)
200 ml (7 fl oz) apple juice
Buttered soft bread rolls, to serve

Mop sauce
250 ml (9 fl oz/1 cup) apple cider vinegar
125 ml (4 fl oz/½ cup) tomato ketchup
60 g (2¼ oz/¼ cup) American mustard
2 tablespoons Worcestershire sauce
2 teaspoons of your favourite hot sauce, such as Cholula or Tabasco
Juice of 1 lemon

Spice rub
1 tablespoon sweet paprika
1 tablespoon soft brown sugar
1 tablespoon sea salt
2 teaspoons mustard powder
2 teaspoons ground black pepper
1–2 teaspoons ground cayenne
½ teaspoon ground cinnamon

Red cabbage slaw
80 ml (2½ fl oz/⅓ cup) apple cider vinegar
80 g (2¾ oz/⅓ cup) mayonnaise
1 small red cabbage, thinly sliced
2 pink lady apples, julienned
1 red onion, thinly sliced
1 handful of flat-leaf (Italian) parsley, coarsely chopped

NOTE

➜ *You'll need natural charcoal and applewood chunks for this recipe.*

Cut *Pork shoulder*
See page 220

RAISED PORK PIE

Prep time *1 hour (plus chilling)*
Cook *5 hours (plus resting, cooling)*

1. To make the jellied stock, combine all ingredients in a large saucepan. Boil, then reduce the heat to medium and simmer, skimming any scum from the surface, for 2–2½ hours. Strain into a clean saucepan and boil for 25–30 minutes until reduced to 300 ml (10½ fl oz). Refrigerate until the stock sets to jelly.

2. Meanwhile, make the pie filling. Fry half the lardons, add the onion and fry for 4–5 minutes, adding garlic in the final minute. Add the mace and nutmeg and cook for 30 seconds until fragrant. Transfer to a bowl to cool, then add the minced pork.

3. Add the pork shoulder and belly to the onion mixture with the thyme, sage, pepper, salt and remaining lardons. Use your hands to mix well. Fry a pinch of the pork mixture, cooking it through. Taste and adjust the seasoning if necessary. As the pie is served cold and the flavours will be muted, season generously. Cover the mixture and refrigerate for 2–3 hours.

4. Meanwhile, make the hot-water pastry. Put the flour mixture in a heatproof bowl. Put the lard with 350 ml (12 fl oz) of water in a saucepan over low heat, stirring until melted. Increase heat to high, bring to a boil, then use a wooden spoon to beat it into the flour until the pastry comes together. When it's cool enough to handle, knead on a lightly floured work surface until smooth.

5. Preheat the oven to 180°C (350°F). Roll out three-quarters of the pastry to 5 mm (¼ inch) thick and line the base and side of a 10 cm (4 inch) deep x 20 cm (8 inch) diameter spring-form cake tin, allowing 1 cm (½ inch) to overhang the edge.

6. Fill with pork mixture, flattening the top. Brush the edges of the pastry with egg wash. Roll out remaining pastry to 5 mm (¼ inch) thick, cut out a 22 cm (8½ inch) disc and lay it on top. Press the pastry together, trim and crimp edges with a fork. Cut out a 1 cm (½ inch) hole in the centre and brush with egg wash.

7. Bake for 30 minutes, then reduce the heat to 160°C (315°F) and bake for 1¼ hours. Carefully remove the side of the spring-form tin, brush the pastry side with egg wash and bake for 20–25 minutes until golden brown. The internal temperature should read 67°C (153°F). Set aside to cool to room temperature.

8. Warm the jellied stock in a saucepan over low heat and season with salt and pepper. Transfer to a jug and gradually pour the stock into the pie through a funnel inserted through the hole in the lid, tilting the pie to help distribute the stock and letting the stock settle before adding more if necessary.

9. Refrigerate for 3–4 hours until the jelly sets and then store in the refrigerator for up to 2 weeks.

INGREDIENTS

750 g (1 lb 10 oz) coarsely minced (ground) boneless pork shoulder

500 g (1 lb 2 oz) boneless pork shoulder (or bone it yourself and reserve the bones for the jellied stock), cut into 5 mm (¼ inch) cubes

250 g (9 oz) skinless boneless pork belly, cut into 5 mm (¼ inch) cubes

150 g (5½ oz) bacon lardons

1 small brown onion, finely chopped

2 garlic cloves, finely chopped

1¼ teaspoons ground mace

¾ teaspoon freshly grated nutmeg

6 thyme sprigs, leaves picked

1½ tablespoons finely chopped sage

2½ teaspoons freshly ground black pepper

1¼ tablespoons sea salt

1 egg, whisked with 1 tablespoon milk, for egg wash

Jellied stock

2 pork trotters, split

1 brown onion, coarsely chopped

1 carrot, coarsely chopped

1 celery stalk, coarsely chopped

3 thyme sprigs

1 teaspoon black peppercorns

2 litres (70 fl oz/8 cups) cold water

Hot-water pastry

550 g (1 lb 4 oz/3⅔ cups) plain (all-purpose) flour seasoned with 1½ teaspoons sea salt

150 g (5½ oz) lard

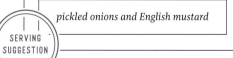

pickled onions and English mustard

SERVING
SUGGESTION

Cut Pork shoulder
See page 220

SERVES 6
~ FENNEL-ROASTED ~
PORK RACK

Prep time *30 minutes (plus overnight drying)*
Cook *1 hour 15 minutes (plus resting)*

1. Score the pork skin at 1 cm (½ inch) intervals with a sharp knife or scalpel, being careful not to cut through to the meat. You could ask your butcher to do this for you.
2. Combine the garlic, orange and lemon zest, 1 tablespoon of the oil and half the fennel seeds in a bowl, season with salt and pepper and rub all over the pork meat. Place the rack skin-side up on a tray.
3. Combine the sea salt and the remaining fennel seeds in a bowl, then rub all over the pork skin. Refrigerate uncovered overnight for the skin to dry out. Remove it from the refrigerator 2 hours before cooking to come to room temperature.
4. Preheat the oven to 220°C (425°F). Combine the potatoes, fennel wedges, onion, half the orange juice and remaining oil in a roasting tin and season generously with salt and pepper. Set the vegetables on the lowest rack of the oven. Place the pork, skin-side up, on a clean, lightly oiled oven rack, directly over the vegetables: all the beautiful fat and juices will drip into the tray. Roast for 20–30 minutes until the skin begins to crisp and crackling forms.
5. Reduce the oven temperature to 160°C (315°F) and leave the door ajar slightly for a few minutes to help the oven to cool. Continue to roast the pork, turning occasionally if necessary so it cooks and crackles evenly, for 40–45 minutes until cooked to medium: internal temperature will read 58°C (136°F) and the meat will continue to cook as it rests. Cover the pork very loosely with foil and set aside to rest for 30 minutes. Cover the vegetables with foil and keep them warm.
6. To carve, place the pork crackling-side down on a board and slice between the rib bones. Squeeze the orange and lemon juices into the resting juices. Serve the pork with roasted vegetables and resting juices, scattered with fennel fronds.

INGREDIENTS

6-rib pork rack, skin on, about 1.5 kg (3 lb 5 oz)
1 garlic clove, finely chopped
Finely grated zest and juice of 1 orange
Finely grated zest and juice of ½ lemon
2½ tablespoons olive oil
1 tablespoon fennel seeds
2 teaspoons sea salt
1 kg (2 lb 4 oz) sebago potatoes, cut into large wedges
2 small fennel bulbs, tough outer layer removed, cut into wedges, fronds reserved
1 brown onion or red onion, cut into wedges

NOTES
→ You'll need to begin this recipe a day ahead to allow the pork skin to dry out and create crisp crackling.

→ To calculate the cooking time for cooking pork rack, after the initial 20 minutes at high temperature, allow 15 minutes per 450 g (1 lb) for medium. The meat will continue to cook as it rests.

→ Any leftover pork and crackling are excellent in sandwiches. If there are leftover roast vegetables too, try making a salad: toss with bitter leaves, leftover sliced pork and a simple vinaigrette dressing.

Cut *Pork rack*
See page 221

SERVES 4

PORK CUTLETS
~ WITH JUNIPER AND ROSEMARY ~

Prep time *25 minutes*
Cook *40 minutes (plus resting)*

1. Remove pork cutlets from refrigerator 30 minutes before cooking to come to room temperature.

2. To make the celeriac purée, put the celeriac, milk and garlic in a saucepan with enough cold water to cover. Bring to the boil, then reduce the heat to medium and simmer for 12–15 minutes, until the celeriac is tender when pierced with the tip of a sharp knife.

3. Drain the celeriac (reserving the garlic and a little of the cooking liquid). Transfer the celeriac and garlic to a food processor with the butter. Purée until smooth, adding a little of the reserved cooking liquid if necessary, and season with salt and pepper. Keep warm.

4. Meanwhile, coarsely crush the juniper, peppercorns and rosemary using a mortar and pestle or with the flat side of your knife. Massage into both sides of the pork cutlets. Season generously with sea salt.

5. Heat a large heavy-based frying pan over medium–high heat. Working with one chop at a time, cook the edge of the cutlet by holding it skin-side down with tongs for 1–2 minutes to render and brown the fat. You should end up with about 1 tablespoon of rendered fat in the pan, which will be enough to cook the chops, but add a splash of olive oil if necessary.

6. Return the chops to the pan and fry for 4–5 minutes on each side until browned and cooked to medium. Transfer to a plate and cover loosely with foil to rest while you make the sauce.

7. Tip out any excess fat from the pan and return to high heat. Pour in the wine, and boil for 1–2 minutes, scraping all the delicious browned bits from the base of the pan with a wooden spoon. Stir in the mustard and simmer for 1–2 minutes until reduced by half. If you like a creamy sauce, add the cream, simmer to combine and check the seasoning.

8. Toss the brussels sprouts, shallot and parsley in a bowl and dress with olive oil and vinegar to taste, then season with salt and pepper.

9. Serve the pork chops with the celeriac purée, pouring the sauce over the pork.

INGREDIENTS

4 pork cutlets, fat on, 2 cm (¾ inch) thick, about 230 g (8½ oz) each
1 teaspoon juniper berries
½ teaspoon black peppercorns
1 small rosemary sprig, leaves picked
150 ml (5 fl oz) dry white wine
1 teaspoon dijon mustard
A splash of pure (pouring) cream (optional)
350 g (12 oz) brussels sprouts, shaved with a mandolin
1 golden shallot, thinly sliced
1 handful of torn flat-leaf (Italian) parsley
Extra virgin olive oil and apple cider vinegar, for dressing

Celeriac purée
1 celeriac, about 800 g (1 lb 12 oz), chopped
375 ml (13 fl oz/1½ cups) milk
3 garlic cloves
7 tablespoons (100 g) butter, chopped

shaved brussels sprouts

SERVING SUGGESTION

NOTE
→ *The excess fat from the pan can be strained and reserved for your next batch of roast potatoes or croutons. Just be careful not to burn the fat, or it will have an acrid taste.*

Cut Pork cutlets
See page 221

248   PIGS

PORK TONKATSU

SERVES 4

Prep time *30 minutes (plus chilling)*
Cook *1 hour 50 minutes (plus resting)*

1. To make the tonkatsu sauce, put all of the ingredients in a saucepan with 100 ml (3½ fl oz) of water over medium-high heat and stir to combine. Bring to the boil, then reduce heat to low. Season with salt and pepper and simmer, stirring occasionally, for 1–1¼ hours until well flavoured and thickened. Purée in a blender or food processor until smooth, then add a dash of extra vinegar to brighten the flavour.
2. Use a meat mallet or rolling pin to flatten each piece of pork to an even 1.5 cm (⅝ inch) thickness.
3. Brush the pork with miso. Put the flour, beaten egg and breadcrumbs in three separate bowls. Working with one piece of pork at a time, dust pork in flour, then egg, shaking off excess. Dip into the breadcrumbs, pressing to evenly cover the pork. Lay the crumbed pork on a tray and refrigerate for 30 minutes to help set the coating.
4. Preheat the oil in a large deep saucepan to 170°C (325°F) or until a cube of bread dropped into the oil browns in 20 seconds. Deep-fry the pork, one piece at a time, turning occasionally, for 4–5 minutes until golden brown and just cooked to medium. Drain on a wire rack lined with paper towel. Rest for 5 minutes.
5. While the pork rests, make the cabbage salad. Whisk the rice vinegar, soy sauce, sesame oil and ginger in a small bowl to combine. Combine the cabbage and spring onion in a large bowl, drizzle with dressing to taste and toss lightly.
6. To serve, slice the pork across the grain, transfer to a plate and serve drizzled with tonkatsu sauce and sprinkled with sesame seeds, with the cabbage salad.

INGREDIENTS

4 pieces of pork loin 3 cm (1¼ inch) thick, about 180 g (6¼ oz) each
1 tablespoon shiro miso (white miso)
Plain (all-purpose) flour, seasoned with salt and pepper, for dusting
2 eggs, lightly beaten
80 g (2¾ oz/1⅓ cups) panko (Japanese) breadcrumbs
Vegetable oil, for deep-frying
Roasted sesame seeds, to serve

Tonkatsu sauce
185 ml (6 fl oz/¾ cup) tomato ketchup
125 ml (4 fl oz/½ cup) Worcestershire sauce
125 ml (4 fl oz/½ cup) rice vinegar, plus extra to finish
125 ml (4 fl oz/½ cup) light soy sauce
80 ml (2½ fl oz/⅓ cup) mirin
75 g (2¾ oz/⅓ cup) soft brown sugar
1 small brown onion, finely chopped
1 granny smith apple, coarsely grated
3 teaspoons finely grated fresh ginger
1 garlic clove, finely chopped
½ teaspoon dijon mustard
1 pinch each of ground cloves, ground allspice and ground cinnamon

Cabbage salad
1½ tablespoons rice vinegar
1 tablespoon light soy sauce
2 teaspoons sesame oil
2 teaspoons finely grated fresh ginger
225 g (8 oz/3 cups) thinly shaved white cabbage
2 spring onions (scallions), thinly sliced

Cut Pork loin
See page 221

PAN-FRIED PORK CHOPS
WITH APPLE AND CRUSHED POTATO

Prep time *20 minutes*
Cook *40 minutes (plus resting)*

1. Remove the pork chops from the refrigerator 30 minutes before cooking to come to room temperature.

2. To make the crushed potatoes, put the potatoes in a large saucepan with enough cold salted water to cover generously. Bring to the boil over medium–high heat and cook for 10–15 minutes until tender. Drain and return to the pan, crush lightly with a masher, add the butter and season with salt and pepper. Keep warm.

3. Heat a large heavy-based frying pan over medium–high heat. Season both sides of the pork chops generously with sea salt. Working with one chop at a time, hold with tongs fat-side down for 1–2 minutes to render and crisp the fat. You should end up with about 1 tablespoon of rendered fat in the pan.

4. Add the butter to the pan and, when it foams, add the garlic and return the chops to the pan. Pan-fry for 3–4 minutes on each side, spooning fat from the pan over the chops every now and then until they are browned and just cooked through. Transfer to a plate and cover loosely with foil to rest. Discard the garlic.

5. Add a splash of olive oil to the same pan, then add the sage and fry for 2–3 minutes until crisp. Transfer to a plate. Pour excess fat from the pan, add the apple and pan-fry, tossing occasionally, for 5–6 minutes until caramelised. Add the shallot in the last minute of cooking. Add the sugar, toss to combine and transfer to a plate.

6. Pour the cider into the pan, boil for 3–4 minutes to reduce by half, then add the vinegar and any resting juices from the pork. Return the apple mixture to the pan to reheat and season with salt and pepper.

7. Serve the rested pork chops with the crushed potato and apple sauce, scattered with the crisp sage.

INGREDIENTS

4 skinless pork loin chops, about 2.5 cm
(1 inch) thick
Sea salt
2 tablespoons (20 g) butter
2 garlic cloves, bruised with the side of
a large knife
Olive oil, for frying
2 sprigs sage leaves
2 granny smith apples, cored and
cut into wedges
1 golden shallot, thinly sliced
1 teaspoon caster (superfine) sugar
500 ml (17 fl oz/2 cups) dry apple cider
2 teaspoons apple cider vinegar, or to taste

Crushed potatoes
800 g (1 lb 12 oz) baby potatoes
4 tablespoons (50 g) butter

SERVING
SUGGESTION

*a simple frisée (curly endive)
salad or steamed green beans*

Cut Pork loin chop
See page 221

~ BARBECUED PANCETTA-WRAPPED ~
PORK TENDERLOIN

Prep time *30 minutes (plus marinating)*
Cook *20 minutes (plus resting)*

1. Combine the pork, olive oil, thyme and garlic in a bowl, season with salt and pepper and mix well to combine. Set aside to marinate for 30 minutes.

2. Meanwhile, to make the piperade, heat the olive oil in a large saucepan over high heat, add the onion and sauté for 4–5 minutes until tender and translucent, adding the garlic in the last minute of cooking. Add the tomato and capsicum and sauté, stirring frequently, for 8–10 minutes until tender, adding a splash of water if necessary. Add the vinegar and Espelette pepper and season with salt and pepper. Set aside until ready to serve.

3. Thread a slice of pancetta onto a skewer, about 1.5 cm (⅝ inch) from the end. Thread a piece of pork on next, then fold the pancetta over the top and thread the skewer through. Repeat threading and folding, so the pancetta interlaces with the pork. Repeat with remaining pancetta and pork.

4. Preheat a barbecue or chargrill pan to medium–high. Drizzle the skewers with a little extra olive oil and season with salt and pepper. Grill, turning occasionally, for 4–5 minutes until browned and cooked to medium. Rest for 5 minutes, then serve with the piperade.

INGREDIENTS

2 pork tenderloins, about 450 g (1 lb) each, cut into 2.5 cm (1 inch) cubes
1 tablespoon olive oil, plus extra for drizzling
2 teaspoons chopped thyme, plus extra leaves to serve
1 garlic clove, finely chopped
8–10 long narrow slices flat pancetta

Piperade
2½ tablespoons olive oil
1 small onion, thinly sliced
2 garlic cloves, finely chopped
4 roma (plum) tomatoes, coarsely chopped
3 capsicums (peppers), deseeded and thinly sliced: a mix of red, yellow and green works well
1 tablespoon red wine vinegar
½ teaspoon Espelette pepper (see note) or hot paprika

NOTES

→ *Espelette pepper is a type of dried chilli from the Basque region of France. It has a mild heat and full fruity flavour. It is available from selected spice specialty shops and delicatessens.*

→ *If using bamboo skewers, soak them in water for 20 minutes before using, to prevent them burning.*

Cut Tenderloin
See page 221

*Glazed Christmas ham
(see pages 258–259).*

SERVES 10–12 WITH SOME LEFTOVERS

GLAZED CHRISTMAS HAM

Prep time *20 minutes*
Cook *1½ hours (plus resting)*

INGREDIENTS

1 leg ham on the bone, about 7 kg (16 lb 12 oz)

NOTES

→ *For step-by-step photographs of this technique, see page 485.*

→ *To store any leftover ham, cover with the reserved skin and place in a muslin (cheesecloth) ham bag or clean pillowcase. Soak the bag first in a light vinegar solution—1 litre (35 fl oz/4 cups) of water mixed with 2 teaspoons of white vinegar—and wring out well before using. Resoak the bag every 2 days and store the ham for up to 1 week.*

1. Prepare your choice of glaze according to the instructions on the opposite page and set aside.

2. To prepare the ham, carefully peel the skin from the fat, starting at the rounded edge: you may need to start with an incision with your knife. Using your fingers, carefully tease and separate the skin from the fat, working back toward the shank. Be careful not to tear the fat.

3. Use a sharp knife to score around the shank, then detach the skin and reserve (use it to cover leftover ham to prevent it from drying out).

4. Score the fat (being careful not to cut into the flesh) evenly with a small sharp knife, maintaining an even depth all over: you can score in parallel lines or in a crosshatch pattern. If you plan to stud the ham with cloves, a crosshatch pattern is the best option.

5. Preheat the oven to 180°C (350°F). Place the ham in a large roasting tin with 250 ml (9 fl oz/1 cup) of water, then follow the glazing and basting instructions for your choice of glaze on the following page, and roast for 1–1½ hours until sticky, golden brown and warmed through. Rest for 30 minutes.

6. To carve the ham easily, make a vertical cut just below the skin on the shank and through to the bone. Cut out a wedge at a 45 degree angle (this can then be sliced), then slice the ham as thickly as you like, ensuring that each slice has some of the glaze.

Cut *Pig's leg (ham)*
See page 222

CIDER AND MUSTARD GLAZE

Combine 750 ml (26 fl oz/3 cups) of dry apple cider, 2 tablespoons of dijon mustard, 55 g (2 oz) of soft brown sugar and a pinch of ground ginger in a saucepan over medium–high heat. Stir and simmer for 20–30 minutes to thicken slightly. Place the ham in a roasting tin and brush with glaze, pouring any remaining glaze over for basting. Roast, basting occasionally with pan juices, until golden brown and warmed through.

PINEAPPLE, RUM AND STAR ANISE

Combine 250 ml (9 fl oz/1 cup) of pineapple juice, 100 g (3½ oz) of soft brown sugar, 60 ml (2 fl oz/¼ cup) of golden rum, 1 tablespoon of dijon mustard, 3 whole star anise and 1 finely chopped bird's eye chilli in a saucepan over medium–high heat and bring to the boil. Place the ham in a roasting tin and brush with the glaze, pouring any remaining glaze over for basting. Roast, basting occasionally with pan juices, until golden brown and warmed through.

QUINCE AND ORANGE GLAZE

Stir 150 g (5½ oz) of quince paste, 60 ml (2 fl oz/¼ cup) of dry white wine, the juice of 1 orange, 1 tablespoon of sherry vinegar and 2 cinnamon sticks in a small saucepan over medium–high heat until melted and smooth. Add 80 g (2¾ oz) of soft brown sugar and stir until dissolved. Season with salt and pepper. Place the ham in a roasting tin and brush with the glaze, pouring any remaining glaze over for basting. Roast, basting occasionally with pan juices, until golden brown and warmed through.

SPICED MAPLE GLAZE

Combine 250 ml (9 fl oz/1 cup) of maple syrup, 120 g (4¼ oz) of soft brown sugar, 80 ml (2½ fl oz/⅓ cup) apple cider vinegar, ½ teaspoon ground cloves, ½ teaspoon ground cinnamon and ½ teaspoon ground ginger in a saucepan over medium–high heat. Bring to a simmer and cook for 5–6 minutes until slightly thickened. Place the ham in a roasting tin and brush with the glaze, pouring any remaining glaze over for basting. Roast, basting occasionally with pan juices, until golden brown and warmed through.

MARMALADE GLAZE

Process 250 ml (9 fl oz/1 cup) of freshly squeezed orange juice, 160 g (5¾ oz/½ cup) of marmalade, 100 ml (3½ fl oz) of golden rum, 1 tablespoon finely grated fresh ginger, 1 garlic clove, 1 fresh bay leaf and ½ teaspoon of ground cloves in a food processor until very smooth, then season with salt and pepper. Place the ham in a roasting tin and brush with the glaze, pouring any remaining glaze over for basting. Roast, basting occasionally with pan juices, until golden brown and warmed through.

STICKY CARAMEL PORK BELLY
~ WITH CHILLI AND LIME ~

Prep time *25 minutes*
Cook *2 hours*

1. Heat the vegetable oil in a large heavy-based frying pan or wok over medium–high heat. Add the coriander root, garlic, chillies and shallot and stir-fry for 2–3 minutes until fragrant.
2. Add the pork, palm sugar, fish sauce, soy sauce and 200 ml (7 fl oz) of water and bring to a simmer. Reduce the heat to medium and simmer, half-covered with a lid, stirring occasionally, for 1–1½ hours until the pork is almost tender. Remove the lid and simmer for a further 15–20 minutes until the pork is glazed in caramel.
3. Add the lime juice and check the seasoning: it should be a balance of hot, sour, sweet and salty. If necessary, adjust with more chilli, lime juice, palm sugar or fish sauce to your liking. Scatter with coriander leaves, sliced chilli and extra shallot, and serve with steamed rice and lime halves.

INGREDIENTS

800 g (1 lb 12 oz) boneless pork belly, cut into 2.5 cm (1 inch) cubes

3 teaspoons vegetable oil

6 coriander (cilantro) roots with some stem attached, soaked and finely chopped, leaves reserved to serve

1 garlic bulb, cloves separated, peeled and bruised with the flat of a knife

3 long red chillies, split lengthways

3 red Asian shallots, thinly sliced, plus extra to serve

110 g (3¾ oz/½ cup) grated light palm sugar (jaggery)

60 ml (2 fl oz/¼ cup) fish sauce

60 ml (2 fl oz/¼ cup) light soy sauce

Juice of 1 lime, plus extra halves to serve

Steamed jasmine rice and thinly sliced bird's eye chillies, to serve

SERVING SUGGESTION

a green mango salad

Cut Pork belly
See page 222

SERVES 6
PETIT SALÉ
AUX LENTILLES

Prep time *25 minutes (plus curing)*
Cook *3 hours 20 minutes*

1. To make the curing mixture, process the ingredients in a food processor to combine, or coarsely pound using a mortar and pestle.

2. Put the pork belly in a ceramic or glass dish and rub it all over with the curing mixture. Cover with plastic wrap and refrigerate to cure for 4 hours for a light salting, or up to 6 hours for a slightly heavier cure.

3. Rinse off the cure and transfer the pork to a large enamelled cast-iron casserole, skin-side down, along with the bouquet garni and enough cold water to cover by about 5 cm (2 inches). Place a plate on top to keep it submerged. Bring to a simmer, half-cover with a lid and cook for 2 hours, skimming occasionally.

4. Turn the pork over in the casserole, add the shallots, celery, carrot and potato and top up with a little extra water if necessary to just cover the vegetables. Simmer for 45–60 minutes until pork and vegetables are just tender.

5. Add the lentils to the pan and simmer for 15–20 minutes until just tender. Discard the bouquet garni and season with salt and pepper. Stir the chopped parsley through the lentils and scatter with thyme leaves.

INGREDIENTS

1 kg (2 lb 4 oz) piece of pork belly, skin on
Bouquet garni, made with 5 thyme sprigs,
    4 parsley stalks and 2 fresh bay leaves,
    tied together with kitchen string
6 golden shallots, halved
2 celery stalks, cut into 5 cm (2 inch) lengths
2 carrots, cut into 4 cm (1½ inch) chunks
2 waxy potatoes, thickly sliced
250 g (9 oz) tiny blue-green lentils
2 tablespoons finely chopped flat-leaf
    (Italian) parsley
Thyme leaves, to serve

Curing mixture
170 g (6 oz/1⅓ cups) sea salt
1½ tablespoons soft brown sugar
2 fresh bay leaves
1 teaspoon each of juniper berries and cloves
½ teaspoon ground allspice
1 garlic clove

SERVING SUGGESTION

*dijon mustard or freshly grated
horseradish, crusty bread*

NOTE

→ *You will need to allow time for the pork to cure, for between four and six hours. Once the pork is cured, you can rinse off the cure and start the recipe the following day if you like.*

Cut *Pork belly*
See page 222

PORCHETTA

Prep time *30 minutes*
(plus overnight drying)
Cook *1 hour 40 minutes (plus resting)*

1. Score the pork skin at 5 mm (¼ inch) intervals using a very sharp knife: score just down to where the skin meets the fat. Turn the pork over and lightly score the flesh with a sharp knife: you only need to make shallow incisions.

2. Dry-roast the fennel seeds and chilli flakes in a small frying pan over medium–high heat, shaking the pan occasionally for 30 seconds to 1 minute until fragrant. Transfer to a bowl to cool, then coarsely crush. Stir in the garlic, herbs, olive oil, lemon zest and 2 teaspoons of the sea salt and mix to a paste. Rub the paste into the flesh of the pork.

3. Place the pork, skin-side up, on a tray. Rub the remaining sea salt into the skin, making sure you get right into the incisions. Refrigerate overnight, skin-side up and uncovered, to dry out.

4. Preheat the oven to 220°C (425°F). Lay the pork belly, skin-side down, on a clean work surface. Roll into a cylinder and tie at 2–3 cm (¾–1¼ inch) intervals with kitchen string. Set aside for 1 hour to come to room temperature.

5. Transfer the pork to a wire rack in a roasting tin, drizzle with olive oil and roast for 30–40 minutes until the skin begins to crisp and crackling forms. Reduce the oven temperature to 160°C (315°F) and open the door to let the heat out. Continue to roast the pork for 45 minutes to 1 hour until cooked to medium: the internal temperature will read 58°C (136°F), and the pork will continue to cook as it rests.

6. Cover the pork loosely with foil and set aside to rest for 30 minutes, then remove the string and thinly slice.

7. While the pork rests, toss the rocket, peach slices and herbs in a bowl. Dress with olive oil and vinegar to taste and season with salt and pepper. Serve with the sliced pork and the lemon wedges.

INGREDIENTS

1 kg (2 lb 4 oz) piece of boneless pork belly, skin on
1 tablespoon fennel seeds
1 pinch of chilli flakes
8 garlic cloves, finely chopped
1 small handful of sage leaves, coarsely chopped
2–3 thyme sprigs, leaves picked
1 tablespoon olive oil, plus extra for drizzling
Finely grated zest of 1 lemon, plus lemon wedges to serve
1½ tablespoons sea salt

Wild rocket salad
3 large handfuls of wild rocket (arugula)
3 peaches, stones removed, sliced into wedges (omit if unavailable)
1 large handful each of flat-leaf (Italian) parsley and mint
Extra virgin olive oil, to taste
Red wine vinegar, to taste

SERVING SUGGESTION
aïoli

NOTES

→ *You'll need to allow a day in advance to dry out the pork skin, which will help achieve crisp crackling.*

→ *The fat from the roast that drips into the pan is liquid gold: use it to roast potatoes to serve alongside the porchetta or strain into a container to use for later cooking. Store in an airtight container in the refrigerator.*

***Cut** Pork belly*
See page 222

VICTOR CHURCHILL'S
~ COUNTRY TERRINE ~

Prep time *40 minutes (plus marinating)*
Cook *2 hours (plus setting)*

1. Clean the pork liver, removing any excess membrane and arteries that may be apparent. Prepare the pork cheeks by removing the skin; check for any bone or cartilage and remove if found.

2. Combine the fleur de sel de Guérande, pink salt and black pepper in a bowl. Coat the liver and pork cheeks with the mixture and marinate overnight in the refrigerator.

3. Preheat the oven to 180°C (350°F). Cut the pork shoulder fat into 1 cm (½ inch) cubes.

4. Bring a saucepan of water to the boil, put the pork fat in the boiling water and cook for 1 minute, then remove the fat from the water and transfer to a dish.

5. Mince the liver and cheeks together through a coarse plate on your mincer. If you do not have a mincer, you can ask your local butcher to do this.

6. In the bowl of an electric mixer fitted with the paddle attachment, combine the liver and cheek mixture with the shallots, parsley and the cooked shoulder fat. Beat for about 2 minutes on low speed until well combined. Slowly add the egg whites and mix them through.

7. Meanwhile, put the milk into a small saucepan over medium–high heat and bring to scalding point (just boiling). Slowly add the milk to the mixture in the bowl while the motor is still running until all is combined.

8. Line an 18 cm (7 inch) oval ceramic or terracotta terrine with 5 cm (2 inches) high sides with the prosciutto or lardo. Fill the terrine with the meat mixture and cover it with the caul fat, tucking it around the edges of the mixture.

9. Stand the terrine in a deep baking dish and bake the terrine for about 30 minutes until the top has a lovely golden to dark brown colour. Then reduce the oven temperature to 100°C (200°F) and add 3 cm (1¼ inches) of hot water to the baking dish creating a bain marie. Bake for a further 1½ hours ensuring the water does not fully evaporate, topping up if necessary. When the internal temperature of the terrine reaches 80°C (175°F), remove it from the oven.

10. Allow the terrine to come to room temperature before refrigerating and allow it to 'set' for a further 24 hours before consumption.

INGREDIENTS

500 g (1 lb 2 oz) pork liver
220 g (7¾ oz) pork cheeks
280 g (10 oz) pork shoulder fat
150 g (5½ oz) prosciutto or lardo, thinly sliced
18 g (⅝ oz) fleur de sel de Guérande (see note)
1 pinch of pink salt
1 pinch of ground black pepper
100 g (3½ oz) golden shallots, chopped
1 large handful of flat-leaf (Italian) parsley, coarsely chopped
100 g (3½ oz) egg white
100 ml (3½ fl oz) milk
100 g (3½ oz) caul fat (see page 468)

SERVING SUGGESTION

crusty bread and cornichons

NOTES

→ *Our charcuterie range is a highlight of our butcher's cabinets at Victor Churchill. This is a classic recipe and great to try at home.*

→ Fleur de sel de Guérande *is hand-harvested from the salt marshes of Brittany, France. Literally translating as 'flower of salt', it is delicate in form and complex in flavour. If you can't find it, use sea salt instead.*

→ *We glaze our terrine with a clarified roasted pork stock mixed with 100 g (3½ oz) of gelatine per litre (35 fl oz/4 cups). Once the glaze has cooled to gelling point, it is poured over the chilled terrine.*

Cut Pig liver, cheek and shoulder fat
See page 220

PORK RILLETTES

Prep time *40 mins*
Cook *5 hours (plus overnight curing)*

1. Process the salt, half the herbs, the shallot and peppercorns in a food processor to combine. Put the pork belly in a container large enough to hold it snugly. Rub the salt mixture all over the pork, cover and refrigerate overnight to cure.

2. Heat the back fat in a saucepan over medium–low heat with a splash of water, stirring occasionally, for 1–1½ hours to render the fat. Strain into a heatproof container. You should have about 350 ml (12 fl oz) of melted lard.

3. Preheat the oven to 150°C (300°F). Rinse the cured pork belly under cold running water and pat dry with paper towel.

4. Cut the pork into 8 cm (3¼ inch) chunks and cover the base of a small deep roasting tin that just fits the meat in a single layer. Add the garlic and remaining herbs and pour the rendered fat over the top. Cover with foil and bake for 3 hours 15 minutes to 3 hours 30 minutes until the pork is very tender and pulls apart easily.

5. Remove the pork from the roasting tin with a slotted spoon and set it aside to cool briefly. Strain the fat through a fine sieve (discarding the solids) and set aside.

6. Meanwhile, dry-roast the fennel and coriander seeds in a small saucepan over medium–high heat for 30 seconds or until fragrant, then crush them in a mortar and pestle.

7. Shred the pork using two forks, pulling it apart along the grain, discarding any sinew or gristle. Transfer to a bowl, add the toasted seeds, season with freshly ground black pepper and drizzle with a little of the reserved fat. Mix with the forks to combine, mashing the meat a little, but still retaining some texture. Spoon into small jars or ramekins, pressing gently to flatten and pack lightly, removing any air pockets. Pour the reserved fat over each jar to cover the pork with a thin layer (place a bay leaf on top of each as a garnish). Refrigerate for 3–4 hours until firm, then cover and refrigerate for up to 1 month.

8. To serve, remove the rillettes from the refrigerator and set them aside for 20 minutes at room temperature to soften slightly. Serve with chargrilled sourdough bread, dijon mustard and cornichons.

INGREDIENTS

800 g (1 lb 12 oz) skinless boneless pork belly, in one piece
200 g (7 oz) sea salt
2 fresh bay leaves, plus extra to garnish
3 thyme sprigs
1 golden shallot
2 teaspoons black peppercorns
550 g (1 lb 4 oz) pork back fat, diced
4 garlic cloves, crushed with the flat of a knife
½ teaspoon fennel seeds
½ teaspoon coriander seeds
Freshly ground black pepper
Chargrilled sourdough bread, to serve
Dijon mustard and cornichons, to serve

a simple bitter leaf salad, dressed with a mustard-spiked vinaigrette

SERVING SUGGESTION

NOTE

→ *Pork shoulder is another good cut to use for rillettes, although it will take a little longer to become tender. The remaining pork fat can be strained and refrigerated for another use.*

Cut Pork belly
or shoulder
See page 222

~ WHISKY AND MAPLE-GLAZED ~
PORK SPARE RIBS

Prep time *30 minutes (plus overnight marinating)*
Cook *3½ hours*

1. To make the marinade, heat the olive oil in a saucepan over medium–high heat, add the onion and sauté for 4–5 minutes until tender and translucent. Stir in the garlic, spices, mustard and chilli until fragrant, then add the remaining ingredients. Bring to the boil, season with salt and pepper and set aside to cool. Blend in a blender or food processor until smooth.

2. Place the ribs in a roasting pan large enough to hold them in a single layer, pour the tomato mixture over and turn to coat. Cover and refrigerate overnight to marinate.

3. Preheat the oven to 120°C (235°F). Cover ribs with foil and roast, basting occasionally with the marinade, for 2½–3 hours until tender.

4. Remove the ribs from the marinade, transfer the marinade to a saucepan and boil over medium–high heat for 4–5 minutes until reduced to a sticky glaze.

5. Heat a barbecue or chargrill pan to medium–high. For the barbecued corn, drizzle the corn with a little olive oil and season with salt, pepper and paprika. Grill, turning occasionally, for 8–10 minutes until charred and tender. Combine the melted butter and lime juice in a bowl, season with salt and pepper and drizzle over the corn. Keep warm.

6. Drizzle the roasted ribs with a little oil and grill, turning and basting occasionally, for 4–5 minutes until glazed and lightly charred. Slice into individual ribs and serve with the barbecued corn, lime wedges and any extra marinade.

INGREDIENTS

1.5 kg (3 lb 5 oz) split American-style pork spare rib racks (see pages 224–225)
Lime wedges, to serve

Marinade
1 tablespoon olive oil
1 red onion, finely diced
2 garlic cloves, finely chopped
1 tablespoon smoked paprika
1 teaspoon ground cumin
1 teaspoon dijon mustard
½ teaspoon dried chilli flakes
300 ml (10½ fl oz) tomato passata (purée)
125 ml (4 fl oz/½ cup) tomato ketchup
100 ml (3½ fl oz) apple cider vinegar
100 ml (3½ fl oz) whisky
80 ml (2½ fl oz/⅓ cup) maple syrup
80 g (2¾ oz) brown sugar
2 tablespoons Worcestershire sauce

Barbecued corn
4 corncobs, husks and silk removed
Olive oil, for drizzling
Paprika, for seasoning
6 tablespoons (80 g) butter, melted
Juice of 1 lime

wedges of lettuce dressed with a buttermilk dressing and a classic potato salad

SERVING SUGGESTION

Cut Pork spare rib racks
See page 221

PORK KNUCKLE
~ WITH SAUERKRAUT ~

1. Combine the pork knuckle, garlic, spices and herbs in a large saucepan, cover generously with cold water and bring to the boil. Season generously with salt and pepper, reduce heat to medium and simmer for 1–1¼ hours until just tender. Remove from the liquid and set aside to cool. Reserve the liquid.

2. When cool enough to handle, score the pork skin horizontally at 1 cm (½ inch) intervals and rub with the sea salt.

3. Preheat the oven to 190°C (375°F). Spread the onion in the base of a small roasting tin to form a trivet, place the pork on top and pour beer and 125 ml (4 fl oz/½ cup) of the pork cooking liquid into the tin. Roast, basting occasionally, for 1–1¼ hours until golden brown. Cover loosely with foil and set aside to rest for 20 minutes.

4. Meanwhile, to make the sauerkraut, cook the lardons in a heavy-based saucepan over medium–low heat to render the fat, then remove the lardons with a slotted spoon. Increase the heat to medium and add the butter. When the butter foams, add the onion and cook, stirring occasionally, for 6–8 minutes until just starting to caramelise.

5. Add the white wine, juniper berries and herbs and simmer for 8–10 minutes until the wine is reduced by two-thirds. Add the sauerkraut, stir to combine and season with salt and pepper. Discard the juniper berries, bay leaf and thyme sprigs and stir the parsley through just before serving.

6. To make the creamy mash, cover the potatoes with cold salted water in a large saucepan. Bring to the boil and cook for 12–15 minutes until the potatoes are just tender when pierced with a sharp knife. Drain, return to the pan and mash well. Bring the butter and cream to a simmer in a separate small saucepan, add to the potato and mix until smooth. Season generously with salt and pepper and keep warm.

7. Take the crackling off the pork knuckle and break it into pieces. Coarsely shred or slice the meat and serve the meat and crackling with sauerkraut, creamy mash and pan juices.

INGREDIENTS

1 pork hock (knuckle), about 1.5 kg (3 lb 5 oz)
1 garlic bulb, halved
2½ tablespoons caraway seeds
1 tablespoon whole black peppercorns
3 thyme sprigs
1 fresh bay leaf
1 teaspoon sea salt
2 brown onions, thickly sliced
375 ml (13 fl oz/1½ cups) amber or dark ale

Spiced sauerkraut
80 g (2¾ oz) speck lardons
2 tablespoons (30 g) butter, chopped
1 brown onion, thinly sliced
185 ml (6 fl oz/¾ cup) dry white wine
5 juniper berries
2 fresh bay leaves
2 thyme sprigs
600 g (1 lb 5 oz) ready-made sauerkraut
Coarsely chopped flat-leaf (Italian) parsley

Creamy mash
1 kg (2 lb 4 oz) coliban or sebago potatoes,
    cut into 5 cm (2 inch) chunks
8 tablespoons (110 g) butter, chopped
100 ml (3½ fl oz) pure (pouring) cream

NOTES

→ *Sauerkraut is available in jars and tins from select delicatessens. Drain off excess liquid.*

→ *Leftover pork knuckle will keep, refrigerated, for up to 3 days. It is perfect to toss through a hash of potatoes and cabbage or add to a white bean soup for a hit of porky flavour.*

Cut Pork hock
See page 223

SPLIT PEA AND HAM SOUP

Prep time *20 minutes*
Cook *2 hours 40 minutes*

1. Heat the olive oil and butter in a large heavy-based saucepan over medium–high heat, add the carrot, celery, onion and garlic and sauté for 8–10 minutes until the onion is tender and translucent. Add 2 litres (70 fl oz/8 cups) of water, the ham hock, split peas, thyme and bay leaf, season to taste with freshly ground black pepper (don't season the soup with salt at this stage or the split peas will take longer to cook) and bring to the boil. Reduce the heat to medium, half-cover with a lid and simmer for 2¼–2½ hours, topping up with extra water if necessary until the split peas are tender and the meat is falling from the bone.

2. Remove the ham hock from the soup and set it aside to cool slightly. Shred the meat into bite-sized pieces (discarding skin, bones and sinew). Discard the thyme sprigs and bay leaf, then purée the soup with a handheld blender or in batches in a food processor until the texture is to your liking, whether that's silky smooth or slightly chunkier. If using a food processor, allow the liquid to cool slightly before puréeing. Thin the soup with a little water, if necessary.

3. Season with sea salt and ground pepper, then squeeze in a little lemon juice to brighten the flavour. Stir in the shredded ham and serve hot, scattered with chopped parsley and with crusty bread or toast to dip into the soup.

INGREDIENTS

1 ham hock, about 800 g (1 lb 12 oz)
2 tablespoons olive oil
2 tablespoons (20 g) butter, chopped
2 carrots, chopped
2 celery stalks, chopped (any tender leaves reserved to serve)
1 brown onion, chopped
2 garlic cloves, finely chopped
320 g (11¼ oz/1⅓ cups) dried green split peas
2 thyme sprigs
1 fresh bay leaf
Freshly ground black pepper and sea salt
Squeeze of lemon juice
Coarsely chopped flat-leaf (Italian) parsley and crusty bread, to serve

NOTES

→ *When fresh peas are in season, they're an excellent addition to this soup. Use two-thirds of the quantity of split peas and add 250 g (9 oz) of freshly shelled peas to the soup in the last 5 minutes of cooking. Alternatively, you could use frozen peas.*

→ *The soup will keep in the refrigerator for up to 1 week, or makes an excellent freezer staple.*

Cut Ham hock
See page 223

PORK SCRATCHINGS
~ WITH SPICED SALT ~

Prep time *15 minutes (plus drying)*
Cook *20 minutes*

INGREDIENTS

400 g (14 oz) pork skin with about 5 mm
   (¼ inch) of fat still attached
1 tablespoon salt

Spiced salt
1 teaspoon cumin seeds
1 tablespoon sea salt
½ teaspoon smoked paprika
Finely grated zest of ½ lemon
1 thyme sprig, leaves picked

1. Lay the pork skin-side up on a clean work surface and use a very sharp knife to score at 1 cm (½ inch) intervals, to just where the skin meets the fat.

2. Place the pork skin-side up on a wire rack in the sink. Boil a kettle of water and pour boiling water over the skin to open the score marks. Pat dry with paper towel, transfer to a tray and rub the salt into the skin, making sure you get right into the incisions. Refrigerate, uncovered, overnight to dry out.

3. Preheat the oven to 220°C (425°F). Cut the pork skin into thin strips, using the score marks as a guide. Lay the strips on a wire rack in a roasting tin, making sure they don't touch one another. Roast for 15–20 minutes until crisp and golden brown.

4. Meanwhile, to make the spiced salt, dry-roast the cumin seeds in a small saucepan for 30–60 seconds until fragrant, then transfer to a mortar and pestle and coarsely grind the cumin seeds. Combine with the remaining ingredients and set aside.

5. Serve the pork scratchings with spiced salt: the scratchings are best served soon after cooking but will keep in an airtight container for a few days.

NOTE

→ *The fat that pools in the base of the roasting tin is excellent for roasting vegetables or as the cooking fat in place of olive oil or vegetable oil. Strain into an airtight container and refrigerate almost indefinitely.*

Cut Pig skin

TONKATSU RAMEN

Prep time *1 hour*
Cook *8 hours*

1. To make the chashu pork, preheat the oven to 140°C (275°F). Season the pork belly flesh then roll into a cylinder. Tie at 2–3 cm (¾–1¼ inch) intervals with kitchen string, securing each with a knot.

2. Combine all of the remaining chashu ingredients with 250 ml (9 fl oz/1 cup) of water in an ovenproof saucepan, large enough to fit the pork quite snugly. The liquid should half cover the pork. Bring to the boil, add the pork and transfer to the oven. Braise, turning pork occasionally in the liquid, for 3½–4 hours, until a skewer inserted meets no resistance. Set aside to rest for 30 minutes in the braising liquid. Remove the string and slice thinly. Reserve the braising liquid.

3. Meanwhile, to make the pork broth, combine the pork bones, trotters and chicken carcass in a large stockpot, cover generously with cold water and bring to the boil over high heat. Tip the bones into the sink to drain. Rinse thoroughly under cold running water to remove impurities and any grey scum. Rinse the pot thoroughly too.

4. Return the bones to the clean pot and add the onion, leek, ginger, spring onion and garlic. Add cold water to cover generously and bring to a rolling boil. Skim off any dark scum that appears on the surface and cook, skimming occasionally, for 15–20 minutes until the dark scum stops appearing.

5. Reduce the heat to medium, cover with a lid and cook at a low rolling boil for 5–6 hours, until broth is creamy and opaque and reduced by about three-quarters.

6. Strain the pork broth through a sieve lined with muslin (cheesecloth) into a clean saucepan. You should have about 1.8 litres (62 fl oz) of broth: return it to the stove and reduce it further if there is more. Add the soy sauce, mirin, ginger, kombu and 200 ml (7 fl oz) of the braising liquid from the chashu pork. Simmer for 45 minutes to 1 hour for flavours to develop. Discard ginger and kombu and season with freshly ground white pepper.

7. Cook the ramen noodles in a large saucepan of boiling water, then drain and divide among hot bowls. Ladle hot broth over the noodles in each bowl, top with chashu pork and 2 egg halves and drizzle with sesame oil. Serve scattered with reserved spring onion, sesame seeds and toasted nori.

INGREDIENTS

60 ml (2 fl oz/¼ cup) Japanese soy sauce
2 tablespoons mirin
5 cm (2 inch) piece of fresh ginger, thickly sliced
1 piece kombu
Freshly ground white pepper
500 g (1 lb 2 oz) fresh ramen noodles or 290 g (10¼ oz) dried ramen noodles
6 eggs, soft-boiled for 6 minutes, peeled and halved to serve
Sesame oil, sesame seeds, roasted nori and thinly sliced reserved spring onion (scallion), to serve (see below)

Chashu pork
600 g (1 lb 5 oz) boneless pork belly, skin on
250 ml (9 fl oz/1 cup) sake
250 ml (9 fl oz/1 cup) mirin
100 ml (3½ fl oz) Japanese soy sauce
100 g (3½ oz) caster (superfine) sugar
6 spring onions (scallions), coarsely chopped
6 cm (2½ inch) piece of fresh ginger, sliced
1 garlic bulb, halved

Pork broth
2 kg (4 lb 8 oz) large pork bones, cut into pieces (ask your butcher to do this)
2 pigs' trotters, split in half
1 chicken carcass, quartered
1 brown onion, skin on, coarsely chopped
1 leek, white and green parts, coarsely chopped
10 cm (4 inch) piece of fresh ginger, thickly sliced
8 spring onions (scallions), white part only (reserve green parts to serve)
1 garlic bulb, halved

Cut Pig bones, trotters and belly
See pages 222 and 223

CHAPTER FOUR

CATTLE

BEEF ~ VEAL

CATTLE

BEEF, VEAL, MILK, SUET, LEATHER, HIDES, HORN, FERTILISER, DRIPPING, SAUSAGE CASINGS

PRIZED CUTS

TO ROAST *Tri-tip*
TO GRILL *Spider steak*
TO BRAISE *Tail*
PRIZED OFFAL *Tongue and cheek*

CUTS TO MINCE FOR A HAMBURGER
Chuck and brisket

COMPLEMENTS TO THE COW

ANCHOVY	SALSA VERDE	ROSEMARY
HORSERADISH	HERBS	THYME
BEARNAISE SAUCE	CHIMICHURRI	MARROW
POTATOES	CAFÉ DE	RED WINE
WATERCRESS	PARIS BUTTER	FENNEL
MUSTARD	CARROTS	MUSHROOMS

DRY-AGEING: Dry-ageing is a process of ageing or 'hanging' a primal (a whole muscle such as the striploin or a rack of ribs), in a temperature- and humidity-controlled room. This process allows the natural enzymes in the meat to go to work on the muscle fibres, making them softer and more elastic. At the same time the flavour intensifies, yielding that elusive fifth taste, umami; not only that, but with dry-ageing the beef will become more relaxed and tender. This is the purest and best way of preparing a steak in the butchery. See page 456.

WAGYU FAMILY TREE

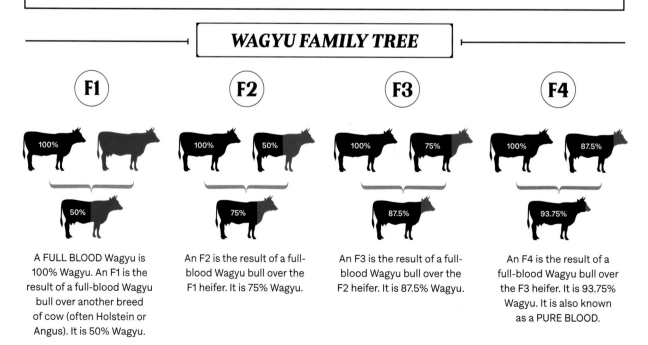

A FULL BLOOD Wagyu is 100% Wagyu. An F1 is the result of a full-blood Wagyu bull over another breed of cow (often Holstein or Angus). It is 50% Wagyu.

An F2 is the result of a full-blood Wagyu bull over the F1 heifer. It is 75% Wagyu.

An F3 is the result of a full-blood Wagyu bull over the F2 heifer. It is 87.5% Wagyu.

An F4 is the result of a full-blood Wagyu bull over the F3 heifer. It is 93.75% Wagyu. It is also known as a PURE BLOOD.

GRASS-FED

A clean, strong beefy flavour,
reflective of the seasons, can be tougher; however,
it is higher in omega-3 and vitamin E.

GRAIN-FED

Rich, buttery, fat coats your mouth, tender,
succulent, consistent flavour
and soft texture.

MORE
ABOUT FEED
PAGE 300–1

—ALL ABOUT—

MARBLING

FAT = FLAVOUR + TENDERNESS

Generally there are two kinds of fat that are of concern in the kitchen: external fat—sitting just below the skin—and intramuscular fat, found within the eye of the meat.

The external fat can be left on for roasting or grilling as it will baste the meat as it cooks and protect it from drying out. You can remove it before serving if you wish.

External fat can be rendered to become dripping. At its simplest, you can add a little fat to a pan to lubricate it for your onions and garlic, then remove it before adding any other ingredients for a braise.

Hard beef fat, or suet, has long played a role in the kitchen as a shortening agent for cakes and pastries. Now it is largely reserved for use in plum pudding.

Intramuscular fat refers to the spider's web of fat running through the inside of the muscle and is known as marbling. The more of this marbled fat there is, the juicier the steak. Intramuscular fat can be influenced by the breed (see, for example, Wagyu), feed and age of the animal. To illustrate the marbling of steaks, pages 492–493 show photographs of steaks with a range of low to high marbling scores.

SELECT & STORE

Look for beef that is cherry red in appearance: the deeper purple the colour, the more stressed the animal was at time of death. A nicely marbled piece of steak—with a spider's web of fat through it—will mean a juicy result. Dry-aged steaks are deeper in colour and have delicious flavour and tenderness. Beef needs to breathe: wrap it in greaseproof paper and store in the fridge with cool, fresh air circulating.

BUTCHER'S TREATS

BONES AND MARROW

CHEEKS AND TAILS

SKIRTS

SPIDER STEAK AND INTERCOSTALS
(BETWEEN THE RIBS)

SIMPLE CUTS VS COMPLEX CUTS

If you imagine how cattle move, you will have a good idea of what the cut will be appropriate for in the kitchen. Basically, the more movement of the muscle, the more complex the cut and the more cooking time required.

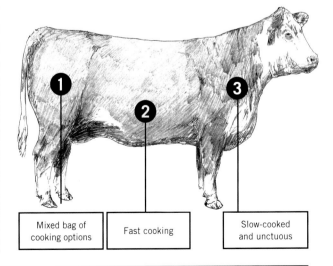

Mixed bag of cooking options

Fast cooking

Slow-cooked and unctuous

TIP: *Bringing your steak to room temperature before cooking is critical to ensure an even doneness.*

HISTORY

Three years in the paddock, six weeks dry-ageing, 10 minutes for a skilled butcher to cut the primal muscle into steaks, seven minutes on a hot grill, three minutes to rest: there is a lot of time that goes into producing the perfect steak. It is for this reason you will find it is often the most expensive cut in the butcher's cabinet.

Beyond the hip pocket, beef has played an integral role in our appetite for meat. A beast of burden as much as of consumption, cows, with their docile nature, are among the earliest domesticated animals: they have been tamed and eaten since Neolithic times. Long ingrained in our daily life, the word 'cattle' comes from the Anglo–Norman word *chattel*, meaning possession.

So revered are cattle by the English, the rallying cry of 'Beef and Liberty' has been used by Englishmen since the eighteenth century; in fact, the French still refer to the English as *les rosbifs*. While it is likely intended as a dig, who wouldn't want to be a roast beef?

In India, the cow is worshipped and, as such, not found on your plate, but rather lolling around their streets; while the Japanese treat their cattle with such reverence they will play them classical music and massage them. Unfortunately for the cows, this does not spare them a role at the dinner table: it's a ploy for the very best marbling (see pages 492–493).

In the butchery, beef also tells an interesting tale. Perhaps due to its size, and thus the multitude of options, it is an animal where the culture of the table has very much dictated the butcher's cuts.

The French, with their continental breeds that harbour less fat than their British cousins and centuries of culinary tradition aimed at getting the very most from each beast, have to work with animals that are lean of muscle, but high in collagen. A frugal nation in the kitchen, they break their animals down, allowing each individual muscle—and its attributes—the chance to shine. It is also through this adversity that we celebrate some of the very best, and perhaps still underrated, steaks: *bavette*, *onglet* and *araignée* (see page 314).

The French were a little late to the dry-ageing game: their wet, lean prime steaks are a source of curiosity, especially when compared to the exquisite care they take with their poultry and pork products. Across the pond, the British focussed their attention on the subprimal cuts (the large muscle groups as they are first separated from the carcass), which are generally kept whole and carefully aged on the bone.

Japanese cattle were so valued for their brawn it was once forbidden to eat them. Coupled with Buddhist ideologies, four-legged animals were rarely eaten in the thousand years leading up to the 1860s: it was not until Japanese soldiers were granted exemption that beef really found its way to the table. The returned soldiers brought with them an appetite for meat; however, their elders still believed that cooking beef indoors was a desecration of the house. Therefore, cooking was taken outdoors, where they heated ploughshares over hot coals, calling it *sukiyaki*, meaning 'spade cooking'. With a time of starvation still in living memory, it is with this mentality of clear restraint that they continue to enjoy beef in Japan.

Americans, with a focus on time efficiency—in the feedlot, butchery and the kitchen—took another approach altogether. Grilling cuts are balanced with their insatiable appetite for the hamburger. Conversely, there is the southern tradition of the barbecue: long and slow cooking of the brisket and short rib to render the meat tender, smoky and unctuous.

South American countries are among the world's greatest beef consumers, from the vast organic grassfields of Uruguay to the high plains of Argentina, they have abundant grassland tracts that make cattle production an easy income source. The *gauchos* (South American cowboys) and, consequently, their *asador*—a large iron cross used for cooking over an open fire—feature widely. There is an old Argentine proverb that says: 'Every creature that walks ends up roasting on the iron cross.' The *picañha*, or rump cap, is a particular favourite for cooking by this method.

In Australia, with wide, varying pastures and British culinary sensibilities, beef production accounts for around half of all farms and agricultural industry. Much of the beef produced in Australia is exported, particularly the hardier cattle of the far north. A tradition of barbecue thrives that is different from that of the Americas, with a historic focus on speed and convenience. This, coupled with a fair climate and outdoor lifestyle, has led to a focus on prime steaks on the table. More recently, Australians are happily exchanging gas for charcoal and flames, and prime steaks for the less-known skirt steaks.

Cattle are social creatures, with clear group structures and hierarchies. For more about cattle on the farm, see page 308.

BREED

It is with an ancient, wild cattle breed known as the aurochs that we start our bovine family tree. In one of the great examples of the ingenuity and adaptability of nature, the ancestors of modern cattle spread out across the world, forming characteristics that have given them the ability to cope in different conditions, climates and environments.

At its most basic, the adaptability of cattle species is seen in the broad divide between the domesticated cattle of Europe—*Bos taurus*—and the humped zebu cattle of India and Africa—*Bos indicus*. *Bos taurus*, broad in both form and muscular structure, has an excellent natural ability to store fat, a win in a cold environment as they build stores for long winters when grass is hard to come by. By happy coincidence, it also makes for wonderful eating.

Bos indicus does somewhat the inverse. Generally scrawnier of body with long, lean muscles, indicus has an innate ability to make the most of meagre supplies when they are available. The hump on their back, akin to that of a camel, is made up of tissue that stores water. Incidentally, this hump is said to produce delicious, honeycombed meat.

From these broad brushstrokes, humans have selected the best characteristics for their own advantage. Cattle have been domesticated for roles in the dairy, in the field and on the plate. Often, as one characteristic was exaggerated, another was sacrificed. With careful selection of specific traits over time (whether for milk production, meat yield, fat development, maternal capability or temperament), new breeds have been created. These breeds are now closely guarded, with registered breed books and pedigree used to ensure their purity. It is one of the earliest and greatest examples of (literally) branded marketing.

One of the oldest, if not the oldest, purebred breeds is the majestic Chianina: a monster of a cow, with bulls standing up to two metres tall and weighing in at a whopping 1800 kg (nearly 2 tons). Chianina date back to the Bronze Age, and have been a part of the Italian landscape for more than two thousand years. The beautiful white cow has become synonymous with the *bistecca alla Fiorentina*, the equally majestic T-bone steak you will find in nearly all Florentine restaurants.

The Aberdeen Angus, perhaps the most prominent breed of cow found on restaurant menus today, is another great example of marketing clout. Originally

→ *A polled animal is one that is lacking horns. This feature has usually been removed through selective breeding.*

developed in Scotland, it was in the 1980s, as the breed was disappearing into obscurity, that the people of Aberdeen decided to throw some money behind it. Now, for better or worse, they're everywhere. Angus cattle have an ability to reach maturity relatively quickly, coupled with the addition of excellent intramuscular fat: a compelling combination.

Japanese Wagyu (in Japanese, *wa* means Japan and *gyu* means cattle) is, by many, considered the Champagne and caviar of the meat world. Bred from native Asian cattle with some British infusions, these cows are treated like royalty, sometimes quite literally. Their ability to develop intramuscular fat—the spider's web of monounsaturated fats ('good' fats) that run through the beef—is unchallenged in the world of beef for its richness. See page 284 for an explanation of the crosses (F1, F2, etcetera) in Wagyu breeding.

As new lands and farming regions have been developed, these breeds have followed; however, there is no escaping the natural selection that first defined them. As the *B. indicus* would freeze in the northern hemisphere winter, so too would the *B. taurus* thirst in the subcontinental heat. And so, in the new world, we have sought to enhance these cattle breeds for our own needs. In America and Australia, this has often meant a combination of both *B. taurus* and *B. indicus*.

In Queensland, where almost half of Australia's cattle are raised, the dry conditions and often scant grasses have seen success for *B. indicus*, while in some distinct packets of rich grassland, such as Tasmania or southern Gippsland in Victoria, there is sufficient rainfall to successfully grow and finish pure *B. taurus* breeds (such as the ubiquitous Angus) on pasture alone.

Across the broad, in part sunburnt, paddocks the Australian Brahman has been developed: lauded for their unique digestive system that allows them to perform more efficiently on low-protein, low-quality feed, they have a strong immune response and thus disease resistance, and also have tolerance of heat and ticks, thanks to their dark pigmented skin, extra sweat glands and pliant, reflective coat.

In a perfect world, that would be enough, but of course we have other market pressures to compete with. We're not actually great at playing with the cards nature deals; we want more. It would also be fair to say this is not just about the want, but also the need. As our population expands and becomes ever more urbanised, the demands on these breeds has shifted.

Enter the feedlot; enter grain-fed beef.

Bos indicus *are best suited to dry, warm conditions. For more about cattle breeds, see page 292.*

HERITAGE BREED MAP: CATTLE

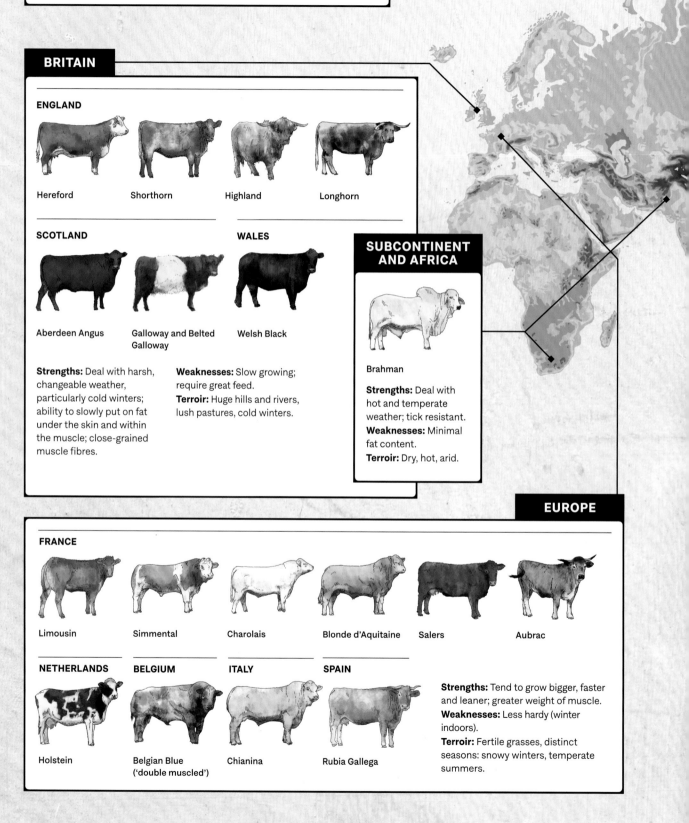

BRITAIN

ENGLAND

Hereford

Shorthorn

Highland

Longhorn

SCOTLAND

Aberdeen Angus

Galloway and Belted Galloway

WALES

Welsh Black

Strengths: Deal with harsh, changeable weather, particularly cold winters; ability to slowly put on fat under the skin and within the muscle; close-grained muscle fibres.

Weaknesses: Slow growing; require great feed.

Terroir: Huge hills and rivers, lush pastures, cold winters.

SUBCONTINENT AND AFRICA

Brahman

Strengths: Deal with hot and temperate weather; tick resistant.

Weaknesses: Minimal fat content.

Terroir: Dry, hot, arid.

EUROPE

FRANCE

Limousin

Simmental

Charolais

Blonde d'Aquitaine

Salers

Aubrac

NETHERLANDS

Holstein

BELGIUM

Belgian Blue ('double muscled')

ITALY

Chianina

SPAIN

Rubia Gallega

Strengths: Tend to grow bigger, faster and leaner; greater weight of muscle.

Weaknesses: Less hardy (winter indoors).

Terroir: Fertile grasses, distinct seasons: snowy winters, temperate summers.

SUBCONTINENT

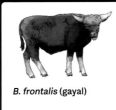

B. frontalis (gayal)

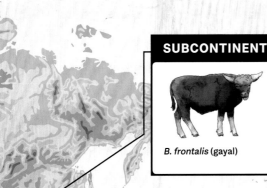

JAPAN

Wagyu

Strengths: Incredible intramuscular marbling.
Terroir: Temperate climate, green and lush fields.

NORTH AMERICA

Santa Gertrudis (Texas: Brahman and Shorthorn cross)

Strengths: Rapid growth, ability to live in hot or humid environments.
Weaknesses: Minimal fat.
Terroir: Hot and humid.

AUSTRALIA

Murray Grey (cross Shorthorn and Angus)

Droughtmaster

Strengths: Heat resistant, tick resistant.
Weaknesses: Lean muscles, a lack of fat.
Terroir: Ranging from the green grasses of Tasmania to the arid paddocks of outback Queensland.

INDONESIA

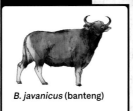

B. javanicus (banteng)

SOUTH AMERICA

Around 300 million cattle are raised in South America each year, particularly in Brazil, Argentina and Uruguay, predominantly using British breeds (Hereford, Angus).

Terroir: Vast grasslands, newer soils, rich in rainforest debris.

FEED

Many factors influence the quality of the meat we eat, but perhaps none more so than the feed they are raised on, particularly in the final stages of their lives. There is debate over the virtues of grass-fed and grain-fed beef. In the mouth, it's generally a question of chasing tenderness over flavour, or flavour over tenderness; in the field it is much more complicated.

Cattle, like sheep and goats, are ruminants: herbivores with a complicated stomach made up of four compartments that helps them to first ferment the grasses they eat before turning them into 'cud'. For pasture-fed cattle, raised in their natural environment, it is the various grasses that yield different protein and energy levels that give rise to differences in the quality of the beef they produce. The farmer must carefully manage the rotation of their cattle through the pastures, watching to ensure that they have enough feed and don't overgraze their environment.

This is not always an easy task and, consequently, a potential downside to pasture-fed beef can be a variation in the quality and marbling of the beef. On the other hand, cattle raised in a feedlot will generally have more consistent marbling and improved tenderness, having spent anywhere between 70 days and the last year of their life in a large, open-air pen with their feed carefully managed.

Beyond the animal's immediate environment, the greater environment is also called into question. Debates rage over the conversion rate of meat production per kilogram of feed, as well as the greenhouse effect from the production of methane and other emissions. To complicate the already complicated, many of the figures we are presented with come from the USA, where the scale of Concentrated Animal Feeding Operations (CAFOs) is vastly different from the rest of the world. The jury is still out, with some studies suggesting that lot-feeding, with the trucking of grain and animals included in the figures, can actually produce less carbon emissions.

One way of identifying grain- or grass-fed beef is to look at the colour of the fat: the whiter it appears, the higher the likelihood of the animal having been grain fed. Grass-fed beef tends to have a yellow tint to it thanks to the chlorophyll in the grass.

GRASS-FED

It is not unusual to meet a cattle farmer who will say his job is actually to grow the grass and then the cattle. There are many ways this can be achieved, starting with

Grass-fed

→ *Clean beefy flavour; stronger taste; reflects the seasons; can be tougher; higher in omega–3 and vitamin E.*

Grain-fed

→ *Rich, buttery; fat coats your mouth; succulent; consistent flavour and cooking.*

pasture quality and good soil and fertility management. With hoofed animals, the ranging technique plays a fundamental role: from cell or rotational grazing in controlled smaller paddocks to ranging, where the cattle are left to roam free and find their own grasses.

The quantity of feed available during the life of the animal plays a large role in the end product. Consistent feed helps to ensure even weight gain. Interestingly, the cattle's bodies and their muscles have a memory for times of adversity; if cattle are starved, their bodies will remember.

When left to forage naturally, with space and a variety of pastures in front of them, cattle can 'finish' (grow to their optimal size and weight before slaughter) well; they will be more relaxed, and, depending on their breed, will form good intramuscular fat. They are naturally very good managers of the soil and of themselves. In a paddock they will seek out what their bodies require, sometimes ignoring lush pastures for the nutrients and fibre of bark or leaves.

The grasses themselves also provide variety, with different grasses growing in summer and winter, each yielding their own nutritional values; from native perennials to foraging crops that can be planted for certain specific attributes to aid health and weight gain. Good rainfall helps to provide nutritious grasses. The animals' weight will also fluctuate with the weather: if it's cold they use their fat stores, while the grass also has to work harder to grow.

Read more about Sir Sidney Kidman and his approach to Australian terroir in The Cattle King, *by Ion Idriess (Angus & Robertson, 1936).*

One of the first lands to rise from the sea, Australia has very old soils with high acidity; in complete contrast to, for example, the soils in South America, where the rainforest debris and newer soils mean luscious grasses. The best farmers work with it, or at least around it, not against it. The earliest drovers in Australia, the frontier men, had to find their feet in foreign, often wild, country. Sir Sidney Kidman—in his early mastery of the channel country where the Northern Territory cuddles up to Queensland, New South Wales and South Australia—achieved this by following the storms, and thus the feed, all the way down Australia in the inevitable times of cyclical droughts. His was a nomadic farming system, largely borrowed from Indigenous knowledge.

Not all farmers today have this great luxury of land. Nowadays they may look to increase calcium to raise the pH of the soil, or move their animals through distinct paddocks, with the soil of old river flats containing nutrients that have been washed down into the valley, or vast tracts of decomposing trees building humus and thus fertile soils. At all times, the stocking density must be carefully managed so as to not denude the soils and desecrate the land.

LOT-FED (GRAIN AND CORN)

Over recent decades many people have developed a preference for grain-fed beef, particularly regarding the tenderness of the meat. Essentially, the extra fat makes the steak more forgiving on the grill. In America, the market is predominantly

corn-fed beef, due to the longstanding and rather complicated corn subsidies. The high percentage of carbohydrates in grain and corn provide good weight gain rates for the cattle.

All lot-fed cattle will start their life on pasture. Cattle will be moved from pasture into the feedlot anytime between 12 and 24 months of age. To manage the shift in the microflora (gut bacteria) of the beast, as one type of feed is replaced with another, the ration of grains or corn (in combination with an assortment of vitamins, minerals and sugars) is slowly increased as the animal and its rumen (the first stomach compartment) adapt to its new environment. These grains and other carbohydrates are generally sourced by price and then manipulated (soaked, cracked, puffed) to help the animal digest them.

In the best feedlots, this is carefully managed: beyond the complications for their rumens, if cattle are given too much grain or corn too quickly, then the desirable intramuscular fat will develop out of proportion to their external fat. The best feedlots are high-tech, with a fierce focus on animal health and stress levels. If an animal is unwell, it will be moved out of the feedlot to be treated.

SUPPLEMENTARY FED

Of course, it is not always a simple choice of grain or grass; and one does not mean the complete exclusion of the other. All grain-fed beasts start their life on grass, while some grass-fed beasts will require supplementary feeding at different points throughout their life. In Europe, it's the snowy winters that prompt supplementary feeding, while in Australia it's harsh summers and drought that creates the need. In some of these cases the alternative, with cattle left on snowy or arid pastures to fend for themselves, does not bear thinking about.

Somewhere in the middle of these two options is a supplementary-fed animal. In this case they will often be allowed the room to range freely with access to grass, while a supplementary feed will be provided to aid intramuscular fat growth. One Australian farmer found this method actually provided a greater weight gain than the feedlot animals, speculating that it was due to their level of relaxation and ability to lie down in the grasses while chewing their cud.

ON THE FARM

Cattle are herding animals, designed to travel distances and follow the grasses in a mob. A herding mentality means community groups; within these groups, bonds are forged. The best farmers are aware of this and will keep the mob together from the beginning until the very end.

The social connections of cattle are formed early and those farmers who follow the practice of keeping the herd together are helping to reduce undue stress on the animals. Introducing new cows to the mob can also result in fights, which—beyond the emotional turmoil—can also damage their hides.

The natural desire to roam in these herds stops their hard hoofs from trampling over one patch of ground and thus desecrating the land. It's also nature's way of providing manure to the soils and grasses, turning over the land, thus putting back into the cycle while they feed.

Most of the beef we eat comes from steers, or castrated males, with the females often saved for breeding stock. These bullocks are generally left to suckle their mothers' milk for the first six months and as such are known as a suckler herd.

As they grow and develop, in the field or feedlot, habits form. They will stick to their friends, and a leader of the herd is often distinguishable. As with the human race, good leaders are an important part of the process and it is in maintaining these social structures that the animals are most relaxed.

The final days in a cow's life are incredibly important to the overall quality of the meat. New people can stir up cattle—dogs too—and in many of the best feedlots and farms over-excitable people and animals are kept to a minimum. The way animals are trucked to the abattoir, and indeed moved through the process, is also carefully considered. Without this careful management, levels of adrenalin rise, raising the pH of the meat, resulting in 'dark cutters'; beef that will be more purple in colour, tougher in texture, with less flavour and a shorter shelf-life. No farmer wants this.

Dr Temple Grandin of Colorado State University has been revolutionary in this field. Her work in reading animal behaviour has resulted in unique designs of circular yards, encouraging a gentle process and natural direction of movement for animals as they pass through the yards. These advances in animal care continue to develop and have greatly reduced stress on the beasts in cattle yards and abattoirs.

AGE AT SLAUGHTER

Generally, the younger the animal the more tender the meat and the milder the flavour.

Bobby veal – a by-product of the milk industry, male calves can be slaughtered at only a few days old, and are most often sent to export. They tend to have a soft texture and milky flavour.

Rose veal – male dairy calves, raised for up to six months on milk and grains. A blank canvas for the creative chef, this is a meat we should respect and eat more of.

Beef – 12 months to three years and sometimes beyond. There is an argument, particularly with British breeds, they need up to 30 months to develop a good amount of intramuscular fat.

Ox – also referred to as a bullock in Australia and India, an ox is most often a castrated male that is trained for draught work. In a culinary sense the term 'ox' became synonymous with some of the secondary cuts (oxtail, ox tongue).

The old dairy cow – Some cultures and butchers insist that an animal will reach its prime much later. The Basques have a tradition of rearing old dairy cows for beef, producing a low-yielding, slow-growing animal that has spent its time on pasture. The tradition allows them to make use of (and respect) an animal that has already spent its life providing milk and calves. This beef has found recent fame and favour in some of the world's best restaurants including Magnus Nilsson's Fäviken and Asador Etxebarri in the Basque country. Generally, these cows will be put back out to pasture following their career in the dairy. This spell will allow them time to regain their condition.

At Bodega el Capricho, in León, Spain, rather than entirely focussing on breeds, José Gordón is all about age: he only works with old cows (from 11 to 15 years old). Furthermore, José, a producer and chef, serves up only castrated males, because he believes testosterone is healthier, with the hormone cleansing the beef of saturated fats. Perhaps the most romantic notion is that he selects his cows on temperament: 'I'm looking for animals with character; they must be docile and noble.'

VEAL

Veal is traditionally a by-product of the dairy industry: a way to find a use for the young bull calves that are not needed at the dairy. A dairy cow must calve once a year to keep up milk production (they will milk for six to seven years): while the female calves will generally be absorbed back into the herd, there is no room in the dairy for the bull calves. Traditionally this was where veal came into play.

As dairy cows are not great at meat production—with their breed selection seeing the focus going into producing milk—young bulls are often sent to cheap slaughter, treated as a commodity. These calves leave the farm as young as a few days old, before being processed as bobby veal, destined for export.

To manage this, many farmers will put a beef bull over the dairy cow and fatten the half-caste calf for veal; however, in some countries, there remains a stigma against eating calves. With a continuing demand and consumption of the best dairy products accompanied by a misguided refusal to eat veal, we are doing wrong by the system to not find a place for these animals at the table. The hypocrisy is infuriating. We need to eat more veal, as it is the only way these bull calves will be viewed as a desired product and therefore respected.

Equally frustrating is the fact that veal is delicious when treated properly: just ask the Italians or the French. Known as the 'chameleon' of French cuisine, the mild flavour and tender meat is put to work in the kitchen to create all kinds of marvels (see pages 378–395). Not to mention the culinary marvel that is veal bones and the collagen they produce.

AT THE BUTCHER

You may have noticed that in Australian, American, British and French cookbooks familiar cuts of meat are given different names: this is generally a reflection of the culinary traditions of the nation. A good butcher will let the animal's structure guide the incisions and will work with the natural lines, a kind of dot-to-dot created by the muscles and the bones.

THE CARCASS

Taking apart a carcass is a logical process. Starting at the front, the **cheeks** are slipped from their socket, while the **clod** (or shoulder) is simply teased away from the blade bone. Just above the shoulder is the **chuck**, or neck, which is beautiful for slow cooking: a favourite for casseroles and stews.

The middle of the carcass is a bit more complicated. Here the meat is pure and free from sinew. The **loin** accounts for about 12 per cent of the cow and deciding where you cut the muscle and bone will change the other options; it is a beefy game of Tetris. The **rib eye** comes down from the neck: it's where we get the **standing rib roast** and rib eye steaks. If the bone is removed it will become a cube roll (which is, in turn, cut into **Scotch fillet** steaks). Moving beyond the rib cage, the loin muscle becomes the **striploin** (sirloin). By virtue of the T-shaped bone the sirloin is connected to, it can be cut laterally with the **tenderloin** or eye fillet, to create a classic T-bone steak.

There are a couple of other cuts from the middle of the animal. These cuts sit lower on the cow, consequently getting more of a work-out than those on the cow's back: here we find beef **short ribs** (the continuation of the rib bones), **skirt steaks** and the **brisket** that runs along the underbelly. These cuts have a lot of flavour.

At the end of the carcass we are back to pretty obvious boundaries with the knife. The **rump** can be cut with or without the cap that sits on top. The cap is a great barbecuing cut and is much more affordable than the sirloin. Around the back of the cow we find the **silverside**, the ultimate piece of meat to pickle. The **topside** (also known as the inside) is nestled in beside the silverside. These both lead down to the **knuckle** which is a fantastic cut to make lean mince from because the texture and fibres are quite resilient. The **shin**, often referred to as gravy beef, is great for stews and slow cooking. At the tail end is, well, the **tail**, with its beautiful combination of bone, collagen and sinews.

BRITISH & AUSTRALIAN CUTS

In Australia and Britain, butchery cuts at right angles to the major muscle groups, cutting through fat deposits and bone.

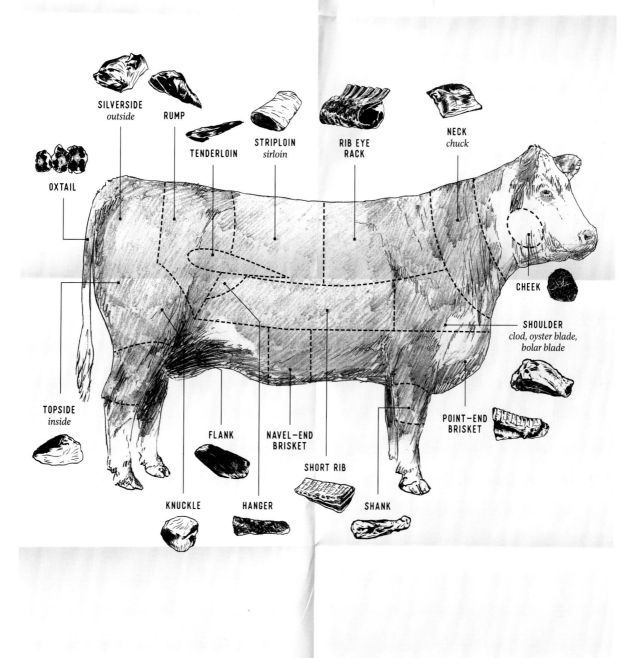

SILVERSIDE *outside*

RUMP

TENDERLOIN

STRIPLOIN *sirloin*

RIB EYE RACK

NECK *chuck*

OXTAIL

CHEEK

SHOULDER
clod, oyster blade, bolar blade

TOPSIDE *inside*

FLANK

NAVEL-END BRISKET

SHORT RIB

POINT-END BRISKET

KNUCKLE

HANGER

SHANK

For more about beef and veal cuts, see pages 318–333.

FRENCH CUTS

In continental Europe, the focus is on complex cuts. The French dissect the individual muscles, providing a higher proportion of cuts for each different cooking method.

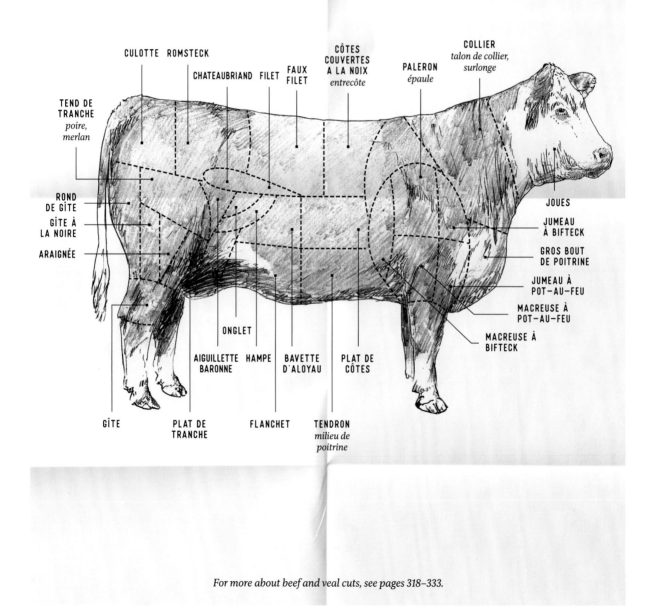

CULOTTE ROMSTECK

CHATEAUBRIAND FILET FAUX FILET

CÔTES COUVERTES A LA NOIX *entrecôte*

PALERON *épaule*

COLLIER *talon de collier, surlonge*

TEND DE TRANCHE *poire, merlan*

ROND DE GÎTE

GÎTE À LA NOIRE

ARAIGNÉE

JOUES

JUMEAU À BIFTECK

GROS BOUT DE POITRINE

JUMEAU À POT-AU-FEU

MACREUSE À POT-AU-FEU

MACREUSE À BIFTECK

ONGLET

AIGUILLETTE BARONNE HAMPE BAVETTE D'ALOYAU PLAT DE CÔTES

GÎTE PLAT DE TRANCHE FLANCHET TENDRON *milieu de poitrine*

For more about beef and veal cuts, see pages 318–333.

AMERICAN CUTS

In the United States, simplified butchery focuses on the grilling cuts,
with much of the rest of the animal used as ground beef or mince
for the ubiquitous hamburger.

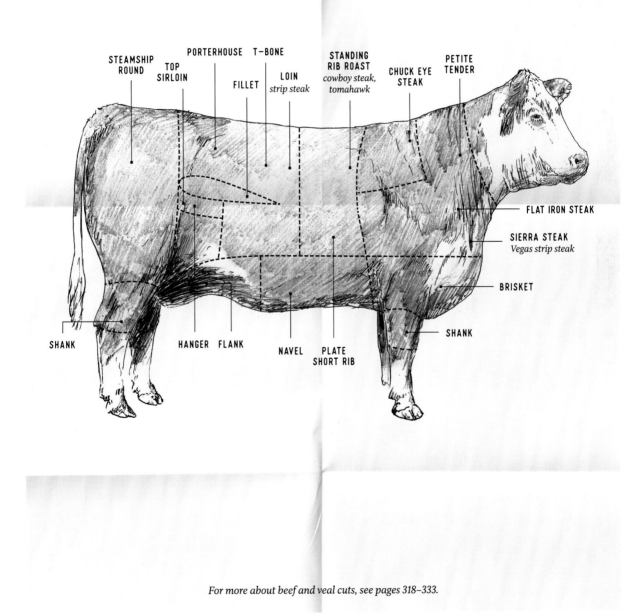

STEAMSHIP ROUND

TOP SIRLOIN

PORTERHOUSE   T—BONE

FILLET

LOIN
strip steak

STANDING RIB ROAST
cowboy steak, tomahawk

CHUCK EYE STEAK

PETITE TENDER

FLAT IRON STEAK

SIERRA STEAK
Vegas strip steak

BRISKET

SHANK

SHANK   HANGER   FLANK   NAVEL   PLATE SHORT RIB

For more about beef and veal cuts, see pages 318–333.

BEEF CUTS

BEEF CHEEKS

The cheeks tend to be a prized part of any animal. They are hard at work in the field constantly chewing and, as such, they are excellent when slowly cooked to allow the connective tissue, sinew and fat to break down and release their flavour. Beef cheeks have the added advantage of being a lovely manageable size, at around 300–350 g (10½–12 oz) each they can easily be cooked whole until they are soft and unctuous. You may need to remove the layer of silverskin from the top of the beef cheek before cooking. Simply slide your knife between the silverskin and meat and, angling the blade upwards, run it along the skin to remove, or you can ask your butcher to do it for you.

CUT WEIGHT: 300–400 G (10½–14 OZ)
BEST COOKED: BRAISED
OPTIMAL FINISH: SOFT AND TENDER
RECIPE: SEE PAGES 336–337

NECK
CHUCK, CHUCK TENDER

Beef neck, or chuck, is the top of a muscle that runs all the way along the spine. At this point the muscle gets a good work-out reaching down for grass. Because of this it is rich in collagen and sinews that melt and become gelatinous with slow cooking, basting the meat in a gooey tenderness that makes these cuts far superior to others when it comes to a stew or ragù. The chuck tender, a small muscle within the neck that sits on top of the shoulder blade, makes a wonderful roast when cooked whole.

CUT WEIGHT: 4–6 KG (9 LB–11 LB 8 OZ)
BEST COOKED: BRAISED
OPTIMAL FINISH: SOFT AND TENDER
RECIPES: SEE PAGES 338–343

SHOULDER
BOLAR BLADE, OYSTER BLADE, CLOD, PALERON, FLAT IRON

The two key muscles in the shoulder offer terrific opportunities for the patient chef. They are both hardworking and therefore sweeter and tastier than many other cuts, but they are both quite different. The largest muscle, the bolar, is cost effective and can make a great family roast. The oyster blade is the ultimate cut of beef for a daube, particularly revered by the French for its riches in connective tissue, marbling and sinew, but the oyster blade has another hidden talent: trimmed and prepared carefully it is a fantastic piece of meat to grill or pan-fry (developed, or at least marketed, by the Americans as a flat iron steak): it's the ultimate Jekyll and Hyde cut.

CUT WEIGHT: 4–6 KG (9 LB–11 LB 8 OZ)
BEST COOKED: BRAISED
OPTIMAL FINISH: SOFT AND TENDER
RECIPES: SEE PAGES 344–345
AND 396–397

Please note that all weights are approximate, as animals will differ based on their age, breed and feed. The internal temperatures given are the rested temperatures. For more information on cooking styles, roasting times, etcetera, see pages 448–455.

RIB EYE RACK
SCOTCH FILLET

Also known as standing rib roast, OP rib (oven prepared), *côte de boeuf* or cube roll (when boneless). This is the cut that ticks every box: flavour, texture, tenderness, juiciness. It is the first of the muscles that run the length of the spine, known as the loin of the cow. It comes down from the neck and connects to the sirloin or striploin. Sitting on top of the cow, it does little work and is naturally tender. Left whole it is a great roasting cut, because of the chain of fat that runs through the centre of the muscle. This bastes the meat from the inside as it roasts. The rib eye cap, which can be found within the layer of fat that sits over the rib eye rack, is worth seeking out.

→ When the bone is removed it's called a cube roll, which, when cut into steaks, becomes Scotch fillet.

→ This is a big cut of beef, so make sure it'll fit in your oven or pan. If not, ask the butcher to trim some of the bone.

CUT WEIGHT: 6-RIB ROAST, 3–6 KG
 (6 LB 12 OZ–13 LB 8 OZ)
BEST COOKED: ROASTED
OPTIMAL FINISH: MEDIUM-RARE,
 INTERNAL TEMPERATURE 55˚C (130˚F)
RECIPE: SEE PAGES 346–347

STRIPLOIN
SIRLOIN

Found between the rib eye rack and the rump, the striploin is one of the most expensive cuts of beef but it's cost effective in its own way: it requires very little intervention in the kitchen. It responds beautifully to quick cooking and, as it has a higher moisture content than tenderloin, it is best to undercook it a little: opt for medium-rare, tending to rare. Look for a sirloin from a mature animal: meat that has been dry-aged, is well marbled and has a deep, rich cherry red colour.

CUT WEIGHT: 4–6 KG (9 LB–11 LB 8 OZ)
BEST COOKED: ROAST
OPTIMAL FINISH: MEDIUM-RARE,
 INTERNAL TEMPERATURE 55˚C (130˚F)

TENDERLOIN
EYE FILLET, CHATEAUBRIAND, FILET MIGNON, TOURNEDOS

This cut is the most tender and the most expensive! What the tenderloin lacks in flavour, it more than makes up for in tenderness. Positioned beneath the sirloin, along the spine, the tenderloin finishes within the rump. As this is one of the least-used muscles on the cow it is not forgiving in the pan so take care not to overcook it.

It's best if you treat it as three separate parts. The thick end at the top of the muscle is known as the chateaubriand or butt tenderloin. It sits almost inside the rump and consequently has the most flavour. The middle of the tenderloin makes round, tender steaks. Finally, the tail of the tenderloin, the filet mignon, is wonderful for steak tartare.

→ To cook the tenderloin whole, fold the narrow tail end up with the rest of the fillet and tie it in place to create an even log and ensure even cooking.

CUT WEIGHT: 1.6–2.2 KG (3 LB 8 OZ–
 4 LB 8 OZ)
OPTIMAL FINISH: MEDIUM-RARE,
 INTERNAL TEMPERATURE 55˚C (130˚F)
RECIPES: SEE PAGES 350–351 AND
 354–355

RUMP
TRI-TIP, RUMP CAP, PICAÑHA, ROSTBIFF, RUMP STEAK, TOP SIRLOIN, FAUX-SIRLOIN

The rump sees a moderate amount of exertion and consequently it has great flavour: it can be fantastic grilled or slowly cooked. It is a complex group of three key muscles: the rostbiff, rump cap and tri-tip.

The rump cap is well marbled and is a favourite to grill or roast (particularly favoured in Brazil, where it is known as *picaña*). It is a lovely size to roast, the fat layer basting it as it cooks (remove this after cooking if you want). The rostbiff, the largest muscle in the rump, is relatively lean, with just a little intramuscular fat. It makes a lovely stand-alone roast or can be portioned into rump steaks; it is great cubed and threaded onto skewers. The tri-tip, a small triangular muscle, can be roasted whole but is also perfect for thin slicing and quick cooking.

CUT WEIGHT: WHOLE, 6 KG (13 LB 8 OZ):
   TRI-TIP, 700 G–1.2 KG (1 LB 9 OZ–2 LB
   10 OZ): RUMP CAP, 1.5 KG (3 LB 5 OZ)
BEST COOKED: ROASTED
OPTIMAL FINISH: MEDIUM–RARE,
   INTERNAL TEMPERATURE 55°C (130°F)
RECIPES: SEE PAGES 352–355

SILVERSIDE
EYE ROUND, GIRELLO, OUTSIDE FLAT OR OUTSIDE, BOTTOM ROUND

The silverside is the ultimate piece of meat to pickle or corn. This muscle is hardworking, but when married with the salty solution it becomes an incredible cut of meat to eat, as it manages to retain a texture that is entirely unique.

Situated under the rump, the silverside is made up of two leg muscles: the outside flat and the eye round. The outside flat is a large fibrous muscle that is best roasted whole or pickled and poached for corned beef (think Reuben sandwiches). The eye round or girello is a smaller missile-shaped muscle that is sought after for bresaola or as a premium cut for corned beef.

CUT WEIGHT: 6–7 KG (13 LB 8 OZ–
   15 LB 12 OZ)
BEST COOKED: POACHED
OPTIMAL FINISH: SOFT AND TENDER
RECIPE: SEE PAGES 356–357

TOPSIDE
INSIDE

While this cut is versatile and has a number of uses, the topside does one thing amazingly well: lean mince (ground beef). The topside sits inside the leg and for this reason is also known as the 'inside'. It is very lean, with only small amounts of fat on the surface.

It is great for dicing, mincing and other applications where lean meat is required. The texture and fibres of this cut are quite resilient. It has the perfect ratio of fat for lean ground mince. This cut can be used in two halves, with one half reserved for bresaola and the other used for beef jerky or biltong.

→ The topside is good for a pot-roast, an economical and very tasty dinner for the family.

CUT WEIGHT: 6–8 KG (13 LB 8 OZ–18 LB)
BEST COOKED: POT–ROASTED
OPTIMAL FINISH: SOFT AND TENDER
RECIPE: SEE PAGES 358–359

SHORT RIB
BEEF SPARE RIBS, CHUCK RIBS, INTERCOSTALS

This section of the rib cage is the continuation of the bones from the rib eye rack that sits above it. It includes a well-marbled, flavour-packed flap of meat on top of the bones, the ribs beneath and the intercostals. It can be sold bone-in or boneless and grilled over high heat to release complex, deep flavours or slowly braised to let the connective tissue melt down.

The intercostals or rib fingers are found between the bones that run from the rib eye rack to the short ribs. This cut is a reservoir of flavour and juiciness.

→ Leaving the bones attached adds flavour; cut across the bone this is popular for a South American asado.
→ Boneless, this cut has found great favour (and flavour) on Korean-style barbecues and Japanese teppanyaki.

CUT WEIGHT: 5-RIB, 1.5–2.5 KG
  (3 LB 5 OZ–5 LB 8 OZ)
BEST COOKED: LOW AND SLOW
OPTIMAL FINISH: TENDER
RECIPE: SEE PAGES 364–365

BRISKET
POINT END, NAVEL END

Brisket, irrespective of the animal, will always deliver. It has an unstructured, unplanned combination of meat and fat and dense muscle fibres. The navel end, an inexpensive cut, can be fatty and fibrous, but when trimmed will reveal a special cut called the karubi plate.

At the point end, where the brisket runs up to the front of the animal, the meat is naturally larger and leaner than the navel end. More sought-after, this cut is wonderful rolled, tied then slowly braised in stock to release flavour from the meat and break down the connective fibres, giving a luscious texture. The brisket is a firm favourite for the low and slow cooking of the Texas-style barbecue.

CUT WEIGHT: 4–6 KG (9 LB–11 LB 8 OZ)
BEST COOKED: BRAISED
OPTIMAL FINISH: SOFT AND TENDER
RECIPES: SEE PAGES 362–363 AND 366–367

KNUCKLE
ROUND

The knuckle runs lengthways down the leg and terminates at the knee bone. Made up of a central eye muscle, the leaner parts of the knuckle can be diced or thinly sliced; however, as with many of the working muscles on the animal, this cut requires slower cooking, but rewards with texture and flavour. The knuckle is super-lean: if that is what you are seeking, this is where you will find it.

CUT WEIGHT: 4–6 KG (9 LB–11 LB 8 OZ)
BEST COOKED: BRAISED
OPTIMAL FINISH: SOFT AND TENDER
RECIPE: SEE PAGES 368–369

Please note that all weights are approximate, as animals will differ based on their age, breed and feed. The internal temperatures given are the rested temperatures. For more information on cooking styles, roasting times, etcetera, see pages 448–455.

SHIN SHANK
GRAVY BEEF, OSSO BUCO

More than any other cut, the shin shank has a huge collection of collagen and sinews and, when properly cooked, it is awesome. It's somewhat disparagingly known as gravy beef, which is a pity, because when approached intelligently it yields silky soft, densely flavoured dishes of braised beef that are impossible to replicate with any other cut. Seamed with connective tissue that breaks down with the long, slow application of heat and liquid, these muscles sit astride the two shin bones and connect between the Achilles tendon and the knee.

The shin shank is made up of the heel muscle and the conical muscle, with the beef tendons running through them. Beef tendon, traditionally seen in Asian soups and stews, has been receiving more attention of late and these days can be found puffed and deep-fried on high-end restaurant menus around the globe.

CUT WEIGHT: 2 KG (4 LB 8 OZ)
BEST COOKED: BRAISED
OPTIMAL FINISH: SOFT AND TENDER
RECIPE: SEE PAGES 370–371

OXTAIL

In Old English, the word ox was used to segregate the classes: words like oxtail and ox cheek were used to refer to the cuts of beef that were available for the poor. The flavour of these cuts tells a different story in the mouth: a working muscle, slowly cooked on the bone, combined with the more pronounced flavour of a 30- to 36-month-old beast makes for excellent eating. It requires at least three hours cooking, but the combination of the bone, providing gelatine and thus viscosity to your sauce, and the full flavour of this hardworking muscle makes for a delicious stew. Because of the blood and bone in this cut, you may want to soak it in cold water before cooking, and you will need to take extra special care to skim it as you bring it to the boil; however, it will reward you with a lovely thick sauce made simply with water and the tail.

CUT WEIGHT: 1 KG (2 LB 4 OZ)
BEST COOKED: BRAISED
OPTIMAL FINISH: SOFT AND TENDER
RECIPE: SEE PAGES 372–373

TONGUE

Both beef and veal tongues are highly revered in the kitchen. Smoke it, cure it, barbecue it, serve it crisp or brine it and braise it: with a multitude of cooking options, tongue may be one of the more underrated cuts of beef! The tongue is a hardworking muscle, meaning that it can be tough, but will also be full of flavour. Slow, gentle cooking will make the most of the complex connective tissues and muscle fibres, but timing is important to keep the textures and flavours intact. If you overcook tongue it can become stringy, mushy and tasteless. If salted, you will want to wash and soak the tongue for 24 hours, changing the water once, before cooking. Often the tongue will be slowly poached, starting with cold water, before it is skinned and then transferred to its final cooking method.

→ With Wagyu, the marbling starts at the front of the beast, and thus the tongue will be the most marbled muscle in the whole carcass.

CUT WEIGHT: 800 G–1.1 KG (1 LB 12 OZ– 2 LB 7 OZ)
BEST COOKED: BRAISED
OPTIMAL FINISH: SOFT AND TENDER (BUT NOT TOO SOFT!)
RECIPE: SEE PAGES 386–387

The skirt steaks *are much admired for their complexity of flavour. See page 327 for more details.*

STEAK CUTS

FLAT IRON

RIB EYE

SCOTCH FILLET

The flat iron steak is a little-known steak that is rightfully revered by butchers and chefs. While the shoulder is traditionally a braising cut, when trimmed and prepared properly it reveals this gem, brought to light in an American beef study in 2002.

Normally the oyster blade is cross-cut into top blade steaks, or feather steaks, but a flat iron is cut from between the two layers of the oyster blade and thus has all the connective tissue removed. Treated this way it is a brilliant grilling cut with great depth of flavour. Furthermore, when cut thin on the bias it showcases its incredible marbling.

AUSTRALIA: OYSTER BLADE STEAK
BRITAIN: BUTLER'S STEAK
USA: FLAT IRON STEAK

Cut from the rib eye rack, this is the cut that's got it all: flavour, texture, tenderness, juiciness. When cut vertically, rib eye steaks (or *entrecôtes* in French) are the result. If the bone is removed, it's called a cube roll, which can be cut into Scotch fillet steaks.

Sometimes you will find the rib eye with the short rib still attached; this cut is known as a tomahawk steak and it is from between the long ribs that the intercostals are cut.

ARGENTINA: OJO DE BIFE
AUSTRALIA: RIB EYE
FRANCE: ENTRECÔTE
USA: COWBOY STEAK, BONE—IN RIB EYE

The Scotch fillet is a boneless rib eye steak. It is easy to recognise due to its natural roundness and the eye of fat that you can see in the middle of the steak. This little nugget of fat is one of this steak's most excellent features, basting it from the middle as it cooks. The Scotch fillet has more beef flavour than a fillet, and is tender, due to the cut's natural marbling.

ARGENTINA: BIFE ANCHO
AUSTRALIA & BRITAIN: SCOTCH FILLET
FRANCE: CÔTE DE BOEUF
USA: RIB EYE, SPENCER STEAK

The optimal steak is around 3 cm (1¼ inches) thick, allowing time for the meat to caramelise without cooking the centre. We suggest cooking steaks to medium-rare, with an internal rested temperature of 55°C (130°F).
For information about cooking steaks, see our barbecuing tips on pages 448–449.

T-BONE

The shortloin, consisting of the tenderloin and sirloin attached together on the spine, can be cut vertically to reveal the much-admired T-bone. You get the contrast in tenderness and flavour between the sirloin and tenderloin; it's cooked on the bone, not just adding flavour but conducting heat through to the centre of the meat; and, finally, there is the sheer awe and beauty of a big, juicy T-bone on the table. T-bones differ greatly in size, depending on which end of the shortloin it is cut from and how much eye fillet is attached. The American porterhouse, for example, is cut from the rear end of the shortloin, and therefore has more tenderloin. Traditionally cut thicker in Tuscany than it is in Texas, we suggest cutting it into 800 g (1 lb 12 oz) portions, perfect for two.

ARGENTINA: BIFE DE COSTILLA
AUSTRALIA & BRITAIN: T-BONE
ITALY: BISTECCA ALLA FIORENTINA
USA: PORTERHOUSE (WITH FILLET)
    OR T-BONE
RECIPE: SEE PAGES 348–349

SIRLOIN

Often playing second fiddle to a rib eye steak, the sirloin is a brilliant steak, but does need a little extra love. Seek out a beautiful dry-aged sirloin from a mature animal and it will be one of the nicest pieces of meat you have eaten. When sold without the eye fillet—which would be a T-bone—but with the bone still attached, it is referred to as a Delmonico, club steak or bone-in sirloin. Tender but resilient, the sirloin has a beautiful texture and a pure beefy flavour.

ARGENTINA: BIFE ANGOSTO
AUSTRALIA & BRITAIN: SIRLOIN
FRANCE: CONTRE-FILET, FAUX-FILET
USA: CLUB STEAK (BONE-IN), NEW YORK
    STEAK, STRIP STEAK

EYE FILLET

What the fillet lacks in flavour, it more than makes up for in tenderness. A long tubular muscle, the middle of the tenderloin is where we find the perfectly round, lean steaks. Known as tournedos in France, they are beautifully tender with a mild beefy flavour (with foie gras, this becomes a tournedos Rossini). The rump end of the tenderloin is also known as the châteaubriand (a classic roast for two), its position within the rump muscle bestowing this end of the tenderloin with a little extra flavour. The rest of the tenderloin can be portioned to make filet mignon (the lower narrow end of the fillet) or butterflied, will become the perfect minute steak.

ARGENTINA: BIFE DE LOMO
AUSTRALIA: EYE FILLET
BRITAIN: FILLET
FRANCE: FILET MIGNON, TOURNEDOS,
    CHÂTEAUBRIAND
USA: TENDERLOIN

RUMP
RUMP CAP, ROSTBIFF, TRI-TIP

Rump steak can be cut laterally from the whole rump, incorporating all three muscles (rump cap, tri-tip and rostbiff); however, split into separate muscles you get to appreciate the different virtues of each muscle. The rump cap, sometimes referred to as the poor-man's sirloin, is particularly revered in South America where it is called the *picaña* (pronounced pee-CON-ya). A star of their churrasco restaurants, it is cut in thirds, folded back over itself, threaded onto the rotisserie with the fat side out (to protect the meat) and cooked over charcoal. The tri-tip is perfect thinly sliced and quickly grilled for minute steak sandwiches and it is one of the most popular cuts for the Korean-style barbecue.

ARGENTINA: CUADRIL, PICAÑA (CAP)
AUSTRALIA: RUMP STEAK
RANCE: ROMSTECK, CULOTTE
USA: TOP SIRLOIN

SPIDER STEAK

When a butcher cuts a side of beef using the 'French cut' method, each muscle is removed separately. The spider steak, known as *bifteck araignée* in French, is a very special muscle found in the hollow of the hip joint alongside *le merlon*, *la poire* and *la fausse-araignée*. These are muscles that do not get much work and are therefore very tender, but also have great flavour. They are difficult to remove as a piece and unusual to find. A true butcher's gem!

AUSTRALIA & BRITAIN: SPIDER STEAK
FRANCE: ARAIGNÉE
USA: OYSTER STEAK

FLANK
BAVETTE

The bavette or flank is the most approachable of the skirt steaks. Situated near the abdominals between the brisket and the back leg, it has a stronger beef flavour than traditional steaks, but not so intense as to scare off your family. Weighing in at around 1 kg (2 lb 4 oz) per bavette, it is a great cut to barbecue whole and then slice at the table. Flap meat or flap steak is another of the skirts taken from this part of the animal.

ARGENTINA: VACIO
AUSTRALIA: FLANK
BRITAIN: GOOSE SKIRT
FRANCE: BAVETTE
USA: FLANK

HANGER

A true individual, the hanger or onglet literally hangs from the diaphragm and is unusual in that it doesn't have a pair: there is only one hanger in each animal. Hanging between the tenderloin and the rib, it sits close to the offal and has an intense flavour. While it is tricky to trim and portion, this cut is amazing caramelised in the pan then roasted whole. The hanger has a looser grain than most steaks, but the flavour is phenomenal. It's one of the very best steaks on offer!

AUSTRALIA: HANGING TENDER

BRITAIN: HANGER

FRANCE: ONGLET

ITALY: LOMBATELLO

USA: SKIRT STEAK, BUTCHER'S STEAK

INSIDE SKIRT AND OUTSIDE (THIN) SKIRT

The inside skirt runs along the inside of the abdominal wall, from the hindquarter through to the navel end point of the brisket, while the thin or outside skirt is the costal muscle of the diaphragm. With a slightly more challenging personality, here you will note a spike in flavour and a more unusual texture. The unique flavour (due to their proximity to the offal) and texture makes them very different from other cuts of beef. The outside skirt may also be referred to as harami and is particularly prized in Korea and Japan. The inside skirt sits beside the thin skirt and is broader in its make-up and has a coarse grain.

→ The 'skirts' are named for their pleated appearance, with wide, open-grained fibres. While this is certainly a family of cuts, they reveal some very different personalities.

RECIPE: SEE PAGES 360–361

The optimal steak is around 3 cm (1¼ inches) thick, allowing time for the meat to caramelise without cooking the centre.
We suggest cooking steaks to medium-rare, with an internal rested temperature of 55°C (130°F).
For information about cooking steaks, see our barbecuing tips on pages 448–449.

VEAL CUTS

NECK
CHUCK

This is a great alternative to beef neck if you are seeking a softer and milder flavour. The neck or chuck is great diced or cooked slowly for a delicately flavoured stew. The firmer textured meat from the forequarter takes time to break down but is absolutely worth the effort. With the neck, we must also mention the head. While not for the squeamish, the French love the head for their classic *tête de veau*, veal brains are beautiful braised and the tongue is a great delicacy the world over.

→ Preorder the head from your butcher to slowly cook the classic French dish *tête de veau*.

→ This cut makes excellent meatballs.

CUT WEIGHT: 4 KG (9 LB)
BEST COOKED: BRAISED
OPTIMAL FINISH: SOFT AND TENDER
RECIPE: SEE PAGES 390–391

SHOULDER
CLOD, BOLAR BLADE, OYSTER BLADE,

An economical roasting cut, particularly if you are looking for a milder flavour with guaranteed tenderness. This is the second of the main forequarter muscles, sitting alongside the neck or chuck, and it's great for dicing and slow cooking. The meat requires much less cooking time than beef as the animal is younger and the meat more tender. The shoulder can be stuffed and rolled to create a roast.

→ Ask the butcher to bone, roll and tie the shoulder for you, or bone it out and supply you with the string so that you can roll and tie it at home.

CUT WEIGHT: BONE IN, 4 KG (9 LB);
　BONELESS, 2.5 KG (5 LB 8 OZ)
BEST COOKED: ROASTED
OPTIMAL FINISH: MEDIUM, INTERNAL
　TEMPERATURE 60°C (140°F)
RECIPE: SEE PAGES 378–379

RACK

A veal rack benefits from a marinade to protect it and create a crunchy exterior. Consisting of seven to eight ribs, a veal rack is more manageable than a beef standing rib roast. It is tender, coming from the top of the back where the muscle is thicker but does little work. Often you will see the rack cut between the bones into cutlets, which are great for the barbecue and particularly wonderful when pan-fried.

→ Ask your butcher to trim or french the rack for you. Make sure the chine bone (spine) is removed, so you can carve individual cutlets at the table.

→ Veal weights range widely. Ask for a suitable cut, factoring in 250–300 g (9–10½ oz) of cutlets per person.

→ Crumb the veal cutlets and pan-fry for the Milanese specialty *cotoletta*.

CUT WEIGHT: 8-RIB RACK, 3 KG (6 LB 12 OZ)
BEST COOKED: RACK, ROASTED;
　CUTLET, GRILLED
OPTIMAL FINISH: RACK, MEDIUM–RARE
　TO MEDIUM; CUTLET, MEDIUM;
　INTERNAL TEMPERATURE 60°C (140°F)
RECIPE: SEE PAGES 382–383

Please note that all weights are approximate, as animals will differ based on their age, breed and feed. The internal temperatures given are the rested temperatures. For more information on cooking styles, roasting times, etcetera, see pages 448–455.

BACKSTRAP
EYE OF LOIN, MEDALLIONS

The ultimate piece of veal for pan-frying, the backstrap is perfect cut into escalopes. Technically the backstrap refers to the whole muscle that runs along the spine, from the neck, through the ribs, and down to the rump. More often than not, veal backstrap refers to the shortloin or the sirloin (as it is known when taken from older beef). The backstrap is ideal for a range of cooking techniques that highlight the amazingly soft texture and sweet milky flavour of premium veal. This is the cut used to create veal saltimbocca.

→ Leave the backstrap and tenderloin attached to the bone and cut chops from it (this is akin to a T-bone).
→ The backstrap is one of the most tender of the cuts of veal and makes the Rolls-Royce of veal dishes: scaloppine. Ask your butcher to cut medallions and gently pound them with a meat mallet.

CUT WEIGHT: 1.5–2 KG (3 LB 5 OZ–
    4 LB 8 OZ)
BEST COOKED: BARBECUED, GRILLED
OPTIMAL FINISH: MEDIUM–RARE,
    INTERNAL TEMPERATURE 55˚C (130˚F)

RUMP

Veal rump is beautiful. Situated at the end of the loin, at the top of the leg, the rump is a combination of three muscles; however, unlike a beef rump, it is rarely broken down into these three components. Rather, the rostbiff and cap are always kept together: left whole for roasting or sliced across the face into steaks. The final muscle is known as the tri-tip: it is the tail that extends off the rump and is a grilling or roasting cut. Roast it whole, or cut it into steaks; the great thing about veal is that you know it is going to be tender.

→ Your butcher can roll and tie the rump into a neat little package for you, which will ensure even cooking.

CUT WEIGHT: 2.5 KG (5 LB 8 OZ)
BEST COOKED: ROASTED
OPTIMAL FINISH: MEDIUM–RARE,
    INTERNAL TEMPERATURE: 55˚C (130˚F)
RECIPE: SEE PAGES 394–395

TOPSIDE, SILVERSIDE AND KNUCKLE

The topside, silverside and knuckle are all quite lean muscles on a calf. They are terrific when thinly sliced for the classic Wiener schnitzel. The topside is often sliced thinly and gently pounded with a mallet. This is a good (and cheaper) alternative to backstrap for escalopes. At the top of the leg, is the silverside—where we cut the outside flat—and a cylindrical cut known as girello or eye round. Italians will traditionally use it to make *vitello tonnato*, a classic dish of gently poached and sliced veal coated in a tuna mayonnaise and anchovies.

→ When preparing these cuts for scaloppine, your butcher will cut across the grain, keeping the knife at a 45-degree angle to ensure the meat is tender.

CUT WEIGHT: KNUCKLE, 2.5 KG (5 LB 8 OZ);
    TOPSIDE, 2.5 KG (5 LB 8 OZ);
    SILVERSIDE, 2.5 KG (5 LB 8 OZ)
BEST COOKED: ROASTED
OPTIMAL FINISH: MEDIUM–RARE,
    INTERNAL TEMPERATURE 55˚C (130˚F)
RECIPES: SEE PAGES 380–381, 384–385
    AND 392–393

BREAST
BRISKET

Somewhat overlooked, the veal breast or brisket is a flavour-packed section of the calf that runs from the end of the rib cage around its belly. Characterised by fibrous meat and delicate pale fat, the breast can be opened out to provide a lovely pocket to stuff, or can be hand-tied and rolled for a classic poached or slow-roasted dish. It's fantastic cooked slowly.

Veal breast can also be cubed and stewed and is used in dishes such as the French classic *blanquette de veau*.

Veal breast should be one of the cheapest cuts of veal, but can be incredibly delicious.

CUT WEIGHT: 4.5 KG (10 LB) WITH BONES. 3 KG (6 LB 12 OZ) BONELESS
BEST COOKED: BRAISED
OPTIMAL FINISH: SOFT AND TENDER
RECIPE: SEE PAGES 378–379

OSSO BUCO
SHANK

This succulent, sweet piece of meat responds well to long, slow cooking, bringing out the gelatinous properties. Leave the shank whole and roast it for a great dish for three or four people; or cut it across the bone and it is the perfect classic braised Italian dish. The traditional oval-shaped sliced shin comes from the calf and not from the cow. Veal sliced laterally from the centre of the shank offers two of life's pleasures: the silky soft meat from the braised shin, and the delicate soft marrow in the centre. The hind shank is bigger and thus has more meat (and marrow) than the fore shank. It is favoured for osso buco.

Chefs also use the veal bones specifically for their gentle flavour; they are slowly cooked for up to 24 hours, often with a few key stock vegetables and a couple of pig's trotters or veal feet for their gelatine, and then reduced to a thick syrupy glaze that is added to almost every sauce they adorn your plate with.

CUT WEIGHT: 600 G–1 KG (1 LB 5 OZ– 2 LB 4 OZ)
BEST COOKED: BRAISED
OPTIMAL FINISH: SOFT AND TENDER
RECIPE: SEE PAGES 388–389

KIDNEY
ROGNONS DE VEAUX

Kidneys are a delicacy in many countries, but do require a little love to get them to a happy place. This is in part due to the work they do in the body: the unpleasant truth is that they can carry an odour of urine. Soaking them in milk will help to dissipate this. It is also important to make sure they are carefully cleaned and trimmed of sinew and their skin is removed.

As far as kidneys go, veal kidneys are milder in flavour than those of the cow or the pig; they are also more tender and perhaps, because of all of this, more likeable! Fresh is fundamental, and here you will find a sweetness, followed by an excellent earthiness.

CUT WEIGHT: 450 G (1 LB)
BEST COOKED: HOT AND FAST
RECIPE: SEE PAGES 396–397

SWEETBREADS

Bearing no relevance to their name, the sweetbreads come from the glands of the animal. There are two varieties: from the throat and from the belly or heart. They both have a delicious creamy taste and, when cooked well, a nice exterior crunch and soft interior. When working with veal sweetbreads the bulk of the work is done at home. While some chefs soak their sweetbreads in ice-cold water (for 2–3 hours), you can also use ice-cold milk to great effect and this helps to remove the blood. You will then need to blanch them for a minute in salted, boiling water (no-one wants a raw sweetbread) before picking over them with a sharp knife to get rid of any gristly or sinewy parts. They are then ready to go; simply pat them dry, dredge in flour and caramelise in a pan with butter.

→ The heart and pancreatic sweetbreads are the more highly prized.

CUT WEIGHT: 200–400 G (7 OZ–14 OZ)
BEST COOKED: HOT AND FAST
RECIPE: SEE PAGES 398–399

MARROW

Fergus Henderson, British advocate for nose-to-tail eating, put bone marrow back on the culinary map with his dish of toast with a parsley, caper and lemon salad and a few roasted marrow bones. For good reason: the rich, creamy, nutty flavour is indulgent beefy butter.

The good news is that the marrow—the soft tissue within the bones—is not only nutrient dense but, while it is very fatty, it is predominantly made up of monounsaturated fats (like olive oil) and it is also simple to cook. Ask your butcher to cut the bones from the femur (thigh bone) of the veal horizontally into 5 cm (2 inch) pieces, or vertically. Put the bones on a roasting tray in a moderate oven and roast for around 20 minutes. You want the marrow to be shimmering, wobbly and soft, but not to melt entirely so you're left with your bones in a puddle of liquid. Spread the warm marrow on a bit of toast with a scattering of salt flakes.

CUT WEIGHT: CENTRE CUT, 5 CM
    (2 INCHES) LONG, 150 G (5½ OZ)
OPTIMAL FINISH: UNTIL WOBBLING,
    NOT RUNNING
RECIPE: SEE PAGES 400–401

LIVER

Veal offal has a delicate, soft and clean flavour, yet it still retains that delicious offal flavour. Ask your butcher to clean the veal liver for you. The butcher will need to devein it, remove the skin and slice it for you.

To cook fresh veal liver: sprinkle slices lightly with salt (or dust with seasoned flour) and heat a frying pan over high heat. When it is hot, add olive oil and the liver slices, cooking quickly until golden on each side, but still tender and blushing pink in the middle. This should take 1–2 minutes in total. Throw in a little knob of butter for the final 15 seconds. Serve with bacon lardons and caramelised balsamic onions.

CUT WEIGHT: 2–3 KG (4 LB 8 OZ–
    6 LB 12 OZ)
BEST COOKED: PAN-FRIED
RECIPE: SEE PAGES 376–377

Please note that all weights are approximate, as animals will differ based on their age, breed and feed. For more information on cooking styles, roasting times, etcetera, see pages 448–455.

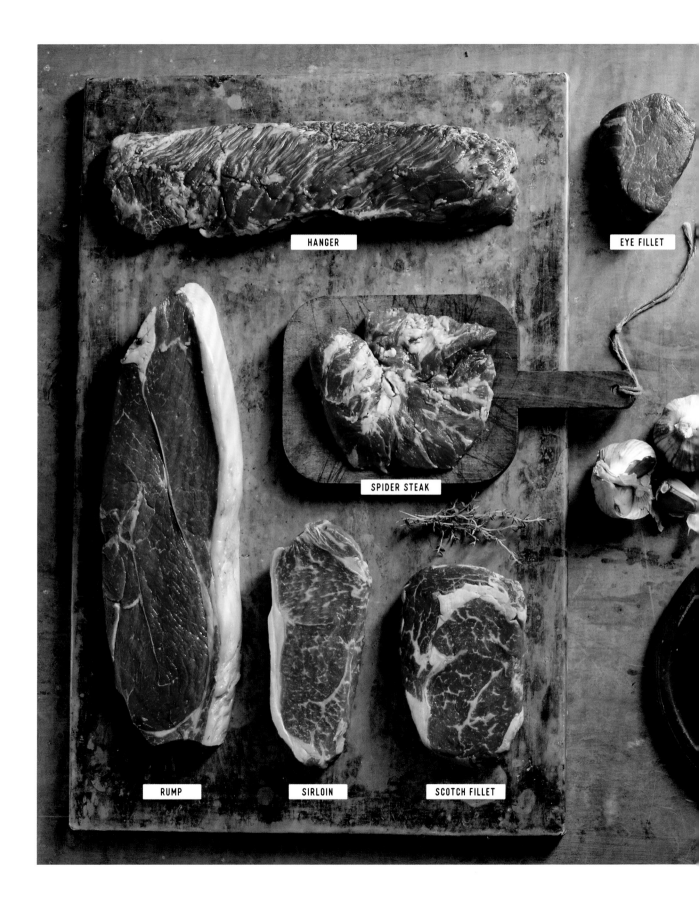

HANGER

EYE FILLET

SPIDER STEAK

RUMP

SIRLOIN

SCOTCH FILLET

OUTSIDE (THIN) SKIRT

FLAT IRON

RIB EYE

FLANK (BAVETTE)

T-BONE

INSIDE SKIRT

IN THE KITCHEN

Whether it's the perfect steak or a large roasting cut to crown your next dinner party, beef can offer some of the most extravagant additions to your culinary repertoire.

SELECT AND STORE

COLOUR

A deep cherry red colour is a good indicator that the cow was raised and slaughtered well. In general, the deeper the colour, the more mature the beast. Older cows will also have more internal and external fat and a deep, beefy flavour.

If the beef is on the lighter side of cherry, it usually means the animal was slaughtered younger—which isn't necessarily a bad thing. In Australia animals are normally slaughtered between 18 and 24 months of age. While it might not have the full force of flavour, the meat will generally be leaner and more tender.

Avoid beef that has a purple tinge with a glossy sheen, indicating it's a 'dark cutter' with a high pH. This is caused by adrenalin and is directly attributable to stress in the weeks before slaughter. The resulting meat will be tough, resilient and chewy.

FAT

Look for external fat that is a creamy white to off-white colour. The more deeply coloured fat will indicate the animal has been grass fed (due to the chlorophyll in the grass—and it's the same for butter) and may also indicate a cow is significantly older, say from three years upwards. If you are buying a grilling cut that's grass fed and 30 or so months, the fat should be creamy off-white due to extra time on pasture. The whiter the fat, the more likely the animal was grain fed. Marbling is also a good indicator of the quality of life an animal has had: there should be some flecks of intramuscular fats in the meat.

SMELL

Dry-aged meat should smell clean, beefy and earthy, akin to freshly turned earth. With wet-aged product you can expect an odour upon opening the packaging; this

Cutting with the grain

→ *Meat is made up of bundles of long muscle fibres that are laid out parallel to one another. This is easier to recognise in some cuts than it is in others; for example, in a bavette (flank).*

→ *If you cut with your knife parallel to the grain, you end up with fibres that are tough for your teeth to break through. Slicing against the grain (perpendicular to the grain) delivers very short pieces of muscle fibre that are barely held together, making them easier and more enjoyable to chew.*

→ *If meat oxidises quickly on being removed from the wet-ageing bag, it generally implies that the meat has been stored for a long time. This is OK; however, if the smell doesn't dissipate after a few minutes, the meat may have been stored too long. Have a word to your butcher.*

will dissipate after a minute or so. (For more on dry-ageing, see page 456.) All meat should have a fresh, bright, clean smell: a strong odour illustrates that it is past its best, or not properly aged.

TEXTURE

Beef should be solid and firm, not sloppy and soft; finely textured with tight grain.

STORAGE

Beef needs to breathe and is best stored in the refrigerator, wrapped in greaseproof or butchers' paper, with cool, fresh air circulating around it. Steaks and roasts can keep stored like this for around three days. If beef is vacuum-packed and frozen you can store it in the fridge for a little longer, but you will need to check with the butcher or the date on the packaging. See pages 478–479 for more information about freezing meat.

VEAL

Veal is all about colour: it should have a nice pink blush to the meat. There will be a fresh smell, which may even be slightly lactic, but don't be put off by this. Quality rose veal is fed a grain and milk-based diet that is low in iron, lending it the paler pink colour and a mild flavour.

Butchery techniques

→ **Dry-ageing** *see page 456*
→ **Marbling and fats**
   see pages 492–493
→ **Beef and veal stock** *see page 461*
→ **Bone marrow** *see page 460*
→ **Mince** *(ground meat) see page 469*

~ RED WINE-BRAISED ~
BEEF CHEEKS

Prep time *20 minutes (plus marinating)*
Cook *4 hours*

1. Combine the beef cheeks, wine, thyme and bruised garlic in a container large enough to fit snugly, cover and refrigerate overnight to marinate (this will infuse the beef cheeks with a beautiful flavour, but if you don't have time, you can marinate them for just an hour or two).

2. Preheat the oven to 180°C (350°F). Render the bacon rind in an enamelled cast-iron casserole on the stovetop, then add the bacon and cook for 4–5 minutes over medium–high heat, stirring occasionally until browned. Transfer to a plate, discarding rinds. Add a splash of olive oil to the casserole if necessary, add the mushrooms and fry over high heat, stirring occasionally, for 6–8 minutes until browned. Remove from the pan with a slotted spoon.

3. Remove the beef cheeks from the marinade (reserve the wine and thyme, but discard the garlic) and pat the beef cheeks dry with paper towel. Season generously with salt and pepper, add to the casserole and sear over medium–high heat, turning occasionally, for 5–6 minutes to brown well all over: the deeper the browning, the better the flavour of the finished dish, so take your time to do this well. Transfer to a plate.

4. Add another splash of oil to the casserole, then add the onion, carrot and celery and fry, stirring occasionally, for 6–7 minutes until tender and beginning to caramelise. Stir in the extra chopped garlic until fragrant, add the reserved wine and thyme, then boil for 5–6 minutes until reduced by half. Add 125 ml (4 fl oz/½ cup) of water and the bay leaf, bring to a simmer, season with salt and pepper and return the beef cheeks to the casserole along with the mushrooms and bacon. Make a cartouche by cutting out a round of baking paper to fit the diameter of the casserole, crumple it up, then wet it under cold running water. Lay it directly on the surface of the mixture, pressing to get rid of any air bubbles, cover tightly with a lid and transfer the casserole to the oven to braise for 3–3½ hours until fork-tender.

5. Remove the beef cheeks from braising liquid. Put the casserole on the stovetop over medium–high heat and simmer for 5–6 minutes until the braising liquid is slightly reduced. Stir in the vinegar and check the seasoning. Coarsely shred the beef cheeks and return the meat to the sauce. Serve scattered with the parsley and orange or lemon zest (if using).

INGREDIENTS

3 beef cheeks, trimmed of sinew, about
   300 g (10½ oz each)
1 bottle (750 ml) full-bodied red wine
3 thyme sprigs
2 garlic cloves, bruised with the flat of a
   knife, plus 2 extra cloves, finely chopped
2 bacon rashers, rind trimmed, sliced
Olive oil, for cooking
200 g (7 oz) Swiss brown mushrooms, halved
1 small brown onion, diced
1 small carrot, diced
1 celery stalk, diced
1 fresh bay leaf
2 teaspoons red wine vinegar
Coarsely chopped flat-leaf (Italian) parsley,
   to serve
Finely grated orange or lemon zest, to serve
   (optional)

*parsnip and potato mash or buttered
egg noodles, such as fettuccine*

SERVING
SUGGESTION

NOTE

→ *If you have the time, cool the braised beef cheeks in the liquid then refrigerate for a day or two to develop the flavours.*

Cut Beef cheeks
See page 318

SERVES 6

GOULASH

Prep time *20 minutes*
Cook *3 hours 15 minutes*

1. Preheat the oven to 140°C (275°F). Heat 2 tablespoons of lard in a large enamelled cast-iron casserole over medium–high heat, add the chilli and fry for 4–5 minutes until beginning to soften, then transfer to a plate.

2. Combine the beef, paprika, flour and caraway seeds in a large bowl, season and toss to coat well. Add beef to the casserole in batches and sear over medium–high heat, turning occasionally, for 3–4 minutes to brown well all over: make sure you don't overcrowd the pan as the meat will stew, rather than caramelise. The deeper the browning, the better the flavour of the finished dish, so take your time to do this well. Transfer the beef to a plate.

3. Add the remaining lard to the casserole, then add the onion and fry, scraping any crust from the base of the casserole and stirring occasionally, for 6–7 minutes until golden. Stir in the garlic until fragrant. If there is any flour mixture left in the bowl from the beef, add it to the pan and stir over the heat for a minute or two to cook out any flouriness. Return the beef to the casserole and add enough water to just cover, stirring to combine.

4. Add the potato, season with salt and pepper and bring to a simmer. Make a cartouche by cutting out a round of baking paper to fit the diameter of the casserole, crumple it up, then wet it under cold running water. Lay it directly on the surface of the mixture, pressing to get rid of any air bubbles. Cover with a lid and braise for 2–2½ hours until the beef is very tender.

5. Return the chilli to the casserole, squeeze in the lemon juice, then simmer over medium–low heat for 15–20 minutes until the sauce thickens slightly. Check the seasoning and serve, dolloped with sour cream and scattered with chives.

INGREDIENTS

1 kg (2 lb 4 oz) beef chuck, cut into 3–4 cm (1¼–1½ inch) chunks
2½ tablespoons lard or olive oil
2 yellow banana chillies, thinly sliced into rounds (see note)
3 tablespoons sweet Hungarian paprika
2 tablespoons plain (all-purpose) flour
2 teaspoons caraway seeds
3 brown onions, thinly sliced
1 garlic clove, finely chopped
2 large floury potatoes, peeled and cut into large chunks
Juice of 1 lemon
Sour cream and finely chopped chives, to serve

NOTE

→ *Yellow banana chillies are often available from selected greengrocers and fruit shops. If they are unavailable, substitute capsicum (red or green peppers).*

Cut Beef chuck or venison shoulder
See page 318 or 422

CHILLI CON CARNE

Prep time *20 minutes*
Cook *4 hours*

1. Dry-roast the dried chillies over medium–high heat in a large enamelled cast-iron casserole, stirring frequently, for 2–3 minutes, until slightly darkened with a deep roasted aroma. Add 750 ml (26 fl oz/3 cups) of water plus the chilli and adobo sauce, bring to a simmer and cook for 5 minutes. Set aside to cool slightly, then blend in a blender until very smooth: depending on the size of your blender, you may need to do this in batches.

2. Render the beef fat in a large flameproof casserole over medium–high heat. Once the liquid fat has rendered out, remove the fat solids. If necessary, add a splash of olive oil or a spoonful of beef dripping. Season the beef generously with salt and pepper, add to the casserole in batches and sear, turning occasionally, for 4–5 minutes to brown well all over: make sure you don't overcrowd the pan or the meat will stew, rather than caramelise. The deeper the browning, the better the flavour of the finished dish, so take your time to do this well.

3. Transfer the beef to a plate, then add the onion to the casserole and fry, stirring occasionally, for 4–5 minutes until softened. Add the garlic, spices and oregano, sauté until fragrant, then return the beef to the casserole along with the chilli mixture and 1 litre (35 fl oz/4 cups) of water. Season generously, bring to a simmer and cover with a lid, leaving it a little ajar, then reduce the heat to medium–low. Simmer, stirring occasionally, for 3–3½ hours until the beef is fall-apart tender. Alternatively, braise in the oven at 120°C (235°F) with the lid ajar.

4. Stir in the masa harina (if using) and simmer uncovered to thicken slightly. Add brown sugar, squeeze in the lime juice and season. Serve hot, scattered with coriander, spring onion and with the avocado on the side.

INGREDIENTS

1 kg (2 lb 4 oz) beef chuck tender, fat trimmed and chopped, meat cut into 5 cm (2 inch) chunks

4 dried chillies, such as pasilla and ancho, stems and seeds discarded

2 small hot dried chillies, such as costeno and New Mexico, stems and seeds discarded

3 tinned chipotle chillies in adobo, plus 2 tablespoons of the adobo sauce

Olive oil or beef dripping, for cooking

2 brown onions, thinly sliced

4 garlic cloves, finely chopped

1 tablespoon ground cumin

2 teaspoons ground coriander

2 cinnamon sticks

2 teaspoons dried oregano, Mexican if you can get it

2 tablespoons masa harina (hominy flour), optional (see note)

2 tablespoons brown sugar

Juice of 1 lime

Coarsely chopped coriander (cilantro) leaves, thinly sliced spring onion (scallion) and chopped avocado, to serve

SERVING SUGGESTION

warm corn tortillas or steamed rice

NOTE

→ *Masa harina is a traditional Mexican flour made from ground dried corn: it acts as a thickener in this recipe. You can leave it out or, alternatively, you can use the same amount of fine polenta to thicken the sauce instead.*

Cut Beef chuck tender or venison shoulder
See page 318 or 422

SERVES 4

SHABU SHABU

Prep time *30 minutes*
(plus freezing, standing)
Cook *10 minutes*

1. Wrap the beef in plastic wrap and put it in the freezer for 2–3 hours until very firm. Remove the plastic wrap and use a very sharp knife to slice paper-thin slices across the grain. Arrange in a single layer on a plate, cover with plastic wrap and refrigerate until required. Arrange the wombok, mushrooms, spring onion and greens on a serving plate, cover and refrigerate until required.

2. Put the kombu in a large saucepan with 1.5 litres (52 fl oz/6 cups) of water and set aside for 15 minutes for the kombu to soften.

3. Meanwhile, to make the sesame dipping sauce, stir all of the ingredients together in a bowl with 2 tablespoons of water and set aside.

4. Bring the kombu mixture to the boil over medium–high heat. Discard the kombu, reduce the heat to low and add the bonito flakes (if using) and the sake. Transfer to a table burner placed in the centre of your dining table and serve with the beef and vegetables for guests to dip and swish in the stock until lightly cooked, then dip into the dipping sauce and eat with the steamed rice.

5. Once all the beef and vegetables are cooked, the broth can be ladled into bowls and drunk. Alternatively, reserve the broth for another use: it makes a lovely base for a simple noodle soup.

INGREDIENTS

300 g (10½ oz) piece of well-marbled beef
   chuck (see note)
¼ wong bok (Chinese cabbage), cut
   crossways into 5 cm (2 inch) strips
6 shiitake mushrooms, stems discarded,
   caps sliced
4 spring onions (scallions), trimmed and cut
   into 5 cm (2 inch) lengths
½ bunch edible chrysanthemum leaves
   or other Asian greens, cut into 5 cm
   (2 inch) pieces
15 cm (6 inch) piece of dried kombu
10 g (¼ oz) bonito flakes (optional)
55 ml (1¾ fl oz) sake
Steamed jasmine rice, to serve

Sesame dipping sauce
80 g (2¾ oz) sesame paste or hulled tahini
2 tablespoons soy sauce
1½ tablespoons rice vinegar
1 tablespoon shiro miso (white miso) paste
2 teaspoons caster (superfine) sugar
2 teaspoons roasted sesame seeds
1 garlic clove, finely chopped

NOTES

→ *Placing the meat in the freezer makes it easier to slice, but be sure to use the sharpest of knives for the job, so your meat is paper thin.*

→ *Lightweight butane-fuelled table burners are available from hardware stores, but if you don't have one, simply bring the pot of hot broth immediately to the table (set on a trivet).*

Cut Beef chuck
See page 318

SERVES 6

BEEF DAUBE
~ WITH ANCHOVIES, ORANGE AND OLIVES ~

1. Heat the olive oil in a large enamelled cast-iron casserole over medium–high heat, add the onion, celery and carrot and sauté for 6–8 minutes until tender and translucent. Add the herbs and garlic, sauté until fragrant, then add the wine and bring to the boil. Reduce the heat to medium and simmer for 10–15 minutes until well flavoured. Cool completely, then add the beef. Cover and refrigerate overnight to marinate, turning the beef in the marinade a couple of times.

2. Preheat the oven to 170°C (325°F). Add the tomatoes, pancetta, sliced fennel, half the orange zest and the bouquet garni to the casserole, season with salt and pepper and stir to combine. Make a cartouche: cut out a round of baking paper to fit the diameter of the casserole, crumple it up, then wet it under cold running water. Lay it directly on the surface of the mixture, pressing to get rid of any air bubbles. Cover with a lid, put the casserole in the oven and cook for 1 hour. Reduce the oven temperature to 120°C (235°F) and braise for 3½–4 hours until the meat falls apart easily.

3. Discard the bouquet garni, skim fat from the surface, then stir in the butter and anchovy mixture to combine. Stir in the olives, add the vinegar, check the seasoning and serve scattered with the parsley, the remaining orange zest and fennel fronds.

Prep time *30 minutes*
(plus overnight marinating)
Cook *5½ hours*

INGREDIENTS

1 kg (2 lb 4 oz) beef oyster blade, cut into
    5 cm (2 inch) chunks
2½ tablespoons olive oil
2 brown onions, chopped
2 celery stalks, chopped
1 carrot, chopped
2 each rosemary sprigs, thyme sprigs and
    fresh bay leaves
2 garlic cloves, finely chopped
500 ml (17 fl oz/2 cups) dry red wine
800 g (1 lb 12 oz) tinned tomatoes, chopped
80 g (2¾ oz) pancetta, chopped
2 small fennel bulbs, thinly sliced,
    fronds reserved to serve
Finely grated zest of 1 orange
Bouquet garni, made with 2 rosemary sprigs,
    2 thyme sprigs, 2 flat-leaf (Italian) parsley
    sprigs and 2 fresh bay leaves, tied together
    with kitchen string
2 tablespoons (30 g) butter, at room
    temperature, mashed with 4 finely
    chopped anchovies
100 g (3½ oz) black olives
2 teaspoons red wine vinegar, or to taste
Coarsely chopped flat-leaf (Italian) parsley,
    to serve

buttered egg noodles, such as fettuccine,
or fennel, parsley and orange salad

SERVING SUGGESTION

NOTE

→ *If you have the time, give the daube a day or two in the refrigerator to develop the rich deep flavours.*

Cut Beef oyster blade
See page 318

ROAST RIB EYE
~ WITH YORKSHIRE PUDDINGS ~

Prep time *20 minutes*
Cook *1 hour 40 minutes (plus resting)*

1. Stir the mustard, rosemary, thyme, garlic and 1 tablespoon of the olive oil in a bowl to combine, season with salt and pepper and rub all over the beef. Set aside at room temperature for 2 hours. Alternatively, cover and refrigerate to marinate overnight, bringing it to room temperature before cooking.

2. Preheat the oven to 220°C (425°F). Spread the onion in the centre of a small roasting tin to form a trivet and stand the beef on top. Roast on the middle rack of the oven for 20 minutes to brown the beef well.

3. Reduce the oven to 160°C (315°F) and leave the door ajar slightly to allow the oven to cool. Continue to roast the beef for 40–45 minutes until cooked to medium-rare; internal temperature will read 48°C (116°F) and the beef will continue to cook as it rests. Remove the beef from the oven, cover it loosely with foil and set aside to rest for 30 minutes.

4. Meanwhile, put the pumpkin wedges in a large roasting tin, drizzle with the remaining olive oil, season with salt and pepper and cook in the bottom rack of the oven.

5. While the beef is roasting, make the Yorkshire pudding batter. Whisk all of the ingredients with 100 ml (3½ fl oz) of cold water in a bowl until smooth, then set aside to rest for 30 minutes.

6. While the beef is resting, increase the oven temperature to 220°C (425°F).

7. Tip 2 tablespoons of the fat from the roasting pan and divide it among eight 125 ml (4 fl oz/½ cup) capacity holes in a muffin tin; alternatively, add 1 teaspoon of vegetable oil or lard to each muffin hole. Put the tin in the oven to heat for 5–10 minutes until the fat is hot. Carefully remove from the oven and quickly divide the batter between holes, filling to half-full. Bake for 20–25 minutes until puffed and golden. At the same time, keep an eye on the pumpkin wedges, removing them from the oven if necessary to prevent burning.

8. To serve, slice the beef from the bone, then slice across the grain. Serve with the roasted pumpkin wedges and the Yorkshire puddings, drizzled with the pan and resting juices from the beef.

INGREDIENTS

1 three-rib beef rib eye rack, about 1.6 kg (3 lb 8 oz)
1 tablespoon English mustard
1 teaspoon each of chopped rosemary and thyme
1 garlic clove, finely chopped
2½ tablespoons olive oil
1 large brown onion, thickly sliced
1.5 kg (3 lb 5 oz) kent pumpkin (winter squash), skin on, seeds discarded, cut into 4 cm (1½ inch) thick wedges

Yorkshire puddings
150 g (5½ oz/1 cup) plain (all-purpose) flour
150 ml (5 fl oz) milk
2 eggs
1 thyme sprig, leaves picked
2 teaspoons salt

SERVING SUGGESTION

crushed steamed peas

N O T E

→ *Leftover roast beef can be thinly sliced and used in sandwiches. Alternatively, use it in a salad: try tossing the meat with leftover roast vegetables, baby spinach and a red wine vinaigrette, or opt for Asian flavours and toss with rice noodles, large handfuls of aromatic herbs such as Thai basil, mint and coriander (cilantro) leaves, along with halved cherry tomatoes, bean sprouts and a lime–chilli–fish sauce dressing.*

Cut Beef rib eye rack
See page 319

T-BONE
~ WITH CHIMICHURRI AND CAFE DE PARIS BUTTER ~

Prep time *30 minutes (plus chilling)*
Cook *15 minutes (plus resting)*

1. To make the café de Paris butter, beat ingredients in an electric mixer fitted with the paddle attachment until combined, season to taste with sea salt and freshly ground pepper and beat once again to combine. Store in an airtight container or roll into a cylinder using plastic wrap, twisting the ends to seal. Café de Paris butter will keep refrigerated for up to 1 month.

2. To make the chimichurri, combine the vinegar, garlic, shallot and chilli in a bowl and set aside for 10 minutes to soften. Stir in the remaining ingredients to combine and season with salt and pepper to taste. Keep chimichurri in an airtight container in the refrigerator for up to 3 days.

3. Season the steak generously on both sides with sea salt and set aside at room temperature for 1 hour. Preheat a barbecue or chargrill pan to high heat and turn off one side of the grill: if using a charcoal barbecue, push the coals to one side.

4. Drizzle the steak with a little oil and chargrill on the hottest part of the barbecue for 4–6 minutes until well browned, then turn and cook for another 4–6 minutes for medium-rare. The internal temperature will be around 52°C (125°F), resting up to 55°C (130°F).

5. Stand steaks up on the bone for another 1–2 minutes (this conducts the heat through the bone for more even cooking) then transfer to a plate. Cover loosely with foil and rest for 10 minutes. Melt a 5 mm (¼ inch) slice of the café de Paris butter over each warm steak.

6. Cut the meat from the bone, then slice across the grain of the meat to divide between plates. Serve with the chimichurri sauce on the side.

INGREDIENTS

2 T-bone steaks, 4 cm (1½ inches) thick, about 800 g (1 lb 12 oz) each
Olive oil, for drizzling

Café de Paris butter
18 tablespoons (250 g) butter, preferably cultured, at room temperature
1 tablespoon tomato ketchup
2 anchovies, finely chopped
1 small golden shallot, very finely chopped
1 small garlic clove, finely chopped
1½ tablespoons finely chopped flat-leaf (Italian) parsley
1 tablespoon finely chopped chives
1 teaspoon finely chopped thyme
1 teaspoon finely chopped tarragon
1 teaspoon dijon mustard
1 teaspoon brandy
1 teaspoon finely grated lemon zest
2 teaspoons lemon juice
1 pinch each of sweet paprika, ground cayenne and curry powder

Chimichurri sauce
100 ml (3½ fl oz) red wine vinegar
3 garlic cloves, finely chopped
1 golden shallot, very finely chopped
1 jalapeño chilli, finely chopped
3 large handfuls of coriander (cilantro) leaves, finely chopped
1 large handful of flat-leaf (Italian) parsley, finely chopped
160 ml (5¼ fl oz) extra virgin olive oil

SERVING SUGGESTION

fat chips and a rocket (arugula) salad

Cut Beef T-bone
See page 325

BEEF WELLINGTON

Prep time *40 minutes (plus chilling)*
Cook *50 minutes (plus resting)*

1. Heat a splash of olive oil in a large frying pan over medium-high heat until smoking. Season the beef generously, add to the pan and sear, turning occasionally, for 6–8 minutes until browned well all over. Transfer to a plate and pat dry with paper towel. Refrigerate and brush with the mustard.

2. Meanwhile, pulse the mushrooms in batches in a food processor until finely chopped, but still with a little texture. Heat the butter in a large frying pan over medium-high heat until foaming. Add the mushroom, season with salt and pepper and sauté for 2–3 minutes until the mushrooms start to give off their moisture. Continue cooking, stirring occasionally, for 4–5 minutes until the liquid evaporates and the mushrooms begin to brown. Add the shallot, thyme and garlic, sauté for 2–3 minutes until softened, then deglaze the pan with brandy, scraping the base of the pan with a wooden spoon. Add the cream and simmer until the mixture dries out. Check the seasoning, transfer to a bowl and chill in the refrigerator.

3. Lay out a piece of baking paper on a work surface. Overlap the prosciutto in a rectangle on top, arranging it so it is the length of your beef fillet and wide enough to completely enclose the meat. Spread the mushroom mixture evenly over the prosciutto.

4. Spread the pâté evenly over the beef. Lay the beef on the closest edge of the prosciutto and roll it into a cylinder, using the baking paper to help roll and enclose the beef (discard the baking paper). Wrap the beef cylinder tightly in plastic wrap and chill in the refrigerator for several hours. Remove the plastic wrap before using.

5. Roll out the pastry on a lightly floured surface to a 30 x 40 cm (12 x 16 inch) rectangle. Lay the prosciutto-wrapped beef on one long side and brush the pastry edges with egg wash. Roll the beef and pastry into a snug cylinder and place seam-side down on a baking tray lined with baking paper. Pinch the pastry ends together to seal and trim off any excess. Brush thickly with egg wash, score in a decorative pattern with a small sharp knife, and chill in the freezer for 30 minutes or in the refrigerator for up to 24 hours.

6. Preheat the oven to 210°C (415°F). Season the beef parcel with sea salt and bake for 20–25 minutes for rare, 25–30 minutes for medium-rare—internal temperature reads 48°C (116°F) for rare or 52°C (125°F) for medium-rare—and the pastry is golden brown. Set aside to rest for 15 minutes. Thickly slice to serve.

INGREDIENTS

1 kg (2 lb 4 oz) eye fillet
Olive oil, for frying
1 tablespoon dijon mustard or English mustard
400 g (14 oz) mixed mushrooms, such as button, Swiss brown and chestnut
3 tablespoons (40 g) butter, chopped
2 golden shallots, finely chopped
2 teaspoons finely chopped thyme
1 garlic clove, finely chopped
80 ml (2½ fl oz/⅓ cup) brandy or Cognac
Splash of pure (pouring) cream
10 very thin slices of prosciutto
70 g (2½ oz) pâté
375 g (13 oz) butter puff pastry
2 egg yolks, beaten with 1 tablespoon water, for egg wash
Sea salt

SERVING SUGGESTION

*roasted baby carrots and
buttered green beans*

NOTES

→ *Many methods for beef Wellington involve wrapping the meat in a thin crepe or blanched cabbage leaves, to keep the moisture contained and prevent the puff pastry from going soggy. A sheet of filo pastry is a simple option.*

→ *This recipe is an exception to the rule of letting the meat come to room temperature before cooking, because you want the beef rare while the pastry is well cooked.*

Cut Beef eye fillet
See page 319

BEEF STROGANOFF

1. Slice the tri-tip across the grain into 5 mm (¼ inch) slices, then cut into 1.5 cm (⅝ inch) strips.

2. Heat a splash of olive oil along with the butter in a large enamelled cast-iron casserole over medium–high heat until the butter foams. Add the onion and sauté, stirring occasionally, for 8–10 minutes until the onion is very tender and light golden. Add the garlic and paprika, stir until fragrant, then transfer to a plate. Increase the heat to high, add a splash of olive oil if necessary, and fry the mushrooms in the casserole for 4–5 minutes until browned, then transfer to a plate.

3. Add an extra splash of olive oil to the casserole if necessary, then add the beef in batches and sear, turning occasionally, for 1–1½ minutes until well browned, but still a little pink in the middle: make sure you don't overcrowd the pan as the meat will stew, rather than caramelise. Transfer to a plate.

4. Deglaze the pan with the brandy, scraping the base of the pan with a wooden spoon to release all the beautiful browned crusty bits, and cook for a minute or so to burn off the alcohol. Add the stock, sour cream, mustard and bay leaf, along with the onion and the mushroom, stir to combine and season with salt and pepper. Reduce the heat to medium and simmer for 2–3 minutes until well flavoured and slightly reduced.

5. Stir in the beef and any juices that have formed on the plate, the lemon rind and a squeeze of lemon juice, bring back to a simmer, and adjust the seasoning if necessary. Scatter with parsley and serve with steamed rice and gherkins.

INGREDIENTS

600 g (1 lb 5 oz) beef tri-tip, trimmed of sinew
Olive oil, for cooking
2 tablespoons (30 g) butter, chopped
1 large brown onion, thinly sliced
1 garlic clove, finely chopped
1 teaspoon sweet paprika
300 g (10½ oz) Swiss brown mushrooms, thickly sliced
100 ml (3½ fl oz) brandy
300 ml (10½ fl oz) beef stock
250 g (9 oz) sour cream
1 teaspoon seeded mustard
1 fresh bay leaf
Finely grated zest of ½ lemon, plus a squeeze of juice
Coarsely chopped flat-leaf (Italian) parsley and steamed rice, to serve
Gherkins, or your favourite pickles, to serve

Cut Beef tri-tip
See page 320

STEAK TARTARE

Prep time *20 minutes*

1. Use a very sharp knife to cut the beef into 5 mm (¼ inch) cubes and combine in a bowl with the Worcestershire sauce, Cognac and Tabasco, season to taste with sea salt and freshly ground black pepper and stir gently to mix well.

2. Divide evenly among four serving plates, forming into a mound, then press a small hollow in the centre of each mound and top with an egg yolk.

3. Arrange little piles of the remaining ingredients around the tartare for each person to add according to their tastes.

INGREDIENTS

350 g (12 oz) rostbiff (or tenderloin)
3 teaspoons Worcestershire sauce
1 teaspoon Cognac
8–10 drops of Tabasco
Sea salt and freshly ground black pepper
4 egg yolks, from very fresh eggs
60 g (2¼ oz) very finely chopped golden
  shallot
40 g (1½ oz) very finely chopped cornichons
3 teaspoons finely chopped baby capers
1 tablespoon finely chopped chives
Dijon mustard, to serve

SERVING SUGGESTION

*croutons or pommes
gaufrettes (waffle fries)*

Cut Beef rostbiff
or tenderloin
See pages 319–320

SERVES 6

CORNED BEEF
~ WITH WHITE SAUCE ~

Prep time *20 minutes*
Cook *3 hours 20 minutes (plus resting)*

1. Combine the silverside in a large saucepan with the vegetables, vinegar, herbs, lemon zest, spices and enough cold water to cover generously. Bring to the boil, reduce heat to low, then cover and simmer, skimming the surface occasionally, for 3–3¼ hours until the meat is very tender. Drain, discarding the liquid, and set the meat aside to rest for 10 minutes.

2. While the beef rests, make the horseradish white sauce. Melt the butter in a saucepan over medium–high heat, stir in the flour and stir for 1–2 minutes until sandy in texture. Gradually whisk in the milk to combine, then bring to a simmer and cook, whisking constantly, for 2–3 minutes until slightly thickened and the mixture no longer tastes floury. Season with salt and pepper and stir in the horseradish.

3. Thinly slice the corned beef across the grain and serve with the horseradish white sauce, scattered with parsley and extra horseradish.

INGREDIENTS

1 kg (2 lb 4 oz) corned silverside, rinsed
1 onion, halved, each half studded with a clove
1 carrot, cut into chunks
2 tablespoons malt vinegar
5 thyme sprigs
2 fresh bay leaves
2 pieces of peeled lemon zest
5 juniper berries
2 teaspoons whole black peppercorns
Finely chopped flat-leaf (Italian) parsley and finely grated fresh horseradish, to serve

Horseradish white sauce
4 tablespoons (50 g) butter, chopped
50 g (1¾ oz/⅓ cup) plain (all-purpose) flour
500 ml (17 fl oz/2 cups) milk
1 tablespoon finely grated fresh horseradish, or 1 tablespoon horseradish paste

SERVING SUGGESTION

roasted baby beetroot (beets), baby potatoes and baby carrots and steamed greens such as peas or baby broccoli

NOTE

→ *Leftover corned beef makes an excellent Reuben sandwich, or add it to a hearty cabbage soup.*

→ *For only a few dollars more, you can up your corned-beef game by requesting wagyu brisket.*

Cut Beef silverside
See page 320

SERVES 1

THE ULTIMATE BURGER

Prep time *10 minutes (plus macerating)*
Cook *1 hour*

1. To make the mustard, combine all of the ingredients except the tarragon in a container and set aside in the refrigerator for 2–3 days to macerate. Blitz in a blender with the tarragon leaves and return to the refrigerator for one more day to mellow.

2. To make the ketchup, put a splash of olive oil in a heavy-based saucepan over medium–low heat. Sauté the onion, celery, chilli and garlic until soft, then add the tomatoes and cook for 45 minutes to 1 hour over low heat.

3. Stir in the basil and blend, in batches, in a food processor until smooth (be careful, it's very hot). Return the purée to the saucepan and add the sugar, vinegar and pepper. Cook over low heat until the sauce is reduced to a thick consistency. Season with sea salt.

4. Heat a barbecue or chargrill pan to medium–high and grill the beef patty for 2 minutes on each side for medium-rare.

5. Assemble the burger: spread mustard on the base of the toasted bun, top with the beef patty and ketchup. Add sliced gherkin and onion and top with shredded lettuce. Finish with the top of the toasted bun and serve.

INGREDIENTS

180 g (6¼ oz) minced (ground) beef patty,
    seasoned with salt and pepper
1 brioche burger bun, toasted lightly
1 large gherkin (pickle), sliced lengthways
A few rings of thinly sliced red onion
1 salad leaf, such as cos (romaine), shredded

Mustard
50 g (1¾ oz) yellow mustard seeds
100 ml (3½ fl oz) cider vinegar
2½ tablespoons white wine
1 teaspoon salt
Honey, to taste (optional)
3 tarragon sprigs, leaves picked

Ketchup
Olive oil, for cooking
1 brown onion, chopped
1 celery stalk, chopped
½ fresh chilli, deseeded and chopped
5 garlic cloves, smashed and peeled
1 kg (2 lb 4 oz) deep red overripe tomatoes,
    skinned and chopped, or 1 kg (2 lb 4 oz)
    tinned tomatoes
1 bunch fresh basil, leaves picked
50 g (1¾ oz) sugar
2½ tablespoons red wine vinegar
1 teaspoon freshly ground black pepper
Sea salt

NOTE

→ *Pour ketchup into sterilised bottles while it's still hot. Ketchup will keep for 2 weeks in the refrigerator.*

For the best burger mince, look for a ratio of 80 per cent meat to 20 per cent fat.
See page 469.

SERVES 6

SKIRT STEAK FAJITAS

Prep time *20 minutes (plus marinating)*
Cook *20 minutes (plus resting)*

1. Combine the lime juice, olive oil, garlic, cumin and chilli flakes in a bowl and season with salt and pepper. Combine half the marinade with the steak in a resealable plastic bag, massaging well into the meat, and refrigerate to marinate for at least 3 hours (and ideally overnight for best flavour). Bring the steak to room temperature before grilling.

2. Combine the remaining marinade with the capsicum and onion in a bowl, cover and refrigerate to marinate.

3. To make the pico de gallo, toss the tomatoes with the salt, transfer to a sieve and set it over a sink to drain for 30 minutes. Put the drained tomato into a bowl with all of the remaining ingredients and season with salt and pepper to taste.

4. Set up a kettle barbecue for direct grilling, heating until the charcoal is white hot, or heat a gas barbecue to high. While the barbecue is heating, remove the steak from the marinade. Grill the steak on the barbecue, turning once, for 8–10 minutes until well charred and cooked to medium-rare: a thermometer should read 52°C (125°F). Cover loosely with foil and set aside to rest for 15–20 minutes; the steak will continue to cook as it rests.

5. Meanwhile, heat a splash of olive oil in a frying pan on the barbecue until smoking (alternatively, you can do this over high heat on the stovetop). Drain the capsicum mixture from the marinade, put it in the pan and fry, stirring occasionally, for 8–10 minutes until tender and beginning to scorch. Set aside. Pour any juices that have accumulated from the resting meat into the pan and set aside.

6. To serve, thinly slice the steak across the grain and serve with the capsicum, pico de gallo, guacamole, coriander, warmed tortillas and lime wedges.

INGREDIENTS

1 kg (2 lb 4 oz) inside skirt steak (see note)
60 ml (2 fl oz/¼ cup) lime juice
2 tablespoons olive oil, plus extra for cooking
4 garlic cloves, finely chopped
2 teaspoons ground cumin
1 pinch of dried chilli flakes
3 capsicums (peppers), thinly sliced: a mix of red, yellow and green works well
1 red onion, thinly sliced
Guacamole, coriander (cilantro) sprigs, warmed tortillas and lime wedges, to serve

Pico de gallo
4 ripe tomatoes, chopped
1 teaspoon salt
1 small white onion, finely chopped
½ cup coarsely chopped coriander (cilantro)
2 jalapeño chillies, thinly sliced
Juice of 1 lime

NOTE

→ *Depending on the length of your steak and the size of your barbecue, you may need to cut your steak to fit.*

Cut Inside skirt steak
See page 327

BULGOGI

1. Purée the nashi, chopped onion, garlic, soy sauce and sugar in a food processor until smooth, then combine in a large resealable plastic bag with the brisket. Squeeze out any air from the bag and seal, then massage the marinade thoroughly into beef, through the bag. Refrigerate to marinate for 1–2 hours, then add the sesame oil and massage well to combine.

2. To make the ssamjang, stir all of the ingredients in a bowl to combine and thin to a dipping consistency with a little water if necessary.

3. Heat a large heavy-based frying pan over high heat, add a splash of grapeseed oil and heat until smoking. Drain the beef and add it to the pan in batches, searing quickly on each side, adding a little marinade toward the end of each batch, then transfer to a bowl. When all the beef is cooked, add the sliced onion and spring onion to the pan and cook for 1–2 minutes until just tender, then add to the beef.

4. To serve, wrap a little of the beef and some rice in a lettuce leaf with some kimchi, ssamjang and sesame seeds.

INGREDIENTS

600 g (1 lb 5 oz) brisket point, trimmed and
   very thinly sliced across the grain
1 nashi, peeled and coarsely chopped, plus
   extra very thinly sliced to serve
1 large brown onion, half coarsely chopped,
   half thinly sliced
3 garlic cloves, crushed
150 ml (5 fl oz) soy sauce
2 tablespoons caster (superfine) sugar
2 tablespoons sesame oil
Grapeseed oil, for frying
3 spring onions (scallions), thinly sliced, plus
   extra to serve
Steamed rice and butter lettuce leaves,
   to serve
Kimchi and roasted sesame seeds, to serve

Ssamjang
2½ tablespoons gochujang (Korean chilli
   paste)
2 tablespoons doenjang (soy bean paste)
2 tablespoons rice wine
3 teaspoons honey
3 teaspoons sesame oil
4 garlic cloves, finely chopped
2 spring onions (scallions), thinly sliced
1 long green chilli, finely chopped

NOTES

→ *Kimchi, gochujang and doenjang are available from Korean grocers and Asian supermarkets.*

→ *If you can't get nashi, you can substitute a ripe green pear.*

Cut Beef brisket point
See page 321

BARBECUED BEEF SHORT RIBS

Prep time *20 minutes (plus marinating)*
Cook *3 hours (plus resting)*

1. Combine the sugar, spices and salt in a bowl and mix well. Rub all over the beef short ribs, cover and refrigerate for 1 hour to allow the flavours to develop.

2. Preheat a barbecue on medium indirect heat. Spread the ribs in a single layer in a large roasting tin and add the beer. Cover with foil and place on the barbecue, cover with a lid and cook for 2–2½ hours until almost tender. Remove the foil and cook for another 30–40 minutes until a bark forms on the outside of the meat.

3. Remove from the heat and rest for 15 minutes, then serve.

INGREDIENTS

6 beef short ribs, about 500 g (1 lb 2 oz) each
2 tablespoons brown sugar
2 tablespoons paprika
2 teaspoons ground cumin
2 teaspoons garlic powder
2 teaspoons ground chilli
1 tablespoon sea salt
300 ml (10½ fl oz) beer

SERVING SUGGESTION

crunchy slaw, creamy potato salad and crisp green salad

NOTES

→ *There'll be plenty of liquid left in the roasting pan, along with a good layer of fat. Skim off the fat and reserve for your next batch of roast vegetables. If you like, you can reduce the pan juices in a saucepan over medium–high heat to intensify the flavours, then season with salt and pepper and squeeze in a little lemon juice to brighten. Serve spooned over the ribs.*

→ *If you prefer, you can cook the ribs in a low oven instead: it will take a similar amount of time at 140°C (275°F).*

Cut Beef short ribs
See page 321

BEEF PHO

INGREDIENTS

250 g (9 oz) round steak, very thinly sliced across the grain, to serve
800 g (1 lb 12 oz) dried rice stick noodles or 1 kg (2 lb 4 oz) fresh rice noodles
6 spring onions (scallions), thinly sliced
1 brown onion, thinly sliced
½ cup coarsely chopped coriander (cilantro) leaves
Lime wedges, thinly sliced bird's eye chillies, Thai basil, Vietnamese mint and bean sprouts, to serve

Broth
2.5 kg (5 lb 8 oz) beef soup bones, such as leg and knuckle
500 g (1 lb 2 oz) piece of brisket or flank steak
2 brown onions, whole, unpeeled
12 cm (4½ inch) piece of fresh ginger
100 ml (3½ fl oz) fish sauce, plus extra for seasoning
1 tablespoon grated palm sugar (jaggery)
6 whole star anise
3 cinnamon sticks or 10 cm (4 inch) piece of cassia bark
1 garlic bulb, halved
1 tablespoon sea salt

1. To make the broth, combine the beef bones and enough cold water to cover generously in a stockpot, bring to the boil and cook for 2–3 minutes to remove impurities (scum will rise to the surface). Drain and rinse the bones thoroughly under cold running water. Return the bones to a clean stockpot, add 6 litres (210 fl oz/24 cups) of cold water and bring to the boil. Reduce the heat to medium so the broth simmers gently, then skim any froth or scum from the surface.

2. Meanwhile, char the onion and ginger over a naked gas flame, turning occasionally, for 8–10 minutes until softened. You can also do this under a hot grill but it may take a little longer. Remove and discard any blackened skin and add the onion and ginger to the stockpot along with the remaining ingredients, including the brisket. Simmer for 1½–1¾ hours until the brisket is just cooked, but not falling apart. Remove from the broth, transfer to a bowl of cold water for 10 minutes, then drain and refrigerate until required. Simmer the broth for a further 1–1¼ hours until well flavoured, then strain (discarding solids). Cool to room temperature, then refrigerate overnight.

3. Soak the dried noodles in a bowl of hot water for 15–20 minutes until soft, then drain well. If using fresh noodles, pour boiling water over, separate the noodles with chopsticks and drain well.

4. Remove and discard fat from the surface of the broth, then bring the broth to the boil in a large saucepan. Check the seasoning, adding extra fish sauce and freshly ground pepper to taste. Thinly slice the brisket.

5. Divide the noodles among deep serving bowls, and top with sliced brisket, spring onion, onion and coriander. Ladle hot broth into the bowls and serve with lime wedges, chilli, herbs, bean sprouts and sliced round steak to add at the table, dipping the steak into the hot broth as you eat.

Cut Beef round steak, brisket, bones
See page 321

RAGÙ BOLOGNESE

Prep time *20 minutes*
Cook *3½ hours*

1. Heat a splash of oil in a heavy-based saucepan along with 2 tablespoons (30 g) of the butter over medium–high heat, then add the celery, onion and carrot and sauté, stirring occasionally, for 4–5 minutes until the onion is tender and translucent. Add the minced beef and minced pork to the pan, season with salt and pepper and brown well for 4–5 minutes, breaking up any clumps of meat with the back of a wooden spoon.

2. Add the milk and nutmeg, season with salt and pepper and simmer gently for 15–20 minutes until milk reduces completely, then add the wine and simmer for 20–25 minutes until completely evaporated.

3. Add the tomatoes, breaking them up with a wooden spoon, then add the bay leaf and season with salt and pepper. Bring to a simmer and then reduce the heat to low so the mixture is barely simmering, with only the occasional bubble breaking the surface. Cook, uncovered and stirring occasionally, for 2–2½ hours until well flavoured. As it cooks the fat will separate from the meat and the mixture may dry out, so add 125 ml (4 fl oz/½ cup) of water every now and again, but make sure to evaporate all the liquid before serving. Check the seasoning.

4. When the ragù is ready, cook the pasta in a large saucepan of well-salted boiling water for 5–6 minutes until al dente, drain and return the spaghetti to the pan with 1–2 tablespoons of the cooking water. Add the ragù and remaining butter, toss to combine well and serve hot, scattered with Parmigiano Reggiano.

INGREDIENTS

350 g (12 oz) coarsely minced (ground) beef knuckle (round)
150 g (5½ oz) coarsely minced (ground) pork shoulder
Olive oil, for cooking
3 tablespoons (40 g) butter, chopped
2 celery stalks, finely chopped
1 brown onion, finely chopped
1 small carrot, finely chopped
250 ml (9 fl oz/1 cup) milk
1 pinch of freshly grated nutmeg
300 ml (10½ fl oz) dry white wine
400 g (14 oz) tinned Italian tomatoes
1 fresh bay leaf
400 g (14 oz) dried spaghetti
Finely grated Parmigiano Reggiano or parmesan cheese, to serve

NOTE

→ *This ragù is even better served a day or two after making and freezes well (without the spaghetti), so making a double or even a triple batch of the ragù is a good idea. A larger batch is also perfect for use in a classic lasagne.*

Cut Beef knuckle, pork shoulder
See page 321, 220

BEEF RENDANG

1. To make the rendang spice paste, dry-roast the dried spices in a small saucepan over medium–high heat for 30 seconds to 1 minute, until fragrant and toasted. Cool slightly and grind into a powder using a mortar and pestle or spice grinder. Transfer to a food processor with the remaining ingredients and process to a paste, adding a tablespoon or two of water, if necessary to help blend.

2. Dry-roast the coconut in a frying pan over medium heat, shaking the pan occasionally, for 5–6 minutes until golden and toasted. Transfer to a mortar and pestle, cool and crush lightly.

3. Heat the coconut oil in a large enamelled cast-iron casserole over medium heat, add the spice paste and fry, stirring frequently, for 12–15 minutes until browned and very fragrant. Season the beef, add it to the casserole with the kaffir lime leaves and lemongrass and stir to coat well in the paste.

4. Stir in the toasted coconut, coconut milk and 300 ml (10½ fl oz) of water to combine well, reduce the heat to very low, cover and simmer, stirring occasionally, for 1 hour. Add the tamarind paste, palm sugar and sea salt and simmer uncovered, stirring occasionally, for 1–1½ hours until the beef is very tender and the sauce is thick and slightly oily. Check the seasoning and serve with the sliced kaffir lime leaves.

INGREDIENTS

600 g (1 lb 5 oz) beef shin, cut into 4 cm (1½ inch) cubes

30 g (1 oz) coarsely grated fresh coconut or shredded coconut

2 tablespoons coconut oil or vegetable oil

6 kaffir lime (makrut) leaves, plus extra leaves thinly sliced to serve

2 lemongrass stems, white part only, halved lengthways

800 ml (28 fl oz) coconut milk

1½ tablespoons tamarind paste

1½ tablespoons grated palm sugar (jaggery)

1 teaspoon sea salt

Rendang spice paste

1 tablespoon each cumin seeds, fennel seeds and coriander seeds

6 green cardamom pods, bruised, seeds reserved and pods discarded

6 whole cloves

4 whole star anise

30 g (1 oz) each fresh ginger, galangal and turmeric, coarsely chopped

6 garlic cloves

4 red Asian shallots or 1 small red onion, coarsely chopped

8–10 long red chillies, coarsely chopped

2 lemongrass stems, white part only, coarsely chopped

steamed rice or coconut rice and steamed Asian greens with a squeeze of lime juice

SERVING
SUGGESTION

Cut Beef shin
See page 322

BRAISED OXTAIL PASTA

Prep time *30 minutes*
Cook *3½ hours*

1. To braise the oxtail, heat a splash of olive oil in a large enamelled cast-iron casserole over medium–high heat, then add the onion, celery and carrot and sauté, stirring occasionally, for 4–5 minutes until the vegetables begin to soften, adding the garlic in the final minute of cooking. Transfer to a plate.

2. Season the oxtail generously with salt and pepper. Add a little extra olive oil to the casserole, then add the oxtail in batches and sear, turning occasionally, for 5–6 minutes until browned all over. Return the vegetables and the seared oxtail to the casserole, add the wine and bring to the boil, then cook for 5–6 minutes until reduced by half. Add the tomatoes, breaking them up with a wooden spoon, then add the oregano and 250 ml (9 fl oz/1 cup) of water, season with salt and pepper and bring to a simmer. Cover with a lid, reduce the heat to medium–low and simmer for 2½–3 hours until the meat falls from the bone.

3. Remove the oxtail pieces from the sauce and skim the excess fat from the surface. When cool enough to handle, shred the meat off the bone, return it to the sauce, then add the vinegar and check the seasoning. Keep warm.

4. Cook the pasta in a large saucepan of well-salted boiling water for 8–10 minutes until al dente, then drain and return to the pan. Toss the oxtail through the pasta and serve hot, scattered with pecorino, lemon zest and oregano, if using.

INGREDIENTS

1.5 kg (3 lb 5 oz) oxtail pieces on the bone; choose equal-sized pieces of oxtail
Olive oil, for cooking
1 brown onion, chopped
1 celery stalk, chopped
1 carrot, chopped
2 garlic cloves, finely chopped
½ bottle (375 ml) full-bodied red wine
800 g (1 lb 12 oz) tinned Italian tomatoes
3 oregano sprigs
1 tablespoon red wine vinegar, or to taste
500 g (1 lb 2 oz) dried rigatoni or conchiglione
Finely grated pecorino cheese, finely grated lemon zest and oregano leaves (optional), to serve

NOTE

→ *Braised oxtail is beautifully versatile: try keeping it on the bone and serve spooned over soft polenta or a creamy mash and scatter with gremolata to cut through the richness (see pages 388–389 for a gremolata recipe).*

Cut Oxtail
See page 322

SERVES 6

HONEYCOMB TRIPE
~ WITH PARMESAN ~

Marcella Hazan is the prima donna of Italian cooking. Hers is the book to turn to for all the classic dishes: she is an exquisite writer, fastidious researcher and a wonderful cook.

1. Rinse the tripe very thoroughly under cold running water and set aside, then drain and cut it into strips 12 mm (½ inch) wide and more or less 7.5 cm (3 inches) long.

2. Choose an enamelled cast-iron or heavy-bottomed pot that can contain all the ingredients. Put in all the oil, 1 tablespoon (15 g) butter and the chopped onion and turn the heat to medium. Sauté the onion until it becomes coloured a pale gold, then add the chopped celery and carrot, stir to coat them well, and cook for about 1 minute.

3. Add the garlic, parsley and rosemary, cook for another minute, stirring once or twice, then add the cut-up tripe, turning it thoroughly to coat it well. Cook for about 5 minutes, stirring once or twice, then add the wine. Bring the wine to a brisk simmer for 20 or 30 seconds, then put in the tomatoes with their juice, add salt, black pepper, chilli pepper or both, give all the ingredients a thorough turning over and bring the liquid in the pot to a slow boil.

4. Cover the pot and cook for about 2½ hours, until the tripe is tender enough to be easily cut with a fork, and has an agreeably chewy consistency when tasted. Control the heat to maintain a slow but steady boil. While the tripe is cooking, check the liquid in the pot from time to time; if it should be insufficient, replenish with 2 or 3 tablespoons of water; on the other hand, if it is thin and watery, continue cooking with the lid slightly askew.

5. When the tripe has become very tender, transfer it to a warm bowl. If you find the juices in the pot to be too watery, turn the heat up high after removing the tripe, and boil them down to a satisfactory density. Pour the contents of the pot over the tripe, swirl in the remaining butter and all the grated parmesan, and serve at once.

Prep time *20 minutes*
Cook *3 hours*

INGREDIENTS

900 g (2 lb) ready-to-cook honeycomb tripe, thawed if frozen

125 ml (4 fl oz/½ cup/6 tablespoons) vegetable oil

3 tablespoons (45 g) butter

50 g (2 oz) onion, chopped finely

50 g (2 oz) celery, chopped finely

115 g (4 oz) carrot, chopped finely

2 medium cloves garlic, mashed lightly with a knife handle and peeled

1 tablespoon chopped parsley

1 teaspoon chopped fresh rosemary leaves

250 ml (9 fl oz/1 cup) dry white wine

255 g (9 oz) tinned imported Italian plum tomatoes, cut up, with their juice or, if very ripe and firm, fresh tomatoes, peeled and cut up

Salt

Freshly ground black pepper or ½ teaspoon dried hot red chilli pepper, to taste

250 ml (9 fl oz/1 cup) home-made meat broth, or 100 ml (4 fl oz) tinned concentrated beef consommé diluted with water to make 250 ml (9 fl oz/1 cup)

85 g (3 oz) freshly grated Parmigiano Reggiano cheese

NOTE

→ *From* The Essentials of Classic Italian Cooking, *by Marcella Hazan, (Alfred A. Knopf, 1992).*

SERVES 4–6
CALF'S LIVER
WITH BACON, LEEKS, APPLE
~ AND CALVADOS ~

Prep time *10 minutes*
Cook *15 minutes*

INGREDIENTS

225 g (8 oz) slab bacon, cut into small lardons
680 g (1 lb 8 oz) calf's liver, cut crosswise into
  5–7 mm (¼–⅓ inch) slices
Salt and freshly ground black pepper to taste
55 g (2 oz/½ cup) plain (all-purpose) flour
1–2 tablespoons canola oil
2 leeks (white parts only), trimmed and diced
1 granny smith or similarly tart apple, cored
  and diced
125 ml (4 fl oz/½ cup) Calvados
185 ml (6 fl oz/¾ cup) veal stock
1 tablespoon unsalted butter

SERVING SUGGESTION

mashed potatoes

Passionate, humble, supportive, encouraging, Anthony Bourdain was the real deal: someone who did his time in the kitchen, loved food and loved people.

1. Place the bacon in a sauté pan (one that has a lid that fits, which you'll need later) over medium heat, adding a splash of water if necessary, and cook, stirring regularly with a wooden spoon, until most of the fat has rendered and the bacon is lightly browned. Remove the bacon to the lined plate to drain; discard the fat and wipe out or wash the pan.

2. Season the liver on both sides with salt and pepper, and dredge it in the flour, patting off the excess. Heat 1 tablespoon of the oil in the pan until it is smoking, then add the liver, working in batches if necessary, and cook for about 1 minute per side, taking care not to overcook it—it should still have a pink tinge inside. If the flour smells like it is scorching or there's anything turning too dark in the pan, add the remaining 1 tablespoon oil. Using tongs remove the liver to a serving platter. Add the leeks to the pan over high heat, stirring and scraping up any brown bits with the wooden spoon. Season the leeks with salt and pepper and add the apple and the bacon, continuing to cook over high heat until all are browned and pan juices have sizzled away.

3. Working decisively, with sleeves and hair and kitchen towels safely secured, and your pan lid close at hand, add the Calvados, which, for safety's sake, you have poured into a second vessel, to the hot pan. If you do it right, you should experience a brief, dramatic flare-up of flame. Don't freak out—it'll disappear quickly. If it's burning too long or too high for your comfort level, put the lid on the pan, which will quickly extinguish the flames. Once the flames have disappeared, let the mixture cook for another 30 seconds then add the stock and let reduce slightly. Add the butter and toss the pan over high heat. Taste and adjust seasoning as desired, then transfer the mixture to the serving platter alongside the liver. (You may wish to cut it into small portions for easy serving.)

NOTES

→ *Special equipment: a plate lined with newspaper.*

→ *From* Appetites: A Cookbook, *by Anthony Bourdain (Ecco/Harper Collins, 2016).*

Cut Calf's liver
See page 331

VEAL BLANQUETTE
~ WITH SPRING VEGETABLES ~

Prep time *45 minutes*
Cook *1 hour 40 minutes*

1. Put the veal in a large enamelled cast-iron casserole with enough cold water to cover generously. Bring to the boil, then tip into the sink to drain. Rinse the veal and wipe out the casserole.

2. Return the veal to the casserole, add the onion, carrot, leek, garlic and bouquet garni. Cover generously with water, season with salt and pepper and bring to the boil. Skim scum from the surface, reduce the heat to medium and simmer for 1–1¼ hours until tender.

3. Meanwhile, blanch the vegetables in separate batches in a saucepan of boiling salted water until tender: 4–5 minutes for baby leeks and baby carrots, 2–3 minutes for asparagus, 1–2 minutes for peas. Remove with a slotted spoon as each vegetable is ready, refresh in iced water and drain well.

4. Remove the veal from poaching liquid, strain poaching liquid through a fine sieve lined with muslin (cheesecloth), reserving the poaching liquid and discarding the solids. Wipe the casserole clean.

5. Melt the butter in the casserole over medium–high heat, stir in the flour and cook, stirring, for 1–2 minutes to cook out the flour. Gradually add 350 ml (12 fl oz) of the veal poaching liquid, whisking constantly to combine. Bring to a simmer, reduce the heat to medium–low, season with salt and pepper and cook for 1–2 minutes to thicken slightly.

6. Increase the heat to medium, whisk in the crème fraîche mixture to thicken, but don't allow it to boil at this stage or the sauce will split. Return the veal to the sauce, stir in the blanched vegetables to warm through.

INGREDIENTS

1 kg (2 lb 4 oz) veal bolar blade, trimmed, cut into 5 cm (2 inch) pieces

1 onion, halved, each half studded with a clove

1 carrot, coarsely chopped

1 leek, coarsely chopped

1 garlic bulb, halved

Bouquet garni, made with 5 thyme sprigs, 4 parsley stalks and 2 fresh bay leaves, tied together with kitchen string

8 pencil leeks, trimmed, halved lengthways and soaked in cold water to remove grit

8 baby carrots, scrubbed, trimmed and halved lengthways

6 asparagus spears, trimmed and halved lengthways

100 g (3½ oz/⅔ cup) fresh or frozen peas

2 tablespoons (30 g) butter

30 g (1 oz) plain (all-purpose) flour

100 g (3½ oz) crème fraîche whisked with 1 egg yolk

NOTES

→ *Freeze the remaining veal poaching liquid to use in recipes that call for chicken stock.*

→ *You can use a mixture of seasonal vegetables to garnish the blanquette: broad (fava) beans, sugar snap peas and small mushrooms would work well.*

→ *Consider scattering finely grated lemon zest over the top to add a burst of freshness.*

Cut Veal bolar blade
or breast
See page 328 or 330

VIENNA SCHNITZEL

Prep time *30 minutes (plus chilling)*
Cook *15 minutes*

1. Preheat the oven to 120°C (235°F). Spread the breadcrumbs on a baking tray and bake for 8–10 minutes to dry out, then set aside to cool.

2. Pound out each piece of veal with a meat mallet to 3 mm (⅛ inch) thick and season generously with sea salt and pepper.

3. Put the seasoned flour, eggs and breadcrumbs in separate bowls, and season the breadcrumbs generously with salt and pepper.

4. Dip each piece of veal in seasoned flour, then egg, shaking off excess. Dip into the breadcrumbs, pressing so the breadcrumbs stick to the veal, coating completely. Place on a tray and refrigerate for 30 minutes to set the coating.

5. Meanwhile, to make the salad, whisk the vinegar, mustard and celery seeds in a bowl to combine. Gradually add the olive oil, whisking to emulsify, and season generously with salt and pepper. Combine the cabbage, radish, shallot, dill and parsley in a bowl, drizzle with dressing to taste, and toss to combine.

6. Heat 5 mm (¼ inch) of oil in a large frying pan over medium heat. Add a little butter, then when butter foams, add a piece of schnitzel. Pan-fry for 1–2 minutes on each side until golden brown. Drain on paper towel and keep warm while you repeat with the remaining schnitzels. Wipe out the pan between each one. Serve with the salad and lemon wedges.

INGREDIENTS

4 pieces veal topside, about 160 g (5½ oz) each
Sea salt and freshly ground black pepper
Plain (all-purpose) flour, seasoned with salt and pepper, for dusting
2–3 eggs, lightly whisked
200 g (7 oz) day-old fine white breadcrumbs
Olive oil, for frying
Butter, for frying
Lemon wedges, to serve

Cabbage and radish salad
2½ tablespoons white wine vinegar
1 teaspoon dijon mustard
1 teaspoon celery seeds
125 ml (4 fl oz/½ cup) olive oil
500 g (1 lb 2 oz) white and/or red cabbage, thinly shaved
6 radishes, thinly sliced
2 golden shallots, thinly sliced
1 small handful of dill sprigs
1 small handful of torn flat-leaf (Italian) parsley

SERVING SUGGESTION

potato salad

NOTE

→ *The same crumbing and frying technique can be used with eggplant (aubergine). Slice the eggplant lengthways, salt both sides and set aside for 20 minutes. Pat dry, then crumb and fry until golden brown, finishing the cooking in a hot oven. The eggplant is excellent served alongside the schnitzel.*

Cut Veal topside
See page 329

CRUMBED VEAL CUTLET
~ WITH PEA SALAD ~

Prep time *20 minutes*
Cook *30 minutes (plus resting)*

1. Bring the veal to room temperature for 30 minutes and season generously with sea salt.

2. Meanwhile, to make the pea salad, blanch all of the peas for 1–2 minutes in a saucepan of boiling salted water until tender and bright green. Drain, refresh under cold running water and drain well. Transfer to a bowl, add the baby spinach or pea tendrils, mint and shallot.

3. Whisk the olive oil, vinegar, lemon juice, mustard and garlic in a bowl, season with salt and pepper and set aside.

4. Preheat the oven to 180°C (350°F). Put the seasoned flour and eggs in separate bowls. Combine the breadcrumbs, parmesan, pistachios, herbs and lemon zest in a separate bowl and season with salt and pepper.

5. Dip each cutlet in seasoned flour, then egg, shaking off excess. Dip into the breadcrumb mixture, pressing so the breadcrumbs stick to the veal, coating it completely.

6. Heat 5 mm (¼ inch) of olive oil in a large frying pan over medium heat. Add half the butter, then when butter foams, add half the veal. Pan-fry for 4–5 minutes on each side until golden brown. Drain on paper towel. Wipe out pan and repeat.

7. Place cutlets on a wire rack on a baking tray and bake for 4–5 minutes. Set aside to rest for 10 minutes.

8. Drizzle the dressing over the pea salad just before serving and toss to combine. Serve the crumbed veal cutlets with pea salad, lemon aïoli and lemon wedges.

INGREDIENTS

4 veal cutlets, about 3 cm (1¼ inches) thick, about 250 g (9 oz) each
Sea salt
Plain (all-purpose) flour, seasoned with salt and pepper, for dusting
2–3 eggs, lightly whisked
180 g (6¼ oz/3 cups) day-old coarse white breadcrumbs
40 g (1½ oz) finely grated parmesan cheese
1 tablespoon finely chopped pistachios
1 small handful of finely chopped herbs, such as flat-leaf (Italian) parsley, oregano and thyme
Finely grated zest of 1 lemon, the lemon reserved for squeezing
Olive oil, for shallow-frying
3 tablespoons (40 g) butter, chopped
Aïoli, brightened with a squeeze of lemon juice, to serve
1 lemon, cut into wedges, to serve

Pea salad
200 g (7 oz) fresh or frozen peas
200 g (7 oz) sugar snap peas, trimmed
1 large handful of baby spinach leaves or pea tendrils
1 large handful of torn mint
1 golden shallot, thinly sliced
70 ml (2¼ fl oz) extra virgin olive oil
1½ tablespoons red wine vinegar
Squeeze of lemon juice
2 teaspoons dijon mustard
1 small garlic clove, finely chopped

Cut Veal cutlets
See page 328

SERVES 6
VITELLO TONNATO

Prep time *40 minutes*
Cook *20 minutes (plus standing, cooling)*

1. To prepare the poached veal, heat the olive oil in a large enamelled cast-iron casserole over medium–high heat. Season the veal generously, add to the casserole and sear, turning occasionally, for 4–5 minutes. Transfer to a plate.

2. Add the vegetables to the casserole and sauté for 6–8 minutes until tender and translucent. Add the wine, bay leaf, thyme, peppercorns and 750 ml (26 fl oz/3 cups) of water. Bring to the boil, cook for 5 minutes, then remove from the heat. Add the veal, ensuring it is completely submerged, and set aside for 25–30 minutes until the veal is firm but springs back when pressed; a thermometer inserted into the centre will read 52°C (125°F) and the meat will continue to cook as it cools.

3. Remove the veal from the poaching liquid and refrigerate to cool completely. Strain the poaching liquid, discarding the solids, and set aside.

4. To make the tuna sauce, process the tuna, egg, capers, olive oil and lemon juice in a food processor until very smooth. Gradually add enough of the reserved poaching liquid to reach a thin mayonnaise consistency and season with salt and pepper.

5. To serve, thinly slice the veal across the grain, arrange on a serving platter and spoon the tuna sauce over. Cover and refrigerate overnight or for up to 2 days to develop the flavours; alternatively, you can serve it straight away.

6. Scatter with capers, anchovies, Parmigiano Reggiano and rocket, drizzled with a little extra virgin olive oil and seasoned with salt and pepper.

INGREDIENTS

1 kg (2 lb 4 oz) piece of veal girello, trimmed of sinew
1 tablespoon olive oil
1 onion, coarsely chopped
1 carrot, coarsely chopped
1 celery stalk, coarsely chopped
1 bottle (750 ml) dry white wine
1 fresh bay leaf
1 thyme sprig
½ teaspoon black peppercorns
Salted baby capers (rinsed) and anchovies, to serve
Shaved Parmigiano Reggiano or parmesan cheese and wild rocket (arugula), to serve
Extra virgin olive oil, to drizzle

Tuna sauce
185 g (6½ oz) tinned tuna in olive oil, drained
2 medium-boiled eggs, broken into pieces
1½ tablespoons salted baby capers, rinsed
125 ml (4 fl oz/½ cup) extra virgin olive oil
Juice of 1½ lemons, or to taste

NOTES

→ *Leftover poaching liquid can be frozen to use in soups and braises in place of chicken stock.*

→ *The same sauce and garnishes are an ideal way to make use of thinly sliced leftover roast veal rack.*

Cut *Veal girello*
See page 329

SERVES 12–15 WITH LEFTOVERS

BOLLITO MISTO

Prep time *45 minutes (plus brining)*
Cook *4 hours*

1. To prepare the brined brisket, stir the salt, sugar, spices, herbs and chillies into 1 litre (35 fl oz/4 cups) of water in a large stockpot, bring to the boil and simmer for 10 minutes over medium heat. Remove from the heat, add another litre of water, cool completely. Add the brisket, weight with a plate to submerge, cover and refrigerate overnight to brine.

2. For the bollito misto, combine the wine, garlic, vegetables, chillies, herbs and spices in a large stockpot, then add the veal tongue and cotechino. Remove the brisket from the brine (discard the brine) and add it to the pot. Top up with cold water, season with salt and pepper and bring to the boil. Skim off any scum that forms on the surface.

3. Reduce the heat to medium–low and simmer for 1–1½ hours until the tongue is tender. Remove the tongue. When cool enough to handle, peel off the skin and trim fat and gristle, then cover loosely with foil and set aside.

4. Continue cooking the bollito for another 1–1¼ hours until cotechino is tender, remove cotechino, cover loosely with foil and set aside.

5. Continue cooking the bollito for another hour until the brisket is tender. Return the cotechino and tongue to the broth to warm through.

6. To serve, remove the brisket, cotechino and tongue from the broth and thinly slice: be sure to slice the brisket and the tongue across the grain. Arrange the meats on a serving platter and strain a little of the broth over to moisten. Serve with cornichons, mustard fruits, crusty bread and salsa verde. Serve bowls of strained warm broth alongside if you like.

INGREDIENTS

1 kg (2 lb 4 oz) beef brisket, fat and sinew trimmed
150 g (5½ oz) fine salt
110 g (3¾ oz/½ cup) white sugar
1 tablespoon peppercorns
1 tablespoon fennel seeds
10 sprigs each thyme and sage
2 fresh bay leaves
2 dried long red chillies
Cornichons and mustard fruits (see note), to serve
Crusty bread, to serve
Salsa verde, to serve

Bollito misto
1 veal tongue, about 700 g (1 lb 9 oz)
1 cotechino sausage, about 500 g (1 lb 2 oz)
1 bottle (750 ml) dry white wine
4 garlic bulbs, halved
3 celery stalks, cut into thirds
2 brown onions, quartered
2 carrots, cut into thirds
1 fennel bulb, cut into thick wedges
4 dried long red chillies
6 thyme sprigs
4 fresh bay leaves
2 tablespoons black peppercorns
1 tablespoon fennel seeds

NOTE

→ *Mustard fruits (*mostarda di frutta*) originated in Cremona, Italy. Poached in a mustard-spiked syrup, they are available from selected delicatessens, but you can use mustard instead.*

Cut Beef brisket, veal tongue, cotechino sausage
See pages 321, 322 and 232

CATTLE

OSSO BUCO MILANESE

1. Preheat the oven to 160°C (315°F). Dust the osso buco in the seasoned flour and shake off excess.

2. Heat a splash of olive oil in a large enamelled cast-iron casserole on the stovetop over medium–high heat and add the osso buco to the casserole. Fry, turning occasionally, for 5–6 minutes to brown well all over: the deeper the browning, the better the flavour of the finished dish, so take your time to do this well. Transfer the meat to a plate.

3. Add the butter to the casserole and when it foams, add the onion, celery and garlic. Sauté for 4–5 minutes until the vegetables are tender and translucent. Stir in the anchovies until they melt and dissolve into the vegetables, then deglaze the casserole with the wine and vermouth and simmer to reduce by half.

4. Add the stock, herbs and osso buco, season and bring to the boil, then remove from the heat. Make a cartouche by cutting out a round of baking paper to fit the diameter of the casserole, crumple it up, then wet it under cold running water. Lay it directly on the surface of the mixture, pressing to get rid of any air bubbles. Cover with a lid and braise in the oven for 3–3½ hours until the meat is almost falling from the bone. Set aside for 10 minutes.

5. Meanwhile, about half an hour before the osso buco is ready, start making the saffron risotto. Heat a splash of oil and the butter in a saucepan over medium heat, add the onion, season with salt and pepper and sauté for 2–3 minutes until tender. Stir in the garlic until fragrant.

6. Add the rice, stir for a minute or two to lightly toast and until the edges of the rice turn translucent. Add the wine and stir until evaporated, then add the saffron and soaking water and stir to combine. Gradually add the hot stock, a ladleful at a time, stirring constantly and adding more stock as it is absorbed for 25–30 minutes until the rice is creamy and just tender. Add the parmesan, stir to combine, season with salt and pepper and keep warm.

7. To make the gremolata, combine the parsley, lemon zest, a squeeze of lemon juice and the garlic in a bowl. Add enough extra virgin olive oil to make a drizzling consistency and season with salt and pepper to taste.

8. Serve osso buco on saffron risotto, drizzled with gremolata.

INGREDIENTS

4 large pieces of veal osso buco, about 300 g (10½ oz each)
Sea salt and freshly ground black pepper
Plain (all-purpose) flour, seasoned with salt and pepper, for dusting
Olive oil, for cooking
2 tablespoons (30 g) butter, chopped
1 large brown onion, chopped
2 celery stalks, chopped
3 garlic cloves, finely chopped
3–4 anchovies
200 ml (7 fl oz) dry white wine
100 ml (3½ fl oz) vermouth
500 ml (17 fl oz/2 cups) chicken or veal stock
1 fresh bay leaf, 1 rosemary sprig and 1 thyme sprig

Saffron risotto
Olive oil, for cooking
2 tablespoons (30 g) butter, chopped
1 brown onion, finely chopped
1 garlic clove, finely chopped
200 g (7 oz) carnaroli (risotto rice)
100 ml (3½ fl oz) dry white wine or vermouth
1 large pinch of saffron threads soaked in 1 tablespoon warm water for 10 minutes
1 litre (35 fl oz/4 cups) hot chicken stock
80 g (2¾ oz/1 cup) finely grated parmesan cheese

Gremolata
1 large handful of flat-leaf (Italian) parsley, coarsely chopped
Finely grated zest of 1 lemon, plus a squeeze of lemon juice
2 garlic cloves, finely chopped
Extra virgin olive oil

Cut Veal, kangaroo or venison osso buco
See pages 330, 423 or 428

MEATBALLS

1. Preheat the oven to 180°C (350°F).

2. For the meatballs, combine all of the ingredients (except the oil) in a bowl and season well with salt and pepper. Use your hands to combine well until the mixture starts to feel elastic. Roll into golf ball–sized balls and refrigerate to rest for 30 minutes.

3. Meanwhile, to make the sugo, heat a splash of olive oil in a large enamelled cast-iron casserole over medium heat, add the onion, season with salt and pepper and sauté for 8–10 minutes until tender and translucent. Add the garlic, cook until fragrant, then add the wine and simmer for 4–5 minutes until reduced by one-third. Add the passata, tinned tomatoes and herbs, bring to the boil, season with salt and pepper and set aside.

4. Heat a splash of olive oil in a large non-stick frying pan over high heat, add the meatballs in batches and cook, turning occasionally, for 2–3 minutes until browned all over. Add to casserole with the sugo, season with salt and pepper and bring to a simmer over medium heat. Transfer to the oven and bake for 20–25 minutes until just cooked through. Discard the herbs, stir in the vinegar, check the seasoning and keep warm.

5. Meanwhile, to make the green polenta, bring 800 ml (28 fl oz) of water to the boil with the milk and salt in a saucepan over medium–high heat. Add the polenta, whisk to combine and season with salt and pepper. Reduce the heat to low so the surface of the polenta is barely bubbling and cook, whisking occasionally to begin with and more frequently as the polenta thickens, for 25–30 minutes until thick and no longer grainy.

6. Meanwhile, blanch the kale in a saucepan of boiling salted water for 1 minute until just tender, adding the spinach for the last 10 seconds of cooking. Drain and refresh in iced water. Drain well and purée in a food processor or blender until smooth, seasoning with salt and pepper. Whisk the parmesan and butter into the polenta, check the seasoning, then swirl the kale purée through.

7. Serve the green polenta topped with the meatballs, sugo and extra parmesan.

8. Meatballs will keep in the refrigerator for up to 3 days and also freeze well, so consider making a double batch. Leftover meatballs are excellent in a meatball sub: warm them in the sugo and stuff into a baguette with grated parmesan and basil.

INGREDIENTS

400 g (14 oz) minced (ground) veal chuck
200 g (7 oz) minced (ground) pork shoulder
50 g (1¾ oz) finely grated parmesan cheese, plus extra to serve
2 tablespoons day-old coarse breadcrumbs, soaked in a little milk
1½ tablespoons coarsely chopped mixed herbs, such as thyme, oregano and rosemary
1 egg yolk
1 garlic clove, finely chopped
Olive oil, for cooking

Sugo
Olive oil, for cooking
1 small brown onion, finely diced
2 garlic cloves, finely chopped
200 ml (7 fl oz) full-bodied red wine
500 ml (17 fl oz/2 cups) tomato passata (tomato purée)
400 g (14 oz) tinned cherry tomatoes
2 sprigs each of oregano and thyme
2 teaspoons red wine vinegar, or to taste

Green polenta
250 ml (9 fl oz/1 cup) milk
2 teaspoons salt
150 g (5½ oz) polenta (not instant polenta)
100 g (3½ oz) kale leaves, torn into bite-sized pieces
1 large handful of English spinach leaves
60 g (2¼ oz) finely grated parmesan cheese
3 tablespoons (40 g) butter, chopped

Cut Veal chuck, pork shoulder
See page 328, 220

MILK-ROASTED VEAL

Prep time *25 minutes*
Cook *2½ hours (plus resting)*

1. Bring the veal to room temperature for 1 hour and season generously with sea salt and pepper.
2. Heat the butter in a large enamelled cast-iron casserole over medium-high heat until the butter foams. Add the veal and cook, turning occasionally, for 8–10 minutes until browned well. Add the prosciutto and fry for 30 seconds to crisp slightly.
3. Add the milk to cover by two-thirds, plus the garlic, thyme, sage and nutmeg, and season well with salt and pepper. Cover with a lid and reduce the heat to medium. Simmer, spooning some of the milk mixture over the veal and topping up the milk occasionally if necessary, for 2–2¼ hours until tender. To check whether it's done, a thermometer will read 58°C (136°F) and the juices will run clear when the meat is pierced with a skewer. Set aside in the casserole to rest for 30 minutes.
4. To make the wilted greens, heat the olive oil and butter in a large frying pan until the butter foams. Add the rainbow chard stalks and the garlic and, as soon as it sizzles, add the leaves and toss to combine. Add a splash of water to the pan, season with salt and pepper and toss for 2–3 minutes to wilt. Squeeze in some lemon juice and check seasoning.
5. To serve, remove the veal from the casserole, discard the string and thinly slice. Serve topped with fried sage leaves, with the wilted greens and some of the pan liquid spooned over.

INGREDIENTS

1.5 kg (3 lb 5 oz) veal topside, tied at 3 cm (1¼ inch) intervals with kitchen string
6 medium-thick slices of prosciutto
4 tablespoons (60 g) butter, chopped
2 litres (70 fl oz/8 cups) milk
1 garlic bulb, halved
3 thyme sprigs
3 sage sprigs
1 pinch of finely grated nutmeg
3 thin strips of lemon zest
Fried sage leaves, to serve

Wilted chard
1 tablespoon olive oil
2 tablespoons (30 g) butter, chopped
700 g (1 lb 9 oz, about 1 large bunch) rainbow chard, stalks thinly sliced, leaves torn into bite-sized pieces (see note)
3 garlic cloves, finely chopped
Squeeze of lemon juice

SERVING SUGGESTION *roasted cauliflower; roast a whole cauliflower or separate into florets*

NOTES

→ *The braising liquid can be turned into a smooth sauce. Squeeze the garlic from its skin into a blender, add 250 ml (9 fl oz/1 cup) of the pan juices, season and blend until smooth.*

→ *You can use a mix of dark leafy greens for the wilted greens. Kale, silverbeet (Swiss chard) and beetroot (beet) leaves work well. Thinly slice and add to the pan with the garlic.*

Cut Veal topside
See page 329

VEAL TAGLIATA

Prep time *15 minutes*
Cook *10 minutes (plus resting)*

1. Bring veal to room temperature for 30 minutes and season generously with sea salt and pepper.

2. Blanch the beans in a saucepan of boiling salted water for 1–2 minutes until bright green and tender. Drain, refresh under cold running water and drain well. Transfer to a bowl, add the rocket and set aside.

3. Heat a splash of olive oil, the rosemary and garlic in a frying pan until smoking hot. Discard the rosemary and garlic, add the veal and pan-fry for 1–2 minutes on each side until browned and cooked rare. Transfer to a plate and set aside to rest for 5 minutes.

4. Tip any resting juices into a bowl, whisk in the extra virgin olive oil and balsamic vinegar, season with salt and pepper and brighten with a squeeze of lemon juice.

5. Thinly slice the steaks across the grain, and add to the rocket and bean mixture. Drizzle with dressing, season to taste, toss to combine and serve scattered with Parmigiano Reggiano and with lemon wedges on the side.

INGREDIENTS

3 veal rump steaks, about 170 g (6 oz) each
Sea salt and freshly ground pepper
200 g (7 oz) green beans, trimmed
2 large handfuls of wild rocket (arugula)
Olive oil, for pan-frying
1 rosemary sprig
1 garlic clove, bruised with the flat of a knife
2½ tablespoons extra virgin olive oil
1 tablespoon aged balsamic vinegar
Squeeze of lemon juice, to taste
Shaved Parmigiano Reggiano, to serve
Lemon wedges, to serve

NOTE

→ *Tagliata is an Italian word referring to the slicing of the steak, rather than a particular cut of steak.*

Cut Veal rump steak
See page 329

STEAK AND KIDNEY PIE

1. Trim excess fat from the beef and cut it into 2.5 cm (1 inch) cubes, reserving trimmings. Refrigerate until required.

2. Melt a little reserved beef fat in a saucepan over medium heat. Increase the heat to medium–high, add the beef and kidney trimmings and the trimmings from the onion and mushrooms. Stir for 3–4 minutes until browned, season with salt and pepper and add 1 litre (35 fl oz/4 cups) of water and the thyme stems. Simmer over medium heat for 1 hour, skimming scum from the surface. Strain and discard the solids.

3. Melt the remaining beef fat in a large enamelled cast-iron casserole over medium heat, adding a splash of olive oil if necessary. Increase the heat to medium–high, add the onion and mushrooms and sauté for 4–5 minutes until tender. Stir in the garlic until fragrant, then transfer to a bowl.

4. Dust the kidneys in seasoned flour, sear them in the casserole for 1–2 minutes, turning occasionally to brown all over. Transfer to a plate.

5. Dust the beef cubes in the seasoned flour, add to the casserole in batches and cook, turning occasionally, for 5–6 minutes to brown all over. Don't overcrowd the pan or the meat will stew rather than caramelise. Transfer to a plate.

6. Return the beef to the casserole and add the onion mixture, kidneys and herbs. Add the beer and 500 ml (17 fl oz/2 cups) of beef stock. Season, bring to a simmer, half-cover and simmer for 1½–2 hours until beef is tender. Discard the bay leaf.

7. Stir the flour, Worcestershire sauce and 60 ml (2 fl oz/¼ cup) of the beef stock in a bowl to make a smooth slurry. Add this to the beef mixture, stirring for 4–5 minutes until smooth and thick. Add the parsley and season with salt and pepper if necessary. Divide the mixture among eight 250 ml (9 fl oz/1 cup) ramekins and set aside to cool completely.

8. Preheat the oven to 180°C (350°F). Roll out the pastry on a lightly floured work surface to 4 mm (⅛ inch) thick. Refrigerate for 30 minutes, then cut rounds slightly larger than the top of the ramekins by about 2 cm (¾ inch). Brush the edges with a little egg wash, lay the pastry over the pie filling with the egg wash–side down and press over the edges to seal. Pierce a hole in the centre of the lid for steam to escape.

9. Brush the pastry with egg wash, put the baking dish on a baking tray and bake for 20–25 minutes for smaller pies until the pastry is a dark golden brown. Set aside for 15 minutes before serving.

INGREDIENTS

1 kg (2 lb 4 oz) boneless beef shoulder

200 g (7 oz) veal kidneys, trimmed, trimmings reserved

2 brown onions, thinly sliced

300 g (10½ oz) Swiss brown mushrooms, trimmed and sliced

3 thyme sprigs, leaves picked, stems reserved

Olive oil

1 garlic clove, finely chopped

Plain (all-purpose) flour, seasoned with salt and pepper, for dusting

1 fresh bay leaf

375 ml (13 fl oz/1½ cups) beer

40 g (1½ oz) plain (all-purpose) flour

2½ tablespoons Worcestershire sauce

2 tablespoons coarsely chopped flat-leaf (Italian) parsley

500 g (1 lb 2 oz) butter puff pastry

1 egg yolk, whisked with 1 tablespoon milk

NOTES

→ *Leftover beef stock can be cooled, reserved and frozen to use in place of veal or chicken stock.*

→ *To make a single large pie, use a 2 litre (70 fl oz/8 cup) baking dish or pie tin and bake for 25–30 minutes.*

Cut Beef shoulder, veal kidney
See page 318, 330

BROWN BUTTER SWEETBREADS
~ WITH RAVIGOTE SAUCE ~

Prep time *30 minutes*
Cook *25 minutes (plus cooling)*

INGREDIENTS

500 g (1 lb 2 oz) pancreatic (heart) or thymus
   veal sweetbreads
2 teaspoons white vinegar
1 teaspoon sea salt
7 tablespoons (100 g) chilled butter,
   chopped
Plain (all-purpose) flour, seasoned with salt
   and pepper, for dusting
Squeeze of lemon juice
1 garlic clove, finely chopped
Toasted or chargrilled sourdough bread,
   to serve

Ravigote sauce
2 handfuls of flat-leaf (Italian) parsley,
   finely chopped
1 handful of chervil, coarsely chopped
2 tablespoons snipped chives
40 g (1½ oz) cornichons, finely chopped
2 tablespoons tarragon vinegar or
   white wine vinegar
2 tablespoons baby salted capers,
   rinsed and finely chopped
1 teaspoon dijon mustard
1 golden shallot, finely diced
1 garlic clove, finely chopped
Finely grated zest and juice of ½ lemon
Olive oil

1. Bring the white vinegar, sea salt and 1 litre (35 fl oz/4 cups) of water to a simmer over medium heat. Add the sweetbreads and gently poach for 10–15 minutes until opaque. Drain and transfer to a bowl of iced water to cool.

2. Drain the cooled sweetbreads well and pat dry on paper towel. Peel off the membrane, trim any sinew and blood. Break into walnut-sized pieces and set aside.

3. To make the ravigote sauce, pulse the herbs, cornichons, vinegar, capers, mustard, shallot, garlic, lemon zest and juice in a food processor until finely chopped. Stir in enough olive oil to make a drizzling consistency and season with salt and pepper.

4. Heat half the butter in a large frying pan until the butter foams. Dust the sweetbreads in seasoned flour, shaking off any excess. Carefully pan-fry, turning occasionally, for 2–3 minutes until golden brown and crisp. Transfer to a plate lined with paper towel.

5. Wipe out pan, add the remaining butter and cook, swirling the pan occasionally, for 3–4 minutes until nut brown. Remove from the heat, squeeze in some lemon juice (be careful as the butter will spit and sputter), then when the spitting dies down, stir in the garlic and season with salt and pepper.

6. Divide the sweetbreads among serving plates and spoon the burnt butter over. Drizzle with ravigote sauce and serve with chargrilled sourdough bread.

NOTE
→ *Lamb sweetbreads are also excellent cooked in this way: they are smaller than veal sweetbreads, so will take less time to cook.*

Cut *Veal sweetbreads*
See page 331

ROASTED BONE MARROW
~ WITH PARSLEY SALAD ~

Prep time *15 minutes*
Cook *20 minutes*

1. Preheat the oven to 220°C (425°F) and put the marrow bones in an ovenproof frying pan or small roasting tin, setting the bones cut-side up. Roast for 15–20 minutes until the marrow begins to shrink away from the bones. Keep an eye on the marrow as, if it cooks too much, it will become liquid in the pan. It should be just quivering!

2. When the bone marrow is almost ready, chargrill or toast the bread. Rub with the cut side of the garlic and keep warm.

3. Combine the parsley, golden shallot, capers and lemon zest in a bowl, add lemon juice and olive oil and season with a little sea salt and freshly ground black pepper. Toss and serve the salad alongside the roasted marrow bones and sourdough toast: scoop the marrow from the bones, spread on the toast and top with parsley salad, seasoning with a little extra sea salt to taste.

INGREDIENTS

8 pieces of whole bone with marrow, cut
    laterally into 6–7 cm (2½–2¾ inch) pieces
8 thin slices sourdough bread
1 garlic clove, halved
1 cup coarsely chopped flat-leaf (Italian)
    parsley
1 large golden shallot, thinly sliced into rings
1 tablespoon drained baby capers in brine
Finely grated zest of 1 lemon
1 tablespoon lemon juice
2 tablespoons extra virgin olive oil
Sea salt and freshly ground black pepper

NOTES

→ *For a more robust flavour, you can use beef marrow bones instead of the veal.*

→ *Ask your butcher to cut the marrow bones into pieces for you.*

Cut Veal marrow bones
See page 331

CHAPTER FIVE

WILD

RABBIT ~ VENISON ~ KANGAROO
~ OTHER GAME

WILD

HIDES, LEATHER, FUR, HORN, FEATHERS, OIL (EMU)

SELECT & STORE

RABBIT

Farmed rabbit meat will be white in colour, while their wild counterparts will have a greyer appearance. Seek out fresh rabbit; speak to your butcher about the best day to get it, based on processing date. Frozen rabbits will generally be better suited to slow cooking or confit.

VENISON

As farmed venison is often younger it can be milder in flavour; wild venison may be tougher but will also have a richer flavour. Much venison is hung or dry-aged before butchery, which is helpful if you plan to freeze the meat as it removes much of the moisture.

KANGAROO

Kangaroo is very lean and should have a vibrant red colour. In the kitchen, aim for quick frying or slow braising.

COMPLEMENTS TO RABBIT

ROSEMARY, SAGE, BAY LEAVES, FENNEL, THYME, WHITE VINEGAR, VERJUICE, BACON, BRANDY, MUSHROOMS, MUSTARD, OLIVES, PINE NUTS, PRUNES, WINE, ONIONS, GARLIC, ALMONDS, FIGS, PANCETTA, LEMON, CORNICHONS.

COMPLEMENTS TO VENISON

OYSTER, JUNIPER BERRIES, BAY, ROSEMARY, CHOCOLATE, BLACK PEPPER, POTATOES, BEETROOT (BEETS), MUSHROOMS, BERRIES, APPLES, RED WINE, CABBAGE, ONIONS, PEAR, ROOT VEGETABLES.

COMPLEMENTS TO KANGAROO

RASPBERRY, PLUM, CITRUS, ALMONDS, WALNUTS, WINE, STAR ANISE, JUNIPER, GREEN PEPPERCORN, CHILLI, SOY, PARSLEY, THYME, ROSEMARY, ANCHOVIES, CAPERS, BEETROOT (BEETS), GARLIC, PUMPKIN (WINTER SQUASH), HORSERADISH.

POPULAR GAME

| VENISON | REINDEER | KANGAROO | HARE | RABBIT | PHEASANT | PARTRIDGE | GROUSE | BECASSE |

LEARN MORE ABOUT DIFFERENT CUTS AND HOW TO USE THEM ON PAGES 417, 421–423 AND 427–429.

Wild animals are generally very lean, which means their predominant flavour comes from their flesh, not their fat.

The extra flavour in game animals means that with too much fat they could actually become too rich. This balance of flavour and leanness is a culinary boon.

The simple cuts are much better appreciated on the rare side of medium-rare, while the more complex cuts will enjoy long slow cooking with extra moisture.

BUTCHER'S TREATS

RABBIT: KIDNEYS

VENISON: SHANKS

KANGAROO: TAIL

—ALL ABOUT—

RABBIT

A fully grown farmed rabbit will weigh between 1.4 and 2 kg (3 lb 2 oz and 4 lb 8 oz) and will feed four to six people, depending on the way you cook it. The most important thing to keep in mind when cooking a rabbit, as with most game, is not to let it dry out! Treat the different cuts of the rabbit differently. The back legs will take the longest, the saddle and forelegs are naturally leaner and more tender. You can wrap the saddle in prosciutto or some other fat such as bacon or caul fat; alternatively you can marinate the rabbit in olive oil and aromatics. Wild rabbit, which is much smaller at 800 g to 1.2 kg (1 lb 12 oz–2 lb 10 oz), can be soaked in cold, salted water—the brine rendering the rabbit more tender.

IN THE KITCHEN

Wild animals will be treated differently depending on their age and condition: young, they can be cooked quickly and served rare, while older animals (or harder working cuts) are used to better advantage in long and slow preparations. This is where you can get creative. There is a myriad of slow braises scattered throughout this book (for the essentials of a good braise, see pages 454–455). These can be adjusted for use with older game animals and harder working muscles. Our complements to each animal will give you some cursory advice about flavour pairings. The less-used muscles (loin, saddle, fillet) generally require quick cooking so as not to dry out. These cuts can also benefit from marinating and barding (wrapping in bacon) or larding (studding with fat) to mitigate any toughness. Get creative!

BEYOND THE BUTCHERY

In each chapter of this book, we have noted other uses for the animals we consume at the table. These are important and, of course, extend to animals from the wild. Making use of the whole animal is part of the respect we show them.

Kangaroo leather has waterproof qualities that other leathers do not. Deer antlers, shed and regrown each year, can be used to make beautiful knife handles, while rabbit fur has long been used for its warmth.

⊣ FARMING THE WILD ⊢

While there are some wild animals that continue to elude the human hand, much of the game we eat is now farmed, or at least in part controlled: from the huge farmed deer industry in New Zealand to the managed pheasant farms of the UK. These animals will generally be milder in flavour and more tender than their truly wild cousins.

TIP: *Beware the shrapnel! If you are purchasing wild shot rabbit, hare or game birds, keep an eye out for shot in the flesh.*

HISTORY

Barnyard animals tell the tale of human intervention: we have trained and tamed their bodies to exist within the framework of agriculture. And yet, there are animals that continue to thrive on their own, animals endemic to the region in which they live. These are wild animals that have been shaped not by the human hand, but by Mother Nature.

While there are many wild animals we don't eat (and those ethical and moral decisions are fascinating), the variety that we do eat is still quite diverse: from the game birds of Europe, many with their annual pilgrimage to warmer climates for winter, to the camels walking the deserts of northern Africa, the reindeer in the snowfields of Lappland and the bison and other prairie animals of the Americas and Africa. These animals generally tell a very different tale of breed, feed, life and death. They have slowly adapted to the climate and geography of their region and, thus, it is natural selection that has chosen the dominant breeds.

Their diet is the grasses, herbs and trees around them: a true taste of their terroir. Free-ranging, game animals tend to be leaner than other animals. They often have stronger muscles as they need to forage for food, build their own nests, or run from their predators. What they lack in fat, they make up for with a distinctive 'gamey' flavour. Their diet plays a role in this flavour: a diet that is rich in nutrients from the earth, often from soils that are untouched by pesticides or herbicides.

Their footprint (or hoofprint) on the environment generally has a lighter touch than animals in commercial agriculture, particularly those that are intensively raised. Their wild existence is intertwined with the environment around them: natural herding or migratory instincts mean their hoofs will turn up the land without overly compacting it. Furthermore, their manure, a natural fertiliser, travels with them; not only is it often lighter, it can even return nutrients to the soil.

A further advantage of wild game is the lack of stress inflicted upon the animal. (You will remember that stress, particularly in the late stages of an animal's life, increases the alkalinity of the flesh, which has a negative impact on both taste and tenderness.) In the wild, the animal should not even know it is in danger until it is too late. It is important to note that harvesting and culling of these animals is now, generally, carefully monitored by government bodies to ensure that herd numbers remain healthy. It is worth considering that a greater threat than the hunter is probably urban spread encroaching on their habitat.

BUTCHERY

In the butchery and the kitchen these animals are collectively referred to as game: by definition, game is an animal hunted for food or not normally domesticated. The act of hunting has not been without controversy and yet this relationship between man and animal is, in fact, the oldest of them all.

The season for certain game can be short (sometimes dictated by legal rights to hunt, at other times by the natural seasons of the animal's breeding cycle) and erratic. The age and condition of the animals can also vary greatly and must be taken into account. This has many ramifications for the way in which they are treated in the butchery and kitchen. In fact, game will often be hung (dry-aged) to help make it more tender; in the case of many game birds, this is done with their feathers still on, to help protect their thin skin.

→ *The chapter on Birds has more information about game birds: see page 69.*

The wait and anticipation is certainly worth it: a nice young pheasant, quickly roasted and well basted, is delicious, or covered with strips of pancetta and roasted slowly until just a blush of pink remains; the bones from these game birds make a deep flavourful stock; rabbit, another winter treat, is exquisite in terrine, flaked into rillettes or as an excellent light stew; while larger game animals such as deer (venison) offer excellent steaks and roasts, particularly when quickly cooked.

Yet we still find cases where the endemic game has not yet found the favour it probably deserves. Take, for example, the Australian kangaroo. Despite a culinary history that enjoyed kangaroo for tens of thousands of years, the flavour of this endemic animal was eschewed when the culinary straitjacket of Britain was applied to the land. And yet, if the kangaroo was French …

AT THE TABLE

Wild animals and game signal the last frontier for the food connoisseur. There is no doubt the ironlike, gamey flavour is a little more confronting than other meats, perhaps because it's a taste that many of us didn't grow up with, or because psychologically the gamier flavour of these animals requires time to adjust to. Think of it a little like acquiring a taste for anchovies or gin; and aren't we pleased we conquered those two!

Beyond the variety of game birds mentioned in the Birds chapter, we have chosen three wild animals to highlight: rabbit, deer (venison) and kangaroo. The story of breed, feed, life and death is largely the same in concept for all wild animals: they are all mainly dictated by providence, not interference.

HERITAGE BREED MAP: WILD

BRITAIN

**Partridge –
Pheasant – Grouse**

A small selection
of the many game
birds. These three
are particularly
prized: cook quickly
and serve pink.

Deer (venison)

Wild deer should
be chosen for the
table, not the trophy
cabinet. Old males
have a strong aroma,
as opposed to the
younger bucks.

EURASIA

EUROPE

Hare

Originally from
Morocco or the
Iberian Peninsula,
hare are larger and
have darker and
gamier meat than
their rabbit cousins.

Wild boar

All pigs are thought
to have originated
from the wild boar.
Wild boars continue
to roam free in many
parts of the world.
See the Pigs chapter.

LAPPLAND & NORDIC COUNTRIES

Reindeer

Farmed with the
lightest of touches
over a number of
countries in which
reindeer are allowed
to roam.

TURKEY, IRAN, PAKISTAN

Goat

With their ability
to thrive in sparse,
rocky lands, goats
have found homes
where other animals
could not dare. See
the Sheep chapter.

AFRICA

NORTH AFRICA

Camel

A rich meat that
is high in protein,
the camel is highly
prized and is used
and respected in its
entirety, from the
offal to the hump.

Guinea fowl

See page 40 of the
Birds chapter.

SOUTH AFRICA

Antelope

Low in fat and very
tender, with a flavour
that is considered
similar to young beef.
This genus includes
both springbok and
wildebeest.

Springbok

The springbok,
a medium-sized
antelope, is often
cooked over the
braai, a traditional
South African
barbecue.

Wildebeest

Another species
of antelope, the
wildebeest is also
low-fat with a slight
gamey flavour. The
meat can be used
for biltong.

ASIA

Water buffalo

With a lower fat content than beef, buffalo is lean and rich. Prized for their milk production, the buffalo meat tends to be a secondary industry.

NEW ZEALAND

Deer (venison)

Deer were introduced to New Zealand in the mid-19th century. This country is now the number one producer of farm-raised venison.

NORTH AMERICA

Bison

With the wild bison population dwindling (farmed bison is 90% of the bison population), there are calls for more free-ranging production to help restore their numbers in the wild.

Turkey

A bird to give thanks for, turkeys are now largely domesticated and are a traditional part of many Christmas and Thanksgiving feasts. (See the Birds chapter for more.)

AUSTRALIA

Kangaroo

A great natural source of lean protein in Australia. A light touch on the environment, prolific breeders, delicious meat.

Emu

As the meat of the emu is a red meat, it will respond well in recipes for beef and other game animals (as opposed to game birds).

Crocodile

Tender of flesh and particularly fatty, crocodile meat is yet to find a place in many kitchens.

Magpie goose

With many culinary links to the goose, this large water bird is rich in flavour.

WORLDWIDE

Rabbit

The European rabbit has been introduced, and has thrived, on every continent except Antarctica. Due to a voracious appetite and prolific breeding they have reached plague proportions across much of the globe.

RABBIT & HARE

The childhood folklore of the rabbit—whether Peter Rabbit, the Easter Bunny or Watership Down—*has caused untold PR dramas for the rabbit in the kitchen; however, as rabbits populated the world breeding like, well, rabbits, the need to eat them started to outstrip the squeamishness.*

Unlike much wild game, well adjusted to live in its own environment, the rabbit can make a pretty good fist of living just about anywhere. Renowned as prolific breeders and thus an easy source of food, particularly for new settlements, rabbits have been taken from their natural environment and introduced all around the world. They have thrived. Sadly, this has not always meant great things for the land.

More than 200 years ago, when European settlers arrived in Australia with their hard-hoofed animals and, worse still, a handful of burrowing rabbits, they sought to tame a land without first understanding its unique intricacies. Over 50 years the handful of rabbits became hordes. This cookie-cutter approach to the land wrought untold damage on the ancient soils, with the hard hoofs compacting the soil above and the rabbits' burrows destroying the scant binding that held together the soil below.

It did not take long for the cracks to literally begin to show. Rabbits were relegated to the domain of pests and eating rabbit became an act of patriotism. Campaigns such as 'eat feral to save rangelands' attempted to put the rabbit into the pot. It was not always successful. Although continental Europe has a long history of delicious dishes made with rabbit, for many the rabbit was stuck somewhere between childhood toy and a dish for the poor: the 'underground mutton' of the Depression years, the pervasive cry of 'rabbit-OH' never far from memory.

This is a travesty. Rabbit is similar in taste, and indeed in size, to the family favourite, chicken. Most often they are sold in their entirety; however, it is best to joint the rabbit, cooking the loin for less time than the legs, so it doesn't dry out. For those seeking a milder flavour, there is now an industry in farmed rabbit, which is paler of flesh and less strong in taste than their wild counterparts. The slightly sweet, slightly gamey taste (somewhere between chicken and veal) pairs well with many flavours.

Rabbit makes a divine terrine served with crusty bread and cornichons, or is beautiful slowly cooked in a casserole with verjuice and fresh herbs.

If you're lucky enough to get your hands on it, rabbit offal is a great addition to a rabbit stew or terrine. Also look to recipes for confit and rillettes, two French preparations that work particularly well with the rabbit.

HARES

Hares, believed to have originated in Morocco or the Iberian Peninsula, are larger than rabbits with longer ears and a notched 'hare' lip. They are members of the same family, but they have never been domesticated. In the kitchen, hare meat is darker, richer and much gamier.

While younger hare can be roasted, older animals are best slowly cooked and should always be cooked through. The shoulders and legs of the hare are very lean and can be hard to work with, beyond stock and flavouring. Thus it is the saddle that you will be most likely to come across in restaurants, often roasted to the rarer side of medium-rare.

Hares are quite bloody to prepare and joint, with the blood often used to thicken and enhance the sauce, particularly in the classic dish of jugged hare, marinated in red wine and juniper berries.

Both rabbit and hare present excellent adventures for the home cook. We should not just be killing them, we should be cooking them.

→ *Alan Davidson, editor of the incredible* The Oxford Companion to Food *(Oxford University Press, 1999), notes the Italian and Spanish use of chocolate in their hare stews; the Belgians use beer and chestnuts or prunes; while the French will roast young hares with marc and grapes or cream, juniper and mushrooms, or braise them long and slow as a traditional daube or civet (jugged hare).*

RABBIT CUTS

Purchased in its entirety, a rabbit can then be jointed much as you would work with a chicken. In the pan, pay careful attention to the saddle. It will require faster cooking to avoid drying out.

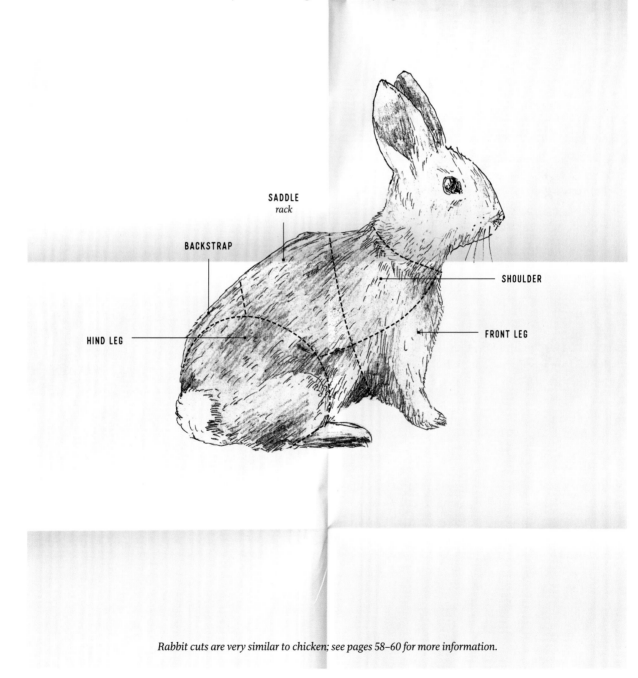

SADDLE
rack

BACKSTRAP

SHOULDER

HIND LEG

FRONT LEG

Rabbit cuts are very similar to chicken; see pages 58–60 for more information.

DEER & REINDEER

The majestic deer and the sentimental favourite reindeer tell two different tales in their path from the wild to the table.

Deer, striking in appearance, were long hunted by the wealthy in the United Kingdom, where it was the preserve of royalty and aristocrats; these animals, and in fact all game, were the property of the monarch. Conversely, Lappland, in the northern reaches of Norway, Finland and Sweden, is the domain of the indigenous Sami people, their lives intertwined with the reindeer in a natural symbiosis: one of the most interesting examples of wild animal husbandry in the world.

In the first case, venison refers to the meat from the deer; however, the word is derived from the Latin *venari*, meaning to hunt or pursue. Originally (and technically) it referred to all game meat, including that from wild pigs, goats, hares, deer and antelopes.

The evidence for hunting in the United Kingdom dates back to prehistoric times, when it was a crucial part of the hunter–gatherer existence. With the birth of agriculture, the need to hunt dwindled but the 'sport' did not. Hounds were trained to catch foxes (although the use of hounds is now largely outlawed in the UK) and, with advances in gun technology, deer stalking and hunting became ever more popular, particularly for people of means, who would pay gamekeepers to create the perfect environment for their hunting parties.

Traditionally a royal sport, the romantic image of pursuing a stag in the highlands proved alluring and thus deer shooting or stalking became a pastime for the gentry. This image of venison as a royal preserve has led to a bit of a PR crisis for the eating of venison. Happily this is beginning to shift, perhaps encouraged by the growth of venison farming, leading to animals that are more consistent with regard to age and condition. This farming is much less intensive, as the deer still require large tracts of land and, therefore, they are often still located in largely wild pastures such as the highlands of Scotland or New Zealand.

Too long considered food only for those with money, the shift to more venison on the plate has taken time. Deer have reached near plague proportion in Canada and

other parts of North America where, as in much of the western world, the culinary focus largely remains on the loin. With a deep, earthy flavour and lean flesh, the loin and rump—especially from a younger animal—are great quickly cooked; yet there is much to be relished in the harder-working muscles. The shoulder is great for stews, and the shin shank can also be cut laterally for osso buco. The dark meat takes well to preservation methods such as pastrami and salumi.

For every rule there is an exception and, in the case of the relationship between wild animals and the hunter, that exception is the reindeer of Lappland and their symbiotic relationship with the seminomadic Sami people. Sami have been herding reindeer in Lappland since the seventeenth century, with herds passed down from generation to generation; however, this herding system is a very different, very gentle approach to animal husbandry.

The animals are largely left to follow their own rhythms and desires, with the Sami surveying their herd from a distance and generally only stepping in when a small group breaks away from the herd and risks getting lost. Their biggest intervention is perhaps the most lovely. Each year, as spring approaches, the reindeer herds head north to return to a specific island to give birth and tend to their young in their infancy. To get to the island, the reindeer must swim a channel: a dangerous undertaking. The Sami now herd the animals onto large boats and ship them across each year.

As with many wild animals, the reindeer have adapted to suit their unique environment. They spend the summer months under the midnight sun, eating two to three times the amount of food they will eat in winter. Then, as the cooler weather approaches, the reindeer, with their bellies full of feed, head south, growing their winter pelt for extra warmth.

Unsurprisingly, given the respect with which the Sami hold the reindeer, they make use of the whole animal. When cooked fresh it is often made into stews, sausages and their own variation of black pudding, using reindeer blood. There is a strong tradition of curing reindeer meat as reserves for times of need. Reindeer milk and cheese are also eaten, while the pelts, hoofs and bones are all put to use, showing true respect for the animal so gently in their care.

VENISON CUTS

Whether the venison was wild or farmed will have a significant impact on its flavour. Ask your butcher about the provenance of the venison before choosing your dish.

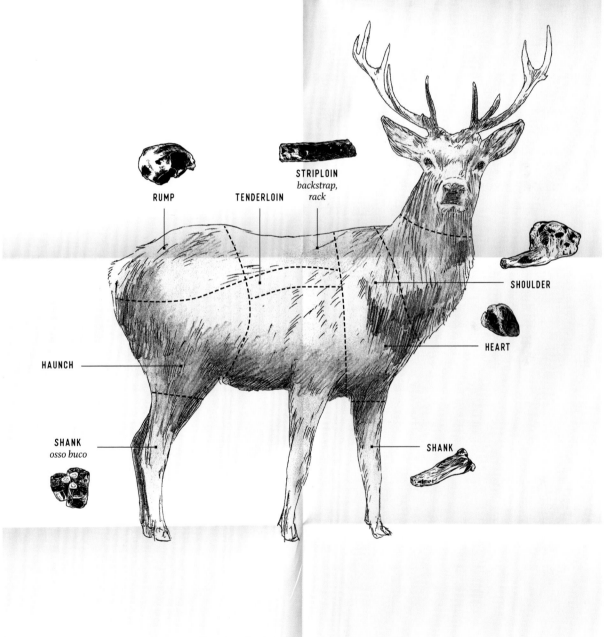

RUMP

TENDERLOIN

STRIPLOIN
backstrap, rack

SHOULDER

HEART

HAUNCH

SHANK
osso buco

SHANK

For more about venison cuts, see pages 422–423.

VENISON CUTS

SHOULDER

Venison shoulder gets a good work-out and is rich in collagen and sinews. It is delicious slowly cooked, whether coarsely or finely chopped. Look to recipes that use beef chuck and adapt them for venison shoulder. It can also be minced and made into sausages, meatballs and burgers.

CUT WEIGHT: 4–5 KG (9–11 LB)
BEST COOKED: BRAISED
OPTIMAL FINISH: SOFT AND UNCTUOUS
RECIPES: PAGES 338–341

BACKSTRAP
STRIPLOIN

Running along the spine of the animal, the backstrap or striploin is revered for its tenderness. This cut is among the most prized. Note that it is different from the tenderloin, which is quite small on a deer compared to, say, a cow. The striploin has good flavour, but is very lean and is best cooked to rare or medium-rare, as is the case with most game meat: overcooking will render it tough.

➙ While the tenderloin is the most tender of the venison cuts—as it is in most animals—it is very small, lean and thus can overcook easily. It's best quickly seared.

CUT WEIGHT: 1.8–2.5 KG (4 LB–5 LB 8 OZ)
BEST COOKED: BARBECUED
OPTIMAL FINISH: RARE, 50˚C (120˚F)
RECIPES: PAGES 434–437

RACK

Due to the size of venison cuts (much smaller than beef and sometimes even than veal) the rib eye rack is not as readily available. Selling the whole backstrap tends to make more sense for both the producer and the butcher; this is why you will see this cut more often than the rack.

If you can find this delicious, tender and rich cut it is best roasted as you would a beef, veal or lamb rack. As with most game, this is best cooked on the rare side of medium-rare.

CUT WEIGHT: 10-POINT, 2 KG (4 LB 8 OZ)
BEST COOKED: ROASTED
OPTIMAL FINISH: RARE TO MEDIUM-RARE, 50–55˚C (120–130˚F)

HAUNCH
RUMP

The hind leg of the deer, including the shortloin, is known as the haunch. This is where you will find the rump, along with the topside, silverside and knuckle. These four muscles collectively (once separated and trimmed) can be referred to as the Denver leg. These muscles are particularly prized and are so soft and tender, they can be sliced and then quickly cooked on the barbecue for a brilliant steak.

The rump is a particular delicacy. It's a small, versatile and extremely tasty cut. It, too, is excellent on the barbecue, but can also be roasted to great success.

CUT WEIGHT: 9 KG (20 LB)
BEST COOKED: BARBECUED
OPTIMAL FINISH: RARE TO MEDIUM-RARE,
50–55°C (120–130°F)

SHANKS AND OSSO BUCO

Venison shanks are excellent braising cuts. Look to recipes for lamb shanks to find culinary inspiration. Keep in mind that a little fruit can help balance out the more gamey flavour of the shanks.

More often cut from the hind legs, which are then cut laterally, the osso buco needs long, slow cooking to bring out its best qualities. This is an excellent cut of venison and can be cooked to great effect in much the same way you would approach veal osso buco.

CUT WEIGHT: 400 G (14 OZ)
BEST COOKED: SLOWLY BRAISED
OPTIMAL FINISH: SOFT AND UNCTUOUS
RECIPE: PAGES 388–389

HEART

The heart is an often-overlooked cut in all animals. Prepared correctly it is delicious: grilled or slowly cooked, it's low in fat and can be tough if cooked anywhere in between. You will need to rinse the heart thoroughly, being careful to squeeze out any excess blood. There is a bit of gristle and fat that you will need to dissect out; work with each chamber of heart individually, slicing away any fat or gristle as you go. You can marinate the heart before cooking, which is particularly successful for quick cooking or grilling. Venison heart is particularly tasty and is worth seeking out.

WEIGHT: 1 KG (2 LB 4 OZ)
BEST COOKED: SLOWLY OR REALLY QUICKLY

Please note that all weights are approximate, as animals will differ based on their age, breed and feed. The internal temperatures given are the rested temperatures. For more information on cooking styles, roasting times, etcetera, see pages 448–455.

KANGAROO

Australia presents one of the most interesting cases for endemic species on the globe. A continent with an enormous land mass, but also an island, it remained largely cut off from the world and thus from the migration of peoples, animals and plants. Australia's endemic animals evolved to suit the unique terroir, without predator or manipulation.

The flavours of Australia's native plants and animals are an amazing untapped resource: they are almost exactly as they were 20,000 years ago, at the time of the last ice age. Working with Australian native ingredients such as the kangaroo is an opportunity to cook with history: with breeds of the utmost purity.

Of course, this is not without its difficulties. Kangaroos have not been crossbred for fat and conformation. In fact, for many years kangaroo wasn't harvested for human consumption except by Indigenous peoples: it was in 1993 that selling kangaroo for the dinner table became legal in the states of New South Wales, Victoria and Queensland. Much of the kangaroo that was killed went, instead, to pet food. There is still no official policy written on offal.

There are 48 species of kangaroo in Australia, with only four that can be commercially harvested:

Red – with the mildest flavour and delicate, savoury notes. This is considered to be the pinnacle of kangaroo meat in terms of eating quality and consistency.

Western grey – medium intensity of flavour.

Eastern grey – robust flavour.

Wallaroo – also known as euro or hill wallaroo, these are tougher and more intense in flavour.

Kangaroos are prolific breeders. One male can service up to 20 females, while the females will have one joey at foot and one in the pouch 90 per cent of the time. Incredibly, they can also hold back the development of the joey in pregnancy during times of severe drought, so that the joey is born at the most opportune time when there is food and water available. Modern farming techniques have provided conditions (such as water and feed) that means these animals thrive. The current

Wallaby

→ *The smallest of the macropod family, wallaby can also be eaten. Predominantly consumed in Australia's southern island of Tasmania, they are smaller and sweeter of flesh.*

Kangaroos *are open-ranging or free-living and not farmed, and there are four species that may be commercially harvested for the table.*

kangaroo population actually exceeds the number that existed at the time of British settlement.

As they are open-ranging or free-living and not farmed, there are no antibiotics, growth hormones or added chemicals in kangaroo meat. Naturally, kangaroos also have a high conjugated linoleic acid (CLA) score; CLA is considered one of the 'good' fats also found in olives and avocados. There is very little difference in fat between the different breeds, with most 'roos having less than two per cent fat. They are a good source of B-group vitamins, including B12, B6, niacin, riboflavin and thiamine.

In order to manage the kangaroo population—conservatively estimated at between 45 and 50 million—Australian state governments allot quotas specific to region and species for culling. This is regulated by the Australian Department of Environment and Heritage and managed by a National Parks and Wildlife Service survey by air. Generally, this will equate to around 15 per cent of the total population, but often only half of what is allowed will actually be culled. The quota is communicated and distributed to landowners via a heavily monitored, tamper-proof tagging system, and the landowners can then select commercial shooters to carry out harvesting.

The harvesting is also very carefully managed, with harvesters required to record the location, date and time of harvest. Shooters must be accredited in order to ensure that they understand microbiology, food safety and butchery. They must also pass a marksmanship accreditation. All harvesting is done at night, with males targeted (many distributors have a strict male-only policy) and kangaroos are killed only by a shot to the head. The kangaroos are eviscerated on the spot, leaving the heart, kidney, liver and lungs for inspection at the abattoir. Refrigerated coolers all around the country store carcasses with data logging to ensure the carcasses are kept chilled at all times. They are hung in the temperature-controlled environment for between two and five days before being sent in a refrigerated truck to the processing facility.

This modern approach to an endemic animal is one to be incredibly proud of. Kangaroo meat is now widely available in butchers and supermarkets, as steak, mince (ground meat) and sausages. (It is also exported to many countries, including Japan, Korea, Hong Kong, Papua New Guinea, South Africa, the United States, Canada and EU country members.) The 'kangatarian' movement is leading a shift in focus from farmed animals to these wild animals, with their light touch and low emissions. There is no question we should be making better use of this lean, delicious animal in the kitchen.

KANGAROO CUTS

An upright animal, the kangaroo does most of its work with its legs and tail,
which require the gentlest cooking.

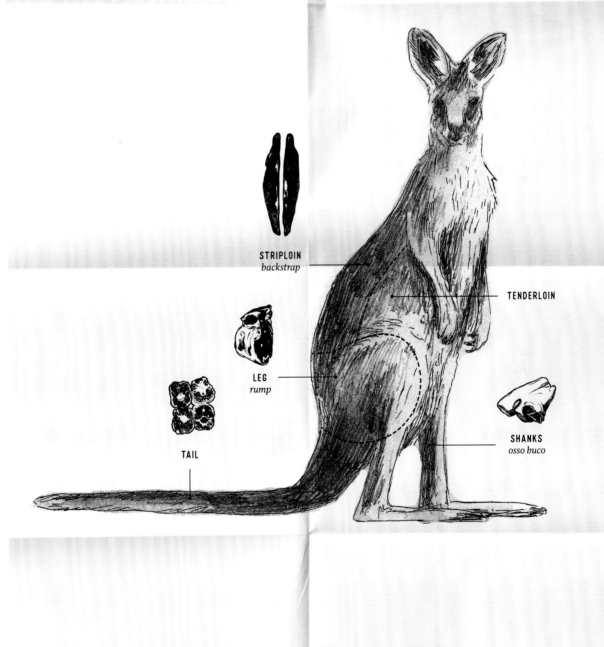

STRIPLOIN
backstrap

TENDERLOIN

LEG
rump

SHANKS
osso buco

TAIL

For more about kangaroo and wallaby cuts, see pages 428–429.

KANGAROO CUTS

STRIPLOIN

One of the prized cuts in the kangaroo, the striploin is lean, requiring quick, hot cooking to serve medium-rare. Note that it has a layer of sinew running on top of it.

Unlike most other animals, the tenderloin in a kangaroo is not prized in a culinary sense: it can be a slippery and sinewy piece of meat. Thus, it is the loin that you should seek out if you are looking for a quick grilling cut.

→ The rack can also be purchased; however, as with venison, this cut is not as popular as striploin, as it is quite small and fiddly.

CUT WEIGHT: 200 G (7 OZ)
BEST COOKED: BARBECUED
RECIPES: PAGES 442–445

LEG
RUMP

The rump on a kangaroo does more work than on other animals, keeping in mind that this is an upright animal, with the two back legs and the tail doing all the work when the animal is moving around.

The rump is a lovely cut for quick grilling, but can work with slower cooking too. It has more flavour than the loin. The rump can also be quickly stir-fried.

The knuckle is another popular cut within the leg. It works well cured or smoked, if it is not being slowly cooked or slowly roasted.

CUT WEIGHT: 3 KG (6 LB 12 OZ)
BEST COOKED: A MIXED BAG!
RECIPE: PAGES 440–441

SHANKS
OSSO BUCO

The shanks—which, when cut laterally, can be used as osso buco—are better suited to slower cooking and stews or to recipes that call for the tail. The addition of the bone is a win for these slower cooking styles.

CUT WEIGHT: 500 G (1 LB 2 OZ)
BEST COOKED: BRAISED
OPTIMAL FINISH: SOFT AND UNCTUOUS
RECIPE: PAGES 388–389

TAIL

WALLABY

The kangaroo tail is a particularly prized cut, especially the tails from the big Red kangaroo. The tail is essentially the third leg of the kangaroo and subsequently is a very hardworking muscle.

It responds well to very slow cooking, allowing the sinews and collagen to break down. It also retains the central bone, adding extra flavour, making it a particularly great soup cut.

CUT WEIGHT: CUT CROSSWAYS, 100–130 G (3½–4½ OZ) EACH PIECE
BEST COOKED: BRAISED
RECIPE: PAGES 438–439

Being physically smaller than the kangaroo, wallaby requires super-quick cooking to keep it on the rare side of medium-rare.

The animal's smaller size means the cuts are all significantly smaller than the equivalent in kangaroos. Wallaby has sweeter meat and is very tender.

BEST COOKED: BARBECUE

Please note that all weights are approximate, as animals will differ based on their age, breed and feed.
For more information on cooking styles, roasting times, etcetera, see pages 448–455.

SERVES 4

RABBIT STEW

Prep time *20 minutes*
Cook *1 hour 10 minutes*

1. Melt the butter in a heavy-based frying pan over medium heat until foamy. Season the rabbit pieces with salt and pepper and fry, in batches so as not to crowd the pan, for 2–3 minutes each until brown on all sides. Transfer to a heavy-based enamelled cast-iron casserole.

2. In the same frying pan, fry the mushrooms over medium heat for 6–7 minutes until they colour, then transfer them to the casserole. Repeat the same process with the shallots and garlic, adding more butter if needed.

3. Deglaze the pan with wine and reduce the liquid by half, then add this to the casserole.

4. Add the cream, stock, juniper berries, thyme and rosemary. Cover and simmer over low heat for 45 minutes or until tender.

5. At this point you may want to reduce the cooking liquid a little. If serving immediately, remove the rabbit and turn up the heat under the liquid until it is reduced to a thick consistency, then return the rabbit to the casserole. If serving the next day, you should allow the rabbit to cool in the liquor first, so it does not dry out, then remove it and reduce the liquid.

6. Finish by stirring in the red currant jelly and sour cream.

INGREDIENTS

1–1.2 kg (2 lb 4 oz–2 lb 10 oz) rabbit, cut into 8 pieces

Butter or rendered chicken fat, for cooking

350 g (12 oz) forest mushrooms, cleaned and sliced (or a combination of mushrooms)

4 golden shallots, sliced

3 garlic cloves, sliced

300 ml (10½ fl oz) dry white wine

200 ml (7 fl oz) pure (pouring) cream

500 ml (17 fl oz/2 cups) game stock or chicken stock

1 teaspoon juniper berries, cracked

1 small handful of thyme sprigs

1 rosemary sprig

2 tablespoons red currant jelly

2 tablespoons sour cream

steamed brussels sprouts and fresh lingonberry or cranberry jam

SERVING SUGGESTION

NOTES

→ *This dish is best when rested overnight to allow the flavours to develop.*

→ *Red wine can be used instead of white for a deeper taste.*

***Cut** Whole rabbit*
See page 417

SERVES 6
RABBIT PAELLA

Prep time *15 minutes*
Cook *1½ hours*

1. Put 70 ml (2¼ fl oz) of the olive oil in a large paella pan with the garlic and thyme and gently cook over medium heat for 5 minutes to flavour the oil and season the pan. Reserve the garlic and the oil separately, discarding the thyme.
2. Brown the rabbit pieces in the remaining oil and transfer them to a heavy-based enamelled cast-iron casserole with the saffron, smoked paprika and enough cold water to cover. Bring to the boil over medium–high heat, then reduce to a simmer and cook for 40 minutes. Remove the rabbit pieces and reserve 800 ml (28 fl oz) of the rabbit stock.
3. Cook the chorizo slices in the paella pan over high heat for 5 minutes until just coloured. Remove the chorizo from the pan and set aside, leaving the flavoured oil behind. Make a *sofrito* (see note) by slowly cooking the onion and capsicum in the paella pan together with the flavoured oils (a combination of both the chorizo oil and the garlic and thyme oil) over low heat for 10–15 minutes.
4. Add the rice, mixing it with the chopped tomatoes and the delicious *sofrito*, then add the reserved stock. Place the rabbit pieces, artichokes and garlic halves (reassemble it in the centre of the pan to look like one whole bulb) in the pan. Cook for 18 minutes or until the rice has absorbed all the liquid and is starting to caramelise in the bottom of the pan, thereby creating the essential *socarrat* (crust) in the base of the pan.

INGREDIENTS

1.5 kg (3 lb 5 oz) rabbit, cut into 14 pieces
130 ml (4¼ fl oz) olive oil
1 handful of thyme sprigs
1 garlic bulb, halved (keeping the top intact)
1 small pinch of saffron threads
1 teaspoon smoked paprika
300 g (10½ oz) fresh chorizo, sliced
1 brown onion, finely chopped
2 red capsicums (peppers), deseeded and
    finely chopped
400 g (14 oz) risotto rice, such as carnaroli
    or arborio
4 very ripe tomatoes, peeled and chopped
400 g (14 oz) artichokes, peeled and boiled,
    or preserved artichokes

NOTE
→ *The idea of a* sofrito *is to gently sweat (that is, cook gently without colouring) the ingredients down to add a sweet base to your braise. See page 455 for more information.*

Cut Whole rabbit
See page 417

SALTIMBOCCA

Prep time *30 minutes (plus chilling)*
Cook *40 minutes (plus resting)*

1. To make the gnocchi, whisk the milk and semolina in a saucepan over medium–high heat until boiling. Whisk constantly for 1–2 minutes until thick. Remove from heat and whisk in the eggs, thyme and 40 g (1½ oz) of the parmesan to thicken. Season generously with salt and pepper, pour into a 20 x 30 cm (8 x 12 inch) buttered baking dish and refrigerate for 1–2 hours until firm. This can be done a day or two ahead.

2. Preheat the oven to 200°C (400°F). Cut out 5 cm (2 inch) rounds of the gnocchi mixture with a pastry cutter and overlap in a buttered 20 cm (8 inch) square baking dish. Top with the melted butter and the remaining parmesan, season with salt and pepper and bake for 20–25 minutes until golden brown.

3. Pound out each piece of venison with the flat side of a meat mallet. You want to pound and stretch the meat, without puncturing holes in it. The best way to stretch the venison is to bring the mallet down flat on the meat and, as it comes in contact, slide in a continuous motion from the centre towards the edge. Repeat this motion, stretching the slice in all directions until 3 mm (⅛ inch) thick throughout.

4. Season venison with freshly ground pepper and a little salt (be judicious with the salt as the prosciutto is salty). Lay a sage leaf on each piece of venison, top with a prosciutto slice, then fold in the ends of the venison and press to seal. Dust lightly in seasoned flour, shaking off excess.

5. Heat half the oil in a large frying pan over medium–high heat. Add the remaining sage and fry for 2–3 minutes to crisp, then remove to a plate with a slotted spoon and set aside.

6. Melt 20 g (¾ oz) of the butter in the same pan and add half the venison pieces to the pan. Fry for 1 minute until golden brown, then turn and brown the remaining side (for about 30 seconds). Transfer to a plate. Repeat with the remaining oil, another 20 g (¾ oz) of the butter and the remaining venison pieces. Cover the plate with foil to keep warm.

7. Pour off excess oil from the pan and return to high heat, then stir in the garlic until fragrant. Pour in the Marsala and scrape the base of the pan to remove the caramelised bits. Reduce by half, add the stock and boil for 4–5 minutes to reduce, adding any juices that have gathered on the plate as the venison rests. Add the remaining butter, a little at a time, swirling the pan to incorporate, and season with salt and pepper.

8. Serve the venison with the Marsala sauce spooned over, scattered with crisp sage and with the gnocchi.

INGREDIENTS

650 g (1 lb 7 oz) venison backstrap, cut into 8 pieces across the grain
16 sage leaves
8 thin slices of prosciutto
Plain (all-purpose) flour, seasoned with salt and pepper, for dusting
80 ml (2½ fl oz/⅓ cup) olive oil
6 tablespoons (80 g) butter, chopped
1 garlic clove, finely chopped
150 ml (5 fl oz) Marsala or dry white wine
250 ml (9 fl oz/1 cup) chicken stock

Gnocchi alla Romana
750 ml (26 fl oz/3 cups) milk
200 g (7 oz) coarse semolina
2 eggs, whisked
2–3 thyme sprigs, leaves picked
70 g (2½ oz) parmesan cheese, finely grated
4 tablespoons (60 g) butter, melted

Cut Venison or veal backstrap
See page 422 or 329

SERVES 4

VENISON CARPACCIO

Prep time *10 minutes (plus resting, chilling)*
Cook *5 minutes*

1. Mix the thyme, juniper berries and pink and green peppercorns in a bowl and set aside.
2. Heat the olive oil in a frying pan over high heat and add the garlic. Season the venison with salt and cook for about 2 minutes, turning, until brown on all sides. Rest the meat on paper towel.
3. When it is cool, roll the venison in the thyme mixture, then roll and wrap tightly with plastic wrap. Refrigerate overnight.
4. Slice the venison as thinly as you can and arrange the slices on a plate with the rocket and shaved parmesan. Drizzle with extra olive oil, a squeeze of lemon juice and some extra crushed peppercorns, if using.

INGREDIENTS

400 g (14 oz) venison backstrap, trimmed
6 thyme sprigs, leaves picked and finely chopped
5–6 juniper berries, crushed using a pestle and mortar
1 teaspoon pink peppercorns, crushed, plus extra to serve (optional)
1 teaspoon green peppercorns, crushed, plus extra to serve (optional)
1 tablespoon olive oil, plus extra to serve
1 garlic clove, crushed
1 handful of rocket (arugula) leaves
Parmesan cheese, shaved, to serve
Lemon juice, to serve

NOTES

→ *You will need to start this recipe one day ahead of serving to allow for overnight refrigeration.*

→ *Try out different combinations of herbs and spices to invent your own flavour.*

Cut Venison backstrap or beef sirloin or tenderloin
See page 422 or 319

JAMES VILES

BIOTA DINING

SERVES 8

KANGAROO RAGÙ JAFFLES

Prep time *15 minutes*
Cook *5 hours 20 minutes*

A dear friend, a great chef and a man who has incorporated hunting and foraging into his cooking in a way unlike many others, James's cooking reflects the land around him: it's a special gift.

1. Preheat the oven to 140°C (275°F). Seal the whole 'roo tails in a hot pan until golden. Remove and place in a baking tray. Cover with rough chopped brown onion, garlic and 3 litres (105 fl oz/12 cups) of water. Then cover with foil and braise in the oven for about 4 hours or until tender. Once cooked, remove from the liquid and pick the meat off the tail. Retain meat and then reduce the liquid to make a sauce.

2. Meanwhile, for the ragù, sweat the onions and garlic in a pot until soft, add the 'roo meat, followed by all the other ingredients, cook on low heat for 1 hour.

3. For the bechamel, melt the butter in a saucepan, add the flour and cook out until it loosens on the side of the pan. Add some hot milk and then whisk in, then add the rest and whisk in. Cook on low heat for about 15–20 minutes then add the grated cheese. Set aside to cool, then chill. Check seasoning.

4. To make the jaffle you can use a traditional iron that goes in the fire, which is what we use at Biota (it gives you a beautiful round jaffle) or you can use a press. Place the buttered bread on the base of the iron followed by the ragù and then the bechamel. Top with a second slice of bread and cook until the bread is golden, add some salt and lemon myrtle when finished cooking and serve hot.

INGREDIENTS

2 kangaroo tails
2 brown onions
4 garlic cloves
16 slices white bread, buttered
Salt flakes, to serve
Lemon myrtle powder, to serve (optional)

Ragù

3 brown onions, diced
4 garlic cloves, minced
10 overripe tomatoes
1 tablespoon + 1 teaspoon Tasmanian
   mountain pepper (optional)
Salt flakes, to taste
60 ml (2 fl oz/¼ cup) olive oil

Bechamel

6 tablespoons (80 g) butter
40 g (1½ oz) plain (all-purpose) flour
500 ml (17 fl oz/2 cups) milk
Salt flakes, to taste
100 g (3½ oz) gruyere or similar

Cut Kangaroo tail
See page 429

O TAMA CAREY AND MAT LINDSAY

LANKAN FILLING STATION & ESTER

KANGAROO JERKY
WITH TRAIL MIX

Prep time *20 minutes (plus marinating)*
Cook *5 minutes (plus drying)*

O Tama and Mat are two of Australia's most talented chefs: an incredible duo. Their collective approach to food is thoughtful, sustainable and entirely delicious. Our food landscape is richer for their contributions.

1. To make the kangaroo jerky, thinly slice the kangaroo across the grain into sheet-like pieces. Combine remaining ingredients in a bowl, season with a pinch of coarsely ground black pepper and add the kangaroo. Mix well to coat, cover and refrigerate overnight to marinate.

2. Drain the kangaroo from the marinade, pat dry with paper towel and arrange in a single layer on the racks of a dehydrator. Dehydrate for 2 hours until dry but not too hard and brittle. Alternatively, you can dehydrate the kangaroo by arranging it on a lightly oiled wire rack on a baking tray and dry it in the oven set to 60°C (140°F). Store in an airtight container until required.

3. To make the native pepper leaf seasoning, dry-roast the ingredients in a small frying pan over medium heat for 1–2 minutes until aromatic. Cool and set aside.

4. Blanch the saltbush leaves in a small saucepan of boiling water for 4–5 seconds until they are bright green, then drain and refresh the leaves in iced water. Pat dry thoroughly with paper towel and dehydrate overnight.

5. Heat 1 cm (½ inch) of vegetable oil in a frying pan over medium–high heat until shimmering, add the saltbush and fry for 30 seconds until crisp. Remove with a slotted spoon and drain on paper towel.

6. To serve, arrange jerky on a large serving platter, season to taste with the native pepper leaf seasoning and scatter with the fried saltbush, dried figs and roasted hazelnuts.

INGREDIENTS

Handful of saltbush leaves, picked (see note)
Vegetable oil, for shallow-frying
5 dried figs, quartered, to serve
40 g (1½ oz/¼ cup) roasted hazelnuts, coarsely chopped, to serve

Kangaroo jerky
125 g (4½ oz) kangaroo rump
3 teaspoons light soy sauce
1 teaspoon ground native pepper leaf (see note)
½ teaspoon sesame oil
½ teaspoon coriander seeds

Native pepper leaf seasoning
1 teaspoon sea salt flakes
½ teaspoon ground native pepper leaf (see note)

NOTE

→ *Saltbush leaves and native pepper leaf are available from specialist suppliers of Indigenous ingredients and Australian bush foods, many of which can be found online. Saltbush leaves are also available from specialist greengrocers and select farmers' markets.*

Cut Kangaroo rump
See page 428

KYLIE KWONG

BILLY KWONG

SERVES 4 WITH STEAMED RICE; 6 AS PART OF A BANQUET

KANGAROO FILLET
WITH BLACK BEAN AND CHILLI SAUCE

The unique combination of personal and national heritage is entwined in all of Kylie's cooking. She has long fought to bring more of Australia's native produce to her restaurant and our tables.

1. Combine the kangaroo with all of the marinade ingredients in a large bowl, cover, and set aside in the refrigerator to marinate for 30 minutes.

2. Heat half the oil in a hot wok until surface seems to shimmer slightly. Add half the marinated kangaroo and stir-fry for 30 seconds. Remove from wok with a slotted spoon and set aside. Add the remaining kangaroo and stir-fry for 30 seconds then remove from wok and set aside.

3. Meanwhile, make the black bean and chilli sauce. Remove seeds and membranes from capsicum, cut into fine slices and set aside. Add remaining oil to hot wok. Add onion, ginger, garlic and black beans and stir-fry over a high heat for 30 seconds, stirring constantly to ensure the black beans do not burn.

4. Return kangaroo to the wok with wine or sherry and stir-fry for 30 seconds. Add sugar, soy sauce, vinegar and sesame oil and stir-fry for a further minute. Lastly, add chilli and reserved capsicum and stir-fry for a further 30 seconds.

5. To serve, arrange kangaroo on a platter and garnish with spring onions.

Prep time *10 minutes (plus marinating)*
Cook *5 minutes*

INGREDIENTS

600 g (1 lb 5 oz) kangaroo striploin,
 cut into 1 cm (½ inch) slices
80 ml (3½ fl oz/⅓ cup) vegetable oil
3 tablespoons finely sliced spring onions
 (scallions)

Marinade
2 tablespoons Shaoxing wine or dry sherry
1 teaspoon sea salt
1 teaspoon white sugar

Black bean and chilli sauce
½ red capsicum (pepper)
1 small red onion, thinly sliced
3 tablespoons julienne of fresh ginger
3 garlic cloves, finely chopped
1 tablespoon salted black beans
2 tablespoons Shaoxing wine or dry sherry
1 tablespoon white sugar
2–3 tablespoons light soy sauce
1 tablespoon malt vinegar
½ teaspoon sesame oil
2 large red chillies, sliced diagonally

Cut Kangaroo striploin
See page 428

BEN SHEWRY

ATTICA

SERVES 8 AS A STARTER
KANGAROO
AND BUNYA-BUNYA

Prep time *40 minutes*
Cook *5 minutes*

Ben's cooking takes Australia's native ingredients into a sphere of their own. From bunya nuts to wallaby, Ben has succeeded in putting them on the pedestal they deserve. He is an immensely talented and thoughtful chef.

INGREDIENTS

400 g (14 oz) kangaroo striploin
½ wong bok (Chinese cabbage)
Purple Dutch carrots, sliced crossways, basil leaves, finely grated lime zest and pepper berry powder, to serve

Macadamia purée
110 g (3¾ oz) macadamia nuts
110 ml (3¾ fl oz) iced water
2 tablespoons macadamia oil

Bunya-bunya purée
175 g (6 oz) macadamia purée
2 bunya nuts, peeled
½ teaspoon white wine vinegar
Lemon juice, to taste
Sea salt, to taste

Miso dressing
50 g (1¾ oz) organic unpasteurised miso
1 teaspoon lime juice
¾ teaspoon white wine vinegar
1 tablespoon canola oil
Sugar, to taste

Hot and sour dressing
3 garlic cloves, finely chopped
25 ml (1 fl oz) canola oil
2 tablespoons Shaoxing cooking wine
80 ml (2½ fl oz/⅓ cup) sweet cabernet vinegar
¾ teaspoon pepper berry powder
3 teaspoons oyster sauce

1. To make the macadamia purée, place macadamia nuts, iced water and macadamia oil in a blender and purée for 4–5 minutes until very smooth—the purée will become warm. Cool to room temperature and purée for another 4–5 minutes until silky smooth, pass through a fine sieve and set aside to cool.

2. To make the bunya-bunya purée, place 175 g (6 oz) of the macadamia purée in a blender with bunya nuts (the seeds of the Australian native bunya pine, these have been used as food by Indigenous people for thousands of years; they are available from selected bushfoods suppliers) and blend for 4–5 minutes until silky smooth, pass through a fine sieve and set aside to cool. Add vinegar, stir to combine, then add lemon juice and sea salt to taste. Store in a covered container in the fridge.

3. To make miso dressing, whisk ingredients and 1½ teaspoons of water in a bowl, season with sugar to taste and refrigerate.

4. To make the hot and sour dressing, sweat the garlic off in a small amount of canola oil for 1–2 minutes over medium heat, until not coloured but garlic no longer tastes raw. Add wine, simmer for 1–2 minutes until reduced. Add vinegar and pepper berry powder, bring to the boil, remove from heat, add oyster sauce and stir to combine. Whisk in remaining oil to combine, check seasoning and set aside. Store in the fridge until serving.

5. Cut the kangaroo loin into 5 mm (¼ inch) dice. Cut one cabbage stalk into 1 cm (½ inch) dice and combine in a bowl with kangaroo loin, a generous pinch of lime zest and a pinch of pepper berry powder. Drizzle with miso dressing to taste, season with sea salt and mix to combine.

6. To serve, spread bunya-bunya purée in the centre of eight serving plates, divide kangaroo among the plates, placing on top of bunya-bunya purée. Drizzle with hot and sour dressing and season with sea salt.

7. Serve with sliced purple Dutch carrots, basil leaves, and a sprinkling of lime zest and pepper berry powder.

Cut Kangaroo striploin
See page 428

444   WILD

CHAPTER SIX

TECHNIQUES

COOKING ~ BUTCHERY ~ TOOLS ~ STORAGE
~ WITH THE KNIFE

COOKING WITH FIRE

Our fascination with fire will always burn. It is the one ingredient that is used in every country, every culture. The basic premise of this type of cooking is that the barbecue itself becomes another ingredient in the cooking, with the flavour imparted by the smoke and fire as crucial as salt or the natural flavour of the meat.

TOP TIPS

1. Beware the naked flame. Use plenty of fuel (wood or charcoal) and allow wood to burn down to charcoal (smoke and naked flame can char the meat and create an acrid flavour) or, if you are starting with charcoal, allow it to become white hot. Trim off excess fat and remove excess oil to help avoid flare-ups: a spray bottle of water can help.

2. Prepare the meat. Bring steaks to room temperature at least 30 minutes before cooking. Salt your meat well. If you are using oil, oil the meat, not the grill, to avoid flare-ups.

3. Soak bamboo skewers in water before cooking over flame to avoid burning. A stripped rosemary branch makes a great skewer and imparts more flavour.

4. Be thoughtful about the plate you carry out to the barbecue with your meat on it: it needs to go back inside and be washed before you put the cooked meat back on it.

5. The hotter the grill the less likely the meat will stick to it. Don't turn the meat over until it comes away easily from the grill: allow it to caramelise. Ideally raise or lower the grill to control heat, or alternatively pile the coals at one end of the barbecue and move the meat around accordingly.

6. Grill marks equal flavour. Caramelisation is the meat sugars burning and thus creating flavour. Charred (burnt) meat is not the same and will leave a horrid carbon flavour in your mouth.

7. To turn or not to turn: don't use tools that will puncture the meat and let the precious juices escape. While the number of turns is hotly debated, if you turn your steak twice on each side (turning 90° each time) you will get attractive crisscross grill marks.

8. Pick up the steak and pinch it between two fingers to determine if it's cooked. Different steaks may feel different according to the grain (for example, a bavette has a much looser grain than a sirloin, so it will feel much looser to the touch). When it is lying flat on the plate or grill it will alter the feeling. For a very simple test, loosely touch your index finger to the pad at the base of your thumb, the amount of give will be close to that of a rare steak on the barbecue. Touching with your second finger is medium-rare, your third finger is medium and your pinkie is well done.

9. Rest the meat for half the time you have cooked it. This allows blood and juices to flow back through the entire steak. If you cut a steak and blood runs out it is under-rested (that blood should have seeped back through the meat creating a juicy steak).

10. While your steak rests it is the perfect time to clean the barbecue, leaving it clean and ready for the next time you want to use it. Use a wire brush, hard fat trimmed from the steak or a lemon to rub the hot grill.

11. Generally it is the more expensive cuts, those that do the least work on the animal, that are best to barbecue quickly (as opposed to the slow Southern US barbecue). Such cuts are most often found in the middle of the animal: these are the cuts that, literally, take a ride on the animal's back.

Heston Blumenthal suggests turning your steak every minute to keep the juices flowing backwards and forwards, but many others suggest once only to capitalise on the caramelisation.

THE ESSENTIALS

Gas

The easiest option, although the food can adopt the flavour of the gas, so it's best to purchase a barbecue with lava rock or ceramic coals between the gas and the grill.

Charcoal

No smoke, good heat and great flavour. Aim for sustainable local hardwood lump charcoal; never use charcoal with firestarter fluid as it will taint the flavour of your meat. Get it hot (for 30–45 minutes) and then cook immediately; open the dampers to increase heat, close them to stifle it.

Wood

Meat will take on the smoky flavour of the wood; change the type of wood for different tastes. Wait for the wood to burn down to charcoal. That said, the pinnacle of cooking with fire is to use live fire. Hard to get right, but incredible when done well.

ROTISSERIE

A rotisserie is a brilliant way to cook: as the meat rotates slowly the juices flow back through the meat, ensuring it stays moist and essentially bastes itself.

A few tips:

→ Balance the meat on the spit rod: if it is off-balance it will put too much stress on the rotisserie; for example, if working with poultry, you can tie the wings and legs to ensure they do not flop around. Ignoring this will shorten the life of your motor.

→ Flavour and season your meat, both inside and out, using salt, herbs and oil (see pages 156–159).

→ Beware of flare-ups, particularly if there is no pan to catch drips. You can have a spray bottle of water on hand to deal with these. Alternatively, place a pan of potatoes under the meat to absorb the delicious juices.

TEXAS BARBECUE

Texans are blessed with four different styles of barbecue.

1. **East Texas** – beef and pork smoked over hickory and glazed with piquant, tomato-based sauce.
2. **West Texas** – 'cowboy style', a cross between grilling and smoking (using low, direct heat), generally over mesquite wood. Mainly beef, sometimes goat and mutton.
3. **South Texas** – Mexican-style *barbacoa* using cheaper cuts (such as calf's head) roasted in a pit of hot coals.
4. **South–central Texas** – flavoured with smoke and salt, beef brisket is king. The cap is left on and the brisket is cooked lean side down, so the fat melts back through. The aim is to produce a *bark*, with a *smoke ring* beneath. You should be able to pull the meat apart with a fork.

QUICK GUIDE TO COOKING A STEAK

APPROXIMATE COOKING TIME FOR A 3 CM (1¼ INCH) THICK STEAK (SIRLOIN, RIB EYE, RUMP), BROUGHT TO ROOM TEMPERATURE AND COOKED OVER A HOT GRILL. THE TEMPERATURE GIVEN HERE IS BEFORE RESTING; IT WILL RISE BY A FEW DEGREES.

Blue	1 minute each side (for caramelisation)
Rare	2–3 minutes each side, internal temperature 47°C (117°F)
Medium-rare	3–4 minutes each side, 52°C (127°F)
Medium	4–5 minutes each side, 57°C (134°F)
Medium-well	about 5 minutes each side, 60°C (140°F)
Well done	about 6 minutes each side, 65°C (150°F)

—SOUTHERN BARBECUE—

→ The **bark** is the crust formed by the rub or marinade and the smoke.

→ A **smoke ring** is a pink layer of colouring just beneath the surface when you cut into smoked meat.

→ **Mopped** means dousing meat in sauce towards the end of cooking.

→ **Dalmatian blend:** salt and pepper.

→ **Hot guts:** a pork and beef sausage owing its origins to German, Czech and Polish settlers.

T-bone steak
A favourite cut for the barbecue or chargrill. Bring steak to room temperature and season well before cooking. Careful management of the coals and a hot grill are fundamental for good caramelisation.

COOKING WITH AIR

There is very little that signals celebration, or family Sundays, like a roast dinner. Roasting is an excellent way to make the most of a prime cut of meat, allowing its simplicity to shine. Happily, the best roast dinners are also relatively simple for a cook to achieve.

THE ESSENTIALS

Cooking vessel – A good heavy-based roasting tin with room for the meat; not too big, or all the juices will evaporate, but not too small, or the meat won't have space for air to circulate and thus to caramelise the outside.

Meat thermometer – for checking the internal temperature. This will change your roasting game and, with expensive cuts, it is worth the comparatively meagre investment.

Utensil – A good long sharp knife for carving.

CARVING TIPS

→ Joint the chicken, laterally slice the breast and don't forget the oysters.

→ Rest pork crackling side up; carve it crackling side down.

→ Carving a lamb leg: cut along the bone in two places, so that you can cut the lamb laterally, giving each person a cross-section of different textures across the cut.

→ Beef: be sure to cut against the grain, through the fibres.

→ Veal is best served just cooked to medium-rare. Adding a sauce will provide some leniency if it is a little overcooked.

TOP TIPS

1. Allow two to three hours for big roasting cuts to come to room temperature before cooking. This is fundamental to achieve even cooking.

2. Large cuts, particularly chicken and pork with skin, can be left uncovered in the refrigerator the night before: the dry air will help the exterior to dry a little and thus form a golden crust (particularly important for a wet-aged cut). Liberally salting the exterior just before cooking will also draw out moisture.

3. Harness the Maillard reaction (for more on this, see page 472) for a golden crust and a deeper flavour. You can caramelise your meat in a frying pan on the stovetop first to encourage the Maillard reaction before transferring to a preheated oven. Alternatively, start (or finish) with a blast of high heat in the oven.

4. Setting the meat on top of a 'trivet' of vegetables will add flavour to the jus and allow a lot of air to circulate around the cut. The trivet can be as simple as a few onions cut in half, as complex as carrots, root vegetables, garlic and woody herbs.

5. Add a little liquid such as wine, stock or water, in the bottom of the roasting pan when cooking; this will combine with the roasting juices, stopping them evaporating too quickly, and it will kickstart your sauce or jus.

6. Bones are great conductors of heat, transferring it to the centre of the joint. This is why meat on the bone will cook more quickly than meat without bones. Also, note that long thin meat cooks quicker than a big round piece of the same weight.

7. Avoid trimming all the fat off your roasting cut before cooking. It will help keep the meat moist and naturally baste it as it cooks. You can remove the fat after cooking.

8. Baste the meat while you are cooking by simply scooping the hot juices from the bottom of the pan and pouring them over the roast. This adds flavour and aids caramelisation.

9. For fast-roasted meat, allow it to rest for half the time you have cooked it. If necessary, you can reheat after it is rested without upsetting the resting process, just as long as you don't restart the cooking process.

10. Be sure to clean the chopping board and knife between working with raw and cooked meat.

RESTING

Resting your roast (generally for half the time you have cooked it) is fundamental. This allows the juices that have contracted in the cooking process to relax and permeate the whole cut. A piece of meat that is not well rested will tend to release juices all over the board when carved: it will have an exterior that is well done and a rare interior.

Rest meat in a warm spot in the kitchen—near the oven or cooktop—loosely covered with a clean tea towel (dish towel) or foil. Rest chicken breast-side down, allowing juices to flow back through the bird, keeping it moist, but rest pork crackling-side up.

COOK'S TREAT

The greatest treat for any cook is the juices that collect at the bottom of the pan. Memories of roasts in Libby's childhood, when her mum, the cook, would sprinkle the shank with a little salt and the kids would fight over it while the meat rested, with little triangles of bread set to soak in the juices of the roast the greatest treat of all.

GRAVY

Today, most gravy tends to be either rustic pan sauces or more refined jus-based sauces. Pan sauces are simplicity itself, made from the caramelised sediment in a roasting pan and a generous splash of stock. More refined sauces will be skimmed of much of the fat and given body and a lovely sheen from the addition of a reduced veal glaze.

QUICK GUIDE TO ROASTING MEAT

FOR LAMB, BEEF OR VEAL, ROAST FOR 20 MINUTES AT 220°C (425°F) TO FORM A GOLDEN CRUST. REDUCE OVEN TEMPERATURE TO 160°C (315°F). ADD A GLASS OF WATER, WINE OR STOCK TO THE ROASTING TIN, THEN APPLY THE APPROPRIATE COOKING TIME BELOW:

Rare 10 minutes per 450 g (1 lb)

Medium-rare 12 minutes per 450 g (1 lb)

Medium 15 minutes per 450 g (1 lb)

Medium-well done 17 minutes per 450 g (1 lb)

Well done 20 minutes per 450 g (1 lb)

—BEST MEAT FOR—

ROASTING

The classic roast is a fast-cooking cut—the rack is the poster child, whether it be lamb, pork or beef—it will cook quickly and evenly to medium-rare. Slow roasting can also make friends of more complex cuts; the collagen and sinews break down and become gelatinous and gooey. This kind of roasting sits somewhere between a braise and a roast, with a little liquid and the addition of steam—by covering the roast with foil—to soften the meat as it cooks.

INTERNAL TEMPERATURES

The temperatures given here tell you when to remove the joint from the oven. Internal temperature will increase by a few degrees (both Celsius and Fahrenheit) as it rests. Insert the probe into the thickest part of the joint, aiming for the centre, but not too close to the bones. Wait for 20 seconds before taking a reading.

Beef, lamb, veal

Rare 46°C (115°F)

Medium-rare 52°C (125°F); rested temperature 55°C (130°F)

Medium 55°C (130°F); rested temperature 60°C (140°F)

Medium-well done 60°C (140°F); rested temperature 65°C (150°F)

Well done 65°C (150°F); rested temperature 70°C (150°F)

Chicken

Medium-well done 70°C (150°F); rested temperature 75°C (165°F)

Pork

Pork can be cooked to medium (internal temperature of 60°C or 140°F), rosy pink in the middle. This is of particular importance with the lean pork we are now rearing, allowing a little more succulence in your cooking. (For more on cooking pork, see page 227.)

COOKING WITH WATER

Braising uses liquid—most often water or stock—and long, slow cooking to break down the collagen and sinews in a complex cut, rendering it soft, unctuous and full of flavour. Time is your master here; there is no hurrying a braise. This is a good reason to do this a day in advance, giving the meat time to tell you it is ready.

TOP TIPS

1. Don't be fooled into thinking the most expensive cut is the best. For a braise, you are looking for muscles that do the most work in the field: cheeks are always chewing, necks are always bobbing up and down for feed, shoulders work hard to pull the animal around. As a rule most of the cuts from the front of the animal, and a few from the tail end, are the best. Collagen and sinews are an asset: as they break down they become gelatinous and gooey.

2. Bones are excellent; they add flavour and body.

3. Be sure to cut meat (if it is bone-in, get your butcher to cut it) to a size that fits your pot. The smaller the cut, the faster the braise will cook; the more surface area, the more caramelisation you can get; but cut it too small and it will disintegrate —it's a balancing act!

4. Caramelise the meat in small batches on the stovetop first: this burns the sugars and amino acids on the outside of the meat, adding flavour and enhancing the levels of *umami* (this process is known as the Maillard reaction: see page 472).

Don't overcrowd the pan as this will lower the temperature of the pan and meat, causing it to stew, not caramelise. Do this in the ovenproof pan you plan to braise in: all the little bits of meat that catch on the bottom are a goldmine of flavour. After cooking a *mirepoix* (see opposite), you can deglaze the pan to help release it. Simply add a little water, wine or oil and scrape the bottom of the pan with your wooden spoon.

5. Lightly flouring the meat before you caramelise it will add body to your braise. Add salt and pepper (or spices) to the flour to season your meat at the same time. Cooking out the flour will add depth to your stew (another consequence of the Maillard reaction).

6. Gently season some of the ingredients as you cook them (for example, the mirepoix, onions and so on); however, don't season the braise until the very end—after it is reduced—or you risk the sauce reducing and the whole dish becoming too salty.

7. Good wine makes sense to spike the dish at the end; if, however, you are adding wine at the beginning you can use a lesser quality wine as you

are going to cook out the alcohol and many of the intricate flavours. That said, you can't cook 'weight' into the dish: if you want body, the wine has to have it in the beginning. Use white wine for lighter meats and red wine or tomato paste (concentrated purée) for heavier meats.

8. Stock can add extra flavour to your braise. Many recipes rely on marinades and water instead, but stock can be used in place of water.

9. Slow means slow: not just cooking for hours, but keeping the pace of the cooking slow. A gentle bubble is correct, not a rapid boil.

10. Braises can be heavy and rich. To mitigate this you can add a dash of vinegar at the end of the cooking process, or some wine for acidity (this is where a good quality wine will be tasted in the dish); alternatively, use a little lemon juice or lemon zest. Consider a tangy side dish such as *salsa verde* to cut through the richness.

11. If you are not serving the dish immediately, let the meat cool in the braise to avoid drying it out. Remove it from the liquid when you reduce the liquid to the desired consistency.

THE ESSENTIALS

Temperature
Low and slow. You can't rush a braise and the meat is boss. You need the collagen and sinews to yield.

Cooking vessel
A heavy-based pot will mean even heat distribution and thus even cooking; the ability to move from the stovetop to the oven (so it should have no plastic parts); ideally it will be a cast-iron casserole with an enamel lining and a lid: Le Creuset is an excellent investment.

Utensil
Wooden spoon. A friend once pointed out the jarring sound metal utensils make on an otherwise gentle process and he was right!

—BEST MEAT TO—
BRAISE

- → On the bone for added flavour.
- → Cuts with plenty of sinew and collagen: the parts of the animal that do the most work in the field. The long cooking process will break down these cuts and render them unctuous.
- → Game meats and older animals that need slow cooking to soften.

MAKE A CARTOUCHE

Cut baking paper to a circle just bigger than the diameter of your saucepan or casserole. Crumple it and wet it before laying it on top of the braise. Add a lid to keep all the liquid inside the pot as it cooks, otherwise much of the flavour will dissipate.

INGREDIENTS

Mirepoix – the French call it *mirepoix*, the Italians *soffritto* and Spanish *sofrito*, in Norwegian it's *de fire store* (four big ones: leek, carrot, onion, celeriac), the Germans say *Suppengrün* (leeks, carrots, celeriac) and in Cajun or Creole cooking it's the 'holy trinity' of onions, celery and capsicum (pepper). Whatever the name, it is clear in the majority of culinary traditions this base is important for slow-cooked dishes. The general ratio for a classic mirepoix is two parts onion to one part each of celery and carrot. The idea is to gently sweat (that is, cook gently without colouring) these ingredients down to add a sweet base to your braise. The longer the cooking time of the dish, the larger the pieces of vegetables can be. For extra depth of flavour, try rendering the excess fat from your meat or the rind from your pancetta and use this to cook the mirepoix.

Bouquet garni – a little parcel of flavour, a bouquet garni can be made from parsley, thyme and bay leaf, wrapped in muslin (cheesecloth) or tied together with a leek leaf so that it can be removed before serving.

Aromatics – herbs, spices, wine.

STOCKS

A STOCK CAN ADD DEPTH OF FLAVOUR AND VISCOSITY TO YOUR BRAISE. READY-MADE STOCKS, FOUND IN THE SUPERMARKET, ARE NOT THE SAME THING: THEY WILL ADD FLAVOUR, BUT LARGELY IN THE FORM OF SALT, WHICH IS A PROBLEM AS THE DISH COOKS AND THE SALTINESS IS EXACERBATED. IF YOU ARE USING GREAT INGREDIENTS—PARTICULARLY MEAT ON THE BONE—YOUR BRAISE SHOULD OFFER UP ITS OWN STOCK. SEE PAGES 460–461 FOR A VARIETY OF STOCK RECIPES.

A QUICK GUIDE TO BRAISING MEAT

1. Chop the mirepoix (and any other vegetables you would like to add).

2. Caramelise the meat in a heavy-based ovenproof casserole over high heat. Do this in small batches so you don't overcrowd the pan (causing the meat to stew, not caramelise). Set the meat aside.

3. In the same pan, sweat the mirepoix until it is soft and translucent.

4. Deglaze with wine or vermouth (optional), scraping up all the goodness from the bottom of the pan.

5. Return the meat to the casserole. Cover with water or stock, add desired aromatics (thyme, bay leaf, star anise, cinnamon, for example) and bring to a gentle simmer. Cook slowly on the stovetop or in the oven for 1½–3 hours, until soft and tender.

BUTCHERY

*The art of the butcher goes far beyond the cutting of the meat.
There are a number of techniques we use in the butchery to
make the most of each animal.*

DRY-AGEING BEEF

It is from days long past that we often find the most delicious culinary serendipity;
and the technique of dry-ageing beef is one such example. Revered by good
butchers, dry-ageing was traditionally a way to hold beef over for weeks, if not
months, when refrigeration was tight or non-existent.

Dry-ageing uses freshly butchered primals (large, distinct sections) or subprimals
(whole muscles), hung in a controlled environment for between four and six weeks
(and in some cases from six to 12 months). Traditionally this would have been
done in a meat locker, but now modern dry-ageing rooms are custom-designed
to maintain a temperature of 0–2°C (32–36°F) and a humidity of 70–75 per cent.

As the moisture slowly evaporates from the beef, the flavour intensifies. A
protective layer forms around the cut; this is not mould, but rather a hard, dark
crust. Scientifically, it is the proteins (more specifically, calpain enzymes) that go
to work on the muscles, breaking down connective tissue and strands of muscle
fibre, busting the protein into amino acids. Thus the flavour intensifies—yielding
that elusive fifth taste, umami—and the beef becomes more relaxed and tender. As
the piece of meat ages and matures those deeper, stronger, beefier flavours emerge.
Some butchers and chefs will paint their dry-ageing cuts in kidney fat, in part to
help reduce waste and in part to help preserve the meat, slowing down the dry-
ageing process so it dry-ages at a slower rate and over a longer period of time.

→ *Dry-ageing increases tenderness
and intensifies flavour.*

This is not a practice you will see everywhere. As you can imagine the weight lost
and the extra trimming required to remove that protective layer means a rib rack
that was around 15 kg (33 lb) to begin with, when dry-aged, trimmed and portioned
will weigh around 7–8 kg (15 lb 6 oz–18 lb), not to mention the six weeks it has been
hanging around for! The cost of dry-ageing is in time, space, shrinkage and wastage.

Instead, most beef is now wet-aged in airtight cryovac bags. Wet-ageing does
improve tenderness; however, it robs the meat of some of the natural juices.

Compared to dry-ageing, which allows the juices and liquids to be reabsorbed into the muscle, in the cryovac bag some of the blood and juices are lost, and this is where much of the flavour is found.

Whether it is dry- or wet-aged, it is important to note that if you are eating beef immediately after it has been slaughtered, you are not eating beef at its peak. Ideally it is at 28–30 days when the beef is at its best.

While traditionally dry-ageing has applied to beef, we are now seeing these principles used with pork and lamb too.

Key principles of dry-ageing
1. *Temperature control* – generally between 1 and 1.5°C (around 34°F)
2. *Humidity control* – generally 70–75 per cent
3. *Bacteria control* – UV lights can destroy airborne bacteria (UV lights are also used to treat water) or ozone gas can be used
4. *Air flow* – it is ideal to have a relatively turbulent environment in your dry-ageing room so there's no stale air; stale air provides a good environment for rot.

Choosing cuts to dry-age
It is generally the more expensive cuts that are worth ageing, otherwise you will turn an inexpensive cut into an expensive cut for no reason. You are most likely to find the rib rack, striploin, short loin (with the fillet) and rump in the dry-ageing room. This choice also comes down to the size and conformation. We are looking for a cut with both good fat and bones: the fat helps to protect the cut, while the bones help it to keep its shape and minimise weight loss.

To cook a piece of dry-aged beef takes slightly longer, as the meat is denser and firmer. Conversely, the resting time is slightly shorter, as there is not as much moisture in the meat.

Cooking dry-aged beef
The best cooking methods for a dry-aged cut are grilling or roasting, where the taste is purer. You are doing less and thus relying on the meat to do the talking (as opposed to braising, mincing and dicing). Cook dry-aged beef to medium-rare.

BONES
There is an old adage that suggests the nearer the bone, the sweeter the meat. This is certainly true in the kitchen: there is much flavour to be found near the bone. When it comes to long and slow cooking, the modest bone brings so much.

Of course, there's the marrow; that intense, beefy butter found in the centre of beef and veal bones, particularly the femur (leg bone). There's also the connective tissue and fat that clings to the surface of the bone, adding flavour to your stew and preventing the meat from shrinking and drying out.

The bones themselves, the actual calcified matter, should also be celebrated. Cheap and on their own quite flavourless, the bones actually play a crucial support role to the meat. They are high in collagen which, with long and gentle cooking, melts to become gelatine. This adds texture and viscosity to an otherwise watery sauce. As the gelatine develops, it also catches small flavour particles of meat, suspending them in the liquid and adding a depth of flavour that you could not otherwise attain. This is why chefs use stocks so liberally in their cooking.

Dry-ageing meat
At Victor Churchill we dry-age our meat alongside Himalayan rock salt bricks to keep the air dry and free of impurities.

Finally, bones—particularly chicken and beef bones—contain that elusive taste: umami. Thus, nearer the bone is not just sweeter, but also more delicious!

BONE MARROW

Braised or roasted until it softens and melts, marrow is a rich and unctuous addition to a dish and ought not to be neglected. In raw bones, it's a yellowish or reddish solid that can be easily seen when long bones such as the leg bones are cut with a butcher's saw. Anthropologists speculate that humans first ate marrow when they scavenged carcasses left by predators, cutting into the bones with stone tools to release the nutrient-dense marrow. Later, it became a delicacy in dishes such as the Italian *osso buco* or as a base for Vietnamese *pho*. Ask your butcher to cut across the bones so that you can easily access the marrow.

→ *For more on marrow, see page 331 and the recipe on pages 400–401.*

STOCK

CHICKEN STOCK

One of the biggest advantages in buying a whole chicken is what lies beneath: the bones for stock, broth or soup. It can be as simple or as complicated as you like; the simpler the base, the more room you have to move down the track. You can reduce your stock, which will enhance the flavour and take up less room in your freezer. Stock will keep in sealed containers in the fridge for three days, or up to three months in the freezer. Store stock in the portions you will use it: one cup, two cups or even an icetray. Label stock with the flavour, quantity and date you froze it.

White chicken stock

A white chicken stock can be as simple as a few chicken carcasses, immersed in cold water, brought to the boil and then simmered for two hours. What you choose to add—carrots, onions, parsley stalks, garlic, peppercorns, thyme and so on—is up to you. All of these will add flavour, but a simple stock with just two ingredients (water and chicken) will also reward. Skim any scum from the surface as you go.

Brown chicken or game bird stock

Brown chicken or game bird stock is made with the roasted bones, to add depth of flavour to the stock. Chop wings at the joints into three small, even pieces to increase the surface area of the chicken wings (thus increasing the flavour) and shorten the cooking time, and roast in a moderate oven, turning regularly, until caramelised. An even brown colour all over the chicken wings will result in a rich flavoured stock. If the wings are not brown enough the stock will lack flavour, and if they burn the stock may develop a bitter flavour. Game bird stocks don't need to be cooked too long, as they will become bitter. One hour is generally sufficient.

Leftover roasted carcass stock

These principles are combined when using the leftover carcass from roast chicken to make a simple broth. Add some wings or another carcass to boost flavour.

BEEF OR VEAL STOCK

→ *Both lamb and pork stocks can be made in the same way as beef stock, but 2–3 hours will be sufficient cooking time.*

Stock is the basis of so many great meat sauces. Beef or veal bones are roasted until golden all over, then transferred to a stockpot, while the pan is deglazed with a little water to scrape off all the tasty morsels stuck to the bottom.

Add this to the stockpot, with a mirepoix and bouquet garni (see page 455) plus a few peppercorns, cover with cold water and slowly bring to the boil. Gently simmer for 3–4 hours, skimming impurities from the top regularly (many restaurants will cook their veal stock for more than eight hours).

Allow the stock to cool before straining through muslin (cheesecloth) and refrigerating overnight. When the stock is cold, most of the fat will have solidified into a layer on the surface, which can be easily scraped away. If you're not using it immediately, divide the stock into batches and freeze. If using stock that has been frozen, thaw it in the refrigerator overnight, or defrost it quickly in the microwave: this minimises the risk of harmful bacteria forming.

Veal *glace* is a heavy reduction of brown veal stock. Heat the completed veal stock in a heavy-based saucepan over high heat until it has reduced by half, skimming the surface regularly. Divide the *glace* into small batches and store in the freezer. This is excellent added to your gravy.

FAT

You will have certainly heard that fat equals flavour, but that's not quite the case: fat doesn't so much equal it, as carry it. In addition, fat makes your meat more palatable, increasing the smoothness and tenderness. As it takes time to digest, fat also helps to keep you satiated longer and thus increases the pleasure of eating.

It is important to note that animal fat is a natural fat, unlike synthetic fats found in junk food and margarine. Different types of fats (and feeds) will have different nutritional properties; for example, the higher levels of oleic acid in intramuscular fat and the omega–3s found in grass-fed lamb and beef.

The natural progression of an animal's fat development is one of the great feats of nature: a young animal will be naturally tender due to the lack of muscle, while an older animal that has spent more time in the field will be tougher. As they develop, their fats develop too, providing balance to this equation. We rely on the extra fat to keep older animals moist and juicy as they roast. There are four stages to an animal's fat development:

Lamb

THIS PAGE
Barnsley chop (see pages 156–157).

RIGHT
Lamb shanks (see page 152).

1. The animal will develop a layer of fat under the skin and around some muscles. This fat is used in the butchery to protect meat from bacteria (allowing it to be hung or dry-aged); it also keeps the moisture in the meat when roasting or barbecuing. Leaving some of this exterior fat on your roasting cut will help protect the meat as it cooks and add extra flavour, and you can remove it after it has rested.

2. The fat around key internal organs grows. This is generally referred to as suet and is the flare or leaf fat found around the kidneys and loin of cows and sheep. If this hard fat is rendered down, it becomes tallow (or more generically dripping). In its solid form, it is used in the Christmas plum pudding; in its rendered or liquid form it can be used as a base fat for all cooking. Dripping was used to make the traditional French fries before vegetable fats took over. In the butchery we sometimes paint it on cuts of meat to protect them through the dry-ageing process. Render it down (see page 468) and store in an airtight jar, or store the solid form in the fridge until you are ready to use it.

→ *Suet should be ordered in advance from your butcher. Beyond the plum pudding, it can be used to great success in pastry. Grating cold suet is the best way to evenly disperse it through your mix.*

3. Development of fat between the muscles (known as intermuscular or seam fat), which keeps the moisture in the meat when roasting.

4. Tiny threads of fat, known as intramuscular fat or marbling, will develop through the meat itself (see pages 492–493). This intramuscular fat is higher in oleic acid, a 'good' fat. In modern agriculture, we can encourage extra marbling as a result of the feed. This is why you generally see more marbling in a piece of grain-fed beef than grass-fed beef; however, keep in mind that grass-fed animals will have higher levels of some nutrients. The threads of fat baste the beef internally as it cooks, making it more tender, juicy and tasty. Marbled beef takes more time and feed to produce, but the fat is a 'good' fat, a monounsaturated fat, particularly in a grass-fed animal, which develops higher ratios of essential omega-3 fatty acids and conjugated linoleic acid (CLA). Marbling can range from small flecks to heavy spiders' webs, graded from 1 to 9+ (only in Japan can meat score above 9+).

At home, fats can be used to protect the cut when roasting or barbecuing, helping to baste the meat as it cooks. If you want, you can trim this fat away before serving. You can also render the fat and use it in place of oils.

PORK FATS

The pig has five distinct types of fat, all with different textures and thus different uses in the charcuterie kitchen.

Shoulder fat – used for lardo, saucisson, sausages. Harder than the loin fat and the first choice for the charcutier.

Loin or back fat – a tender fat similar to the shoulder fat, but softer and used for sausages and terrine. The peculiarity of these two fats is that when you mince them they keep their texture and don't turn to paste, and they will hold temperature without melting. Good for curing, the loin fat lasts for a long time.

**Honeycomb
beef tripe**
*See page 374 for
Marcella Hazan's recipe.*

Top belly fat or flare fat (inside the belly) – used for rillettes, and confit. When it's cold it's hard, but in a pan it turns to a butterlike consistency. This is thanks to its low melting point (similar to beef and lamb), making it the traditional pork lard. If you melt and whip it you will come up with the original butter.

'Chewy fat' or, in French, **la mouille** – found at the bottom of the belly and the top of the pork legs this is excellent for pork pâté. Physically, it's not the prettiest and somewhat resembles chewing gum, so in order to transform it you need to poach it to break it down.

Caul fat or **crépine** – the filigreed lace tissue that surrounds organs makes a good wrap for minced meat or for extra fat. Soak caul fat overnight in the fridge in a bowl of salted water to remove any trace of blood.

→ *Caul fat has merits beyond the ability to add moisture and protect the meat: it is used to shape, mould and protect charcuterie or to hold a parcel of meat together, with its free form allowing more freedom to the chef than the sausage shape of an intestine.*

RENDERING FAT

Somewhere in the middle of last century a debate started about the value of sugar over fat. The tale is sordid, the results even more so: it turns out it wasn't hard to convince people that fat would make you fat, but this is not the case. Happily, this argument is now shifting as we realise the health benefits of natural fats over refined sugars and, indeed, the hydrogenated fats made in a lab.

Sadly, it appears the traditional pot of lard in the kitchen—rendered beef fat—was a silent victim in this process. The larder was originally the lard house, or the place where the fat was stored. We want to bring it back. You can use the trimmings of external fat in place of olive oil or butter as the lubricant to cook your onions, to brown your meat, to roast your potatoes: simply put the fat trimmings in a heavy-based pan over gentle heat, and allow the liquid fat to gently render out. Strain, if necessary, and discard the fat solids. This can also be done to good effect with the rinds of bacon or pancetta. Note that these rendered fats can either be used instead of olive oil or butter, or in conjunction with them.

RENDERING DUCK FAT (AND CHICKEN FAT)

Often sold in jars or tins, at a premium, people don't realise just how easy it is to render your own, using the bits and pieces that come from a whole duck you've purchased. Rendering the fat simply means turning it from its solid form to a liquid form.

To render your own duck or chicken fat, remove excess fat from the cavity of the bird and put it in a small saucepan with a little water (to stop the fat catching on the bottom of the pan), add aromatics of your choice (bay leaf, thyme, some smashed garlic) and heat slowly. Strain the rendered fat and use it in place of oil where the distinct rich flavour will be of advantage; in particular, with roasted potatoes, or for pan-fried croutons. Alternatively, a lot of fat will naturally render from a whole duck that is roasted. Simply strain the fat, chill, remove any impurities, and keep it in the fridge. This technique can also be used with chicken fat, also known as schmaltz.

Confit duck leg

→ *Confit, a term derived from the French verb* confire *meaning 'to preserve', most often refers to a confit duck leg, seasoned with an aromatic salt mix then very slowly cooked in its own fat. This is a great way to use legs, if you are cooking the breast separately. The meat can be stored (traditionally for the winter months) under a protective layer of fat. You can also shred the confit meat and make rillettes (see recipes on pages 106–107 and 268–269).*

MINCE

Minced (ground) meat has been given a bad rap as a way to use up all the leftover trimmings that the butcher couldn't sell. Good mince, created from the right cut, can make a hamburger that rivals a steak in gustatory satisfaction and flavour.

What you are looking for is a cut that has a good ratio of fat to meat, which is generally 80 per cent meat to 20 per cent fat: you can always add a little fat to a leaner cut. When using great-quality fresh meat, you will find that mince is one of the most versatile of products.

The best cuts for mince:
→ Lamb shoulder or leg
→ Pork shoulder
→ Beef chuck, topside, knuckle, rump, brisket

When meat is minced, the surface area that is exposed to the air is greatly expanded, and thus so is the risk of bacteria finding somewhere to grab on to. It is for this reason that freshly ground mince is best; it is also why the use-by date on mince is significantly less than whole cuts. Use mince quickly; if you don't plan to use it straight away you can freeze it for up to two months.

→ *The quality of the mince is also reflected in the way it is cut or ground. Putting your mince through the coarse plate of the mincer twice (or asking your butcher to do it for you) will result in a particularly delicious burger.*

→ *Traditionally the pinnacle of burger patties is a combination of 50 per cent brisket and 50 per cent chuck (resulting in the golden meat-to-fat ratio of 80:20); however, there are also very excellent deviations from the rule, such as the addition of a little bit of rump, short rib or intercostal into the blend.*

SAUSAGES

Sausages, or bangers as they became known during the war—when sausage meat was padded out with water and they would explode in the frying pan—are a family favourite. As with mince, sausages that come from great-quality meat, in many cases coarsely ground, will be a treat for everyone, not just for the children.

Natural sausage and salami casings most often come from the pig's or lamb's intestines, while cattle intestines can also be used for specific sausages and salamis where their size is the boon. An amazing feat of nature, these natural casings are strong enough to act as a barrier against contaminants but are porous enough to breathe. If you are lucky to have a great butcher, with excellent sausages, you can substitute good quality flavoured sausage mince (for example pork and fennel) in the place of mince: this is particularly handy for sausage rolls. Simply squeeze the meat out of the casings and use in place of the mince. These days most commercial sausages are made with synthetic casings.

SALT

'Salt, one of those items in everyone's daily life, is completely quiet, resting inside a shaker on the kitchen counter or box in the cupboard, never calling attention to itself, plain, prosaic, no dramatics, humble—a rock, after all.' So begins Michael Ruhlman's chapter on salt in his fantastic book, considered one of the great guides to charcuterie among chefs and home cooks alike. Given that salt is the cornerstone of all preservation, it's not surprising to find, following that introduction, that Ruhlman devotes an entire chapter to the subject.

→ Charcuterie: The craft of salting, smoking & curing, *by Michael Ruhlman and Brian Polcyn, (W. W. Norton & Company, 2005).*

This 'humble' ingredient has caused quite a stir through history: Gandhi marched across India for it, the Romans paid their soldiers with it (the etymological root of the word salary lies in salt), the Vikings used it to keep their army strong (and alive); it's the only rock crystal that we eat and yet we are very proud of it: you can be 'worth your salt' or 'salt of the earth', both delightful compliments.

Of course, there is nothing silent about the role salt plays in the kitchen, it is the ultimate amplifier. Not only does it enhance and strengthen the impression of aromas, bringing out the savoury as much as it highlights intricacy in the sweet, it also suppresses bitterness.

In general, there are two types of salt: rock salt, which is mined from deposits that have formed from old seas, and sea salt, created by drawing seawater into shallow ponds and allowing the water to evaporate by the natural forces of the sun and wind as it passes through the ponds (a little unromantically, this process is now mechanised). They are all derivations with the same element at heart: sodium chloride, a mineral present in our oceans, our former oceans and our aquifers.

In the days before refrigeration, curing meats in salt, especially beef and pork, guaranteed the supply of food throughout the warmer months when spoilage was a constant danger. It was a feature of most European smallholdings, where they would kill one animal to last the household for a year. Salt plays its part in destroying pathogens, removing water from the meat (and thus removing a home for bacteria), enhancing the fermentation process and, in its own way, 'cooking' (or curing) the meat. It is the magic that turns pork belly into bacon and beef brisket into corned beef. For more on the art of charcuterie, see pages 230–237.

Salt plays a role beyond charcuterie: we use salt bricks in the dry-ageing room to keep the air dry and free of impurities; it's also used before smoking meat to help the smoke 'stick'; but most importantly it is used every time we cook.

As salt draws out the moisture in a cut, it is important not to salt your steak or chop too early. Do be generous with the salt: this is the key to those great steaks you have in a restaurant. Conversely, if your aim is to get great crackling or crisp chicken skin, you will want to harness these dehydration qualities and you can salt a day in advance.

BRINING

When it comes to brining meat, the salt's work is slightly different. Instead of taking the moisture out of the animal, a brine will actually contradict the science and add moisture in, while also seasoning the cut from the inside. This is particularly important for potentially tough birds like the turkey, for lean cuts such as the pork loin or for adding flavour to a chicken that may not have had as much access to grubs and grits as you would like. See pages 113–115 for our recipe for brined Christmas turkey.

In a brine:
→ The salt penetrates faster.
→ It is more effective because it can get right into the centre of the cut.
→ The salt water makes each cell plump up, allowing it to hold more moisture, which makes it a little more lenient in cooking; for example, this allows the chicken thighs to cook completely while the breasts stay moist. It results in a juicier finished dish.

As the salt is dissolved in water it actually becomes more powerful, so use it with care! A brine will also change the skin colour and make it more susceptible to burning, so you may want to use some foil during the cooking process to protect it.

1. Make a brine by combining 225 g (8 oz) of salt—you can also add 125 g (4½ oz) of sugar if you want—with 4 litres (140 fl oz/16 cups) of water plus any aromatics you desire (the flavour of these will also penetrate the meat). Heat to dissolve and then cool completely before adding the meat (the water needs to be colder than the meat, so you will need to chill it in the refrigerator). You can test the brine by putting a potato in the water: if it bobs on the surface your brine is ready to go, but if it sinks there is not enough salt.

2. Completely submerge the meat in the brine and chill it in the refrigerator. You want the brine to be dispersed evenly through the meat: the time this takes ranges from a couple of hours for small cuts, up to a day for bigger cuts.

Good cuts for brining:
→ Turkey (whole)
→ Chicken (whole)
→ Pork loin, shoulder
→ Beef brisket

SMOKE

Smoking is a time-honoured technique used to preserve meat. Smoking adds flavour but also helps to preserve the cut by a chemical reaction between the meat and the smoke. Wood smoke contains more than 200 components, including acids, alcohols, phenolic compounds and some toxins. These toxins can be a good thing, helping to slow down and inhibit the growth of microbes, while the phenolics retard fat oxidisation, especially in conjunction with salt curing.

Salting the meat before you smoke it is an important part of the process. The salt must then be carefully washed off and the cut patted dry, thus creating the pellicle: a slightly sticky surface that attracts and holds the smoke. The smoke doesn't actually penetrate the meat, it sits on the outside and if the meat is not dry the smoke will stick to the moisture with a smoky smudge which will later rub off.

Cold smoking imparts flavour to the meat with no heat. Meat is hung in a smoker, with smoke generated in a separate chamber, and the temperature is kept low, generally a little warmer than room temperature. The process can take days or even weeks. The meat is usually salted or brined prior to smoking to help keep bacteria away. The texture of the finished product varies according to how long it is smoked, but the meat tends to taste salty. Bacon, for example, is cold-smoked and, as with many cold-smoked foods, needs to be cooked before eaten.

Hot smoking is where the meat is enclosed in a smoker along with a fire or pit of coals. Often, aromatic woods are added (cedar, hickory or apple wood, for example) to generate scented smoke. The heat cooks the meat while the smoke gives it flavour. It is not uncommon to marinate or brine before hot smoking. Hot smoking also cures the meat, creating shelf-stable meat (that can be stored in more variable conditions). Ham is often hot smoked.

CHOOSING THE WOOD

Lignin is a compound found in all trees which, when ignited, creates these phenolic chemicals. Some softwoods contain toxic resins and can create harsh acrid notes, so hardwoods are generally preferred. Beyond that, the tree choice will largely come down to your surrounds. In Australia it might be ironbark, while in America it's often hickory, maple and pecan, with mesquite (and its strong aromas) used sparingly. Oak is a great smoking wood and is a favourite where it grows, while fruit trees are an excellent source of mildly flavoured woods. This is all about experimentation. There are also some great alternatives to wood, that can be used in small doses: tea, hay, pine needles, bay, rosemary, juniper leaves.

THE MAILLARD REACTION

The Maillard reaction, named for the French chemist Louis-Camille Maillard, is the chemical reaction that gives caramelised or browned food its unique flavour. This does not just apply to meat but also baked bread, coffee beans and dark beers.

In meat, this reaction occurs between the melting sugars and the amino acids on the surface of the meat when intense heat, from 140°C (275°F) upwards, is applied. Much in the same way that sugar turns to caramel with heat, so does the surface of the meat caramelise. But the resulting flavour is not necessarily a sweetness, but rather a deep savouriness: umami.

This reaction is intrinsic to the best-tasting steaks, braises and roasts. It is for this reason we start the roasting process on high heat, brown the meat before a braise and worship the grill marks on a steak.

MARINADES AND RUBS

Marinating meat is a great way to add flavour while keeping your dish pretty simple. It's also a lovely opportunity to experiment with a dash of this or a spoonful of that: this is all about creative licence.

→ *Browning meat in small batches before braising; char marks from a hot grill; and a delicious golden exterior on your roast are all examples of the Maillard reaction at work. See pages 448–449 for tips on harnessing the Maillard reaction to achieve great carmelisation on the barbecue and pages 452–453 for your next roast.*

One of the big misconceptions is the time you need to marinate something. While often it is great to take time to marinate overnight, you can also add flavour in just a couple of hours, or even simply by cooking the meat with the marinade on it.

If you are using fresh spices, lightly toast them in a dry frying pan to bring out their flavour. Bruising the herbs (by rubbing in your hands) before adding them to the marinade mixture will help release the essential oils in their leaves. If you want to use your marinade as a dipping sauce, be sure to bring it to a rolling boil and cook for a full minute before using.

Finally, don't fall into the trap of thinking that marinating is a way to disguise poor quality meat, it's not! Bad meat will always be bad meat and no coating will cover it.

WHEN TO USE A MARINADE

To add flavour – Generally you are going for a balance of sweet, salty, sour, and acid. For example, bruised or chopped fresh herbs (rosemary and oregano for lamb, thyme and bay leaves for pork and game), alliums (garlic, chives, onions, shallots), dry spices (crushed, fresh whole seeds), and oil to bind.

To form a crust – Sticky marinades and glazes are great friends with spare ribs or pork chops. These make use of a little sugar or honey to form a caramelised exterior on the cut.

What not to use
Be wary of marinating for too long with acids including lemon, wine and vinegars as they can strip the meat of natural juices (essentially cooking it) and thus making it dry rather than moist. If marinating with these ingredients you also want to avoid storing the meat in a reactive container, such as tin, copper or aluminium, as this will taint the meat.

Dry rubs
A dry rub is a great way to encourage a flavourful crust on your meat, especially if you are without a barbecue. Adding a little sugar to the mix will help to form the crust. Common spices include pepper, sweet or smoked paprika, ground cumin and chilli powder. In the deep south of the USA, ground coffee is a favourite.

THE BUTCHER'S TOOLS

If a poor workman blames his tools, then it follows that a good one will cherish useful tools that are chosen wisely. When selecting your butchery equipment, keep this in mind.

KNIFE

For most of the techniques we have included in this book, a good quality chef's knife will get you through; however, you can also purchase a quality boning knife for the smaller jobs.

While there are plenty of beautiful (and expensive) butchery knives to be purchased, you can also pick up a utility chef's knife pretty cheaply. Due to the hard work they do, they often get chipped. They are quite flexible, so they can get in and around bones and muscles, and shaped a little like a sabre. They are relatively cheap and thus easy to replace.

Using a steel (honing rod) maintains or polishes the edge of your knife rather than actually sharpening it. Use it regularly to keep the edge burr free and, if you don't have a sharpening stone, aim to have your knife professionally sharpened regularly. Follow these rules to ensure a good job:

Heel to tip: Every time you sharpen your knife always run the whole knife across the steel: from the heel to the tip.

Balance: For every stroke you do on one side of the knife you must repeat on the other.

Angle: Work at a 15–20 degree angle from the knife to the steel.

Technique: Fingers behind the guard, work slowly, not too much pressure, holding the steel on a chopping board and using downward strokes or held in front of you, away from your stomach, parallel to the floor.

➔ *'A good butcher is gentle with his tools, whether he is sharpening his knives or butchering a carcass.'* Ginger Pig Meat Book, *by Tim Wilson and Fran Warde (Mitchell Beazley, 2011).*

Finally, a couple of quick tips to keep your knife in good condition:

→ It's true what they say about the dishwasher. Always hand wash your knife after use and dry it immediately to avoid any rust forming. By resting the sharp edge of your knife on the side of the sink you will minimise the chance of slipping and cutting yourself.

→ Use a wall magnet or knife pouch to store your good knives. Avoid storing them loose in a drawer, where they will be bashed around.

CHOPPING BOARD

In commercial kitchens chopping boards are plastic and colour-coded according to their use: yellow for poultry, red for raw meat, brown for cooked meat, green for vegetables, and so on. They're easy to clean (generally dishwasher safe) and light. They are most likely made from polyethylene.

And yet, butchers have traditionally used wooden butcher's blocks; in fact, they are one of the few components of a commercial kitchen that can still be made of wood. They're solid, stable and durable (if well maintained). Many woods have natural antibacterial properties. They are also kind to your knife. When looking for a good wooden board go for a tight-grained hardwood board. Be conscious of the thickness: a wooden board will need thickness to balance its size, otherwise it will warp. That said, if it is too heavy, you won't enjoy using it (if you battle to carry it to the sink) and if it is too high it will change the height of your work surface.

You will have to take good care of it: oil your board regularly to keep it from drying out, to block up any of the small holes and to prevent odours and bacteria from sneaking in. You can buy specific oils for this, although you do want to be careful as many kitchen oils will eventually go rancid. The exception to the rule is walnut oil. A light rub all over with the oil on paper towel is sufficient.

Make sure you give the board a good scrub with hot soapy water after each time you use it. Don't soak your board, as this will warp it. Perhaps most importantly, make sure it dries properly after each use. Finally, with a wooden board, little cracks and fissures are the enemy, this is where any germs will gather and multiply.

OTHER TOOLS

In the butchery we make use of a number of specialised tools. Some of these are pictured on the following pages for reference, but many will be surplus to requirements for the home cook.

KEY BUTCHERY TOOLS

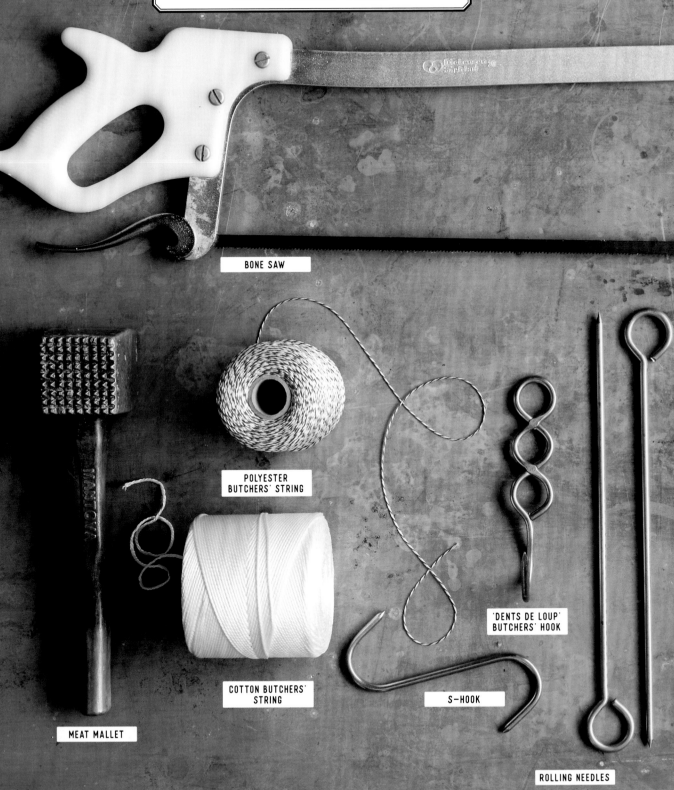

BONE SAW

MEAT MALLET

POLYESTER BUTCHERS' STRING

COTTON BUTCHERS' STRING

'DENTS DE LOUP' BUTCHERS' HOOK

S-HOOK

ROLLING NEEDLES

BENCH SCRAPER

BONING KNIFE (SEMI-FLEX)

BONING KNIFE (FLEX)

BONE DUST SCRAPER

STEEL OR
HONING ROD

BUTCHERS' KNIFE

CLEAVER

STORAGE AND HYGIENE

Good hygiene practices in your kitchen are fundamental when it comes to working with meat.

Of particular importance with meat safety is the separation between raw and cooked product. There are a few easy tips to ensure these two products don't come into contact:

→ Always wash your chopping board (you can have a specific board in your kitchen for raw meat) and knife with hot soapy water after dealing with raw meat.

→ Never chop anything else on the same board until it is clean.

→ Always wash your hands after touching raw meat.

→ Store raw meat on a shelf in the fridge below any vegetables that aren't in a crisper drawer, to avoid spillage and contamination.

→ Always store meat in the fridge and be conscious of use-by dates (ask your butcher when you purchase). Up to three days in the bottom of your fridge is a general rule of thumb.

→ Be careful when it comes to carrying your meat to the barbecue: always have a clean plate for the cooked meat, not the plate you carried out with the raw meat!

For poultry hygiene see page 67.

Refrigerating portioned vacuum-packed meat

→ **Beef:** *5–7 days*
   Chicken: *2–3 days*
   Lamb: *4–5 days*
   Pork: *3–4 days*

→ *Always store meat in the coolest part of your refrigerator.*

FREEZING MEAT

Ideally, we encourage people to buy their meat as frequently as possible to avoid freezing it; however, the reality is that all of us have a moment when we get our hands on a great special or an amazing product that is rare or unusual and want to freeze it. Here are a few things to keep in mind.

WHAT HAPPENS WHEN YOU FREEZE

→ Water expands when it freezes, so the ice crystals can tear and push apart the fibres of the meat, negatively impacting the texture.

→ When you defrost the cut, and again when you cook with it, this water will leach out, taking with it some of the flavour of the meat.

HOW TO FREEZE

→ Preferably buy dry-aged meat, as it has less moisture and thus will freeze better.

→ The faster you freeze your meat, the smaller the ice crystals (and better the result). If you have a fast-freeze button, this is when to use it. Alternatively turn the freezer down for the initial few hours. Also, be sure not to try and freeze too much at once (this will raise the temperature of the freezer and thus make the process take longer).

→ Wrap meat tightly with plastic wrap or freezer paper: air incites freezer burn and, as such, is the enemy. Follow with a layer of foil and then a resealable plastic bag, with the air pushed out.

→ Always label the packaging with the date, the type of meat and the cut; meat can look the same when frozen.

→ As a general rule, larger cuts such as roasts can be frozen for up to six months; smaller cuts such as steaks for up to four months; mince and stocks can be frozen for up to three months.

HOW TO DEFROST

→ Slowly is the key here. Defrost meat in the bottom of your refrigerator at least overnight, making sure it is on a plate so it won't drip and contaminate any food in the fridge. Defrosting on a kitchen work surface is not an option, as it can encourage harmful bacteria.

WITH THE KNIFE

Despite the way many view it, butchery is a gentle craft. It is more about the small knife strokes and patience than it is about the bandsaw. This is all very achievable at home, but requires practice. Here are a few simple techniques for the home cook to start working with.

There are two key guiding lights for the butcher: the bones and the natural seams between each muscle. Cutting along the lines that nature has provided, you will be able to work around the muscles and find your way around an animal.

A BUTCHER'S LEXICON

The following terms are commonly used to describe the work of a butcher.

Boning, deboning – The term used for cutting meat away from a bone.

Rolling – The procedure of rolling a meat product and securing it into an even size and shape for the purposes of cooking.

Seaming – Separating muscles with a little aid from your knife. This is done by following the natural 'seams' in the muscles.

Frenching – This term is a shortened version of 'French trimming', quite simply removing the meat from a bone for the purposes of presentation. Frenching is most commonly seen with a rack of meat, whether pork, veal, beef or lamb.

Butterflying – Describes the act of opening any piece of meat to resemble a butterfly. This gives product with uneven thickness a very even appearance, thus helping to ensure that it will cook evenly.

Trussing – Using butchers' twine to hold together a product for cooking. Generally used to prepare a chicken or any other bird for the oven.

Joint cutting – Cutting through the joints of a product such as chicken legs.

Scoring – Making shallow incisions partially through the skin or outer layer of fat to allow moisture to escape, resulting in a crisp finish.

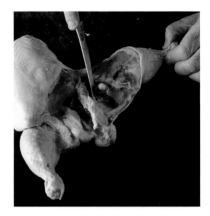

1. Remove the wings by running your knife through the loose flesh between the wing and the breast, down to the bone, pull the wing away from the bird and cut through the joint (reserve for stock).

2. Pull the Maryland (leg quarter, with both the drumstick and the thigh) away from the body and make a cut through the skin.

3. Putting pressure on the Maryland, pop out the ball joint. Continue to carefully cut around the joint to trim the thigh and leg away. Repeat on the other side.

4. Place the Maryland skin-side down and cut diagonally through the joint, to separate the drumstick and thigh.

5. Cut away the spine bone with poultry shears or a large sharp knife.

6. Cut down one side of the breast bone to separate the breasts. Cut each breast in half through the bone.

1. To bone a Maryland (leg quarter), place it skin-side down on a work surface. Feel with your fingers where the bone runs through the thigh. Cut an incision through to the bone with a boning knife.

2. Make small incisions each side of the bone, then hold the end of the bone and scrape down the bone to separate the flesh, working towards the joint. Use delicate strokes, holding your knife like a pen. Work down to the joint.

3. Locate where the thigh bone and drumstick meet and, using the force of your hand, pop or twist the joint out, using your knife if necessary to detach. Be careful not to cut through the flesh and leave the drumstick bone intact.

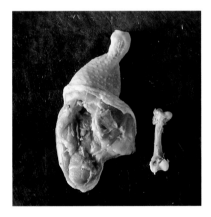

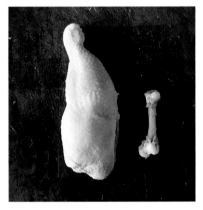

4. At this point you can stuff the ballotine (see pages 90–91 for our ballotine recipe) before cooking.

5. The ballotine can be tied with kitchen string or wrapped in prosciutto before cooking.

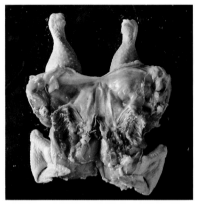

1. Place the chicken on a chopping board breast-side up. Insert a large knife inside the cavity from between the legs to the neck and cut down each side of the backbone (you could also use a pair of kitchen shears). Reserve for stock.

2. Turning the chicken breast-side down on the chopping board and taking one side in each hand, open it like a book, exposing the cavity of the bird. The breast bones should crack a bit.

3. A butterflied chicken (the process is the same for all birds) is ideal for cooking over direct heat, such as on a barbecue or chargrill plate, because it encourages even cooking. This helps to render the bird moist, tasty and succulent.

NOTES

→ *See pages 118–119 for our recipe for butterflied squab.*

→ *Be careful not to tear or put a hole in the skin when boning or butterflying a chicken, especially if you want to put some butter or stuffing under the skin before cooking (a very delicious addition).*

1. Carefully peel the skin from the fat. Start with an incision from your knife under the rounded edge of the ham. Use your fingers and knife, if necessary, to carefully tease the skin away, working back towards the shank. Be careful not to tear the fat.

2. Use a sharp knife to score around the shank, then detach the skin and reserve (use it to cover the leftover ham to prevent it from drying out).

3. Score the fat evenly (being careful not to cut into the flesh) using a small sharp knife, maintaining an even depth all over: you can score in parallel lines or in a crosshatch pattern.

4. If you plan to stud the ham with cloves, a crosshatch pattern is the best option. You can also stud the ham first, to help create a guide for your knife.

1. Locate the knuckle, where the shank meets the rest of the lamb leg, by running your finger along the shank bone. Make an incision one finger width above the knuckle, through to the bone (about 2 cm or ¾ inch).

2. Remove the shank by cutting across the bottom of the leg. If you are cutting at the right spot, the knife will pass through like a hot knife in butter. The shank can be saved in the freezer.

3. Lay the lamb skin-side down. Locate the two ends of the femur bone: running between the two ends, you will find a seam that you can follow with your knife, cutting down to the bone. This may take two or three gentle sweeps with your knife.

4. Cut the meat from the bone, separating the knuckle and silverside from the bone, keeping your knife strokes small and tight up against the bone.

5. Once the bone is cut away from the meat, pull it up towards you and then carefully cut around the ball of the bone. Remove the bone.

6. Open the lamb leg out with your hands, teasing the meat apart following any natural seams, carefully pulling the meat apart until it lies flat on the chopping board.

7. Cut away the chain of fat between the topside and the silverside muscle, in the middle of the leg by gently sliding the knife underneath it, then use your hand to pull it back as you cut it away from the lamb. There is a small blood vessel here you will also need to cut away.

8. You can now butterfly the topside muscle and the silverside muscle, by running your knife through the centre of the muscle and opening them up. Each time you do this, take stock of the shape and cut in a direction that will fill the gap; you are aiming for a nice even rectangle of meat.

9. A butterflied lamb leg, marinated if possible, is a fabulous meat cooked over the barbecue. See pages 184–185 for our recipe.

NOTE

→ *A leg of lamb is made up of four different muscles: the knuckle, the topside, the silverside and the rump (which is most often removed). By butterflying the leg, you will bring all these cuts into some uniformity of size, making it perfect for your barbecue. Ask your butcher for a bone-in lamb leg, with the chump off and the aitch bone removed.*

1. Remove the skin and skin stamp by carefully teasing the skin away with your knife, pulling at the skin as you go. Trim the fat to make it a nice even layer around the lamb (about 5 mm or ¼ inch).

2. Lay the loin skin-side down and run your knife along the spine to remove the tenderloin, gently pulling it up and away from the loin as you work with your knife. Use your fingers to remove any excess fat and sinews from the tenderloin and set aside.

3. Remove the central chain of fat, by cutting down each side of it, being careful just to be working away the fat and not cutting through the lamb.

4. Turning the loin over so it is skin-side up, run your knife along the spine bone, tight up against the bone, until it meets the central bone (the T in the T-bone).

5. Turn the lamb on its side, so the flat of the bone is on the chopping board. Use your free hand to pull the meat away from the bone, while you run your knife down the bone to release the lamb.

6. Remove the chain of gristle along the top of the lamb loin and discard.

  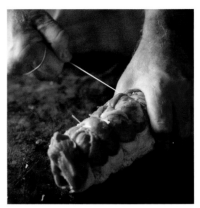

7. Place the tenderloin in the centre of the loin, marrying the narrow end of the tenderloin with the thicker end of the loin, so the meat is nicely balanced.

8. At this stage you can stuff the loin, as in the recipe on pages 178–179, or simply roll it tightly, without any stuffing.

9. Tie the loin at 2 cm (¾ inch) intervals with butcher's twine or kitchen string. You can do a simple double knot or a double slip knot. Make it snug but not so tight that the string cuts into the lamb during the cooking process.

NOTE

→ *Other cuts to tie: a whole eye fillet benefits from being tied, as the narrow, tapered end can be folded back up into the centre of the fillet for even cooking. Tying a standing rib roast or cap-on lamb rack will help to keep the muscle together as it cooks: simply tie between the bones.*

BLUE

COOK: 1 MINUTE EACH SIDE
   FOR A 3 CM (1¼ INCH) STEAK

RARE

INTERNAL TEMP: 50°C (120°F)
COOK: 2–3 MINUTES EACH SIDE
   FOR A 3 CM (1¼ INCH) STEAK
REST: 3 MINUTES

MEDIUM-RARE

INTERNAL TEMP: 55°C (130°F)
COOK: 3–4 MINUTES EACH SIDE
   FOR A 3 CM (1¼ INCH) STEAK
REST: 4 MINUTES

MEDIUM

INTERNAL TEMP: 60°C (140°F)
COOK: 4–5 MINUTES EACH SIDE
   FOR A 3 CM (1¼ INCH) STEAK
REST: 5 MINUTES

MEDIUM-WELL

INTERNAL TEMP: 65°C (150°F)
COOK: 5 MINUTES EACH SIDE
   FOR A 3 CM (1¼ INCH) STEAK
REST: 5 MINUTES

WELL DONE

INTERNAL TEMP: 70°C (160°F)
COOK: 6 MINUTES EACH SIDE
   FOR A 3 CM (1¼ INCH) STEAK
REST: 6 MINUTES

1. When a cut of meat rests, the juices flow throughout the cut, ensuring a nice even blush and moist meat. During the resting process the meat will continue to rise in temperature, sometimes a further 5–10°C (9–18°F).

2. Without proper resting, the cut will leak a lot of the delicious juices, rather than them being dispersed through the meat. The eye of the muscle may appear more rare, while the meat closer to the edges will be overdone.

BEEF MARBLE SCORE COMPARISON

BMS1

BEEF MARBLE SCORE 1

BMS3

BEEF MARBLE SCORE 3

BMS5

BEEF MARBLE SCORE 5

BMS7

BEEF MARBLE SCORE 7

BMS9

BEEF MARBLE SCORE 9

BMS9+

BEEF MARBLE SCORE 9+

THE FUTURE AND THANKS

The future will undoubtedly hold test-tube 'meat', more intensive farms, huge monocultures and, of course, arguments as we tackle the difficulties of feeding a growing population. Through these challenges, we believe that animals must remain integral to the cycle of the planet and to our biodiversity. Sustainably reared meat can and should remain at the pinnacle of the kitchen: a special and wonderful treat, handled with care by the best farmers and butchers and eaten with respect.

This integrity will be upheld by innovators, thinkers and custodians of the land, a number of whom we met in the writing of this book. We would like to pay special acknowledgment to the following:

ON THE FARM
Taylan and Megan Atar, *Seven Hills Tallarook*
David and Ben Blackmore, *Blackmore Wagyu*
John Bruce, *Cape Grim*
Bruce Burton, *Milking Yard Farm*
Michael and Constance Frydrych, *Springfield Deer Farm*
Ray Borda and Clayton Graham, *Paroo Premium Kangaroo*
Andrew Hearne, *Near River Produce*
Vince Heffernan, *Moorlands Biodynamic Lamb*
Matt O'Connor and his family, *O'Connor Beef*
David and Lucy Sheridan
Katrina and Sam Sparke, *Redleaf Farm*
Luke Windsor, *Tathra Place Free Range*

AT THE BUTCHER
Victor Puharich: the man, the mascot, the inspiration
The wider team at Vic's Meat and Victor Churchill, with special mention to Anita, Darren, Mick and Terry, for their help, support and advice

IN THE KITCHEN
The brilliant chefs and friends who created recipes for our kangaroo chapter:
O Tama Carey ~ Kylie Kwong ~ Mat Lindsay ~ Ben Shewry ~ James Viles

And all of the cookbook authors and publishers who generously granted permission to reproduce their work:
Mark Best ~ Anthony Bourdain ~ Elizabeth David ~ Marcella Hazan ~ Fergus Henderson ~ Simon Hopkinson ~ Janni Kyritsis ~ David Thompson

Our heartfelt thanks also go to the incredible team who helped create this book: Emma Knowles for her tireless energy in researching and writing the incredible recipes and styling the photographs for the food shoot—you're amazing, Em; Nick Banbury for his support in the kitchen; Alan Benson for traversing the country to bring our words to life through your beautiful photographs; Jacqui and Dan at Northwood Green for their creative direction and beautiful design; and, finally, the team at Murdoch Books, specifically Jane, Lou, Julie, Viv, Lou P., Estee, Tina, Carol and Melody, for their support, counsel and belief in such an ambitious project. We can't thank you enough for all your help, professionalism and dedication.

FROM LIBBY

I met many incredible people while writing this book. Thank you to my friends at Kaya Kaya in Pantelleria, who fed me coffee, wine and the staff lunch while I wrote; Amy and Hayden who kept me sane while I researched in London; my beautiful French family, the Dumonts and Rorpachs in Paris; Louis, Viv and the Cargills in Rayol; Thomas, that kitchen window, the team and the myriad customers I met at Auberge de Chassignolles; Marko for opening my eyes to the pigs and peka of Croatia; and the ever-delightful O Tama in Sri Lanka. These are people who kept me satiated both in mind and body, who indulged my need for meat conversations and who inspired me to look further.

Back home, it is my incredible family, friends and neighbours who provide unwavering love, support and encouragement, with special mention to Moyz, for sharing so much of his knowledge and Lou, who is always there to prop me up, bounce an idea off and make me chuckle.

And, finally, to Anthony: from the fantastic conversations we had in the early years to the friendship that has developed in the later years. Never satisfied, always questioning, more than just meat knowledge, you have taught me to push for that extra one or two per cent in everything I do. This book is the reflection of that.

FROM ANTHONY

Thank you to my mum and dad, Victor and Stephanie Puharich, for the many sacrifices they made as hardworking immigrants who came to Australia to build a future for themselves and their children. They instilled many great values in my early childhood years, including my interest and passion in meat, good food and business. Over the past 20 years their belief, faith and trust in me to lead our family business is something I will always cherish, remember and never take for granted. Thank you also to my sister, Anita Puharich, who keeps the wheels turning at Vic's Premium Quality Meat so I can go off gallivanting around the world to pursue my vision, seek opportunities and complete amazing projects like writing this book.

To Libby Travers, I never would have—and more importantly never would have wanted to—write this book without you. You are a beautiful and brilliant writer, thinker, agitator and co-author. The manner in which you have effortlessly and intuitively interpreted my 20-plus years in the meat industry, and the four generations that came before me, and woven it all together into a story that is informative, interesting, thought-provoking and inspiring is a credit to the amazing person and writer you are. Thank you. xx

To Costakis Nemitsas, for your friendship, support, counsel and for always being there for me over the last 20 years. You are truly my brother.

To the countless chefs and restaurateurs with whom I have had the privilege of working over the last 20 years: thank you for your custom and, more importantly, your support. You have all fuelled my passion for the industry I so desperately love and have been the driving force behind my dedication to be the best and most innovative meat wholesaling and retailing business in the world.

I would also like to acknowledge the meat industry as a whole, both domestically and internationally: the producers, farmers, growers, abattoir workers, butchers, retailers, wholesalers, journalists, media and everybody else I have been fortunate enough to meet along the way. Thank you for inspiring me, challenging me and igniting the fire that burns within me every day for this great industry and craft.

To all of our amazing customers, whether you eat at the fine establishments we supply across Australia, visit our two retail stores or buy meat from us online, I'm grateful for your support of our family business. You are the reason I get out of bed every morning to do what I do.

Last but by no means least, I would like to thank my beautiful, supporting and loving wife Rebecca who has been by my side from day one, through the good and bad, the ups and downs. I love you deeply and wouldn't have been able to accomplish any of the success I have enjoyed without you. To my children, Maxxamillion, Alessandra, Jet and Piper, I hope I have made you all as proud as you have made me.

INDEX

Text copyright © 2018 by Anthony Puharich and Libby Travers (except as noted below). The moral rights of the authors have been asserted.
Design © 2018 by Murdoch Books
Photography © 2018 by Alan Benson
Images on pages 6 and 11 © Paul Gosney

First published in 2018 by Murdoch Books, an imprint of
Allen & Unwin
First American Edition 2019

Publisher: Jane Morrow
Editorial Manager: Julie Mazur Tribe
Creative Direction: northwoodgreen.com
Editor: Melody Lord
Photographer: Alan Benson (with the exception of images on pages 6 and 11, which are by Paul Gosney)
Illustrators: Carcass and breed map illustrations by Matt Canning/The Illustration Room. Meat cut illustrations by Heather Menzies as well as supplied by Victor Churchill
Recipe Developer and Stylist: Emma Knowles
Home Economists: Nick Banbury, Maxwell Adey and Sarah Mayoh
Production Director: Lou Playfair

Color reproduction by Splitting Image Colour Studio Pty Ltd.
Clayton, Victoria
Printed by C & C Offset Printing Co. Ltd., China

The Countryman Press
www.countrymanpress.com

A division of W. W. Norton & Company, Inc.
500 Fifth Avenue, New York, NY 10110
www.wwnorton.com

978-1-68268-489-4
10 9 8 7 6 5 4 3 2 1

Credits:
Page 70: From *Roast Chicken and Other Stories,* by Simon Hopkinson with Lindsey Bareham. Published by Ebury Press, 1999. Reprinted with permission from David Higham Associates.
Page 86: © David Thompson. From *Thai Food,* by David Thompson. First published by Viking Australia in 2003. Reprinted by permission of Penguin Random House Australia Pty Ltd.
Page 174: From *An Omelette and a Glass of Wine,* by Elizabeth David. Published by Grub Street, 2009. Reprinted with permission from Grub Street Ltd.
Page 186: From B*est Kitchen Basics,* by Mark Best. Published by Hardie Grant, 2016. Reprinted with permission from Hardie Grant Publishing.
Page 190: *The Complete Nose to Tail,* by Fergus Henderson © 2012 by Fergus Henderson and Justin Piers Gellatly. Reprinted by permission of HarperCollins Publishers.
Page 241: From *Wild Weed Pie,* by Janni Kyritsis. Text Copyright © Janni Kyritsis. First published by Michael Joseph 2006. Reprinted by permission of Penguin Random House Australia Pty Ltd.
Page 374: From *The Essentials of Classic Italian Cooking* © 1992 by Marcella Hazan. Used by permission of Alfred A. Knopf, an imprint of the Knopf Doubleday Publishing Group, a division of Penguin Random house LLC. All rights reserved. Any third party use of this material, outside of this publication, is prohibited. Interested parties must apply directly to Penguin Random House LLC for permission.
Page 376: From *Appetites: A Cookbook* © Anthony Bourdain, 2016. Reprinted by permission of HarperCollins Publishers.
Page 438: © James Viles
Page 440: © O Tama Carey and Mat Lindsay
Page 442: © Kylie Kwong
Page 444: © Ben Shewry